ISBN 978-1-332-78500-1
PIBN 10447478

Forgotten Books is a registered trademark of FB &c Ltd.
Copyright © 2018 FB &c Ltd.
FB &c Ltd, Dalton House, 60 Windsor Avenue, London, SW19 2RR.
Company number 08720141. Registered in England and Wales.

For support please visit www.forgottenbooks.com

TWENTY PAGES   PRICE, POST FREE, 3s. 6d.

THE ROMAN CENTURIATION
IN THE MIDDLESEX DISTRICT

With Map

BY MONTAGU SHARPE
Chairman of Quarter Sessions and County Council, Middlesex

"The Centuriation of a district was its division into rectangular parcels
of a more or less uniform size, and was for the twofold purpose of
access by means of roads, and of convenient subdivision into estates.
Mr. Sharpe has found many traces of these divisions shown by existing
roads, lanes, hedges, and so on.   The result is a most valuable contribution to the early history of Middlesex."—*The Home Counties Magazine.*

THE BRENTFORD PRINTING AND PUBLISHING
COMPANY, LTD., ALBANY WORKS, BRENTFORD, W.

CONTENTS.

NOTICES.

It is particularly requested that all communications for the Editor be addressed to him *by name* at 5, Stone Buildings, Lincoln's Inn, W.C. The *Office* of the Magazine is at 44, Chancery Lane, W.C., where all communications for the Publishers should be sent.

The annual subscription to the Magazine is 6s. 6d. post free. Quarterly Parts, 1s. 6d. net each, by post, 1s. 8d. Cases for binding, 1s. 6d. each, can be obtained from the Publishers.

Copies of some of the Plates which have appeared in the Magazine are for sale, and certain Blocks can also be purchased at moderate prices.

REYNELL & SON, 44 Chancery Lane, W.C.

THE HOME COUNTIES MAGAZINE
VOL. XI

THE
HOME COUNTIES
MAGAZINE

Devoted to the Topography of London,
Middlesex, Essex, Herts, Bucks,
Berks, Surrey, and Kent

Edited by W. PALEY BAILDON, F.S.A.

VOLUME XI, 1909

LONDON: GEORGE BELL AND SONS
YORK HOUSE, PORTUGAL STREET, W.C.

Sir John Barnard.

From a mezzotint by J. Faber, after Allan Ramsey.

TWO LORD MAYORS OF LONDON.

By W. L. Rutton, F.S.A.

[Continued from vol. x, p. 267.]

SIR JOHN BARNARD, Kt.

OUR second portrait is that of one of the most eminent and estimable of the Lord Mayors, the four hundred and ninth. He was equally distinguished as merchant, magistrate, politician, financier, and philanthropist. Of his parentage we only learn that his father and mother were of Reading, members of the Society of Friends, usually, though unhandsomely, called Quakers. The best traits of that respected sect were preserved by him through life, although as a thoughtful youth of eighteen he decided to adopt the more expressive Established Church. When fifteen he was placed in the wine business of his father, and by ability and assiduity made rapid progress towards its management. For some twenty years, however, his course, though prosperous, was ordinary, and not until his thirty-sixth year does he seem to have come into public notice as a strong and able man. Then, in 1720, he was chosen by his fellow-merchants to present a petition to the House of Lords against a bill which had been passed by the Commons adversely affecting their trade. His readiness of speech and argument on this occasion formed his passport to public life, his fitness to represent them in Parliament being made apparent to the citizens of London. His election followed in 1722, and for nearly forty years he represented the City, taking first rank as an authority in financial matters, and boldly expressing his opinions when adverse to the policy of the great Prime Minister, Sir Robert Walpole. By his courage, independence, and eloquence, he commanded the deference of the House, and what he had to say he determined should be heard; a litttle story to this effect, though oft told, must be repeated. Once when speaking he observed the Prime Minister whispering to the Speaker, who deferentially leaned towards him on the arm of his chair. "Mr. Speaker! Mr. Speaker!" cried out Sir John, "I address myself to you and not to your chair. I will be heard. I call that Right

Honourable Gentleman to order." Whereon the Speaker adjusted his position, begged pardon of the Member for London, and desired him to proceed.

Bills presented by him had as their object better regulations for merchant-seamen, the improvement of gaols, the relief of poor debtors, the reformation of the London police. His chief measure, perhaps, was one of finance, viz., the reduction of interest on the National Debt from four to three per cent., which, although unsuccessful in 1737—and even at that time the cause of temporary unpopularity to Barnard—had, when eventually carried, the effect of so much enhancing his reputation as a financier that, in 1746, the Chancellorship of the Exchequer was offered to him. That high position, however, he declined.

In the City his career was thus marked: Alderman of Dowgate Ward, 1728; Knighted by George II, 1732; Sheriff, 1735; Lord Mayor, 1737; "Father of the City" as Alderman of Bridge Without, 1749. On attaining the latter dignity, the London merchants, to testify their respect, erected his statue in the Royal Exchange, an honour previously accorded only to sovereigns, and one so inconsistent with his own modesty, that ever after he transacted his business outside the building.[1] This great distinction, meant to crown his noble public conduct, had probably special reference to his high patriotism in 1745, when, to avert panic in the City and a run on the Bank, caused by the temporary success of the Pretender and his advance from Scotland, Barnard headed a band of 1,600 merchants who guaranteed the payment of the Bank's notes and obligations.

As a magistrate he was vigilant, just and humane. Always religious and faithful to his early principles, he promoted the observance of Sunday; but his deference to the clergy was not allowed to affect his constant impartiality. It is related that on one occassion when a "reverend" offender brought before him appealed for consideration in canonical garb, he was told that the sanctity of his profession had aggravated his offence, and the penalty should not be relaxed.

Lord Stanhope, in his *History*, describes Sir John Barnard as the type of an honourable British Merchant. The Earl of Chatham—when Mr. Pitt—called him "the great commoner," a

---

[1] This statue doubtless perished in the fire of 1838. An existing picture of it scarcely causes regret for its disappearance.

soubriquet afterwards attached to the Earl's own son, the illustrious Prime Minister. Sir Robert Walpole reckoned him a doughty opponent in Parliament. Other Ministers, Granville and Pulteney, sought his advice at Clapham. Lord Palmerston (the first) sanctioned the marriage of his son with the daughter of Sir John, who afterwards became the guardian of the son's son, the second Vicount.

In 1754 was his last election by the City to Parliament; it was urged upon him against his desire. He retained his seat until 1761; but previously, in 1758, his age being seventy-three, he resigned his civic duties, and in some degree sought retirement in his home at Clapham. Here he lived kindly and hospitably with his neighbours, chiefly fellow-merchants, meeting them weekly at a club, riding out with them on Saturdays and Mondays, and occasionally taking part in the pastime of the bowling-green. And at times, as said above, he was visited by distinguished politicians.

In his family he was exemplary. His wife was Jane, daughter of John Godschall, a City merchant. He had the misfortune to lose her in the year of his mayoralty, and it appears that she died at his City residence, for it is recorded that the funeral procession to Clapham was attended through the City by the children [*i.e.*, the Blue-coat Boys] of Christ's Hospital, of which Sir John was many years President (*A New and Gen. Biog. Dict.*, 1767, vol. xii, 69). The remains, however, were not finally deposited at Clapham, but (eleven days after death) in Mortlake Church, as noted in the register: " Sep. 1, Dame Jane Barnard, Lady Mayoress of yᵉ City of London was buried." The choice of place just then seems rather curious, for the daughter, Jane Barnard, was not yet married to the Hon. Henry Temple, of East Sheen, in Mortlake. That marriage, however, was celebrated so soon after as September 12th (*Gent. Mag.*), and it connected Sir John with Mortlake. For his son-in-law, Lord Palmerston's only son, died ere two years were completed, and we readily imagine the father's visit to his widowed daughter, who lived at East Sheen with her only son (the future second Lord Palmerston), to whom Sir John was guardian. This lady lived to see her grandson, the third Viscount, who was to be famous as the Prime Minister of Queen Victoria; he was about four years old when his grandmother died on January 25th, 1789 (*Annual Register*). I here correct an error of date taken from Lodge in my *Temple Grove* paper [vol. ix, p. 136]. She, too, was buried at Mortlake, "The Honb^{le} Jane Temple," February 5th, 1789.

The elder of Sir John's two daughters was Sarah, the wife of Sir Thomas Hankey, Kt., of London, and in their descendants is now represented the venerated Lord Mayor of 1738, for John, his only son—to whom we shall presently refer—left no issue.

Sir John Barnard died on August 28th, 1764. The contemporary record of the *Gentleman's Magazine* cannot be here omitted :—

> "At Clapham, in a very advanced age, Sir John Barnard, Knt., sometime Father of the City. He served the office of Lord Mayor in 1737 [and 1738], represented the City in six Parliaments with great honour to himself and with the highest approbation of his constituents, and was ever justly revered and esteemed as a gentleman of consummate abilities and inviolable integrity."

He was buried with his wife in Mortlake Church, September 4th, 1764. The simple entry in the register is the only memorial there; even his grave is now unknown. This we regret, and think discreditable to those who should have preserved it. The words *Humani Generis Decus* were added to the inscription on his statue in the Royal Exchange, but both Exchange and statue perished in the fire of 1838.

Some details of his will, at Somerset House, may be interesting. Very solemnly he commits his soul to God, and directs that his body may be buried at Mortlake near the remains of his dear wife, in a very private and inexpensive manner. His only son, John, had already been equipped "for his advantage in the world," and his two daughters, Dame Sarah Hankey and the Hon. Mrs. Temple, had had their marriage portions; they have now further sums, and Dame Hankey having died her share is to be divided between her six children. Thomas Suttton, his grandson [? by Hankey marriage], has the money arising from the sale of his [Sir John's] furniture in the house in Broad Street; this grandson has a further legacy, and each grandchild is similarly benefited. There are bequests to nieces Dowson and Mary Goffe, to cousins Hannah Thomas, Mary Willes of Marlborough, and Dr. Thomas, to the Governors of Christ's Hospital and of the Foundling Hospital, to his servants, to the Rev. Mr. Stonehouse [afterwards Baronet], Rector of Clapham, the Rev. Mr. Mapletoft, curate of same, and the assisting curate of Mortlake, five guineas each in lieu of burying fees. The residue of his personal estate, his goods and chattels, his freehold, copyhold, and leasehold lands and tenements [not named] he leaves to his dear son John, who with his worthy friend, John Small, of Clapham, are appointed executors with special legacies. By a codicil there is a legacy to his son-in-law, Sir Thomas Hankey, Knight, and bequests to the poor of Clapham, Mortlake, and East Sheen. The will was made April 24th, 1763, and proved September 10th, 1764.

From Sir John's pen there is extant a little volume entitled : *A Present for an Apprentice, or a sure guide to gain both esteem and an estate, by a late Lord Mayor of London* (1740) ; it is described in *Dict. Nat. Biog.* as " a curious medley of Christianity and Commerce." Also : *Considerations on the Proposal for reducing the Interest on the National Debt* (1750), and, in his retirement, *The Nature and Government of the Christian Church from the Word of God* (1761).

JOHN BARNARD, the son, lived, apparently unmarried, as a rich man and collector of works of art, in Berkeley Square, London. What we learn of him is derived from his will and two notices in the *Gentleman's Magazine,* 1785 (pp. 64, 155), written shortly after his death. Here he is referred to as " son of the patriotic Sir J. Barnard, many years Father of the City of London." A portion of his will is quoted. He is said to have died worth £200,000, and that having no issue he left his real and personal estate to his nephew, Thomas Hankey, Esq.

The will contains the names of many legatees, and some interesting particulars. After pious committal of his soul, he desires the burial of his body in the most private and inexpensive manner possible, in woolen according to law, and where it will occasion the least trouble. To his " cousin " Joshua Payne, he leaves his estate called Playhatch, in the parish of Sunning, Oxfordshire, and the other of his freehold and leasehold estates are left to his nephew, Thomas Hankey. To his sister, the Hon. Jane Temple, he leaves £2,000 ; to his three nephews, Henry, Lord Viscount Palmerston, John Hankey and Robert Hankey, certain life annuities. Legacies to his " cousin," Jane Johnson, of Mortlake ; to Mrs. Godschall, his cousin [of his mother's family] ; to his good friend the Earl of Portmore ; to his friend Isaac Pilleau, a clerk in the Bank of England ; to his friend William Baillie, Esq., Commissioner of the Stamp Office; to Captain Thomas Baillie, late Deputy Governor of Greenwich Hospital [the bequest quoted in *Gent. Mag.*] " as a small token of my approbation of his worthy and disinterested though ineffectual endeavours to rescue that noble national charity from the rapacious hands of the basest and most wicked of mankind " (not named). Legacies also to his friend John Bertels, a native of Brussels, and one of the proprietors of the auction room in King Street, St. James's Square; to Mr. John Greenwood, painter and auctioneer in the Haymarket; to Mr. Dominic Serres, of Warwick, painter of sea-views; to Alice Lewry, an old servant of my late father; to his dear friend Nathaniel, Lord Scarsdale, his picture of the "Holy Family," by Simon Cantarini, "which I esteem one of the best of my historical pictures, begging him to keep it as a small remembrance of the friendship and esteem I had for him"; to his worthy friend, John Kendrick, Esq., a' Commissioner of the Stamp Office, "all my entire collection of prints and books of sculpture as they stand distinguished in my catalogue from my other books, begging him, as they were collected by me with great trouble and expense, that he will keep them entire as long as he shall live, and leave them at his decease to such as he thinks will be most likely to do the same. Charitable bequests are made to the Marine Society for putting out poor boys to sea; to the Society for the discharge and relief of the persons imprisoned for small debts in Craven Street in the Strand; to the Governors of the Lock Hospital, called the Asylum, near Westminster Bridge; to the poor of whatever parish shall be the principal place of his residence at the time of his decease; and there are liberal bequests to his servants. The rest and residue of his monies, government securities, long annuities, and life annuities in the Exchequer, his goods, chattels, and personal estate whatever, are left to his aforesaid nephew, Thomas Hankey, whom he appoints his sole executor.

By codicil he leaves legacies to Mr. Joseph Nollekens, statuary in Mortimer Street; to Mrs. Susannah Pilleau, sister to Mr. Isaac Pilleau above mentioned; to Mr. Simon Beauvais, miniature painter in Market Street, St. James's; to his worthy friend, John Peachey, Esq., son of Sir John Peachey, Baronet, his picture of the "Finding of Moses," by Paolo Veronese, desiring him to accept it as a small token of the respect he had for him.

By a later codicil he makes a further handsome bequest to his youngest nephew, Robert Hankey, in some compensation for the great loss he had sustained in his trade and partnership. He revokes the legacy to the Earl of Portmore, as he had not found his friendship such as he had thought it.

And by a still later codicil he revokes his bequest to Mr. Joseph Nollekens, and gives legacies to John and Dominic Serres, the two sons of Mr. Dominic Serres, the painter of sea-views mentioned in his will.

John Barnard died in Berkeley Square in November, 1784, and on December 1st was buried in the vault under the chapel of the burying-ground of his parish, St. George's, Hanover Square, on the Uxbridge Road (*Registers*). I have not found any memorial. The will was proved by the executor, Thomas Hankey, November 26th, 1784 (? before the deposit of the remains in the vault). In the British Museum is found: *A catalogue of the superb and well known Cabinet of Drawings of Iohn Barnard, Esq., late of Berkeley Square, deceased. To be sold by auction by Mr. Greenwood in Leicester Square, February 16th, 1787.* The produce of the sale is noted on the catalogue as £2,472 15s. 6d.

Memoirs of Sir John Barnard were published in 1776, and these were reprinted in 1855 by his great-great-grandson, Thomas Hankey, Esq., of Portland Place, London, who wrote a Preface and included biographical sketches from Orridge's *Citizens of London and Their Rulers*, Heath's *Grocers' Company*, and Rees' *Cyclopædia*. Also Chalmers' *General Biographical Dictionary* (1815), and, indeed, all works of that nature down to the latest and greatest, the *Dictionary of National Biography*, record and do honour to this noblest of Lord Mayors.

THE HAMPSTEAD ASSEMBLY ROOMS IN WEATHERALL PLACE.

By Alfred Stanley Foord.

THE Hampstead Assembly Rooms in Weatherall Place consisted of the "Long Room," which is contained in Weatherall House, and the "Assembly Room" or "Ball Room," now merged in Nos. 7 and 9 Well Walk. During the hundred odd years in which they have been used as private houses, many alterations, both external and internal, have been made in them by different owners, but not so as to obliterate all traces of the purpose for which they were originally designed. Probably the very fact of their having passed into private ownership ·has contributed to their preservation, and notwithstanding the lapse of time—some portions âre alleged to be of late seventeenth century age—few signs of decay are apparent.

When the original Long Room and Pump Room on the east side of Well Walk were transformed into a place of worship in 1725, the inhabitants and their visitors found themselves for the time being deprived of a suitable building in which they could hold their dances and assemblies. It was not very long before a fresh site was forthcoming, a little farther away from the Heath in the same road, in that part of it which, until 1800, had no specific name. From that date until 1870, or perhaps rather later, it was called Weatherall Place,[1] and since then the whole length of the road has' been designated Well Walk. There were buildings already existing here, (built in part in the seventeenth century,) which, by adaptation, and with the addition of new erections, provided all the accommodation required for public entertainments.

The history of the property is very clearly set forth in an admirable little book on Hampstead Wells,[2] by Mr. George W. Potter, who, in his capacity of a Trustee of the Wells and of the Campden Charity, enjoyed the advantage of access to the local and other archives. He says that the earliest mention of the premises which he was able to find, occurs in the Manor Court Rolls for 1727. In this document they are spoken of as "a newly-erected building," which, it is pretty certain, is that now standing and formerly known as the Long Room; the term "newly erected," Mr. Potter is careful to add, might be applied to a building some years old. The property is again mentioned, remarks the same author, in 1753, in connection with the will of one Henry Vipont, (who was admitted to it in 1734,) in these words; "there had been erected upon the said premises

[1] In the *London Suburban Directory* for 1868, Weatherall Place is mentioned, but in that for 1872, (they were issued every fourth year,) the name had disappeared.

[2] *Hampstead Wells; a short history of their rise and decline,* by Geo. W. Potter ; 1904.

another messuage or tenement fronting the way leading from Flask Walk to Hampstead Wells, and also a new room called the Assembly Rooms." The language is not very explicit, but there can be no doubt, from the situation indicated, that this new messuage was the large Georgian Room, now incorporated in Weatherall House, and that the new room was the block now divided and numbered 7 and 9 Well Walk. The Long Room is certainly of older date than 1753, having apparently been only converted into a place of entertainment.

The entire group of buildings can be plainly made out in the Hampstead section of Rocque's plan of London (1741-45); also in the plan in Park's *Topography of Hampstead* (1814). Copies of these, numbered 1 and 3, and lettered to correspond with the large-scale plan, c. 1761, No. 2, accompany this article. The fact that Park's plan is undated, having been compiled from various surveys, which are not named, detracts somewhat from its historic value. His description of the Weatherall Place Rooms, from whatever source it was taken, (for he could not himself have seen them before they were converted to private use),[1] is written with some minuteness of detail, and the inference may be drawn from it that the assemblies were more like a social club than a public resort. He says:— "Here the gentry used formerly to meet every Monday Evening to play at cards, and here they had likewise an assembly, beginning at Whitsuntide and ending in October. The Ball Room [*i.e.* the Long Room] was seventy-five feet long by thirty-three feet wide, and adorned in a very elegant manner. On each side of the entrance were two small but neat rooms for tea and cards. A guinea subscription admitted a gentleman and two ladies to the Ball Room every other Monday. To non-subscribers admittance was half-a-crown each night. The Master of the Ceremonies had an annual benefit, when the tickets were five shillings each; on this occasion a concert usually commenced the evening."

Towards the middle of the XVIII century a praiseworthy effort appears to have been made to keep the society of Hampstead as select as possible, "care being taken, (as Seymour relates) to discourage the meaner sort from making it a place of rendezvous, that it is now become, after Scarborough, Bath,

[1] Park was born in 1795, the year in which Thomas Weatherall senior, was admitted as tenant of the property, which included the Long Room.

and Tunbridge, one of the politest places in England.[1] But in whatever way the reform was brought about, the class of persons patronising these later Assembly Rooms was very different from that of most of the frequenters of the older rooms in the Wells Walk. The poet Rogers[2] testifies to this when he says that in his youth (*circa* 1783), he used to go to the Hampstead Assemblies, "which were frequented by a great deal of good company," and that he himself danced four or five minuets there in one evening. To these gatherings came Mark Akenside, about 1760, during his residence at North End, and here it was that Pope, Arbuthnot, and other literary celebrities resorted. Dr. Johnson's wife came also, from "the last house southward in Frognal" where she lodged in the year 1748, indulging herself in country air and nice living, and although the presence of the gifted man himself is not actually recorded, it is more than probable that he went in his "bushy, grayish wig, brown clothes, black stockings, and plain shirt," a solecism among the beaux resplendent in lace ruffles and embroidery. Fanny Burney was here in the person of her heroine Evelina, if not in her own; indeed her description of the Long Room seems too circumstantial to have been written merely from hearsay. She writes of it probably as it appeared to her before 1778:— "This room seems very well named, for I believe it would be difficult to find any other epithet which might, with propriety, distinguish it, as it is without ornament, elegance, or any sort of singularity, and merely to be marked by its length."[3] This impression of the Long Room is quite at variance with what Park says of it, as "adorned in a very elegant manner." Perhaps the adornment, whatever it may have been, was unnoticed by Miss Burney, who suffered from short sight. She was, moreover, a closer observer of people than of places, and consequently she gives very little more actual description of such public resorts as the Marylebone Gardens, Vauxhall, and Ranelagh, than of Hampstead.

After a public career of sixty years or more, this second set of Assembly Rooms gradually declined in popularity, and passing into other hands was, about 1800, converted into private houses. When Mr. Charles Cooper came into posses-

[1]Robert Seymour: *Survey of London and Westminster*, 1734-35, Appendix.
[2]Samuel Rogers : *Table Talk*, Edited by A. Dyce, 1856.
[3]*Evelina*, Edit. 1903, (Macmillan), p. 268.

sion of the premises in 1810, they are described in the copy ot Court Roll as " The Long Room with a large garden, the Assembly Rooms, and also a new room called the Assembly Room." This second Assembly Room is that adjoining the Long Room, and is now used as the drawing room of Weather-all House. Being on the garden side of the house, it is only partly visible from the road.

The most interesting of the new Wells Assembly Rooms, from its early associations, is, of course the Long Room. It was originally a long, low, white structure of timber, brick and mortar, but when the late Mr. Goodwin Rooth bought the property in 1876, he had it encased in red brick, making the lower walls eighteen inches thick. The ground floor, before it was turned into a private residence, consisted of an entire room, with two small ante-rooms, one on either side of the entrance, used tor tea and card parties. The great length of the Long Room—seventy-five feet—is still easily discernible. It has been sub-divided by wainscots into a dining room, hall and two smaller rooms ; all fronting the road. Along the whole length of these rooms, in the middle of the ceiling, run huge beams of oak, cased in moulded timber. The whole of the front of the house is believed to be of one date. The portion of the Long Room now forming the central hall is supportd by six pillars ; the walls, like those of the dining room, are panelled from floor to ceiling. There was probably another entrance at the north east end of the Long Room, some foundations having been dis-covered when a window was put in by Mr. Rooth. The family have a theory that at the end of the hall, opposite to the pre-sent main entrance, was a musicians' gallery, open to the floor above, where there is now a landing, reached by the staircase built by Mr. Rooth : one of the evidences that a gallery existed, is a large hook still fixed in the landing ceiling, such as might be used to carry a chandelier, which would serve as an over-head light for the orchestra. Over the greater part of the Long Room were five card rooms, originally communicating with one another by means of central doors. These rooms were, about one hundred years back, converted into bed-rooms. The old flight ot stairs, formerly outside the Long Room—a ' lean-to,' but now roofed over—by which the guests gained access to the upper rooms, has been preserved intact, as also has the arched fan-light of the outer or street door. Mr. Rooth had this stairway, which rises at the side of the passage on the ground floor, where the great beams end, 'capped' with wood and the lower steps turned sideways into the passage: they formerly ran straight up. The entrance gate stood a few yards to the west of the present tradesmen's entrance—on the street.

It will be seen from the foregoing that when Mr. Rooth took the house some thirty years ago, he carried out many structural and other alterations, such as building a new staircase, inserting a window, putting in a fireplace, and a number of other minor changes. In fact the place underwent a thorough restoration at his hands. Yet, with all this, he succeeded admirably in preserving the characteristic features of the building as he found them. The rare taste and judgment observable in the fabric itself are equally manifest in the decorations of the interior, and nothing could be more appropriate than the beautiful antique furniture.

Near Weatherall House, at the corner of the road leading to New End Square, is Burgh House. So far as is known, it had no special connection with the Assembly Rooms, but being included with them in the frequent references to the property which occur in the Court Rolls, some description of it seemed only proper. Unfortunately there is very little to relate. The house stands back from the main thoroughfare, and has a spacious quadrangle in front. The façade is rather imposing, overtopping the neighbouring houses. It was built in 1709, but has not been called Burgh House for more than sixty years at the most, being so named after the Reverend Allatson de Burgh, (afterwards Burgh, the prefix "de" being dropped), who in later years resided in it. He was Vicar of St. Laurence Jewry, to which he was appointed in 1815, and held the living till his death in 1857 at Hampstead. He was a musical amateur of knowledge and skill, and built a large room for his organ, which is now used as a library. This house was at one time used for a Militia Barracks, at which time, (1863), two projecting wings abutting upon the roadway were added to the old mansion, and were used as an armoury and storehouse, the officers occupying Burgh House itself, which now belongs to Mr. Rooth, and is again a private residence.

Associated with the Long Room, and standing only a few yards away from its north-eastern end, was an elongated building, marked in Chatelaine's print of 1745 by a projecting bay at each extremity, and having a mansard roof. This building has been already alluded to in the quotation from Henry Vipont's Will as "a new room called the Assembly Rooms," which "new room" seems to answer to the one referred to by Seymour in his *Survey*, published in 1734-35, when he says, "to add to the entertainment of the Company, there is, besides the Long Room, in which the Company meet publicly on a Monday Evening to play at cards, etc., a new Dancing Room, built this year—1735—by Mr. Vipand (sic), the owner of the other, [*i.e.* the Long Room]. This room is·sixty feet long and thirty feet wide, well adorned with chandeliers, etc." This Dancing or Assembly Room seems to have been that portion of the building now known as No. 9 Well Walk, as the title deeds of that house, in the possession of the Rooth family, mention it as having been "converted out of a building formerly known as the Assembly Room." But as the frontage of Nos. 7 and 9 together measures 120 feet, there is a length of 60 feet still to be accounted for. The most probable explanation seems to be that this was built after, and not before, Vipont's Dancing Room, namely, some time between the years 1735 and 1745, in which latter years the entire block appears in Chatelaine's drawing. The building originally consisted of a lofty ground floor, with a top story, (which is still panelled), and a basement; the present middle floor was inserted in the centre part of the block, but apparently not in the wings, when it was transformed into a dwelling house.

The outward appearance of these semi-detached houses at the present day does not differ materially from Chatelaine's picture, except for the insertion of the front doors and rose windows in the south bay of No. 7, put in by a late owner, Mr. Henry Barrett-Lennard, who took the house some time between 1876 and 1880. Some years previously, (certainly before 1872), the southern half of the block—now No. 7,—was subdivided into two houses, and numbered 3 and 5, some of the steps leading up to the front door of the last mentioned house being still *in situ*, and in the garden there are remains of the dividing wall. No. 7, answering to the modern No. 9, seems always to have been one house. In the Suburban Directory for 1880, No. 3 only appears, Mr. Barrett-Lennard having thrown the two houses—3 and 5—into one; he also made extensive alterations in the inside, among these being the lengthening of the dining room, and the formation of a passage leading to a large new room, which he built out at the back of the house. The drawing room, which occupies the southern bay, and is the largest room in the house, rests on massive brick vaulting. It measures forty feet long by fourteen feet wide, and has had the ceiling raised. The lighting is by a window at each end, probably as at first planned, and above each of these—front and back—is a rose window. The hall and main staircase leading up to the first floor are panelled in oak, and the bannisters are a good example of the carving of the period. The older stairs leading down from the top rooms have been closed. On the landing and in an upstairs room there are unsuspected doors and cupboards, concealed by wall paper, reminding one of the secret hiding places met with in some old Tudor and Jacobean houses. No. 9 has been slightly altered in front, where the bay, corresponding with that of No. 7, instead of projecting, stands flush with the centre part of the house. As seen from the back, however, the houses seem to have retained most of the salient features of the old Assembly Room.

The best, if not the only view extant, of the Long Room and Assembly Rooms, is the print by Chatelaine, a copy of which, taken from Lysons' *Environs of London* (1795-1800), serves to illustrate this article. In her *Life of Josiah Wedgwood* (1865-6), Miss Meteyard describes the service of china made by him in 1773 for the Empress Catharine II of Russia, decorated with views of English scenes. Among them are no fewer than twenty-one views of Hampstead and the vicinity, bringing in the Long Roon, Assembly Rooms and Burgh House. The collection is understood to be in the Hermitage Palace at St. Petersburg. William Howitt also mentions the service in his *Northern Heights of London* (1869), adding a list of pieces containing the Hampstead views.

As these pages profess to deal only with the later Assembly Rooms, it is unnecessary to describe that part of the plan of 1761—No. 2—which shows the original Wells Buildings. Permission to reproduce this plan from his *History of Hampstead Wells* was kindly granted by Mr. G. W. Potter, and for the reproduction of Chatelaine's print and the plans numbered 1 and 3, by the Guildhall Library.

The writer, in conclusion, desires to express his special

obligations for the kind assistance given him by Miss Rooth, of Weatherall House, Mr. Ernest Wallis, of No. 7 Well Walk, Mr. George W. Potter, formerly of Hampstead, and Dr. Williamson, of Burgh House.

SOME FAMOUS LONDON WELLS.

By J. F. Leask.

THE encroachment of modern building on the environs oᵢ the former metropolis has caused many antiquarian associations to be dropped into oblivion, and not the least important and interesting amongst these deserving special notice might very well be mentioned the numerous wells which surrounded London.

To the antiquarian hunter and keen observer there are, however, still some land-marks which link the present to the past, and cause us to stop a while and picture to ourselves the life of the earlier inhabitants of London.

In dealing with this subject of wells, it must be borne in mind that, although the modern Londoner is not greatly interested in the sources of our water supply, yet in the not so excessively remote past, when our present elaborate system of water conduit had not sprung into being, it was necessary to a great extent to resort for the water supply of the Metropolis to surrounding springs and wells, some of which will be touched upon. The present remarks, however, will more especially be confined to those wells which were famous for their medicinal qualities.

KILBURN has become a byword to many in consequence of the popularity of the motor omnibuses which were pioneer in the field on the main thoroughfare of this district. Kilburn was famous not only for its mineral wells, no remains of which now exist, but also for its ancient Priory, which was founded in the reign of Henry I by Godwin, the hermit, who built the hermitage of Cuneburn, now Kilburn, which he afterwards ceded to three nuns, Emma, Christena and Gunelda, and hereafter the hermitage became a nunnery of the order of St. Benedict. About the time of the dissolution, the possessions were valued at £741 per annum, and the land was granted to John, Earl of Warwick. There are now no visible relics of the Priory, the occupants of which extended so much hospitality to travellers, but its memory is perpetuated in the name of the road which now occupies its site, namely, Priory Road.

The Kilburn Wells were situated near at hand to the Priory, on the east side of Edgware Road, being, as the ancient records tell us, " a morning's walk from the centre of the metropolis, two miles from Oxford Street." The old site of the Wells is now occupied by a Bank, standing a little to the north of the Kilburn station on the L. & N. W. Railway, on the east side of the road, and the only indication of the interesting association is a tablet with inscription, on the wall of the Bank, as shown in our illustration, reading, " This was the site of the Kilburn Wells." From a newspaper cutting dated 1795, we learn that at that time this well was famous on account of its purgative qualities, and celebrated for its rural situation with extensive prospects, and for the acknowledged efficacy of its waters, which were more strongly impregnated with carbonic acid gas than any known spring in England. Close by the well existed a house set apart for the recreation and entertainment of people visiting the Wells, and in the season numerous concerts and balls were arranged.

Journeying across country a few miles to the east of Kilburn upon a hill existed another well in equal favour as the one at Kilburn, being known as the HAMPSTEAD WELLS. Hampstead has now become a select residential quarter, and its picturesque heath still draws crowds of holiday seekers as in former days, when people journeyed out from London to this conspicuous amongst health resorts, to recuperate and to enjoy quietly the pure air of this high altitude, with its delightfully rural appearance; and also to drink of its life-giving waters. This Chalybeate Well was situated on a part of the heath which has since been encroached upon and is now covered with houses; but the remembrance is still with us in the name Well Walk, which lies on the west side of the heath. But there is also another denoted in the shape of a fountain, which is situated where Gainsborough Gardens runs into the Well Walk. The water, which flows from this fountain from the side, as shown in our illustration, is the only remains of the well, and is forbidden to the public, having become contaminated. How-

Kilburn Wells.

Hampstead Wells.

ever, one can still obtain a refreshing drink from another fountain placed against and adjoined to the same erection, and at the same time meditate on bygone times. It is interesting to observe in passing how the present Gainsborough Gardens derives its name. In the year 1698 the Earl of Gainsborough vested, we are told, in trustees for the use of the poor of the district, six acres of heath land, which was situated round about the medicinal wells, and it is probable that Gainsborough Gardens now occupies part of this land.

St. Chad's Well, though its surroundings were uninviting, yet having an attraction all its own, was situated at the end of Gray's Inn Road, near Battle Bridge, King's Cross, where the present St. Chad's Lane lies, the only memory of the wells. The wells were opened in 1772, and were in great esteem, being visited not only by people of the district but by strangers. They were accessible by descending from Holborn Bars to the very bottom of Gray's Inn Lane, and their position was by the side of a hill, on which, we are told, "were wont to climb and brouse certain mountain goats." Curiously enough, this hill consisted of an accumulation of ashes, it was the largest heap of cinder dust in the neighbourhood or in London, and was formed by an annual deposit of some 100 cart loads. It is not generally known that this heap of cinder dust, after being razed to the ground, was exported to Russia for making bricks to rebuild Moscow after the burning of that city on the entrance of Napoleon. Opposite to this unsightly hill, and on the right hand side of the road, was an anglewise sign-board bearing the inscription, "St. Chad's Wells," and underneath, "Health restored and preserved." A poor wooden gate led into a scene which an unaccustomed eye might take for the pleasure ground of the "Giant Despair," for trees stood as though it was not their nature to vegetate; hedges without foliage, with numerous weeds straggling upon unlimited borders. But the reassuring octagonal sign-board was not a mockery, for St. Chad's, although with such a forbidding external, drew many persons to drink the invigorating waters, one pint, it being said, was sufficient, and many people in the neighbourhood who would not otherwise stir themselves to breathe the fresh morning air yet resorted to this spot for their health.

St. Agnes Le Clare, near Hoxton, so named from a spring of water which was dedicated to that Saint. The spring was situated at the end of Pitfield Street in Old Street, City Road. From the transparency and salubrity of its water it was denominated St. Agnes Le Clare, or, vulgarised, "Anniseed Clear." In the reign of Henry VIII it was thus named *Fons voc' Dame Agnes a Clere*, and it is suggested that it had been used to advantage by priests of former times. In a survey of the possessions of the Prebendal estate of Halliwell, *alias* Finsbury, it was called "Dame Agnes the Cleere," and by a previous survey taken in 1650 it is mentioned as lying in waste land, the owner of which was Charles Stuart, late King of England. The neighbouring Charles Square is no doubt named after that monarch. The waters were turned into a cold bath in 1774, and were recommended for nervous complaints and for the cure of rheumatism, etc. The bath, we are told, was thirty feet long and twenty feet broad and four feet six inches deep, and the water being continually running was capable of being rendered higher or lower by a contrivance of sluices.

Not far from St. Agnes Le Clere existed the PEERLESS POOL, and it is interesting to note the origin of the nomenclature of the district, namely, Bath Street and City Road, and Peerless Street and Old Street, for the square formed by these four roads enclosed the site. The Peerless Pool, once known as the Perilous Pool in consequence of its having been a source of danger to the public, consisted of a spring which overflowed its banks and caused the death of many persons by drowning. To prevent these frequent accidents it was filled up in the year 1743, and through the instrumentality of a Mr. Kemp was converted into one of the completest swimming baths in the world then, and it was the only one of its kind in Christendom, The bath, we are told, was 170 feet long and over 100 feet broad and five feet deep in the middle, and was descended to by a grand staircase of marble steps. The bath was in the open air and was surrounded by numerous dressing apartments, and the ground in the immediate vicinity was laid out as a garden with many fine lime trees. Besides the above mentioned swimming bath there was also a cold bath for gentlemen, supposed to be the largest of its kind in England, being forty feet long and twenty feet broad, with an approach of two flights of marble steps, and a dressing room at the end. At four feet depth was a bottom of lattice wood, under which was five feet of water. To these the ingenious originator added a well-

stocked fish-pond 320 feet long for the diversion of the subscribers who were fond of angling. This was also surrounded
by terraces with stately lime trees, and at the end of the garden,
we are told, existed a genteel public house, adjacent to which
the son of the projector afterwards lived.

To the above might be added other wells surrounding
London, equally in repute in their time as places of amusement,
recreation, and as health resorts, such as the wells of Acton,
Richmond, Sydenham, Dulwich and the Beulah Spa, Norwood
etc., etc.; but in the above selection the writer has limited himself
to those wells which were in or near the main arteries to and
from London, and in consequence perhaps were the better
known and more frequented.

CHESFIELD AND ITS RUINED CHURCH.

By CORNELIUS NICHOLLS.

NEAR to the town of Stevenage in Hertfordshire, and
east of the high road leading to Baldock, lie the ruins
of the ancient church of Chesfield, a parish which
although united with that of Gravely since the time of
Henry VI, in 1445, was formerly quite distinct. So ancient is
the manor of Chesfield that even the name under which it has
been known for centuries has, with regard to its origin, long
been a stumbling-block to local historians, who seem to have
failed in satisfactorily accounting for the name it now bears, and
in reconciling that with the name under which it figures in
Domesday Book. This, its manorial history, shows to have been
identical with " Escelveia " or " Scelva."

It will be found amusing, if not always convincing, to compare the various attempts made to elucidate this matter, which
seem, in their extremes, to range between an engaging simplicity and what has been styled " a peremptory roundness of
assertion."

The earliest writer of a description of Hertfordshire, John
Norden, " Surveyor of His Majesty's Woods " to James I, and
author of the *Historical and Chorographical Survey of Middlesex*

and Hertfordshire, gives, amongst other place-names, the following curious derivation of Chesfield : "Chesfeyld, *forte* Choisfeyld *(ager delectus)* for the rich scituation in so fertile a corne soyle." This recalls a similar etymological triumph to be found in the pages of Fabian's *Chronicle*, on the derivation of Constantinople : "Then this Constantyne removed the emperyall see unto his cytie of *Constantyne the noble :* and there for the more partye kepte his emperyall honoure ; and other emperours in lyke wyse after hym. By reason whereof the emperours were longe after called emperours of *Constantyne noble.*"

In quite another style is the assumption of Sir Henry Chauncy, who, after tracing the manorial succession from *Domesday Survey* to the time of Henry III, proceeds—" Then these manors [Graveley andChesfield] came into the possession of William de Chives, who erected a seat upon this hill and called it by his own name to perpetuate the memory thereof to posterity." The next paragraph however suddenly changes this name into " William de Monte *Caviso*" ; thus quite reversing the usual progression of place-names. Salmon's history of the county, an abridgment and continuation of the former to the year 1728, slightly modifies the foregoing statement, thus : " In the reign of Henry III William de Monte Caviso united these manors, and having built himself a seat upon the hill called it by his name, Cavisefield, corrupted since to Chisfield, dropping the old name of Escelveia."

It seems to have fallen to the lot of Clutterbuck, whose history appeared in 1821, to call attention towards the various errors in Chauncy's book. He speaks of Chauncy's frequent digressions, total omission of many important particulars of church history, defective genealogical sketches and numerous errors in tracing the descent of property. One is not surprised, therefore, to find that he differs entirely from the foregoing statement, nor to hear that " The authorities quoted by Chauncy prove his facts to have no connection with the manor." [1] His own theory is that " Chesfield is a slight contraction of Chellsfield or Chillsfield ; Chells being the name of a small adjoining lordship." This opinion is also adopted in the recently published volume of the *Victoria County History*.

These later views on this subject certainly seem more con-

[1] Clutterbuck's *History of Herts*, vol. ii, p. 297.

Chesfield Church.

Photographs by Arthur J. Shorter.

vincing, though requiring some further support. This, we believe, is afforded by the fact that " manors continued to be created until the eighteenth year of Edward I, and numerous parcels of land which now form manors of themselves, at the time of *Domesday Survey* must have been parcels of other manors still in existence." [1] In this way, out of a larger Escelveia or Scelva, or from the original manor of Chells itself, may have been created the separate manor of Chesfield, which would then carry on the old name in its modified form.

Unsatisfactory as have been the efforts of local history to account for the origin of Chesfield's name, it has preserved for us some fragmentary account of Chesfield's ancient church previous to its demolishment. This took place in 1750, under a licence granted by the Bishop of Lincoln, in whose diocese the church then was, upon the representation of the Rector and Churchwardens, who alleged the ruinous and unsafe condition of the building for worship. There seems to have been no suggestion of repairing the fabric which had been the burial place, and contained many memorials of former lords of the manor. This Bishop was Dr. John Thomas, who, in 1753, was also responsible for the pulling down of Shenley Church tower, and the removal of the chancel and nave arches. And, again, in 1757, for the abstraction of the XIV century glass from the Churches of Stanstead Abbots and Eastwick, in order to replace them by modern windows. Fortunately, perhaps, for this diocese he was, in 1761, translated to Salisbury.

As late as the time of Sir Henry Chauncy's history, and up to about the year 1728, the church was still used, though it had suffered much during the rebellion of 1642, quaintly alluded to as " the zeal of the times." According to both Salmon and Chauncy there were in their time still existing, various monuments and painted windows. Under the arch dividing the chapel from the chancel, stood a tomb two feet high, supposed to be that of the founder. In the chancel east window two headless figures, one of them representing St. Edmund. On the north side a Bishop, supposed to be Thomas à Beckett, with his crozier in his hand, and some remains of coats of arms. Another window showed the crest of the Barrington family, who were for a long period lords of this manor. There was also a memorial to John Hurst of Baldock, married to a

[1] Ellis's *Introduction to Domesday Survey*, vol. i, p. 41.

daughter of John Throckmorton; and an old stone bearing the inscription :—

> *Thomas de Blommule gist icy*
> *Dieu de sa alme eit merci.*

This old French form attests its antiquity.

Paintings, memorials, and "storied windows" have disappeared; Clutterbuck, writing in 1821, says—"What remains of the church now is a miserable heap of ruins; the roof is gone, the walls are broken, not one of the windows is entire; the arms and inscriptions above mentioned are lost. The churchyard is thrown open. The following inscription is the only one which remains." This is, or rather was, on a stone, possibly the lid of a stone coffin or tombstone :—

> *Uxores inter*
> *Hic jacet Guli Goodwin*
> *Patriæ Præceptor,*
> *Ickleford et Purton*
> *Villarum Pater;*
> *obiit xx Martii*
> *Ætatis lxxxi*
> *MDCCXXXI*
> *Sequi præpari.*

At the present time but little of this remains, for the stone has been recklessly broken. One silent witness of the past, not previously alluded to, still exists. It is an old stone coffin without lid, slightly sunk below the ground level, showing a chiselled circular cavity for the head.

So remorselessly has all this demolishment been carried out, that one could well imagine Talus himself had been set to work, and had

> "———With his iron flale at it let flie."

> . . . .

> "And all the hewen stones thereof defaced
> That there mote be no hope of reparation
> Nor memory thereof to any nation." [1]

Yet over this "shapeless mass of ruins" grows the kindly ivy, hiding all deformity with its trailing grace.

In common with other churches, Chesfield was twice despoiled of its goods by order of "Protector" Somerset, who, having enriched himself and built Somerset House with the proceeds of

[1] *Faery Queen*, Bk. v, c. 11.

ecclesiastical property, was also eager for the State. After his first Inquisition, in the second year of Edward VI, which still left the church much property, these robberies soon spread beyond his control. "Private men's halls were hung with altar-cloths; their tables and beds covered with copes instead of carpets and coverlets. Many drank at their daily meals in chalices; and no wonder if in proportion it came to the share of their horses to be watered in rich coffins of marble."[1] This state of things roused Somerset and his Privy Council to send out another Inquisition to fine and punish the offenders, and to sweep what was still left into the Treasury. It was then found that some portions were "utterly imbezeled, by some parties not detectable, so cunningly they carried their stealths; seeing every one who had nimmed a church bell did not ring it out for all to hear the sound thereof."[1]

When the Commission came to Chesfield there was found only "A Chalysse of Silver weighing x oz., a Vestymente of Blewe Chamlett, an other Vestyment of White fuschien, an old Cope of Stayned Clothe, Two Bellys in the Steple."[2] From which meagre account there would seem to have been some foundation here for the suspicion of "embezelment."

Before leaving this part of the subject it is interesting to notice that near to the church and the old manor house of Chesfield formerly stood one of the beacons of the county; others being placed at St. Peter's Church, St. Albans, Therfield near Royston, Amwell, and Hertford Heath. This at Chesfield must have been standing shortly before the beginning of the XVIII century, and is clearly denoted on the map of Hertfordshire appended to Chauncy's *History*, who thus alludes to it: "Near the manor house a fair beacon might have been lately seen, which was wount by a light burning fire, to give notice to all the inhabitants round about when any enemies were coming."

The population of this parish is now only about 450, including the picturesque hamlet of Cory's Mill. In this hamlet, lying on the boundary line of the town of Stevenage, there still lingers a curious tradition of its having been the site of one of the first paper mills established in the county; a belief which seems to find expression (under the head of "paper" in Chambers' *Encyclopædia*.

[1] Fuller's *Church Hist.*, chap. vii, sec. 11.
[2] Cussans, vol. ii, p. 69.

23

HAREFIELD.

With regard to the charities of the parish, it is recorded by Cussans [1] that "Edmund Jordane of Chisfield gave by will, dated 12 June, 1626, an annual rent charge of four shillings for the benefit of the poor. It is settled on an acre of land in Graveley Bottom, abutting upon Span Mead." There was another benefaction which now appears to be lost. It was devised by Andrew Cater for the benefit of Sawbridgeworth. This man was a Rector of Chesfield at the time of the Commonwealth, being deprived in 1662, and is described as a "Sectary and a great preacher who keeps conventicles on the Lord's-day." By his will, dated 26 June, 1700, he gave five acres of land and a cottage in Graveley-cum-Chesfield, the annual rent of which was to be given to the poor of Sawbridgeworth. One half was to be expended in teaching four poor children to read, and the remainder in purchasing certain religious books, named by him, for their benefit. This latter bequest seems to have proved a *damnosa hæreditas*, for, according to the same authority, "this gift has long been lost to Sawbridgeworth, probably on account of difficulty in obtaining copies of the books named," and also, apparently, difficulty about the five acres.

HAREFIELD.

By Mary F. A. Tench, F.R.A.I.

THERE are few more interesting and picturesque places to be found in the neighbourhood of London than Harefield, lying about midway between Uxbridge and Rickmansworth. Picturesque, with the soft wooded beauty of a quiet English landscape; interesting from its historical, literary and antiquarian associations. The church, though restored, and a not very impressive example of the Decorated period, is of old foundation, as is proved by its many brasses and monuments, for the most part in an excellent state of preservation, of which a short account will be given later; but the historical records of the neighbourhood must first be touched on.

Consulting the *Domesday Book* we find that at the date of its

[1] *Hist. of Herts*, vol. ii, p. 70.

compilation Harefield belonged to the Earl of Briou, "Richard, son of Gilbert, the Earl (of Briou) holdes Herefelle, which is taxed at five hides . . . . there are three cottars and three slaves, and two mills yielding 15s. rent, four fisheries yielding 1,000 eels, meadow equal to one carucate, pasture for the cattle of the manor, and pannage for a thousand hogs. The total annual value is 12l.; it was only 8l. when entered on by the present owner; in King Edward (the Confessor's) time being then the property of the Countess Goda it was 14l."

From the Norman earl the property descended successively to the Bacheworths, Swanlands, and Newdigates, in each case through marriage with an heiress. In the XVI century the head of the last-named family exchanged his heritage with that of another house, who sold it to the Lord Keeper Egerton, the tomb of whose wife (she was daughter of Sir John Spencer, of Althorpe, and widow of Ferdinando, Earl of Derby) is to be seen in the south-east corner of the chancel of the parish church, and is a heavy cumbrous structure, such as was popular at the time of her death. Whilst the wife of Sir Thomas Egerton she had the no doubt costly honour of twice entertaining Queen Elizabeth, then nearing the end of her reign. The first of these visits was paid in 1601, and amongst the amusements provided for the royal guests was a "Lotterie presented before ye Queene's Majestie." A "marriner," we are told, with "a boxe" under his arm, came into the presence singing a song, which began:—

> "Cynthia Queene of seas and lands,
> That Fortune everie where commands."

Before the lottery took place the "marriner" addressed the feminine portion of his audience in these words: "Come, ladies, try your Fortunes, and if anie light vpon an vncomfortable blanke, let her thinke that Fortune do but moke her in these trifles, and meanes to pleasure her in great matters."

Indeed the motto attached to one of the "vncomfortable blankes" was quite a cheery one running as follows:—

> "Nothinge's your lot, this more than can be told
> For nothinge is more precious than gold."

Amongst the treasures in the box we find a "plaine" gold ring, a "paire of sizzers," a mirror, and other small articles.

All during this visit seems to have gone as merry as a marriage bell; but in the following year, when the Queen came again to " Harevile," we are told that it rained without ceasing for the whole three days of her stay there.

Notwithstanding this unpleasant state of the weather the brave old woman (for she was then about seventy years of age) sat on horseback for hours at a stretch receiving the homage and addresses of her subjects, and seems to have taken no hurt. For Sir Fulke Greville, who was one of the party at Harefield Place, says, in a letter to the Countess of Shrewsbury, " the beste newes I can write your ladieship is of the Queene's health and disposition of bodie, wch, I assure you, is excellent goode, and I haue not seene her in euery way better disposed these manie yeares."

Indeed, though this was within a few months of her death at a good old age, Elizabeth seems to have been in a very light-hearted frame of mind, for we read of a little prank played by her which would have been more in keeping with a middle-class schoolgirl, than with the elderly majesty of England. Noticing that Lady Derby wore a miniature suspended from her throat she demanded to be allowed to examine it. On her hostess objecting she seized it, and having opened it and finding that it contained a portrait of Mr. Secretary (though what the wife of the Lord Keeper meant by wearing Cecil's picture on her breast the chronicler does not state), she tied it in the first instance to her shoe, and later, fastening it to her elbow, wore it thus for the remainder of the day. In regard to this occurrence, Cecil wrote and presented to his sovereign a flattering set of verses, such as, notwithstanding her many masculine qualities and lion heart, Elizabeth dearly loved. In fact, although to quote some lines out of many written, about her visit " poor St. Swithin now," dared " to show his cloudy brow," these three days did not pass by any means drearily. On the occasion of the Queen's departure there was a rustic ceremony, in which " Herfel " was shown mourning for her departure, the rain being attributed to the many tears which it shed at this sad misfortune. During the visit a Morality Play was acted before her Majesty by the Lord Chamberlain's players, brought down specially from London for the occasion, and since Shakespeare belonged to this company, it is thought that he may have been amongst the actors, though there is no evidence that such was the case.

But if the appearance at Harefield of England's and, indeed,

Brass of William Assheby and Jane his wife,
Harefield Church.

Brass of George Assheby and Rose his wife,
Harefield Church.

HAREFIELD.

The scatter'd lead pursues the sight,
And death in thunder stops their flight ;
His spaniel of true English kind
With gratitude inflames his mind ;
This servant in an honest way,
In all his actions copied Tray."

The whole is a handsome tribute, not only to the worth of a valued dependent, but also to the good qualities of man's truest and most faithful friend, who here indeed seems to be given the higher, not the lower place.

On entering the church let us first go to the chancel where is the tomb of the Dowager Countess of Derby, who, though she died at an advanced age, is here shown with the golden brown hair of her youth flowing over her shoulders, and with a face fair and unlined. She lies full length, clad in a crimson robe of the fashion of the period, and with her head (encircled by a coronet) resting on an embroidered cushion. In niches underneath kneel her three daughters, Lady Chandos, and the Countesses of Bridgewater and of Huntingdon, and all over the tomb are to be found the arms blazoned of Stanley and Spencer, of Egerton, Bridgewater and Hastings, the whole effect though interesting being, to modern eyes, heavy and indeed rather wanting in good taste. This "ladye of high degree," was a notable personage in her day, being, according to Harrington—

" Fruitful and faire and of so cleare a name,
That all this region marvell'd at her fame,"

and he adds that she—

" Took such sweet state vpon her,
All eares, eyes, tongues, heard, saw and spoke her honour."

Lady Derby appears to have been of a charitable disposition, for she it was who founded, shortly before her death in 1637, the picturesque almshouses for six old women, which stand beside the road leading to Harefield village, endowing each with £5 a year and £1 for repairs, a larger sum in those days than in these. She gave besides to the curate, whose stipend only amounted to £6 13s. 4d. per annum, a yearly sum of £5 and a house, on condition that he read prayers twice a week to the poor almswomen.

Close to the imposing monument just mentioned is another and more interesting one, an altar tomb without date to John Newdigate and Anne his wife, who kneel opposite to each other, with behind them a train of thirteen sorrowing sons and daughters. On the stone table in front are some helmets and gauntlets of ancient date.

The south aisle, which is known as the Brackenburye Chapel, so called from the family of de Brackenburgh, who, in the XIV century, leased a messuage and lands in Harefield from the de Swanlands, contains many interesting monuments of the old and honourable house of Newdigate. In the north-east wall is a XVI century table-tomb of one of its members and of Amphilicia his wife, who were the parents of no less than fourteen children. The brasses are in good preservation; but, unfortunately, are nearly entirely hidden by a modern stall which is placed in front of the tomb. Very clear and perfect is another brass which ornaments the south wall, and represents Edetha, widow of William Newdigate, who died in 1444. Richard Newdigate, commemorated in a very long Latin inscription, lived in stirring and troublous times, Whitlock, in his memorials, giving a vivid account of various passages in his life. At the date of the execution of Charles I he was a Serjeant-at-law, and was summoned with other barristers into the presence of Cromwell, who announced his intention of making them judges; but they declined the honour, asserting that they could not act under his commission. Upon this he turned from them angrily, saying: "If you of the red robe will not execute the law, my red coats shall," so they all cried out, "make us judges, we will be judges." But Newdigate was shortly after deprived of his post, for being sent on the northern circuit at a time when many cavaliers were tried for bearing arms in the cause of the Stuarts, he refused to sentence them, saying that he "knew no law which made it high treason to levy war against a Lord Protector." However, some years later he became Chief Justice of the Upper Bench, and on the restoration received a baronetcy (the ordinary fees being remitted) from Charles II, who was by no means so ungrateful as some would have us believe, and also that monarch's warmest thanks for kindness shown to his friends during "the worst of times."

Sir Richard, shortly before his death, which occurred in 1678, purchased the house and lands of Harefield, which had been exchanged by his grandfather for another property; it was at the time in possession of the heirs of the Dowager Countess of Derby, and it has belonged to the Newdigate family ever since.

William Assheby's **Children.**

George Assheby's **Children.**
Harefield **Church.**

HAREFIELD.

It may be of interest to readers to recall that the father of "George Eliot" was land agent to Francis Newdigate, Esq., at Arbury, in Warwickshire, which had been received in exchange for Harefield Place by his ancestor, John Newdigate, and that the celebrated novelist was born at Arbury Farm.

Space does not permit of a notice of all the tombs to be found in the Brackenburye Chapel, for the north aisle claims our notice. In it are to be seen many monuments to the family of Ashby of Brakespere or Braekspeare, though none quite so old as the earliest of the memorials to the Newdigates, already mentioned as bearing the date 1444. There are, however, several brasses of the XVI and XVII centuries in a capital state of preservation, notably those of George Asheby, "Clerke of the Sygnet to Kynge" Henry VII, and also to Henry VIII, to whom he was "Counseller" as well. The tomb bears no date, but is said to have been placed in the church in 1514. George Ashby's wife, Rose, and their children are also represented. Another very perfect memorial is that to Willam Ashby and Jane his wife, the inscription, oddly enough, being placed upside down. Close by are many other brasses, the latest, which is to the memory of John Sheron, "surgeon," dating from 1755, and several mural monuments; whilst on the west wall of the passage leading from the Ashby aisle to the nave, may be seen one to the Rev. John Prichett, who, after serving as Vicar of the parish for thirty years, was raised to the See of Gloucester in 1672, dying in 1680.

The church has been lately whitewashed and otherwise cleaned, which, though probably necessary and desirable, has somewhat spoiled its old-world appearance, but this is a fault which will no doubt be cured by time; it is full of memories of the past, which will endear it to the heart of the antiquary.

The information in regard to Harefield's past has been principally drawn from two sources, *The Progresses of Queen Elizabeth*, and *An Historical Account of those Parishes in the County of Middlesex, which are not described in the Environs of London.* My thanks are due to the Vicar of Harefield for permission to take rubbings; to Mr. Gustavus A. Handcock, of the Public Record Office, and to Mr. George Watts, under whose able ciceronage I first made the acquaintance of Harefield, as well as to various residents in this charming and most interesting spot.

THE CULPEPERS IN KENT.

By A. Leland Noel.

NO genealogist," says the well-known archæologist, Mr. William Smith Ellis, in his *Early Kentish Armory*, "has yet explained the origin of the name and family of Culpeper. No such local name has been met with either in England or Normandy. The probability seems to be that the Culpepers rose to their high position by a wealthy alliance, and in that way acquired their coat armour with their property, but through what channel is at present unknown."

On this text I wish to make a few remarks. That it was a remarkable family needs no demonstration, seeing that the " high position " to which they attained is made evident by Camden's remark that there were no less than twelve knights and baronets of that name living in his time. And after his time one branch of the family reached the peerage.

They first appear in the page of English history in the person of Thomas de Colepeper, who was a judge of assize in the reign of King John, that is about the year 1200. They disappeared in the person of John Spencer Culpepper, who was born December 18th, 1740, and died unmarried. There is not known to be a single male descendant left in England. During this period of five centuries and a half they were the owners of six estates in Kent, one in Sussex and one in Rutland, together with numerous manor houses in Kent, Sussex, Surrey, Rutland, and Linconshire. And of them Dugdale says : " this family has for many ages past flourisht with great esteem in the counties of Kent and Sussex."

Their coat of arms is mentioned by the poet Drayton in his *Baron's Wars.*

> "And Colepeper, with silver arm inrailed,
>   Bore thereupon a bloody band engrailed."

In heraldic language this reads " Argent, a bend engrailed gules."

These arms are first mentioned as borne by John Colepeper in 1330. Dugdale informs us that they were set up at Whitehall by Henry VIII for the valor of members of the family at the battle of the Spurs. And Hasted tells us that they were more than once carved on the roof of the cloisters of Canterbury Cathedral.

Brass of **Edith** Neudigate, Harefield.

THE CULPEPERS IN KENT.

As regards the origin of the name: the earliest form in which it appears is "Colepeper," with some ten after variations. But none of these give us the needful hint how the name arose. We find "Cole" in many combinations, *e.g.*, "Cole Abbey"; while the second half "peper" is part of the name of a parish in Surrey, "Peper-Harrow." But as this Peper in Peper-Harrow is said to de derived from one Pipard, it does not help us in the matter.

The family was best known as landed proprietors, though among its members some were in the army, at the bar, and in the Church. They had, however, no representative in literature, unless we can dignify with that name the strange book published in 1653 under the title of *Culpeper's Complete Herbal.* The book was republished as a curiosity in 1835, with a portrait of the author showing the long hair, white collar, and general dress of a Puritan, and with a picture of the house in London in which he lived and died. There is a reference to it in the *Gentleman's Magazine* of February, 1836. And it appears to have been one of the books read by the youthful Livingstone, as in his autobiographical sketch he refers to it as "that extraordinary old book on Astrological Medicine, *Culpeper's Herbal.*"

The first property which came into the hands of the family, of which mention is made, is that of Bayhall, in the parish of Pepenbury (now Pembery, near Tonbridge Wells), which was owned by Sir John Colepeper in the latter end of the XIII century. Of him we know nothing. But his son, Sir Thomas, was in 1309 appointed Bailiff of Ashdown Forest. The Bailiff had two sons. The elder, Thomas, who inherited Bayhall, was Castellan of Leeds Castle, near Maidstone, for Lord Badlesmere, and was beheaded in 1324 at Winchester for obeying his lord's orders to refuse the admission to the castle of Queen Isabella, wife of Edward II.

He was succeeded at Bayhall by his son, John, who was the first to bear the family arms, as mentioned above; which arms are engraved on old Pembury Church, which he is supposed to have built, and they can be seen there to-day.

He was followed at Bayhall by his son, another Sir Thomas, who was one of the Commissioners for resisting the rebels under Wat Tyler.

He, Thomas, married Joan, daughter of Sir Nicholas Green,

and in her right became possessed of Exton Park, Oakham, in Rutland. He was succeeded at Exton by his son, Sir Thomas, whose daughter, and only child, carried the estate to the Haringtons, whose eventual heiress, Mabel Harington, married Sir Andrew Noel, from whom descends the present holder of Exton, the Earl of Gainsborough.

Sir Thomas, having inherited Exton, sold Bayhall about 1450, to Humphry Stafford, Duke of Buckingham, from whom it passed through several hands to Charles Browne, who died there in 1753.

The second son of the Bailiff of Ashdown Forest, Walter, was the owner of several manors round about Tonbridge, amongst others of Fairlawn, now the property of Mr. William Casalet.

Walter's eldest son, Thomas, appears as the first holder of Preston Hall, near Aylesford, but as he left no children, the estate passed to his brother, Sir Jeffery, who served as High Sheriff of Kent in 1366 and again in 1374.

Jeffery's grandson, Sir John, was judge in the Court of Common Pleas in 1406. From him through several generations Preston passed to Sir Richard, who had three danghters, the second of whom, Joyce, married Lord Edward Howard, and was the mother of Queen Catherine, fifth wife of Henry VIII.

Preston Hall passed to Sir Richard's younger brother, William, and from him to his great-grandson, Thomas. This Thomas was a man of varied parts. He figures as Chief Bailiff and Park Keeper of the Manor of Tonbridge, whilst it was held by the Duke of Buckingham; and when the Duke was attainted by Henry VIII, Thomas shared in his disgrace, his offices being granted by the King in 1542 to Ralph Fane.

Having become accustomed to the management of a park when Thomas lost his position at Tonbridge he rented Knole Park from John Dudley, Duke of Northumberland, until 1553, when the tenancy ceased on the sale of the property by the Duke to King Edward VI.

On the accession of Queen Mary, Thomas, in company with the sons of Lord Cobham, joined in the rebellion under Sir Thomas Wyatt; and in consequence his house, Preston Hall, was handed over to Mr. Cartwright the Under-Sheriff, whilst he himself was confined in the Tower of London. He had there as a fellow prisoner Thomas Fane, who had married his cousin,

Elizabeth Culpeper. They appear to have been martyrs to their Protestant principles, for Dugdale records that they cut on the stone wall of the cell these words : " Be thou faithful to the end and I will give you a crown of eternal life—1554, T. Fane, T. Culpeper, of Ailsford, Kent." We must pardon the prisoners their somewhat hazy remembrance of Rev. ii, 10.

In spite of their forebodings they appear to have been pardoned, for Fane lived to be Sir Thomas Fane of Mereworth Castle, and Culpeper became a Revenue Commissioner; and in 1561 he was " Purveyor of Rochester Bridge." Preston Hall seems to have been restored to him, for his grandson, Sir William, is described as of Preston Hall.

This Sir William was created a baronet in 1627—it is noticeable that in the patent the name is spelt Colepepyr. He was succeeded by his son Sir Richard as second baronet, whose son, Sir Thomas, was third baronet. Sir Thomas died in 1723 without children, and he left the property to his sister Alice. This Alice married four times. When the last baronet died and left her the estate, she was the childless widow of his cousin, Thomas Culpeper of Hollingbourne, and he doubtless thought that, as there were no direct heirs, she would leave her estate to her late husband's branch of the family.

But within six months of his death, that is, in October, 1723, the wily Dr. Milner induced the old lady, then sixty-six years of age, to accept him as her fourth husband, and to settle all her property upon him. This done, Dr. Milner died the following year, and bequeathed the estate to his brother Charles, also an M.D. Charles Milner died at Preston Hall in 1771, leaving the property to his nephew, the Rev. Joseph Butler, from whom it passed to Henry Robert Milner, who held it in 1847. He, or his heir, sold it to Mr. E. L. Bates, who sold it to Mr. Henry Brassey. Mr. Brassey pulled down the old hall and erected the present grand modern house.

The Sir Thomas Colepeper who through his wife Joan Green became possessed of Exton, and whose eldest son inherited Exton, had a second son, Walter, who served under Sir William Bourchier at the siege of Harfleur in 1415. When the war terminated at the battle of Agincourt, Walter returned to England, married Agnes, daughter of Edmund Roper, of St. Dunstan's, Canterbury, and settled down as a country gentleman at Goudhurst. But his fighting temper, untamed by thirty-five years of peaceful life, led him, in company with his sons, John and Richard, to join the rebels under Jack Cade in 1450. His eldest son John married Agnes, the heiress of Bedgebury, and so came into possession of that property; while his second son, Richard, and his third son, Nicholas, became in succession the owners of Wakehurst in Sussex.

By Agnes Bedgebury, of Bedgebury, this John was the father of two sons, the eldest, Alexander, succeeding to Bedgebury; while the younger, Walter, through his marriage with Ann Aucher, becoming owner of Losenham, in the parish of Newenden.

We will first follow the line at Bedgebury, and then revert to the line at Losenham.

Sir John (husband of Agnes) died in 1483, and was succeeded, as stated above, by his son Alexander. This Alexander's son, Thomas, married twice, and both his wives being heiresses, they brought a number of manors into the family. By his first wife, Eliza Haute, he had two sons and one daughter; the elder of the sons, Alexander by name, followed him at Bedgebury; while the daughter, Elizabeth, married Thomas Fane (afterwards Sir Thomas Fane of Mereworth Castle) who was in the rebellion with Sir Thomas Wyatt in 1553, as mentioned above. By his second wife, Helen Somerset Hendley, he had a daughter, who married Christopher Sackville, ancestor of the Duke of Dorset.

But, unsatisfied with having secured a number of properties by his two wives, this Thomas Culpeper is notorious in history as a barefaced trafficker in the manors of the dissolved monasteries. No less than twenty-nine of these transactions are on record. It would be wearisome to go into the details of these grants, purchases, and sales of manors all over the county; but the result was that Thomas became perhaps the richest squire in Kent.

He was buried at Goudhurst, and in the church there there is a large monument commemorating "the eldest son of ould Sir Alexander."

He was succeeded at Bedgebury by his eldest son, Sir Alexander who entertained Queen Elizabeth at Bedgebury in 1573.

It was at this period, I think, that the family reached its highest point as landed proprietors. For although they were

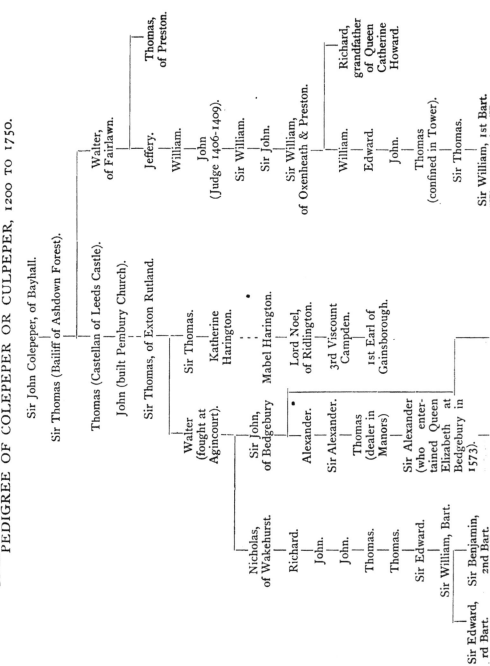

John Spencer
(died unmarried, the last male
representative of the Colepeper
family).

afterwards to obtain two baronetcies and a peerage, yet as a family of squires they were, in 1573, the owners of more estates than at any time either before or after. There was a Thomas at Crawley, a George at Balcombe, a William at Worth, a Richard at Onstye, and a William at Hunton. Francis was living at Greenway Court; Sir John was the owner of Losenham, in Kent, and of Wigsell, in Sussex; Thomas was flourishing at Preston Hall; while Edward, of Wakehurst, was at that time a boy of eleven, whose inherited property was accumulating during his minority, so that in 1590 he was able to rebuild Wakehurst, and turn the modest home of his ancestors into "one of the most stately houses in Sussex."

Sir Alexander, of Bedgebury, died in 1599, and was succeeded by his son, Sir Anthony.

This Sir Anthony began dissipating his father's large estate, and his grandson, Thomas, sold Bedgebury and died childless.

The above Anthony's fourth son was Colonel Sir Thomas, who in 1637 bought Place House. He married Lady Barbara Sidney, daughter of the Earl of Leicester, and widow of Viscount Strangford. By her he had a son, Thomas, who, in 1675, sold Place House to Edward Hales, whose great grandson, Sir Edward Hales, Bart., pulled down the old house and built the large one now in the occupation of the French Jesuits.

We hear no more of this Thomas, and with him that branch of the family appears to have died out.

We must now revert, as proposed, to Walter, the second son of Sir John of Bedgebury, who, as seen, became owner of Losenham. Of his descendants the most prominent was Sir John Culpeper, who, in 1644, was created by Charles I, Baron Culpeper of Thoresway, Lincoln. His three sons, Thomas, John, Cheney, were successively second, third, and fourth Barons. The last-named died unmarried in 1725, and the title became extinct.

There was another line at Greenway Court and Hollingbourne, which manor was bought by Francis, second son of William, of Losenham. The son of Francis, known as Sir Thomas of Hollingbourne, bought Leeds Castle; but, it seems, continued to live at Hollingbourne Manor House. His three daughters are known to fame as having embroidered the velvet altar cloth of Hollingbourne Church, the colours of which, though the work is 250 years old, are still brilliant. The room in which they did the work is known in the manor house to this day as " The Needle Room." They were engaged upon it during the days of the Commonwealth, but they did not dare present it for public use until the Restoration. The subject of the embroidery is the twelve mystic fruits of the tree of life.

Sir Thomas died in 1661, and his great grandson, John Spencer Culpeper, sold Greenway Court and all his property at Hollingbourne.

This John Spencer, having got rid of all his family property, took up his abode in 1739 at the Charterhouse in London as Receiver.

He married in 1743 Ruth Webb, by whom he had one son, John Spencer, his wife Ruth dying at her son's birth. In 1752 he married secondly Mary Webb, by whom he had one son, Richard, who died unmarried. The second John Spencer died unmarried, and with him the wide-spread family of Culpeper, as regards male representatives, became finally extinct.

There are many families in English history who, after becoming prominent, have failed to leave male heirs to carry on the name. But I do not think there is any family who occupied so much land, and held so many public positions during a period of five hundred years, who have been so entirely obliterated as the descendants of Sir John Colepeper, who was the owner of Bayhall at the end of the XIII century.

NOTES ON THE EARLY CHURCHES OF SOUTH ESSEX.

By C. W. FORBES, Member of the Essex Archæological Society.

[Continued from vol. x, p. 260.]

I PROPOSE in this article to complete the series of churches lying between Grays and Stanford-le-Hope, viz:—Grays Thurrock, Little or East Thurrock, West and East Tilbury, all of them being churches of early foundation.

Little Thurrock Church.

West Tilbury Church.

Forbes

EARLY CHURCHES OF SOUTH ESSEX.

GRAYS THURROCK.

The church at Grays Thurrock, commonly called Grays, is situated close to the railway station, a few yards to the south; it is cruciform in shape, built of flint and chalk. The tower, with its dwarf broached spire, is on the north side, and contains three bells. There are two entrances: south door with porch, and a plain north door. In 1846 the church was to a great extent rebuilt and considerably enlarged, the portions lying to the west of the south porch being new work. The interior contains chancel, with a modern wooden screen of no particular merit, dividing the altar from choir; a nave of four bays, with north and south chapels, one on each side of the chancel.

The east end of the church, the two chapels, and the lower portion of the tower, also the octagonal font, are attributed to the XIII century. So far as I have been able to learn there is no trace of an earlier structure.

An Early English arch divides the north chapel from the aisle. The chancel arch is round and rather low; it is believed that a similar XIII century one lies underneath, but covered in with modern work. The south chapel also has a modern brick division, the eastern portion being now used as a priest's vestry; the western end, forming a part of the choir, has a small piscina and an aumbry.

The interior is very poor as regards monumental work, but has one brass, *circa* 1510, to a civilian with two wives and several children.

In digging the foundations for the station master's house close by, a very fine tesselated Roman pavement was discovered some few years back; also portions of Roman masonry. Doubtless the Romans had a settlement here close to the river.

This pavement, in its entirety, now forms the floor of the priest's vestry; it is in very good preservation.

LITTLE THURROCK.

One mile to the east, on the the road to Tilbury Docks, is the small church of East or Little Thurrock. The town of Grays has grown rapidly the last few years, and practically absorbed this small village.

The structure is a small one, dating from the XII century, containing chancel and nave only, and an early XIII century door with porch on the north side, on the east side of the interior wall of which is the remains of a Holy water stoup. The south doorway on the opposite side of the church was bricked up during the early part of the XVII century.

In the chancel is a small priest's door now fastened up.

There was originally a small wooden western spire which was destroyed at the restoration in 1878, being replaced by the present low stunted tower of no great beauty; in fact it rather mars the appearance of the church from the roadway.

On entering, we notice traces of a large arch on the south wall, now built in. No information is available as to what this arch really was; it is supposed to have been at one time occupied by a tomb. This, however, is only conjecture.

The pulpit is very plain, dated 1700. The font to the west of the north doorway is a plain octagonal one, and presumed to be XIII century work.

The arch dividing the nave and chancel is a plain rounded one, probably original XII century work. It is believed that at one time another arch was placed in front of this, remains of which can be seen at the present time on the south side. These remains were uncovered at the late restoration, and traces of a curious old fresco were discovered on them.

The best piece of work in the church is a handsome three-seated sedilia, and a large trefoil-headed piscina with an ogee ornamental top added. The sedilia has curious figure-heads carved in the stone on the arches.

WEST TILBURY.

Continuing on our journey towards the ferry, we next arrive at West Tilbury. This church stands at the top of a hill. On a clear day a very fine view of the river Thames and the county of Kent can be seen from the top of the tower.

The renowned Archbishop Laud was at one time, *circa* 1615, Rector of this parish. It is stated that owing to this fact the building was despoiled, and partially destroyed by Lord Fairfax and his troopers in 1648, when on their way to the siege of Colchester. The building, like many others, was used as stables for the horses of his troopers.

The present church, restored in 1883, contains a chancel and nave, and an embattled western tower with clock and five of the old bells, with dates 1621 to 1694. The early portions of

East Tilbury Church.
Photographs by C. W. Forbes.

the structure, viz., the outer walls, north door, and some of the windows, are XIII century.

A modern lychgate admits us to the churchyard. Built into the first buttress, to the east of the north door, is the stone framework of the remains of a trefoil-headed piscina; this at one time was doubtless in the chancel, thrown out during the destruction in 1648, and at a later period inserted here to preserve it.

The north doorway has the remains of a Holy-water stoup plainly visible on the west side.

The interior has now little to interest the archæologist; the present font dates from the restoration; but outside in the churchyard is an old pedestal font of the Georgian period. In the chancel is a plain two-seated sedilia. There are no other features of ancient work left worth mentioning.

The Communion plate has two chalices, dated 1762 and 1797, and a flagon, *circa* 1800.

The registers date from 1540.

EAST TILBURY.

We now pass to the last of the churches in this corner of the county, situated about a mile and a half from what is called Low Street, an ancient Roman road. This church, from the point of view of the historian, is certainly the most interesting in this part of Essex. It is quite close to the river, and near what is called Coalhouse Fort, built by the illustrious military hero, General Charles Gordon, while in command of the Thames forts, 1866 to 1871.

The ancient parish of East Tilbury, and its church, may really be regarded as possessions of national importance. Tracing its history back to very early times, we read that A.D. 43, the Roman Emperor, Claudius, crossed the Thames by the ferry here, and took command of the army of Aulus Plautius, preparatory to his march upon, and capture of, Camelodunum (or Colchester). Traces of the ancient causeway on the opposite side of the river from Rochester to Higham, point directly to East Tilbury as the site of the ancient Roman ferry.

Later we find the Venerable Bede referring to two centres of St. Cedd's or Ceadda's spiritual work, viz., Ythancester and Tilbury. The first-named place has been identified with the site of the Roman fortress of Othona, which was situated near a small place called "Bradwell juxta mare," at the north-east corner of the Hundred of Dengie. As regards Tilbury, at that time called Tilaburg, Bede states that Cedd was, *circa* 655, at the request of Segibert, King or chief of the Kingdom of Essex, sent here to preach and baptize. He afterwards became the third Bishop of London, and is credited with building the first church here and a monastery, no traces of which are now in existence. Later we find that, *circa* 1042-1066, *temp.* Edward the Confessor, the parish was one manor subsequently divided into five, one of which still exists under its ancient name of Gobyons.

The church, down to the middle of the XVII century, consisted of a nave, chancel, north and south aisles, and a lofty western tower; there was also a chantry attached, founded and endowed, *circa* 1328, by Sir Thomas Gobyons, the then owner of the manor; some remains of this can still be seen.

In 1667 the Dutch fleet, under the celebrated De Ruyter, sailed up the Thames and Medway and caused considerable damage to the English fleet and dockyards at Sheerness and Chatham during the battle between the English and Dutch fleets, which took place in what is called the Lower Hope. The fine and lofty tower and south aisle, also the Vicarage, were fired on by the Dutch sailors and utterly wrecked. The foundations are still clearly visible, and numerous cannon balls can even now be picked up in the churchyard and surrounding fields.

Until the year 1893, when about £1,000 was spent on the restoration, the church was simply a patched ruin, the roof was open in many places to the sky, the water stood in pools in the north aisle and nave after heavy rain, and the windows were so shattered that it was necessary to fasten a covering over them to keep out the wind and rain. After every firing of the guns at the adjoining fort and battery, large portions of the ceiling fell from the inside of the roof, and many tiles were dislodged from the outside.

It is estimated that a further sum of at least £1,500 is necessary to rebuild the tower, etc., on the original sites, and complete the restoration.

The body of the church is Norman work dating from the middle of the XII century. The walls, however, contain portions of earlier ancient masonry, probably Saxon or pre-Norman; also fragments of Roman bricks and flanged roofing tiles. Additions and alterations were made in the XIV and XV centuries.

The north doorway by which we enter is Early English with an ancient porch.

There are three small lancet windows in the chancel, and one larger one which is now bricked up; also an early-pointed priest's door. To the west of this is a low-side window of the XIV century, with an additional square-topped one built over it, forming a curious double window.

The nave on the north side has one small lancet window similar to those in the chancel, the others being two and three light windows in the Decorated style.

In the chancel is a trefoil-headed piscina with shelf and rose-basin.

The north aisle is separated from the nave by three pillars, two being round and the centre one octagonal. The ornamental carved stone work at the top of each pillar is different.

In the south wall are visible the remains of two arches which formed part of the south aisle. The wall, however, and the two windows in the Decorated style inserted in it, have been built up very roughly out of the old materials and stone work.

The font is a fine octagonal one of the XIII century.

There are no monuments or brasses now left in the interior; but scattered about the western end are portions of two ancient stone coffins and a number of pieces of stone work which formed portions of early tombs which doubtless existed. The pulpit is Jacobean.

In 1389 the living of East Tilbury was appropriated to Lord Cobham's College in Kent by authority of a bull of Pope Urban II.

The reputed stone coffin of St. Chad, *circa* 667, is said to be in the churchyard, although I have not as yet been able to trace it.

Nearly all the churches along the river from London to Shoebury had, it appears, originally strong stone towers, built and used as means of defence. It was probably owing to the tower at East Tilbury being used for this purpose that it was fired upon by the Dutch.

Near by are remains of ancient earth works, also portions of the embankment or sea wall, built by the Danes to prevent the overflowing of the river.

[To be continued.]

SOME EAST KENT PARISH HISTORY.

By Peter de Sandwich.

[Continued from vol. x, p. 275.]

BUCKLAND.

1580. [See under Badlesmere, vol. vii, p. 212.]

1605. We have a [Prayer] Book and a Bible, but we want a book of Homilies. We say our carpet was lately stolen away, and we will speedily provide another. We have not the Ten Commandments as yet [set up in the church].

Our church is somewhat at reparations wanting tileing and glazing, which hereafter shall shortly be repaired.

We have not yet a table of degrees [of marriages forbidden] but will provide one.

We have not a pulpit cloth, for it was lately stolen away.— (Fol. 3.)

That for the space of these five weeks we have had no service in the forenoon in our parish church.

We have had no service on Wednesday and Fridays, and seldom on holydays this twelvemonth.

He is beneficed and allowed preacher and preacheth every Sunday, but not at Buckland.

We have no youth catechised in our parish this twelvemonth.

An answer to the presentments made against the Vicar of Buckland by the churchwardens.

The Vicar saith that he only omitted to read prayers two Sundays in the morning nor more as he thinketh, the reason whereof was partly for that he was not in health. That there is not a large Bible, with a surplice in the church, that divers times he requested the churchwardens to provide one, but they would not.

He saith that on Holy-days for the most part they have had prayers, but for none come to the church.

He is ready and willing to catechise the youth of the parish, but have none come to the church before evening prayer.— (Vol. 1604-5, fol. 214.)

1637. We present Robert Clegat and his wife for that they have often neglected to come to our parish church on Sundays and Holydays to hear divine service; and especially for their absence from church on the feast day of the Purification of the Blessed Virgin Mary ; and on the feast day of St.Mathias, 1636; and on Sunday, 2 April, 1637; and Sunday, 23 April; and on St. Mark's day.

Also we present Robert Clegat for that he suffereth his mill to go on Sundays and Holydays, albeit he hath been often warned to the contrary, to the great disturbance of the minister and people, especially on St. Matthew's day and on St. Mark's day.

Also we present Robert Clegat and Sarah, his wife, and Elisabeth Thomas, his maid-servant, for not receiving the Holy Communion at Easter last.

On 23 November, Robert Clegat appeared in Court and said :—That by the necessary affairs of his calling he is often occasioned to be absent from home both Sundays and week days, sometimes a whole quarter of a year together, but at such times as he is at home he duly keeps his church upon Sundays, but for Holy-days it is the generality of the parish that is to blame as well as he for not keeping their church those days.

That his mill never goeth in prayer time on the Sundays, nor that he permits on Holydays; nor, indeed, on the Sundays from morning till toward evening.

That he and his wife were from home the last Easter and abode here at Canterbury at his father's in St. Andrew's parish ; but shortly after, she being at Newcastle, received the Communion there, as appears by a certificate under the minister's hand. But he received it in his own parish church of Buckland last Whitsuntide, and had received it there with his wife and maid-servant on Low Sunday; but because there were no more in the parish to receive but only they, not a convenient number to communicate alone, their Pastor refused to call or hold a Communion for them.—(Vol. 1636-39, fol. 113.)

1640. We do present Whittingham Fogge[1] of the parish of Buckland, gent., for not paying his cess for the reparation of our church, which sum is ten shillings upon hin cessed the 7 May, 1639, for 120 acres of land lying in our parish, at one penny an acre.—(Vol. 1639-66, fol. 51.)

[To be continued.]

[1] See *Archæologia Cantiana*, vol. v, for the Fogge Pedigree, etc.

THE KING'S OLD BARGEHOUSE.

By Ethel Lega-Weekes.

[Continued from vol. x, page 304.]

THE plot of land, which, in the last Ordnance Survey Map (London, five feet scale, Sheet VII, No 74) is marked "Site of the King's Old Bargehouse,"[1] appears to me, as I have said, to lie too far to the west to coincide with the actual site of the building in question. For, although it is on the east side of the "Parlimentary Borough Boundary" between Southwark and Lambeth, indicated in the 1875 O.S. and other modern maps, it is distinctly on the west side of the *original boundary*, as shown in earlier maps, down to 1768.

The fact that this plot is in the possession of the Duchy of Cornwall would, moreover, seem to indicate that it was anciently within the manor of Kennington and parish of Lambeth, whereas the actual site of the King's Bargehouse, as stated in the Cromwellian Survey, and as established by the old Court Rolls, was "*within the parish of St. Saviour's.*"

The obvious geographical boundary was the wide ditch which is so conspicuous a landmark in the early views, running north, or, more correctly, north-west, from St. George's Fields into the Thames, and which must have been of very ancient construction, if, as I gather from a passage in Allen's *Lambeth* (p. 357), it coincided with part of the so-called "Canute's Trench."

In most of the Elizabethan maps, *e.g.*, the Guildhall original, 1562,[2] Braun 1572, and Norden 1593, and in the Manorial Plan of 1627, its entire length is exposed to sight; but in most of the later ones its northern end—beyond Narrow Wall—disappears from view, though it presumably pursued its straight course subterraneously, as it does, I am informed, at the present day, in the guise of a sewer. In one "Plan of the City in the time of Elizabeth" (reproduced in Besant's *London Under the Tudors*, p. 188) its upper end deviates to the westward, forming

---

[1] The lettering on this sheet, I may mention, covers a space having about 100 feet river-frontage, but is no doubt meant to apply only to the narrow strip on which the same title is inscribed in the 1875 O.S.

[2] This map has generally been attributed to Agas; but Overall, in the preface to the reproduction, contends that the date ascribed to it by Vertue, 1560, is too early for it to have been by Agas, and appears to be of opinion that it is probably "the carde of London" entered on Gyles Godhead's list, 1562; and that if by Agas, it cannot have been made before 1591.

a sharp loop suggesting the curvature of the modern Parliamentary boundary, but I think that this must be a faulty modification of Van de Keere's,[1] where—as in other and more modern maps—two branches turn off to the left, bordering Narrow Wall, while the remainder of the main ditch is not delineated. The same bend to the westward appears in Faithorne's map, but here we plainly see the main ditch debouching close to the Bargehouse. In Bray's "Ancient Plan" (the date of which is unknown), the main ditch, with its western off-shoots and its straight continuation into the Thames, are most distinctly shown. The discrepancies between the divers representations of the minor ditches are too numerous and too complicated for discussion here. That the old parochial boundary coincided with this main ditch may be seen in the Ogilby-Morgan map of 1677, where the dotted line bordering the ditch,[2] as far as that is visible, is produced thence direct to the river. The same line is followed by the dotted (? manorial) boundary in the Survey by R. Summersell, 1768, at the Office of the Duchy.

In the 1627 plan of the Manor of Paris Garden, the ditch is exposed, and runs straight, its full length; and that it was then the *proprietary* boundary seems implied by the fact that none of the land to westward of it is tinted.

Nevertheless, a piece of ground on the Lambeth side of the ditch must have belonged, in some sort, to the Manor of Paris Garden; for, among schedules of Copies of Court Roll deeds[3] concerning copyhold lands held of that manor, I find in Sched. VI, No. 1 :—20 Jan., 1st Edw. VI, Indenture of Lease, whereby Martin Bowes, junior, Goldsmith, of London, and Frances, his wife, one of the heirs of Robert Amadas, late Goldsmith of London (according to the grant of a licence dated 23 Oct., 36 Hen. VIII, by Henry Marwood, deputy to Sir Richard Long, High Steward of the King's manor of Paris Garden), demised to Robert Mott, Blacksmith, "all that messuage some time called

---

[1] Drawn 1593 for Norden's *Speculum Britanniæ*.

[2] Along its western edge.

[3] At the office of Messrs. Lethbridge Money & Prior, Abingdon St., Westminster, who hold them for Edward G. Baron Lethbridge, Esq., of Tregeare, Egloskerry, Cornwall, the owner of part of the manor of Paris Garden, formerly possessed by the Baron family; this property having descended to Mr. Baron Lethbridge through the marriage of his grandfather to Miss Baron, of Egloskerry.

a mill, within the manor of P.G., and all the herbage upon the banks round about the said manor, also one acre of meadow in Lambeth Marsh, and one acre of pasture in St. George's Fields." The same is probably refered to in Sched. (1 ?) No. 3 (4 Eliz.), when Bryan Stapleton, Esq., surrendered at a Court of the Manor of P.G., among other holdings . . . . "*one acre of Customary land lying in the Parish of Lambeth,* which premises were late the estate of one Robert Amadas, Citizen of London." No. 4 (8 Eliz.) also mentions " 1 acre of meadow on Lambeth Marsh."

In 1542, Henry VIII [1] had granted to William Basely of Paris Garden, Gentleman, for the remainder of a term (of twenty-one years?) all that messuage or farm called Paris Garden, with all buildings, all closes, fields, gardens, etc., including "the Bolyng Alyes," and with thirty-four acres of meadow and marsh, *parcel of the Manor of Kennington,* late in the tenure of Robert Drueston; all which farm and other premises, etc., were parcel of the possessions of the late dissolved Hospital of St. John of Jerusalem.

I must, however, repeat that the wide ditch was the recognised proprietary as well as parochial boundary; for, apart from maps, there is authoritative verbal evidence on this point.

At the Office of the Duchy of Cornwall is a survey made by John Norden,[2] in 1615, of the Manor of Kennington, which he divides into two parts; the second—corresponding, I think, to the Prince's Mead—being thus defined :—

" Incipiendum juxta fluvium Thamesis ad os cujusdam aque cursus qui dividit manerium de Parres Garden et manerium istud de Kenington ; et, ab ore dicti aque cursus, per fossatum aquaticum subtus Murum Viridum tendens a Paries Garden, versus Campum Sancti Georgii, usque ad alium fossatum aquaticum secundum a dicto campo ; et per dictum fossatum versus Austrum usque ad viridem venellam [*Marginal Note :*—Medietatem istius viride venellae pertinere manerio de Kenington existimo] quae ducit a villa de Lambeth Marshe, usque ad mariscum de Lambeth bori-occidentaliter, et per venellam illam usque ad Rivulum Tamisie, ad emissarium sive. locum cognitum per nomen de le Sluse ; et inde per littus fluvii, usque ad os sive exitus communis aquae cursus qui dividit maneria de Paries Garden et Kennington, ut supradictum est."

[1] Exchequer Augmentation Office, Misc. Book, 214, page 34 *b*. See also Calendar of State Papers, Domestic, 1542, p. 700.

[2] Mr. Peacock informs me that the text shown me was the original, and that no plans or drawings in connection with it exist at the Office, or are known to have existed.

THE KING'S OLD BARGEHOUSE.

That is to say, beginning by the River Thames, at the mouth of a *certain water-course which divides the Manor of Parres Garden and the Manor of Kenington;* and from the mouth of the said water-course by a ditch of water under the Green Wall,[1] leading from Paries Garden towards St. George's Field, to another ditch of water hard by the said field ; and by the said ditch, towards the south, to the Green Lane (half of which Green Lane belongs to the Manor of Kenington), which leads from the village of Lambeth Marsh to the marshes of Lambeth, north-west ; and by that lane, to the River Thames, to an outlet or place known by the name of the Sluice; and thence by the river-side to the mouth or issue of the common water-course which divides the manors of Parres Garden and Kennington, as stated above.

This may be compared with the Parliamentary Survey of 1649[2], in which we find, under " Particulars of all such lands and tenements belonging to the Manor of Kennington as are under demise or grant " :—" The Prince's Mead, containing 22 acres, M[r] Daniel Goodersay, under-tenant ; now divided into two several closes, adjoining unto the common or highway [*i.e.*, Broad Wall], leading from the Bankside unto St. George's Fields on the east, unto Lambeth Marsh on the south, unto the Earl of Arundel's Garden on the west, and unto the River Thames on the north. . . . There are standing upon the said closes, called the Prince's Meadow, 37 willow trees, which wee valew to be worth £3 14s. 0d."

This portion of the Manor of Kennington intervened between the Liberty of Paris Garden and the Church Manor of Lambeth, the boundaries of which are given in the following Parliamentary Survey of 1652 :—[3]

" The Manor of Lambeth, late belonging to the Archbishop of Canterbury, hath on ye west side ye River of Thames, and extends towards the King's Bargehouse by the Thames side to ye shore (*i.e.*, ditch) eastward ; and there, leaving a peece of meadow of the Prince's Manner on the east, it turneth south-east by the ditch of the Prince's said Meadow, to the Bancke

---

[1] Another name for the Broad Wall, as stated on a map accompanying Middleton's *Survey.*
[2] Record Office, *Surveys and Rentals, Surrey*, No. 33.
[3] Parliamentary Survey, Surrey, 49. Printed in the *Collections of the Surrey Archæological Society*, vol. xii, p. 35).

that goeth from the King's Bargehouse to St. George's Fields; and thence, along by St. George's Fields, to the Lord Mayor's Stone by the Royall Forte." [1]

There is an apparent discrepancy between the above and that which Nicholson, in his *New Survey of London*,[2] sets down thus:—

"The bounds or circuit of Lambeth Palace, as I had it from M[r] Gennaway,[3] the only person I can hear of who perfectly knows it, is as follows :—

" From the landing-place, northward and eastward along the water-side *to the old Bargehouse*, and thence to the corner of St. George's Fields; and so, on the westerly side of the ditch, to the Lord Mayor's Stone by the 'Dog and Duck,' . . . ." etc.

The difficulty, however, disappears, if for " Bargehouse " in the last account we read *Bargehouses*; for the premises so-called (being timber-yards, etc.) occupied the northern border of the tract which, in Nichols' *Lambeth*, 1786 (p. 25), is styled the WALL LIBERTY ; *i.e.*, the Narrow Wall, from the King's Old Bargehouse to Cupar's Gardens, and the distinction observed by Nichols between the " Wall Liberty " and the " Prince's Liberty," or " Prince's Mead," apparently did not exist as early as 1649, since the " Prince's Mead " in the Parliamentary Survey of that date, is described as " bounded on the north by the Thames." Indeed, the Prince's Mead, according to its boundaries, must have included " the Bargehouses," though these are separately specified.

The " Shore " with its " Sluice," mentioned in the foregoing surveys, is the one—conspicuous on old maps[4]—that debouched close to Cupar's Stairs, just where the triangular northern extremity of Cupar's Garden touched the river; and this, again, accords with the specification of the Earl of Arundel's Garden as the western boundary of the Mead.

For the Garden that in 1636 was the freehold of Thomas Howard, Earl of Arundel,[5] was afterwards kept as a public

---

[1] There was one fort near the junction of Dirty Lane with Blackman Street, and not far from the windmill at the north-east angle of St. George's Fields. Others stood near the " Dog and Duck " and Vauxhall Gardens.

[2] Published in 1708 ; vol. ii, p. 386.

[3] Lambeth Burial Reg. :—1671, Feb. 6, Eliza, dau. of W[m] Gennaway.

[4] See Ogilby-Morgan, 1677, and Strype's *Stow*, 1720.

[5] Ducarel also tells us that the Earl also occupied the Prince's Meadow adjoining, and Allen states that in 1636 he had a house on Prince's

pleasure resort hy his tenant and former gardener, Boydell Cupar, whence it became known as "Cupar's," and later as "Cupid's Garden," or "Cupid's Bowling Green," as marked on an undated map at the Duchy of Cornwall Office. It was suppressed in 1753, and its site is said to be covered by the timber wharves of Belvedere Road, near the approach to Waterloo Bridge.

Among inhabitants of the "Prence's Leberty" who paid Hearth Tax in 1662, I find "Boyden Cooper [1]—6 hearths."

The embanked way bordered by ditches, called Narrow Wall, that followed the course of the river round to Lambeth Palace, and that the topographers tell us was a work of great antiquity, is marked on Bray's "Ancient Plan," "The Waye leading to Lambeth." I am not sure that I have found it called "Narrow Wall" in any map before Roque's; but in Lambeth Burial Registers I have noted the entries: "1655, Feb. 25, Thos. Atkins from the Narrow Wall"; "1673, Oct. 16, Fulke Morris,[2] from the Narrow Wall," and other instances.

A part of "Upper Ground," also, would appear to have belonged to the parish of Lambeth, if we might accredit with accuracy the terms of a deed of endowment cited by Ducarel whereby it is stipulated that the overseers of a certain school in the Marsh Liberty, founded by Major Richard Lawrence, are to be "four able men in Lambeth Marsh and *Upper Ground within the said* [Lambeth] *parish*. In the Lambeth Burial Register I note: "1659, Ap. 11, Richard Arthur, from the Upper Ground."

[To be continued.]

Meadow; while my extracts show that he was tenant of a large amount of land within the manor of Paris Garden.

[1] The Lambeth Registers contain the following extracts:—1652, June 29, Bur. Jacob, the sonne of Boyden Cuper; 1659, June 4, Bapt. Sarah, the dau. of Abraham Cuper; 1674, May 8, Bur. Abraham, son of Bodwin Cuper.

[2] In 1662, Folck Morris paid tax on 5 hearths, in the Prince's Liberty, in the parish of Lambeth.

SHAKESPEARE'S GLOBE PLAYHOUSE MEMORIAL.

AN appeal has been made by The Shakespeare Reading Society of London for funds, whereby the site of the Globe Playhouse of Shakespeare may be worthily commemorated. The site is covered by the brewery of Barclay, Perkins and Co., Ltd., Park Street, Southwark, who have given permission for the erection of a tablet upon their premises, which face the public thoroughfare. A view of the tablet as it appears in the full-size plaster model is shown herewith. The model has been executed by Professor Lanteri of the Royal College of Art, South Kensington, from a design of Dr. William Martin, F.S.A., and will be cast in bronze, its dimensions being five feet six inches in length and three feet six inches in breadth. The view depicts, in relief, Bankside, Southwark, in the time of Shakespeare, with the " Globe " in the foreground, a medallion-bust of the poet appearing in one corner. A suitable incription is also added.

The view is largely based upon the Norden map of London of 1593, in which a playhouse, probably the " Rose," and the Bear-garden are shown on opposite sides of a ditch (see *H.C.M.*, vol. ix, p. 85). Other map-views and prints of the time have been drawn upon for detail. As regards the shape of the Globe, a cylindrical playhouse is shown in an inset to a map of Great Britain in Speed's *Theatre of Great Britain*, 1611, the map bearing the name of Hondius with the date 1610, no name, however, appearing on the inset. It is assumed that the cylindrical playhouse represents the Globe. A similarly shaped structure may be seen in other views, *e.g.*, that by Delaram, and on the title-page of Baker's *Chronicles* (*H.C.M.*, vol. ix, p. 81 and p. 201).

There is no evidence that the Globe, which was burnt down in 1613, was polygonal in shape, as is so often represented to be the case; the polygonal building occurring in the map-views of later date, would represent the theatre as re-erected.

As regards the site of the Globe, the so-called " Ryther " map in the Crace Collection of date later than 1612 (*H.C.M.*, vol. ix, p. 81), seems correctly to indicate where the theatre stood, viz., in the angle formed by what is now known as Park Street and the thoroughfare which, now no longer existent, bore the name of Bandy Leg Walk. The site was more accurately

The Globe Playhouse Memorial.

determined by the late Dr. Rendle from certain Sacrament Token Books of the early years of the XVII century, which are preserved in Southwark Cathedral. These books contain lists of the inhabitants of the parish, arranged in order of their residence, and also contain incidental mention of the Globe in such a way that the situation was calculated. Although no view would appear to be known in which the round Globe, as opposed to the later polygonal Globe, and the Bear-garden, are shown along with the Rose, yet the Rose is known to have been contemporary with the Globe. The three structures are represented in the tablet. The bust is an adaptation of the Droeshout Portrait from the First Folio of the Plays. It will be seen that Professor Lanteri has invested the portrait with the intelligence which the Dutch original somewhat lacks.

The project for commemorating the Globe has been approved on all sides. Surprise has been expressed that in these days of mural tablets, no indication has yet appeared upon the site of what the late Halliwell-Phillipps characterised as "the most celebrated theatre the world has ever seen."

The tablet will be vested in trustees on behalf of the public. To enable the unveiling to take place on Shakespeare Day, April 23rd, 1909, the executive committee desires it to be known that donations should be forwarded at an early date. The subscription list is open both for small and large amounts. The fear is expressed that the numerous admirers of the Poet have delayed subscribing under the impression that the necessary fund will easily be raised, with the result that the donation list has suffered. To produce the tablet and to provide a fund for maintenance and cleaning, the sum of about £300 will be required. Donations should be sent to the Honorary Treasurer, Mr. Cecil F. J. Jennings, 27 Walbrook, E.C.; or to the Honorary Secretary, Miss Gardner, 1 York Gate, Regent's Park, N.W.

BRUCE CASTLE, TOTTENHAM.

By C. EDGAR THOMAS.

BRUCE CASTLE, Tottenham, is, at the present day, like many more once handsome edifices, only a relic of what it originally was. That is from the point of view of a fashionable, aristocratic residence, for the structure, like many more belonging to the good old times, is still in excellent preservation. From being a splendid nobleman's estate with all its requisite grandeur, it has, through the ravages of time, lost all its former fame and brilliancy, and gradually sunk down into ignominious decadence. Thomas Robinson, the historian of Tottenham, thus mourns its altered state in his *History of Tottenham* :—" And thus, in the compass of a few short years, a mansion which had for so many centuries opened its portals only to nobles, princes, and kings, sunk for ever from its proud splendour and magnificent hospitality, and became lost in the long extended list of country houses, to which undistinguished, though opulent individuals retire after the fatigues of business." But still, a short account of its origin, former extent and splendour, its many distinguished owners and varied vicissitudes may not be altogether without interest. The mansion is pleasantly situated among a cluster of noble trees; in fact very little of it is visible until one is in the grounds, and once through the little gateway the castle is displayed in all its glory, with its large windows and old-fashioned shutters, its picturesque gables, and other innumerable architectural peculiarities of old houses which cannot perish, although the surroundings may. If it were not for the modern park which the estate has been converted into, one would imagine they were back in the period to which the historic old building belongs. One can picture the jolting canter of a cavalcade of royalty and nobility coming up the drive, and the smiling, genial host on the steps welcoming them to "my humble dwelling," and beseeching them to partake of "my poor hospitality." But, alas! we awake from this charming revery, and, with a sigh, painfully remember that the days that saw such picturesque gallantry and chivalry are no more, and that we are in the enlightened twentieth century, which, unfortunately, does not cater for such happenings.

Bruce Castle, as its name implies, was intimately associated with the illustrious Bruce family; but the intimacy did not

54

extend, as is often erroneously supposed, to the present building. There is a tradition that the foundation of the mansion
was laid by Earl Waltheof, the celebrated warrior who married
Judith, niece to William the Conqueror, and who was ultimately
executed A.D. 1076 for conspiring against the life of the King.
At any rate, according to the *Domesday Book*, the manor of
Tottenham was part of the possessions of Earl Waltheof in
the reign of King Edward the Confessor. After the death
of Waltheof, the manor came into the possession of his wife,
Judith, who was also heiress to Huntingdon, and ultimately
into the hands of their only child, Matilda or Maud. She
married a Norman nobleman, by name Simon St. Liz, and on
his decease, in the reign of Henry I, she took for her second
husband, David, King of Scotland. Her first husband, Simon,
left two sons, from one of whom, Simon, the King took the
Earldom of Huntingdon and gave it to David, the King of
Scotland, husband of Maud (?). She died in 1130, leaving a son,
Henry, who was the possessor of Huntingdon until his death,
which occurred in 1153, and his family still retained possession
of it until about 1174. King Henry II then ordered an army
to besiege Huntingdon, and to return it to the family of Simon
St. Liz, the rightful owners from whom it had been taken. The
Castle soon capitulated, but on doing so there ensued such a
scene of animosity between William, the descendant of Maud,
who then owned it, and Simon St. Liz, that the King, who was
present, declared that neither should have it, and ordered it to
be destroyed. His wrath, however, seems to have soon abated,
for some time after he confirmed the Earldom to Simon, and on
his death without issue returned it to William. Isabel, second
daughter of David, Earl of Huntingdon, married Robert Bruce,
great grandfather of the celebrated King Robert Bruce of
Scotland. Thus the property at Tottenham came into the
possession of the eminent Bruce family. She also brought to
her husband, in England, the manors of Writtle and Hatfield ;
also those of Conington and Huntingdon, Exton in Rutland,
and Jarioch in Scotland. Their son was Robert Bruce, commonly known as the "Competitor." He succeeded to the
lordship of Annandale on the death of his father in 1245, and
married Isabel, daughter of Gilburt de Clare, Earl of Gloucester.
Being involved a great deal in Scottish affairs, consequently his
active career was distributed between the two kingdoms. In

BRUCE CASTLE, TOTTENHAM.

1290 he was one of the aspirants for the throne of Scotland; but, unfortunately for him, he had a rival in this respect in the person of John Baliol, his cousin. On Baliol being adjudged the rightful heir, and ultimately crowned King, Bruce retired from Scotland, and settled on the estates of his father at Tottenham. He improved and repaired his property, and gave it his own name. Dying at Lochmaben, his castle, in 1294, he was buried in the family burial-place, Guisborough, in Cleveland. His son, Robert Bruce, Earl of Carrick, distinguished himself at the Crusades, and on his return in 1270 married Marjory, Countess of Carrick, and their son eventually become the distinguished King Robert, of Scotland. He died 1303-4, and was buried at Holmecultram in Cumberland. Bruce Castle remained in the possession of Robert Bruce for a very short time, for the property was forfeited to the crown on his asserting the throne of Scotland in 1306. From that time to the great epoch in its history, that dawned with the accession of the Comptons as owners, Bruce Castle had been granted to and possessed by numerous individuals. A description of all of them is utterly impossible; consequently, the most important are briefly recounted. Edward I granted to John de Brettigny the castle, town, and manors of Tottenham. These manors formerly comprised Pembrokes, Bruses—Bruce Castle, D'Awbenys, Mockings, and Dovecotes, and the owner was Lord of the manor of Tottenham. Roger de Waterville, in 1326, had committed to him by Edward II the custody of the manor of Tottenham. Edward III gave to Richard Spigurnal one third of the manor of Tottenham, and this was declared by writ of privy seal at York, October 12th, 1335. It appears that Walter de Shepedon had it for some time, for at the suit of Thomas de Hethe, in 1340, Edward III granted to him the reversion of all the lands and tenements in Tottenham, forfeited by Robert Bruce, and lately held for term of life by Walter de Shepedon. Thomas de Hethe, not content with what had already been granted to him, claimed the third portion of the property that had been before granted to Spigurnal. There is every reason to believe that the Spigurnals lived long about Tottenham and in Essex. The property seems to have come into the hands of John de Bello Monte, for, in 1343, he died possessed of the manors of Tottenham and Greenfield. Some time later Richard II granted to Robert de Cheshunte, "the manors called

BRUCE CASTLE, TOTTENHAM,

Le Bruses in Tottenham." In the reign of Henry V, to be exact, 1421, "Alice, the wife of Elmungus Legett, died seised of a manor in Tottenham, called Bruses." Still a few years later, 1426, Elmungus Legett, the husband of this lady, possessed sixty-nine acres of land in Tottenham, being part of the manor of Bruses. In 1455, John Teynton granted to Joan Gedeney, widow of John Gedeney, Alderman of London, the reversion of all the manors of Pembrokes and Bruses in Tottenham. Richard Turnant—Joan Gedeney's son by a former husband—inherited the property through his mother, and on his son-in-law, Sir John Risley, dying without issue, the manor escheated to the crown. John Stockton, Alderman of London, in 1466, remitted to the Bishop of Winchester his right in the manor of Bruses. About 1474, in the reign of Edward IV, Richard Cumberton held one third of the manor of Tottenham.

In 1514 Bruce Castle came into the hands of Sir William Compton, a clever soldier and Groom of the Bedchamber. It was granted to him by Henry VIII. Sir William was the son of Edmund Compton, of Compton, in Warwickshire, and at his father's death, he then being about eleven years of age, Henry VII appointed him to wait on his son Henry, Duke of York— afterwards Henry VIII—whose special favour he had acquired. He remained in personal attendance on the King from 1509 to 1523, and occupied the position of absentee Chancellor of Ireland, as well as that of Keeper of the Privy Purse, and during the latter part of his life he distinguished himself in the Scottish war, taking part in the Earl of Surrey's expedition. He owned three seats or manor-houses:—Bruce Castle, in the church of which his daughter Margaret lies buried, 1517; Battishorne, near Windsor; and Compton in Warwickshire. So great was his favour with Henry VIII that the great Cardinal Wolsey became jealous and suspicious lest he might endanger his own, and on this account, he contrived to send him away; but he was soon recalled. Whilst Bruce Castle was in his possession extensive alterations were made, and he practically rebuilt it, and two years after it had been granted to him, 1516, it is recorded:— "On Saturday after Ascension Day in that year, King Henry VIII met his sister Margaret, Queen of Scots, at Maister Compton's house beside Tottnam." When the Castle came by inheritance into the possession of Henry Compton,

grandson of Sir William, it was honoured by a visit from " Good
Queen Bess." This happened in the spring of 1578. It will
thus be seen that Bruce Castle could boast of a fair amount of
royalty among its guests.

Sir William Compton married Werburgh, daughter of Sir
John Brereton, and left one son, Peter, at his death, which
occurred in 1528, in the forty-seventh year of his age. If
he had lived longer he would in all probability have been
raised to the peerage, for at the time of his death he was in
nomination to be elected a Knight of the Garter. His son, Peter,
married Anne Talbot, daughter of the Earl of Shrewsbury, and
had one son, Henry, created Baron Compton, who owned the
Castle when Elizabeth paid a visit to it. Henry had a son by
his first wife, William, who was created Earl of Northampton,
by James I in 1618. Henry, Baron Compton, took for his
second wife Anne, daughter and heiress of Sir John Spencer.
She survived him, ultimately marrying Robert Sackville, Earl
of Dorset, and living at Tottenham until her death in 1618.
She left to William, her first husband's son by a former wife,
the manors of Tottenham. It appears that he either sold or
mortgaged them to Thomas Sutton and Thomas Wheller.
The last that can be traced of the illustrious Comptons in
relation to the property is that William Compton, Earl of
Northampton, held the manor of Mockings, and died in 1630.
In later years the Compton family—probably the last-named
William—assumed as a crest a fire beacon with the legend,
" *Nisi Dominus.*"

During the latter part of the XVII century, Bruce Castle
was owned by the Hare family, coming into the possession of
Henry Hare, second Lord Coleraine, though whether by inheritance or purchase is very problematical. Hugh Hare, the
founder of the house of Coleraine, was created, at the early age
of nineteen, Lord Coleraine by Charles I. He married Lucy
Montague, second daughter of the first Earl of Manchester, and
from them descended the Lords Coleraine. He is chiefly remembered as a celebrated but eccentric Royalist, who supplied
the King with funds amounting to considerably over £40,000.
His son Henry, second Lord Coleraine, rebuilt the edifice,
and his lady, Sarah, Dowager Duchess of Somerset, founded
Tottenham Grammar School, and at her death left a large sum
for improving it. Naturally Lord Coleraine removed the arms

of the Compton family from their position over the old portico, when the property came into his possession, but out of respect for the eminent Comptons, he placed them elsewhere in the house. In front of the mansion there used to stand a detached brick tower, and the Comptons are credited with having been the erectors of this. Henry died in 1708. He built, in 1696, "with great expence and difficulty," a vestry at the east end of the north aisle of All Hallows, the parish church, and also a vault for his family. Being interested in antiquarian topics, he corresponded a great deal with Dr. John Woodward, the antiquary. He was succeeded in the property by his grandson, Henry Hare, third and last Lord Coleraine. He was born at East Betchworth, in Surrey, in 1693, and was the son of Hugh Hare, son of the second Lord Coleraine, who died in 1708. He was a renowned antiquary, and there is no doubt that he carried out many of his antiquarian researches at his estate at Tottenham. Being a good classic, and well versed in civil and ecclesiastical law and history, he was admitted a gentleman commoner of Corpus Christi College, Oxford. He was Lord of the manor of Tottenham, Bruce Castle being then known as the manor-house. Henry Hare attained some fame as a writer, being the author of an account of the " History and antiquities of the town and church of Tottenham," which was unearthed from his MSS. in the Bodleian Library, Oxford, and printed in the second edition of Dyson's *Tottenham*, 1792. He was a member of the Republica Letteraria di Arcadia, and became acquainted with the Marquis Scipio Maffei, who renewed the intimacy at Bruce Castle. After his first wife, Anne Hatcher, left him owing to domestic troubles, he entered into a solemn engagement with Rosa Duplessis, the daughter of François Duplessis, a French clergyman, and to their only child Henrietta Rosa Peregrina, born in Italy, he bequeathed Bruce Castle, in his will dated 1746, and executed at Rotterdam. His valuable library was purchased at his death by Thomas Osborne, the bookseller, who appropriated many private deeds and papers secreted in presses behind the bookcases. Lord Coleraine died in 1749, and Mrs. Duplessis, on behalf of her daughter, entered on the estates. The Lords of the Treasury, however, filed a petition against Rosa Duplessis inheriting them, on account of her being an alien; it was appealed against in 1752, and subsequently dismissed through the instrumentality of

HOUGHTON CONQUEST.

Chauncy Townsend, Esq., who was intimately associated with the then Lord Holland. Rosa Duplessis, or Hare, married James, son of Chauncy Townsend, Esq., and a grant was made of the estates to Mr. and Mrs. Townsend, and this was later confirmed by an Act of Parliament.

[To be continued.]

HOUGHTON CONQUEST.

By CONSTANCE ISHERWOOD.

THIS picturesque village, two miles from Ampthill, nestling at the foot of a high ridge of hills that cross the centre of Bedfordshire, and command a very fine and extensive view of the Vale of Bedford, possesses a most interesting history on account of its literary and antiquarian associations, which invest the place with a romantic glamour. From time immemorial this parish had been separated into two parts, one of which was called Houghton Franchise (Free), and the other Houghton Gildable (Taxed). There were also two rectories (but only one church) which were united during the period when Dr. Archer, a famous cleric in his day, was the Rector, 1589–1620. When the two rectories were united the names Franchise and Gildable were dropped, and the name Conquest was substituted, after the ancient family of the Conquests, who possessed the manor of Houghton in the XII and XIII centuries, and who resided at Conquest Bury, a noble mansion, built on a plateau on the slope of the hill overlooking the village. Of this lordly mansion, with its "eves, curiously carved," no trace remains, the site alone being marked by a clump of fir trees. Fragments of the house, however, are still to be seen, having been built into some of the farmhouses and cottages in the neighbourhood. The homestead near the site is called the Bury Farm, which preserves the ancient name. Sir John Conquest was one of the Knights of Bedfordshire who served in the army of King Henry III, and members of the Conquest family are interred in the beautiful church of All Saints. Houghton Park, formerly the property of the ancient and noble family of St. Amand, who owned much valuable property in this county in the XIII and XIV centuries, was occupied by Sir Edmund Conquest, as Keeper and a lessee under the Crown. In the year 1605 his Royal Master, King James I, honoured him with a visit at his mansion, Conquest Bury, and his Majesty was attended on this occasion by a retinue of noblemen, including the Duke of Lennox, the Earls of Northampton, Suffolk, Salisbury, Devonshire and Pembroke; Lords Knolles, Wootton and Stanhope, and his Almoner, Dr. Watson, Bishop of Chichester. On July 28th, 1605, "being our town feast day," the Sunday after St. James' Day (July 25th), his Majesty attended Divine Service at the parish church, in state, accompanied by his retinue. The Rector of Houghton Conquest, the celebrated Dr. Thomas Archer officiated, and the sermon was preached by Mr. Baly, Chaplain to the Earl of Suffolk. The King joined the Queen at Haynes Park, the residence of Sir R. Newdegate, the following day, and on the Tuesday Dr. Archer preached the sermon at the service at the Church of St. Mary, Haynes, taking for his text "Take us the foxes, the little foxes, that spoil the vines; for our vines have tender grapes." (Cant. ii, 15, "Song of Solomon"), which bore allusion to the Gunpowder Plot in the previous November. The King was so pleased with the sermon that the very same day he commanded Dr. Archer to be "sworn and admitted one of his chaplains-in-ordinary" (Haynes Park is about six miles from Houghton Conquest). Nor was this the last time that he preached before the King and Queen, for when their Majesties visited Toddington, three years later, in 1608, he preached the sermon at Divine Service in the Church of St. George, on July 24th, taking for his text: "Seek those things that are above;" and, four years later, in 1612, during the visit of their Majesties at Bletsoe, he preached the sermon, on July 26th. This worthy Rector appears to have not only preached himself into the King's good graces, but also into the Rectory of Meppershall (about eight miles from Houghton Conquest), which, in those days, was a valuable living. This, in conjunction with the united rectories of Houghton Conquest, must have brought in to Dr. Archer a good income, so that he ought to have been a wealthy man. In the Archer MSS., which are preserved at Houghton Conquest Rectory, the following extraordinary entry is to be found :—"Died—Master Richard Reynar, Rector of

HOUGHTON CONQUEST.

Meppershall, in County Bedford, 19 Sept., 1613, Service there held by me, Thomas Archer. Text i, col. ix, 24, ' So run, that ye may obtain.' In whose place I succeeded Parson, presented thereunto by our Sovereign Lord, King James, my most gracious Lord, and I his most unworthy Chaplain, and I was instituted into the Rectory of Meppershall in Nov., A.D. 1613." Dr. Archer continued to reside at Houghton Conquest, and employed a Curate to attend to the spiritual needs of his parishioners at Meppershall. The fine Rectory house, which he built, was surrounded by a moat (now filled in). The approach is both beautiful and dignified. A magnificent avenue of lime trees, that meet overhead, leads up to the front door, with its flight of stone steps, forming a very charming *coupe a'oeil*.

Another famous Rector of Houghton Conquest was Dr. Zachary Grey, the editor of *Hudibras*, whose prolific pen pourtrayed such a wide range of subjects. He was instituted to the living of Houghton Conquest in 1725, and subsequently became Vicar of the Church of SS. Peter and Giles, Cambridge, which living he held in conjunction with the former, so that it will be seen that the Rectors of Houghton Conquest were notorious pluralists. Notwithstanding his clerical duties, which must have heavy, Dr. Zachary Grey, contrived to accomplish much literary work, and also to carry on a voluminous correspondence with other learned men. The list of his writings is a long and interesting one, and, with the exception of *Hudibras* and the attacks on Neal, are anonymous : (1) *A Vindication of the Church of England*, by a Presbyter of the Church of England (in answer to James Peirce), 1720 ; (2) *Presbyterian Prejudice Displayed*, 1722 ; (3) *A Pair of Clean Shoes for a Dirty Baronet ; or, an Answer to Sir Richard Cox*, 1722 ; (4) *The Knight of Dumbleton, Foiled at his own Weapon by a Gentleman and no Knight*, 1723 ; (5) *A Century of Presbyterian Preachers*, 1723 (a collection from sermons preached before Parliament in the Civil Wars) ; (6) *A Letter of Thanks to Mr. Benjamin Bennet, a mere Pretender to History and Criticism, by a Lover of History*, 1724, etc. Number twenty-four on the list is the celebrated *Hudibras*, in three parts, "written in the time of the late Civil Wars, corrected and amended ; with large annotations and a preface, adorned with a new set of cuts by Hogarth," which was published by subscription in 1744, and is said to have produced £1,500. A second edition of *Hudibras* appeared in 1764, and a " Supplement " in 1752. Dr. Grey's knowledge of Puritan literature enabled him to illustrate his author by profuse quotations from contemporary authors, a method comparatively new. Fielding, in the preface to his *Voyage to Lisbon*, calls it the " single book extant in which above 500 authors are quoted, not one of which could be found in the collection of the late Dr. Mead." Dr. Grey, through the medium of their mutual friend, James Tunstall, the Public Orator at Cambridge, borrowed some notes from Warburton, who said that he gave them expressly to oblige Tunstall. Although Dr. Grey "made proper acknowledgments in his preface," Warburton took umbrage at some supposed slight or omission, and gave vent to his feelings in the preface to his *Shakespeare* (1747), by saying that he doubted whether so "execrable a heap of nonsense had ever appeared in any learned language as Grey's commentaries on *Hudibras*." Dr. Grey, who was born at Burniston, Yorkshire, May 6th, 1688, is said by Cole to have possessed a charming and genial personality, and a sweet, communicative disposition. He was "admitted a pensioner at Jesus College, Cambridge, 10th April, 1704, but migrated to Trinity Hall, where he was elected a scholar, 6th Jan., 1706–7. He took his LL.B. degree in 1709, and his LL.D. degree in 1720, but never obtained a Fellowship." He was twice married, his first wife being a Miss Tooley; and his second wife, Miss Susanna Mass, a relative of Dean Mass, by whom he had one son, who died in 1726, and two daughters, one of whom married the Rev. William Cole, of Ely; and the other to the Rev. M. Lepipre, Rector of Aspley Guise, Beds. Dr. Zachery Grey died on November 25th, 1766, aged seventy-eight years, and was interred in Houghton Conquest parish church, where a mural tablet was erected to his memory.

Before describing the church, we must note the curious fact that, though dedicated to All Saints, the Dedication Festival is celebrated on St. James' Day, July 25th, and the village feast is "kept" on that day.

The exterior of this beautiful and ancient church is built of red sandstone (which rich-coloured material is so largely used in this county for the building of churches, as it is both durable and picturesque) faced with bath stone. The tower, which is embattled, has an octagonal angle turret, and

HOUGHTON CONQUEST.

is supported by massive buttresses. A double row of battlements adorns the nave, and a single row ornaments the chancel; while Greek crosses of various design surmount the gables of the nave, chancel, and transepts. The porch, which is also embattled, is surmounted by a Greek cross below which is a niche, richly ornamented with crockets with a statue sculptured therein, evidently intended to represent our Lord. Sculptured at the angle of the cornice, which is decorated with a design of roses, are angels bearing shields; while grotesque gargoyles are carved in the stonework at the junction of the cornice with the wall of the nave. The arch moulding terminates in two corbels, one being the head of a king wearing a crown, and the other that of a bishop wearing a mitre.

The corbels of the arch mouldings of the windows of the church are very quaint and curious. A notable feature of the south wall of the chancel is an altar tomb, surmounted by a canopy which is built of stone, and projects slightly from the surface of the wall, being protected by the buttress at the angle at the east end.

Roughly inscribed on a slab above the tomb are the words: "Thomas Awdley, January 22, 1531." This tomb was repaired in 1624 by a descendant and namesake of this gentleman, who must have been a benefactor to this church for his tomb to have been placed in this position, embedded in the outer wall of the sanctuary. There was also a monumental brass of Thomas Awdley and his lady, with one son and two daughters, in the church; but this has long since been removed. The interior of the church, which is both beautiful and spacious, possesses many features of antiquarian interest, which are, for the most part, in an excellent state of preservation.

[To be continued.]

AN UNEDITED FRAGMENT OF THE HISTORY OF LINCOLN'S INN.

By W. C. BOLLAND.

THE Black Books of Lincoln's Inn are the official records of the proceedings of the Benchers, the governing body of the Inn. The still extant ones go back as far as 1422 ; and there were undoubtedly earlier ones which have perished. I have had reason to wish more than once that in supplement of these minutes of the Bencher's meetings—for that is what the Black Books amount to—it had been somebody's duty through the centuries that have gone by since Lincoln's Inn came into being to keep a log-book of events happening in the Inn which never came under the purview of the Benchers in formal meeting assembled. I am inclined to think that the interest of such a chronicle to students of the times would have been little, if any, less than that of the Black Books themselves, and we should certainly have had preserved to us many a fact which we should now be glad to possess, and many a valuable sidelight on the manners and customs of our predecessors. It is one of these little fragments of the Inn's history, of which the Black Books take no notice, but which such a log-book or journal as I have hinted at would have chronicled, that I wish to record here. My knowledge of it comes from the old newspapers of the time. There is no other memorial of it, so far as I know. For several months during 1682, almost every county and municipal authority and other organized societies considered it their duty to send to Charles II addresses of protest against and dissent from " the Association," found, or alleged to have been found, among Lord Shaftesbury's papers. The effect of this Association would have been, says Bishop Burnet, that " the King, if it had taken place, would have reigned only at the discretion of the party " ; but the Bishop is clearly of opinion that Shaftesbury had nothing to do with it. If any one wants, by the way, to compile a complete glossary of all the terms of abuse known to our forefathers of 1682 he can scarcely do better than get together as many of these " Loyal Addresses " as possible, and then extract from them the adjectives applied to the " Association."

The Inns of Court, to be in the fashion, set about preparing and forwarding Loyal Addresses. There seems to have been no hitch or trouble about the matter so far as the two Societies of the Temple and Gray's Inn were concerned. But at Lincoln's Inn things did not go quite so smoothly, for it happened that Lord Shaftesbury was a Lincoln's Inn man himself; and he apparently had sufficient friends there to make something of a fight for him—so, at least, we gather from the following extract from *The Loyal Protestant and True Domestick Intelligence* of May 27, 1682.

" *Lincoln's-Inn, May 25.* This day an abhorrence of that most detestable *Association* found in the E. of S.'s Closet, was brought into the Hall of this Honourable Society and debated; and the Gentlemen who promoted it desiring a Poll, the Opposers (doubting of their strength) thought it convenient to withdraw at that time. Two of the Benchers, and almost 100 Worthy Gentlemen of that Society, have already subscrib'd it, and very speedily a Council of the Benchers will be call'd, to take it into further consideration; it being not in the least doubted but this good work will be carried by the majority, there being not above 160 Chambers in the whole House."

This extract from the old newspaper is of interest from another point of view, as it gives us the approximate number of chambers in the Inn in 1682. Apparently only tenants of chambers were allowed to vote. There is no record in the Black Books of the Council of Benchers announced by *The Loyal Protestant*, and so, presumably, it did not take place. Somehow or other, however, the Address was drafted and adopted, and the *London Gazette* tells us that it was presented, with several others, to the King at Windsor on the 6th of June, and gives us the text of it. It runs as follows:—

" To the King's most excellent Majesty.

" We, your Majesties most loyal and dutiful Subjects, the Benchers, Barristers, and Students of the Society of Lincoln's-Inn, whose names are hereunto subscribed; Observing your Majesties unparall'd Justice, Mercy and Goodness; and being Partakers of that Great Liberty, Peace and Happiness which your Majesties Subjects have always enjoyed since your Majesties happy Restauration; the like whereof no People in the World did ever pretend, or can hope to enjoy: And also remembering that great and particular Honour your Majesty was pleas'd to do our Society by your gracious Condescension in Recording your Royal Name amongst us.[1] We of all People did think our selves under such high Obligations of Loyalty, Duty and Obedience, that to make any publick Profession thereof might give an unnecessary trouble to your Majesty, and seem in some measure to draw into question that which we thought no person could doubt: But being convinced (by that Treasonable Paper, and Hellish Project of Rebellion lately produced at the Proceedings against the Earl of Shaftesbury, a member of this Society, and which was then by good, and unquestionable Witness positively sworn to be found in his Lordship's Closet) that no Obligations can be sufficient to keep and detain some Men in their Duties: We therefore humbly claim leave to assure your Majesty, that we utterly Abhor, Detest and Abominate all such Base Ingratitude and Villainous Treasons, resolving to Defend your most Sacred Majesty, and your most Excellent Government as it is now Establish'd, your Heirs and Lawful Successors, with our Lives and Fortunes against all such Conspiracies and Associations, the Contrivers and Abettors of the same."

The Loyal Protestant gives us the further information that this " Address in *Abhorrence* of the *Damnable* and *Treasonable Association* " was carried to Windsor by Sir James Butler and several other Persons of Quality. Sir James Butler, K.C., was successively the Queen's Solicitor and Attorney General. He was elected Treasurer of the Inn in 1673, and he again filled that office from June 24th to November 28th, 1703, the Treasurer for the year, Mr. John Weddell, having died during his term of office. As I cannot find that the " Loyal Addresses " have been preserved at the Public Record Office, I am unable to say anything as to the number and names of those who subscribed the Address from Lincoln's Inn.

---

[1] When, accompanied by the Duke of York, Prince Rupert, and a distinguished suite of peers and gentlemen, he visited the Inn in 1671.

THE CHRONICLE OF PAUL'S CROSS.

BY W. PALEY BAILDON, F.S.A.

[Continued from vol. x, p. 314.]

1538, December 22.   "Allso this yere, the Sonday afore Christmas Daye, Henry Daunce, bricklayer, which did use to preach in his house this sommer past, bare a fagott at *Paules Crosse* for heresye, and two persons more with him, one beinge a preist, for heresy allso."—(Wriothesley's *Chronicle*, vol. i, p. 93.)

The same authority tells us that "this yeare [1538], in June and July, a bricklayer, called Henry Daunce, in White Chappell parishe without Algate in London, used to preach the Worde of God in his owne house in his garden, where he sett a tub to a tree, and therein he preached divers Sondayes and other dayes early in the morninge and at 6 of the clocke at night, and had great audience of people, both spirituall and temporall; which sayd parson [person] had noe learninge of his booke, neither in Englishe nor other tongue, and yet he declared Scripture as well as [if] he had studyed at the Universities. But at the last, the Bishops had such indignation at him, by reason [that] the people followed him, that they sent for him to my Lord of Canterbury [Cranmer], where he was demaunded many questions; but they coulde laye nothinge to his charge, but did inhibit him for [from] preachinge, because of the great resorte of people that drue to his sermons."—(*Ibid.*, p. 82.)

Circa, 1538.   Among the "Reminiscences of John Louthe." "Ther ys a lytle paryshe (I thynke called St. Margaret) in the ende of Estchepe, in the wych served a curate of as good religione as lyvyng, for bothe were sterke nowght, as any man by wych folowyth may judge, *si homo ex fructibus*. . . . A commandement was gyven that all curattes (what so ever) should not be at sermones nor servyce longer than ix of the clocke, that then the curattes with the paryshes myght come to *Poles Crosse* and here the prechers. To this sayd this good curatt—'I wyll (quod he) make an ende of service at the proscribed hower gladly, seing I muste needes so doo. But so longe as any of these heretykes preche at the *Crosse* as nowe adayes thei do, I wyll never here them, for I wyll not come there. I will rather hange.' "—(*Camden Soc.*, vol. 77, p. 23.)

1539, July 6.   Thomas Warley to Lord Lisle :—" My dewty moste humbly rememberyd both to yo[r] good Lordschip and to my synguler good Lady, Pleasith it yor Lordschippe to be advertysed of the newes here currant; this ys to sertefy the same. . . . Allso this day one George, a prest, bare a fagot at *Powlles Crosse*, whos opynyon was that Chryst nor any creatur had any meryt by his Passion, and allso that exorsysyng of holly water or holly bred wer execrable and detestable before God. And after the sermond was ended, he deliveryd the fagot and cast it to the Somer [Sumner], whiche he shuld have caryed where he recevid it, but he wold not for any thyng they could do. . . . Written in hast at London, the vj day of July, w^t the rude hand of yor most humble and faithfull servant

to my poer
Thomas Warley.

To the Right Honorable and my synguler good Lord and M^r, the Vicount Lyssle, at Calleis."—(*Lisle Papers*, vol. viii, No. 41.)

1539, July 23. John Hilsey, Bishop of Rochester, to Cromwell:—"*Gracia Dei tecum.* Ryght Honorable and my syngular good Lorde. Thes be to put yor Lordshyppe yn remembrans off my sute unto you for an ordre to be taken for sermons att y^e *Crosse*; for, sens ye Parleamentt, I cowd nott gett own [one] to preache a sermon there, savynge myselfe or own off my chaplens; except own day only y^t Doctor Byrde, at long sute, prechyd one sermon. I promysyd to wrete a booke to yor Lordshyppe for ye sayd sermons, the wch I have sent here wythe thys bylle, and yff hytt please yor Lordshyppe to subscrybe hytt and commawnde hytt to ye Bysshoppe off London [Stokesley], for he can make provysyon for prechurs bettre then onny els (as hys chaplens reportythe) and as I yndeade thynke, for mennye doothe refreyne to preache there because y^t he hathe nott ye ordre theroff; and off the oy^r [other] syde, when I or onny off myn preache there, we ar soe untrewely reporttyd, y^t we dare nott wythowt fere to preche onny more there. For whereas a chaplen off myn prechyd a Sonday last att y^e *Crosse*, nowe he ys a cytyd to apere afore ye Bysshoppe off London a Fryday next; but I trust he hathe nothynge prechyd agenst Godes lawys nor ye Kynges; and a Sondey next, for lacke off own to preache, I must preache there myselfe, wythe more fere then ever I dyd yn my lyff. Nottwythstandyng, the mattre thys brokyn, yor Lordshyppe shall commaunde and ordre me, nott only yn thys matters, but yn alle thynges, as yor Lordshyppe shall thynke best, as longe as my lyff shall endure; and therwyth shall alsoe pray to God for yor prosperyte off body and sowle. Wretyn yn Lambhethe Marshe, ye xxiij day off July.

Yo^r Lordshyppys humble Oratour,
J. Roffen.

To hys Ryght honorable and especyall good Lord, my Lord Privye Seale, thys be yevyn."—(*Letters and Papers*, Henry VIII, vol. 152, fo. 207.)

1539, August 4. "This yere, the 4th day of August, dyed the Bishopp of Rochester [John Hilsey],[1] which sometyme was a Blacke Fryer, and came from Bristowe [Bristol], and was Pryor of the Blacke Fryers in London, and was one of them that was a great setter forth of the syncerity of Scripture, and had occupied preachinge most at *Pawles Crosse* of any Bishopp; and in all the seditious tyme, when any abuse should be shewed to the people, eyther of idolatrye or of the Bishop of Rome, he had the doeynge thereof by the Lord Vicegerentes [Cromwell's] commaundement from the Kinge, and allso had the admission of the preachers at *Pawles Crosse* theise 3 yeares and more."—(Wriothesley's *Chronicle*, vol. i, p. 104.)

1540, March 7. "The life and story of William Hierome, Vicar of Stepney, and Martyr of Christ. . . . It so happened that the said Hierome, preaching at Paul's on the fourth Sunday in Lent [March 7] last past, made there a Sermon, wherein he recited and mentioned of Agar and Sara, declaring what these two signified. In process whereof he shewed further how that Sara and her child Isaac, and all they that were Isaacs and born of the free woman Sara, were freely justified; contrary, they that were born of Agar the bond woman were bound and under the law, and cannot be freely justified. . . . This Sermon finished, it was not long but he was charged and convented before the King at Westminster, and there accused for erroneous doctrin. . . . The knot found in this rush was this, for that he preached erroneously at *Paul's Cross*, teaching the people that all that were born of Sara were freely justified, speaking there absolutely without any condition

[1] His death is usually assigned to 1538.

either of baptism or of penance, etc. Who doubteth here but if St. Paul himself had been at *Paul's Cross*, and had preached the same words to the English-men which he wrote to the Galathians in this behalf, *ipso facto* he had been apprehended for an Heretick for preaching against the Sacrament of Baptism and Repentance."—(Fox, *Martyrs*, vol. ii, p. 441.)

1540, March 7. " Th'effecte of certain erroneous doctrine taught by the Vicar of Stepney [William Jerome] in his sermon at *Polles Crosse* upon Sonday was sevenight, which was the vij^th day of March. . . . A summe of thiese articles is that the first persuaded makith obedience to prynces an outwarde behavour oonly, which is but a playe eyther for feare or manersake. The secounde engendrith such an assured presumption and wantonnesse, that we care not gretly whether we obey God or man." Memorandum by Stephen Gardiner.—(*Letters and Papers*, Henry VIII, vol. 158, fo. 50.)

1540, March —. " Be it knowen to all men that I, William Hierome [Jerome], on myd [Lent] Sonday last past have preached erronyouslie, pernycyouslye, and . . . . [at] *Paules Crosse*, to the utter perverting of the . . . .; which dampnable doctryne I utterlie deteste and re[fuse, desiring] hertelie, w^t ernest purpose, to preache the contrarie to the [utmost] of my power . . . ."—(*Letters and Papers*, Henry VIII, vol. 158, fo. 120.)

Jerome was executed on July 31st, 1540.

1540, March —. " Be it known to all men that I, William Heirome, on Midlent Sunday last past, have preached erroneously, perniciously, and . . . . at *Paules Crosse*, ..."—(*Calendar of Letters and Papers*, vol. xv, No. 411.)

1540, March 7. " The effect of certaine erroneous doctrines taught by the Vicar of Stepney in his sermon at *Polles Crosse* upon Sunday was sevennight, which was the vij^th day of March."—(*Calendar of Letters and Papers*, vol. xv, No. 345.)

1540, April 4. " Also on Low Soundaie following, the Person [Parson] of St. Martin's at the Well of Tow Buckettes in Bishopsgate, called Doctor Wilson, preached at *Poules Crosse*. . . . ."—(Wriothesley's *Chronicle*, vol. i, p. 114.)

THE CHRONICLE OF PAUL'S CROSS.

1540, April 11. "Also, the 11th daie of Aprill, being Soundaie, preached at *Powles Crosse* the Bishopp of Wynchester [Gardiner]; and in the sermon tyme was a fraye made betwene three or fower serving men in the said church yearde, and some hurt, to the great disturbance of the said sermon."—(Wriothesley's *Chronicle*, vol. i, p. 115.)

1541, March 6 & 27. "Stephen Gardiner, hearing that the said Barns, Heirome and Garret should preach the Lent following, *Anno* 1541, at *Paul's Cross*, to stop the course of their Doctrine, sent his Chaplain to the Bishop of London the Saturday before the first Sunday in Lent [March 5], to have a place for him to preach at Paul's, which to him was granted, and time appointed that he should preach the Sunday following, which should be on the morrow; which Sunday was appointed before for Barns to occupy that room. . . . This sermon of Stephen Winchester finished, Doctor Barns, who was put off from that Sunday, had his day appointed, which was the third Sunday next following [March 27], to make his sermon. . . . In the process of which sermon he proceeding, and calling out Stephen Gardiner by name, to answer him, alluding in a pleasant allegory to a cock-fight; terming the said Gardiner to be a fighting cock, and himself to be another, but the garden-cock (he said) lacked good spurs; objecting moreover to the said Gardiner, and opposing him in his Grammar Rules; thus saying, that if he had answered him in the Schools so as he had there preached at the *Cross*, he would have given him six stripes."—(Fox, *Martyrs*, vol. ii, pp. 441, 442.)

1541, October 16. "This yeare, the sixtenth daie of October, tow priestes wente a procession afore the *Crosse* in Poules, and stoode all the sermon with tapers and white roddes in their handes; the cause was [that] they maried one Mr. Heringes sonne, a Proctor in the Arches, to a yong gentlewoman, in a chamber, without license or asking. . . . This matter was examyned in the Starre Chamber in West-minstre, before the Kinges Counsell, and by theim the said preistes were enjoyned penance."—(Wriothesley's *Chronicle*, vol. ii, p. 130.)

1541, —. "W. Tolwine, Parson of S. Antholine's. Presented and examyned before Edmund Boner [Bishop of London], for permitting Alexander Seton to preach in his church, having no license of his Ordinary, and also for allowing the sermons of the said Alexander Seton, which he preached against Dr. Smith. To the said Tolwine, moreover, it was objected that he used, the space of two years, to make holy water, leaving out the general Exorcisme, beginning *Exorciso te*, etc. . . . against this objection thus Tolwine defended himself, saying, that he took occasion so to do by the King's Injunctions, which say, that Ceremonies should be used, all Ignorance and Superstition set apart. In the end, this Tolwine was forced to stand at *Paul's Cross* to recant his Doctrine and doings.

"This same time also Robert Wisedom, Parish Priest of S. Margaret's in Lothbury, and Thomas Becon were brought to *Paul's Cross*, to recant and to revoke their Doctrine, and to burn their Books."—(Fox, *Martyrs*, vol. ii, p. 450.)

[To be continued.]

NOTES AND QUERIES.

UNPUBLISHED MSS. RELATING TO THE HOME COUNTIES IN THE COLLECTION OF P. C. RUSHEN.

[Continued from vol. x, p. 315.]

1799, May 1. Lease of Possession for one year by John Larking, of Clare House, East Malling, Kent, Esq., to Thomas Andrewes of East Malling, Esq., of a messuage, &c., in East Malling Street, formerly occupied by . . . . Workman, since of . . . . Lee, then late of . . . . Cooper, and then of John Buchanan ; and an oasthouse and hopground (then lately fenced off from a hopground containing three acres belonging to a messuage in East Malling, then late of James Tomlyn, Esq., deceased, and purchased by the lessor with other hereditaments from the devisees of the said Tomlyn), the said fenced land containing from east to west along the highway 78 ft., and from east to west along the hopground 60 ft., and from north to south 60 ft., abutting on the high road from East to West Malling north, to premises of Sir John Twysden, Bart., east, and to the said hopground south and west.

1812, Aug. 14. Lease of Possession for one year by Alexander Smith, shop-keeper, to Joseph Hopkins, junior, Gent., both of Cholsey, co. Berks, of a messuage and orchard, &c., in Cholsey, then used as two tenements lately occupied by Mary Titcomb, and then by Richard Jones, Joseph Leader, and the lessee ; which premises (except a piece of land formerly called "Hog Close," containing 36 p., then forming part of the said orchard) were purchased by the lessor of Thomas Irons, and the said close with the barn thereon were likewise then lately purchased of the Rt. Hon. William, Lord Kensington.

REPLIES.

1812, Dec. 15. Lease of Possession for one year by the Rt. Hon. Charles, Earl of Romney, only son and heir of the Rt. Hon. Charles, Earl of Romney, deceased, to Sir Richard Neave, of Dagnam Park, co. Essex, Bart., and Thomas Neave, of Broad Street Buildings, London, Esq., of a messuage on the west side of Arlington Street, in the parish of St. George, Hanover Square, formerly occupied by the said Earl, deceased, and then by the Earl of Pembroke; containing from east to west 221 ft.; abutting west on a piece of land thereinafter described to have been granted by the Crown and laid into the garden; east on Arlington Street; north on a messuage then occupied by John Pitt, Esq.; and south on a messuage then late in the possession of or belonging to the Duke of Newcastle; and also a piece of land on the east of the garden belonging to the demised messuage, and abutting west on the Green Park, and held jointly with a piece of land adjoining the garden of the said John Pitt; which pieces of land were held by warrant from the Treasury, at will, at 14*s*. yearly.

[To be continued.]

JACKSON FAMILY.—Information wanted as to who are the present representatives of James Jackson, of 17 Furnival's Inn, London, Attorney, who either died or retired from practice in 1779. He acted for the Molyneux and Sherard families.

Office of Arms, Dublin.   PEIRCE GUN MAHONY, *Cork Herald.*

HAMPSTEAD ASSEMBLY ROOMS.—We regret to say that the drawings illustrating Mr. Foord's interesting paper have been accidentally mislaid, and we are therefore unable to reproduce them in the present number.—EDITOR.

REPLIES.

ARCHERY IN THE HOME COUNTIES—HERTFORDSHIRE (vol. ii, pp. 12-16).—Lady Banks bequeathed several volumes of cuttings, notes, etc., on Archery to the British Museum. In Add. MS. 6318, fo. 28, is the following reference to the Hertfordshire Society :—

"The Hertfordshire Archers. Ladys' prize: a gold heart, on one side a bow and shaft, set with spark diamonds; on the other side a shaft, do. The Marchioness won this prize.

Gentlemen's prize, a silver arrow, won by :—

Wm. Prior Johnson, Esqr., 2 August, 1790.
John Cotton, Esqr., 8 August 1791.
Matthew Raper, Esqr., 6 August, 1792.
Marquis of Salisbury, 5 September, 1792.
John Cotton, Esqr., 6 September, 1792.
George Stainforth, junr., Esqr., Sepr. 7, 1792.

Copied at Hatfield House, September 10, 1815."

E. E. SQUIRES, Hertford.

REVIEWS.

MUCKING (vol. x, p. 259).—The derivation of this name suggested by Mr. Forbes will not do. Place names in *ing*, with or without a suffix, almost without exception denote ownership, and are derived. from a personal name. The popular theory that *ing* always means *meadow* has been exposed by Professor Skeat and other philologists over and over again. Mucking is simply the long genitive form of a personal name, Muck or Mock, and probably records the first Saxon settler or owner. Compare Moxhall (co. Warwick), Moxby (co. York), Mugginton (co. Derby; Domesday, Moginton), and the surnames, Mogg, Moggs, Moxon, and Muggins.—PHILOLOGUS.

THE PAGEANTS OF THE HOME COUNTIES (vol. x, p. 310).—There is one error which should be corrected in Mr. Anderson's excellent article in the October number of the *Home Counties Magazine.* The name of the Master of the St. Albans Pageant is *Jarman*, not *Farman.* He is Mr. Herbert Jarman of the Lyric Theatre. If the promoters of one of next year's pageants should be so fortunate as to obtain his services as Pageant Master, I feel sure that their pageant ought to be as great a success as ours.—WM. R. L. LOWE, St. Albans.

THE FINCHLEY FONT (vol. x, p. 316).—Perhaps your correspondent may be satisfied with an additional authority to ours on this matter. In Sperling's *Church Walks in Middlesex* (1853), page 115, we read :— " A marble vase has superseded the ancient font, whose octagonal and arcaded bowl lies desecrated in the belfry ; it is of First Pointed date."—W. BOLTON, Croydon.

Mr. J. P. Emslie also sends the quotation from *Church Walks in Middlesex.*—EDITOR.

In answer to Mr. Letts' enquiry, I have ascertained that the old font is in the back garden of Mr. Wells, Ballards Lane, Finchley, the present occupier of Mr. Plowman's house (builder), where it was no doubt put when the church was restored under Mr. Billing in 1873 (see *H.C.M.*, vol. iii, p. 128). If Mr. Letts is interested in Finchley topography I shall be glad if he will communicate with me.—A. HEAL, Nower Hill, Pinner.

REVIEWS.

TYBURN TREE, Its History and Annals, by Alfred Marks Brown, Langham & Co.; pp. xi, 292.

The recent "improvements" (save the mark!) at Marble Arch have brought the name of Tyburn once again into notice. Much has appeared in the public press as to the history of the famous gallows and the precise spot at which it stood. For the most part this has been crude and ill-digested stuff, founded on no sort of evidence, and written rather for the sake of advertisement than for giving information. Mr. Marks' book is of a very different calibre. Learned, sober, and methodical, he had treated his somewhat gruesome subject in most admirable fashion. Some ghastly details are inevitable in such a work, if it is to be truthful, but they are not unduly obtruded. We may consider this book in three aspects, topographical, historical, and juridical; and in each it must be pronounced a notable success. As a valuable contribution to London topography (which is slowly being re-written), we can best compare it to Mr. Holden Mac-Michael's work, than which there is no higher praise; as history it collects and arranges a vast number of facts, gathered from very many sources; while the initial essay on capital punishment and kindred subjects in England is a most excellent and scholarly piece of work. It is a little startling to read that on a moderate computation 50,000 persons have been hanged at Tyburn, but our astonishment is lessened when we remember that there were at one time 200 offences for which the penalty was death by hanging. That the law made such savage reprisals in many cases that nowadays would be punished only by a short term of imprisonment, seems very shocking to modern ideas. We are perhaps inclined to err in the opposite direction; for, provided some spice of sentiment or romance can be rightly or wrongly discerned, the most brutal and callous murderer is sure of obtaining thousands of signatures of old women, of both sexes, to a petition for reprieve. The petition is some times successful, and is always a good advertisement for the solicitor. In the "Annals" Mr. Marks gives us a succession of stories, from 1177 to 1783, the date of the last execution on Tyburn Tree. The reproductions of old maps and prints are a great addition to the book, on which the author is to be highly congratulated. There is a good index.

EARTHWORK OF ENGLAND: Prehistoric, Roman, Saxon, Danish, Norman, and Mediæval, by A. Hadrian Allcroft, M.A. Macmillan & Co.; pp. xix, 711; 18s. net.

To every book-lover it must from time to time have occurred, on reading a new work, to wonder why the subject had not been dealt with long before; and in a few cases he will congratulate himself and the world at large that it has been reserved for his present author. It certainly seems strange that, with all our wealth of earthworks scattered over the country—here numerous, there scanty, but never very far to seek—no book should hitherto have been written dealing with the subject generally. Such a work, for instance, might have been produced under the auspices of the Victoria County History people, had they been less obsessed with the parochial spirit which leads them to record solemnly, in forty-two volumes, that flies and mice are found in the houses, and buttercups and daisies in the fields of each county in England. We may, however, congratulate ourselves that these pundits thought as they did, for otherwise we should probably be the poorer by not having Mr. Allcroft's admirable treatise. The two introductory chapters are most interesting reading; they contain a clear and concise account of what is known of prehistoric man in Britain, his manners and customs, his pursuits and his culture. The first type of earthwork to be considered is that of the so-called "promontory forts." These, as

REVIEWS.

the name implies, occupy the extremities of headlands, spurs, or peninsulas, with an artificial protection only on the landward side. A good though small example of this type may be seen on the East Hill at Hastings. Inland examples also occur in rocky districts, and by the sides of rivers. "Contour forts" are the next type dealt with. These, whether on hill tops or plateaus, have artificial defences on every side; they are very numerous and of endless variety. Many camps of similar design are also found on relatively low ground or even in valleys. Roman camps and stations are exhaustively described; likewise Saxon and Danish earthworks, Norman castles, and moated homesteads. The chapter on Dewponds and the question of water supply to camps on high ground is of great interest. Mr. Allcroft sees no difficulty in the matter; dewponds would supply some, and the remainder would be carried. He mentions certain African tribes who carry the water they require in calabashes; and he might have added, by way of further illustration, that many of the castles on the Rhine and elsewhere were dependant on carried water; the copper vessels used for this purpose until recent years may be sometimes seen in London curiosity shops, where they are sold for umbrella-stands! We have been specially impressed by two chapters of this admirable book, those on "Prehistoric Fortification" and "The Primitive Homestead." These two essays are of the highest order, and will rank with the very best archæological work of modern times. Mr. Allcroft has a pretty turn for quotation, and here and there a touch of dry humour. "Cæsar and Noll [Oliver Cromwell] and Old Nick between them claim a most unfair share of the nation's antiquities," for example; could anything be neater? Well printed, equipped with over 200 illustrations and a first-rate index, this book will be indispensable to every student interested in the development of civilisation in Britain.

ENGLISH HOUSES AND GARDENS in the 17th and 18th centuries; a series of bird's-eye views reproduced from contemporary engravings by Kip, Badeslade, Harris, and others, with descriptive notes by Mervyn Macartney, B.A., F.S.A. Batsford; sixty-one plates; pp. xvi, 34; 15s. net.

We have always had a particular liking for the engravings of the kind and period here reproduced. Stiff, formal and conventional as they undoubtedly are, there is yet a charm about them which appeals alike to the antiquary, the architect and the artist. Kip, who is our prime favourite, is represented by thirty-eight plates. The reproductions, though much reduced in size, are wonderfully clear, and the publisher's claim—that the special process employed " not only represents faithfully the detail of the original engraving, but also preserves much of its spirit and brilliance "— is fully warranted. Many of these beautiful old houses have been burnt or pulled down, and others have suffered so much from the ambitious architect as to be unrecognizable; while most of the quaint and formal gardens were destroyed during the senseless rage for landscape-gardening, which has done so much to spoil the picturesqueness of the English country house. These engravings, therefore, have a historical value which is hardly to be over-estimated, and Mr. Batsford's beautiful reproductions should be welcomed by many who cannot hope to possess the originals. Mr. Macartney gives an interesting and adequate sketch of the general subject in his introduction; while his descriptions of the plates and notes on the architecture and history of the various houses are so good that we should have preferred them a little less condensed. The get-up of the book, like all Mr. Batsford's productions, leaves nothing to be desired.

REVIEWS.

THE PARISH REGISTERS OF ADDINGTON, CHELSHAM AND WAR-
LINGHAM, Surrey, transcribed and edited by W. Bruce Bannerman,
F.S.A. The Surrey Parish Register Society ; pp. 94, 62, 117.

Thanks to the untiring energy of Mr. Bannerman, this society's publications are
beginning to make a good show, the present volume being No. 5. The permanent
preservation of records of such value as our parish registers cannot be too highly
estimated. An unprinted register is always at the mercy of destruction by a chance
fire, though damage by neglect is probably a thing of the past. A photograph of
the first book of the Addington registers shows the deplorable state to which it had
been reduced. Photographs of the three churches are given, and there are full
indices of names and places.

THE CHURCHYARD SCRIBE, by Alfred Stapleton. Vol. iv of the
"Genealogist's Pocket Library"; pp. 106; 2s. 6d. net.

The author divides his work into three sections. I. On recording the inscriptions
in a churchyard or burial-ground. II. Hints on reading apparently illegible inscriptions. III. Typical and authentic examples. The first section is a thoughtful and
well-reasoned plea for the copying of all monumental inscriptions. Such a work is
of great importance to the genealogist, and we should like to see followed in every
county the excellent example set by the East Herts Archæological Society. Mr.
Stapleton discusses the various systems adopted in copying inscriptions. Personally,
we are strongly in favour of the verbatim inscription, with the omission of verses and
texts, unless these contain some information, e.g., "the only son of his mother, and
she was a widow." Mere selections should be sternly discouraged. Section II
will be invaluable to the novice, and contains many hints that the fairly expert will
find useful. Section III contains a good selection of examples from the genealogical
and biographical point of view.

"SAINT" GILBERT : The Story of Gilbert White and Selborne, by
J. C. Wright. Elliot Stock; pp. 90; 2s. 6d. net.

A nice, chatty little volume on an evergreen subject, with many well-chosen
quotations from White himself and his numerous biographers, editors, and commentators, and some pretty illustrations. While not containing anything very new, it is
pleasant reading, and may serve to introduce its readers to the *Natural History* if
they know it not. The title, which is not very happy, is explained by a paragraph
in the preface :—"It may be permissable to regard White as the patron saint of the
little village where he spent the greater part of his life."

RUINED AND DESERTED CHURCHES, by Lucy Elizabeth Beedham.
Elliott Stock; pp. 106; 5s. net.

A good idea, and well carried out. Miss Beedham writes with great charm and
sympathy, and the twenty reproductions from photographs are well representative of
different epochs. The story she has to tell is a melancholy one, and, as her work
does not pretend to be exhaustive, it might easily be extended to much larger size.
We hope to see further volumes on the same lines from Miss Beedham's pen, for,

REVIEWS.

unfortunately, there is no lack of material. Hundreds of towns and villages have remains of these desecrated shrines, whether as actual ruins, or converted into barns or dwelling houses, or worse. And the process, as the author hints, with quite unnecessary delicacy, is still going on. Bishops and parsons who allow disused churches to become common doss-houses for tramps and dumping-grounds for village refuse (such as we have seen not a hundred miles from London) are not likely to be thin-skinned at a little wholesome and outspoken criticism. Particularly good are the chapters on "Early Christian Oratories," "Some Barns and their Story," and "Guild, Wayside, and Chantry Chapels"; but the whole book is well worth reading.

SELBY ABBEY; a *Resumé*, A.D. 1069, A.D. 1908, by Ch. H. Moody, Organist of Ripon Minster, with illustrations by E. Ridsdale Tate, York, and a Preface by the Rev. Maurice Parkin, Vicar of Selby. Elliot Stock; pp. 114; 1s. net.

This is the best shilling's-worth we have ever seen. The text contains a good account of the great church, both historical and architectural, with some useful appendices, and lists of Abbots and Vicars. The account of the unfortunate fire in October, 1906, must have been sad writing for an organist; for at Selby, as at so many other places, the fire originated in the organ. Mr. Moody records the un-availing exertions of four fire brigades to extinguish the flames; and it is a curious fact that if no attempt had been made to do so, the actual damage would have been infinitely less. It was the cold water on the hot stone that did most of the damage. It is fervently to be hoped that the renovated church will have an orchestra instead of an organ, and that if *(absit omen!)* there is another fire, it will be allowed to burn itself out. Of Mr. Tate's beautiful drawings it is impossible to speak too highly; they are all that pen-and-ink work of the highest class should be. The photographic reproductions are also good, and those showing the results of the fire form an interesting record. A marvellous shilling's-worth.

THE VILLAGE OF EYNSFORD; illustrations by Herbert Cole and Fred. Adcock. Simpkin, Marshall & Co.; pp. 92; 1s. net.

Another excellent shilling's-worth. No author's name appears on the title page; the introduction is signed by " H. H. B.," who states that the bulk of the material was collected by Mr. E. D. Till, of the Priory, Eynsford, and describes the book as " a plain narrative of the incidents of the village life since Saxon and Norman days." This last phrase rather led us to expect chronicles of the village-pump-and-"small-beer" order. We were therefore agreeably surprised to find that it is the result of much careful research. Many documents are quoted, and the book is a useful con-tribution to Kent local history. References are not always given, which is a mistake, and there are some curious misprints which should be corrected in a second edition. The account of the descent of the estate of William de Eynsford is unfortunate, for we fail to see how his property could pass " by marriage of *his ward's* daughter to Sir Nicholas de Crioll," as suggested on p. 13. As a matter of fact, the Close Roll of Edward I, cited on the same page, makes it quite pretty that de Enysford left two co-heiresses, one of whom married Nicholas de Crioll, and the other William de Hering, and that both these ladies were then dead, leaving infant heirs, whose wardship belonged to the King. Eynsford seems to have more than its share of interesting buildings—a church with some good Norman work, a ruined castle, several interesting examples of half-timbered houses and others of later date, and some delightful cottages; all these are prettily illustrated.

REVIEWS

THE HERTFORDSHIRE WONDER, or Strange News from Ware. W. B. Gerish, Bishop's Stortford ; 1s. net.

This is another of Mr. Gerish's useful reprints of old Hertfordshire pamphlets ; the present one was "printed for J. Clark at the Bible and Harp, West Smith-Field, near the Hospital Gate, 1669." The nature of the story sufficiently appears from the lengthy title-page, beloved of the seventeenth century :—"Being an exact and true Relation of one Jane Stretton the Daughter of Thomas Stretton of Ware in the County of Herts, who hath been visited in a strange kind of manner by extra-ordinary and unusual fits, her abstaining from sustenance for the space of 9 Months, being haunted by Imps or Devils in the form of several Creatures here described, the Parties adjudged of all by whom she was thus tormented and the occasion thereof, with many other remarkable things taken from her own mouth and confirmed by credible witnesses." Mr. Gerish has an interesting prefatory note on the subject of mediæval and modern fasting performances.

CONTENTS.

NOTICES.

It is particularly requested that all communications for the Editor be addressed to him *by name* at 5, Stone Buildings, Lincoln's Inn, W.C. All communications for the Publishers should be sent direct to them.

The annual subscription to the Magazine is 6s. 6d. post free. Quarterly Parts, 1s. 6d. net each, by post, 1s. 8d. Cases for binding, 1s. 6d. each, can be obtained from the Publishers.

Copies of some of the Plates which have appeared in the Magazine are for sale, and certain Blocks can also be purchased at moderate prices.

GEORGE BELL & SONS, YORK HOUSE, PORTUGAL ST. W.C.

Hendon House.
From an old print.

HENDON & SIR WILLIAM RAWLINSON, KNIGHT, One of the Keepers of the Great Seal of England, 1640-1703.

By W. H. Wadham Powell.

WHEN, in 1665, the Judges of the London Law Courts were driven out of the city by the Great Plague, which, according to the Bills of Mortality, left 68,000 people dead behind it, they not unwisely betook themselves to the breezy heights of Hampstead, in search of a purer and healthier atmosphere.

There, beneath the shade of an avenue, or grove, of elm trees, they held their court, much in the same way, it may be presumed, as the Tynwald Hill in the Isle of Man is used for a similar purpose at the present day.

This avenue, or promenade, has ever since been known as "The Judges' Walk." It is situated upon a terrace of high ground, overlooking the western portion of Hampstead Heath. The elms, or their successors, are still there, though, alas, in a somewhat decadent condition; and as the judges paced up and down and surveyed the charming and extensive landscape which lay before them to the northward, consisting of a far-spread range of well wooded and undulating country, stretching away to the Hertfordshire hills on the distant horizon, the only building probably to meet their gaze in that direction would be the gray square tower of the old church at Hendon, situated on rising ground, about a couple of miles distant from where they stood, and forming then, as it does still, the most conspicuous object in the middle distance of this wooded and pastured landscape.

Like so much of the fertile land about the metropolis, portions of the country about Hendon were occupied in the thirteenth and fourteenth centuries by the Knights Templars and their successors the Knights Hospitallers of St. John of Jerusalem. By an inquest taken in 1331, it was found that this last-named order of knights possessed some 140 acres of arable land in Hendon and Fynchele, at a value of 4*d*. an acre, yearly rent, as well as two acres of meadowland, and other five acres as well, and in 1388, one Guy de Hoddeston made a release or quitclaim to the then Prior of the said

Order, John Radyngton, of all lands at Hendon which were formerly held by Gilbert de Brauncestre. And it may also be remarked, as regards this deed of quitclaim, that a Richard de Breynte was one of the witnesses to it, showing that the name of Brent, which is the name of the stream running through Hendon, and which also gave its name to the old Brent Street (now completely modernized, though the name is still retained), is one which has long been a local name in Hendon, and was indigenous, as one may say, to the soil. The old order changeth, here as elsewhere, but the names of a locality seldom change, and often remain now the same as they were centuries ago.

> You may break, you may shatter
> The vase as you will,
> But the scent of the ointment
> Will cling to it still.

And in this connection, it may also be interesting to notice that the Templars' rule in Hendon is still kept in record by the name of Temple Fortune, a hamlet about a mile from Hendon itself, towards the now well known Finchley Road, and close to the very modern buildings of the so-called Garden City, but no other trace of the white-robed knights seems now to be found in the neighbourhood.

In 1410 Hendon was included with other lands in an assignment to Henry, Lord Scrope of Masham, for the maintenance of the servants and horses of his lordship, who was then attending Parliament on the King's service, and no doubt the inhabitants at that date would duly appreciate the honour thus conferred upon them.

There is nothing especially remarkable about the church itself, which is dedicated to the Virgin Mary, but it contains a capacious font which is a fine specimen of the Norman period, and is decorated with the small interlacing circular arches which are so characteristic of Norman work.

In 1650 the parsonage of Hendon was worth about £170 a year, and it then belonged to Sir Percy Herbert, who is described by Lysons as a "recusant convict."

In the church registers, extracts from which have been published, are many well known names. Among these may be mentioned the entries relating to the Powys family, to Joseph Ayliffe, the Antiquary (1781), and to Sir Jeremy Whichcote and his family (1677). There is a monument to Nathaniel Hone, the miniature painter, in the churchyard

(1784), and in the church is a memorial slab to Edward Fowler, Bishop of Gloucester (1714); there are also many other monuments to more or less well-known people of various dates.

Probably, however, the most important and interesting monument in the parish church of Hendon is that to the memory of Sir William Rawlinson, of which more particular mention may now be made.

This monument to Sir William Rawlinson takes the form of a stately recumbent effigy in white marble, said to be by Rysbrach, which is placed under a north window at the chancel end of the church. He is represented in his robes as a Commissioner of the Great Seal, and with one arm he leans on his Official Box, which has the arms of England carved upon it.

A small shield on one side is blazoned with the arms of Rawlinson, which are: Sable, three swords in pale silver, the hilts gold, two of them erect with the points upwards, the middle one with the point downwards; a chief indented of the third.

The inscription on the monument is as follows:

Effigies honoratissimi viri Gulielmi Rawlinson,
Militis, servientis ad Legem, hic infra posita est,
qui in omni re literariâ et jurisprudentiâ
insignis ad summum pro Magni Sigilli custodiâ,
Munus a serenissimis Gulielmo et Mariâ
Principibus primo regni sui anno (inter alios
Commissionarios) ascitus est.
Quo quidem munere cum fide et dignitate
defunctus, rerum forensium pertæsus, vitæ
quod superfuit in religionis cultû et
amicorum observantiâ cum leni otio et
securitate exegit.
Vixit annos 63. Obiit 11° Maii Anno 1703.
Sepulchrum quod sibi testamento decreverat,
posteri ejus integrâ fide posuerunt, Anno 1705.

This Sir William Rawlinson was born in 1640. He was created a Serjeant-at-Law in 1686, and when the Revolution of 1688 had become an accomplished fact, he was appointed by King William as one of the three Commissioners to whose hands the custody of the Great Seal of England was entrusted.

He was knighted by the King at Hampton Court in 1688-9. In after life, "rerum forensium pertæsus," as the inscription on his monument so pathetically expresses it, he retired to Hendon, where he purchased the old house in Brent Street which belonged to the ancient family of the Whichcotes, and he died there on the 11th of May, 1703.

Sir William was twice married; by his first wife, of whom no detailed information seems to be available, he had two daughters, named Elizabeth and Anne respectively, both of whom married and had descendants, Anne, the second daughter, marrying the Right Honourable Sir John Aislabie, of Studley Royal, Yorkshire. She died in 1742.

Sir William's second wife was Jane, daughter of Edward Noseworthy of Devon. She died in 1712 and is buried at Ealing.

To return to the elder daughter by Sir William's first wife, Elizabeth Rawlinson. This lady was sought in marriage by William Lowther, Barrister-at-Law, who probably made her acquaintance when they were both living in London. He was born in 1659, and matriculated at Queen's College, Oxford, in 1687-8. There was no issue of this marriage, and after William Lowther's death, Mrs. Lowther married Giles Earle, of East Court, Wilts, and they had a son William, who was Member of Parliament for Malmesbury.

This William Lowther was the second son of Sir John Lowther of Lowther, Westmoreland, Bart., by his second wife, Elizabeth, daughter and co-heiress of Sir John Hare of Stow Bardolph, by Elizabeth, only daughter of Thomas, Lord Keeper Coventry, and relict of Woolley Leigh, Esquire, of Addington, Surrey.

At his death in 1675, this Sir John Lowther left his widow, Lady Lowther, the sum of £20,000, "in lieu of dower," with which she purchased the estate of Ackworth, in the West Riding of Yorkshire, and she resided there until her death in 1700.

It is by the care and labour of this remarkable lady that a long series of most interesting letters relating especially to the Lowther family, copied for the most part in her own handwriting into two large folio volumes, and dated from 1682 to 1692, have been preserved. A few of these letters which relate to the marriage of her son William Lowther with Elizabeth, daughter of the Sir William Rawlinson whose monument, as has been already mentioned, forms such a conspicuous feature of interest in the old Parish Church of Hendon, are now by the kind permission of their present owner, Sir J. W. Ramsden, Bart., printed for the first time; and it will be found that they throw a very interesting light on the courtship and marriage of the aforesaid William Lowther and Elizabeth Rawlinson.

The first letter is addressed by William Lowther to his mother, Lady Lowther, from which it would appear that, then as now, the course of true love seldom did run smooth, though, as not unfrequently happens on these occasions, the *dénouement* was of a quite satisfactory character to those immediately concerned.

The first of these letters is written by

William Lowther, Esq., Barrister-at-Law, to Lady Lowther.

No date, but probably 1687-8.

Honoured Mother,

I shewed my Cousin Hare the letter, and he says he has not seen the young lady, nor so much as heard anything of her, since the last Long Vacation, neither does he know where she is at present, but he believes it will be much against the mother's mind. So that there is but small hopes and encouragement for me—A Knight of 1000 *li.* a year was refused; he says that also Sir Christopher Wandesford is very ill, the other night an impostume broke in his stomach with coughing &c [*sic*].

Your Ladyship's most dutiful and obedient Son.

WM. LOWTHER.

Sir William Rawlinson himself now appears upon the scene, and the next letter is a most charming one from Sir William to Lady Lowther; there is a fine old world fragrance and courtesy about it, which is most delightful. It appears from this epistle that the Knight with the £1,000 a year had now quite lost his place in the running, and that young Lowther had gained the day and become the affianced bridegroom of the "very very good girl" who would now shortly become Mrs. Lowther.

The affair had so far advanced that the marriage articles had been signed, and we learn from another of these interesting documents that the marriage settlement was dated the 28th of December, 1687, the contracting parties being William Lowther of the Middle Temple, William Rawlinson, Serjeant-at-Law, Dame Elizabeth Lowther of Ackworth Park, Sir John Lowther of Whitehaven, Baronet, John Sharpe, Doctor of Divinity and Dean of Norwich, and John Rawlinson, Esquire Secretary to The Honourable the Master of the Rolls.

HENDON & SIR WILLIAM RAWLINSON, KNIGHT.

By this document £7,000 was settled on Elizabeth Rawlinson by Mr. William Lowther, and £3,000 on her by her father, making a considerable dowry when the value of money in those days is taken into consideration. This document is signed by William Lowther and (Sir) John Lowther.

Sir William Rawlinson, Knight, to Lady Lowther.

The last day of the old year, 1687.
Chancery Lane.

Madam,

I forebore the acknowledgement of the receipt of your letter received some time ago until I could doe it in such manner as I thought might suit Your Ladyship as well as my own inclinations. And I now send you this scribble to tell you that by the modesty of the young persons concerned on both sides, we have had some difficulties, as well as many delays, to bring the matter towards a conclusion. Yet I think I may not only wish Your Ladyship a merry Christmas, but also present you with a very very good girl for your daughter, and for a new year's gift, assuring Your Ladyship that, as I do not doubt, but (that) she will do likewise upon all occasions. I will endeavour to make your son William, as he was born, so also that he may continue, a happy new year's gift to you and your family.

We have advanced so far, as that the other day your Son and I sealed the Articles, and this evening my brother Sharp, and my own brother John, have likewise sealed as Trustees.

We are now going to your true friend as well as Son, Sir John Lowther, for him to seale, and then shall send them down for Your Ladyship's approbation.

The honest Dean of Norwich desired to join with me in our most hearty respects and humble service to you, and to the good company with you, and what remains shall be to testify the Honour I have for Your Ladyship and your son William, yet further to assure you that I am, Madam,

Your Ladyship's ever faithful friend,
and most humble servant,

WM. RAWLINSON.

The next letter is from William Lowther to his mother, informing her that he and his wife had taken up their residence close to Gray's Inn, and saying that his wife's sister, Anne Rawlinson, "a very good humoured young woman" was staying with them.

William Lowther to Lady Lowther.

January, 1687-8.

Honoured Mother,

Your Ladyship's acceptable letter I received about ten days ago, and since that I received one from Sir John Lowther, which I have enclosed in this to you. My Wife also received a very kind one from my Lady Lowther. Both which I look upon to be very great favours, and could not but let you know of them. I am now removed from the Temple to Gray's Inn, the Sergeant has put me into very good Chambers of his that were formerly Sir William Jones's—it was his pleasure that I should remove, it lying more convenient for business with the Northern Attorneys. My Wife and I have taken Lodgings in Grevell Street, which lies on the back of Gray's Inne Lane, and the Sergeant is pleased to be so kind as to let my Wife's Sister stay with us, who is a very good humoured young woman.

We have been gone from the Sergeant these 10 days, but God be thanked, he still continues his wonted kindness to us, and I must and will always say so. My Father presents his service to you, and my Wife her duty. Both our services to the good family with you.

I rest, craving your Blessing,

Your most dutiful and obedient Son,

WM. LOWTHER.

This letter is followed by another letter from Sir William Rawlinson addressed to Lady Lowther, from which it appears that young Lowther was a man of business and had already started for the Northern Circuit, leaving his wife in charge of Sir William.

Sir William Rawlinson to Lady Lowther.

1st March, 1688.

Dear Madam,

I send you these few lines not only to acquaint Your Ladyship that I received the Counterpart of the Articles, but to give you my hearty thanks for your great favour and kindness to my daughter Lowther, and for your encouragement to her, not doubting but you will ever find her a very dutiful and affectionate child. And for your further comfort and assurance, that I have the same good hopes of my son Lowther, and to assure Your Ladyship that they shall both of them have all the encouragement and hearty assistance that shall lie in my power, to befriend them withall, and to promote my son's welfare, which I will tender as my own, and which by his good demeanour I do already find he shall deserve from me, and I do cheerfully hope, God will bless them together.

I will take care of his wife in his absence, and I look upon it as a good amends for the trouble of his Circuit that he hath the opportunity of paying his duty to Your Ladyship, and to his other relations with you.

The rest will not be so much of the profit of what his practice will amount unto, as to give him opportunity to make observations of what passes in the Circuit, and to increase his acquaintance, which I hope will insure him to a way of further advantage, which I doubt not he will obtain unto, and shall want no assistance I can contribute to, and I doubt as little the concurrence of the rest of his relations.

I give Your Ladyship no further trouble, save my most unfeigned and hearty respects, and the assurance that I am, dear Lady,

Your Ladyship's most affectionate and humble Servant.

WILL^M RAWLINSON.

The next and last letter of this series is from Lady Lowther to Sir William Rawlinson, expressing her satisfaction at the marriage—things moved slower in those days than they do now—and apologizing for her " illegible scrawl," and it may be added, that a sight of the original would convince any one that her ladyship did herself no injustice in this respect.

*Lady Lowther of Ackworth, Yorkshire, to
Sir William Rawlinson.*

The 25th of March, 1688.

Most dear and Honoured Brother,

I am bound to return you my most true and hearty thanks for your great care and kindness to my Son, and think myself very happy in the alliance, and if my age and many infirmities and disagreement of the Town's air did not discourage me from taking so great a journey, I should attend personally to give you and my dear daughter a visit, and thereby better to express my sense of my son's happiness than I can manifest by my scribbles.

All I can say is, I hope he will ever be governed by you, and though this Circuit is not encouraging to young lawyers, yet future advantages may follow, and your directions observed cannot want a good effect, if his parts and industry do well second them, as I hope his good nature and obligations will prompt him to, and my advice shall ever concur.

I am ashamed to interrupt your most weighty occasions by my impertinent illegible scrawls, so beg your pardon, and return from myself and whole family our most obliged due services to your self and your Lady, and rest,

Your most affectionate Sister and Servant,

E. LOWTHER.

All that the space at our disposal will now permit us to do, is to add a few lines with reference to Hendon House itself, the residence, as has been already stated, of Sir William Rawlinson, while he lived at Hendon, and we desire here to express our thanks to the late occupier, Mrs. Burgess, for her courtesy in permitting us on a recent occasion to inspect the house and grounds.

The original mansion is said to have been built by John Norden, the celebrated antiquary, who wrote a history of Hendon, and who resided there in the time of Elizabeth.

To him succeeded the family of the Whichcotes, who are the subject of many entries in the parish registers, say from 1654 to about 1698. At what date Sir William Rawlinson bought Hendon House is not quite clear, but at all events in 1694 the grant was confirmed to him by William and Mary of all the charters of their predecessors, which freed the inhabitants of Hendon from all markets, fairs, bridges, river, and other tolls, so that at that date Sir William may have been probably a resident there. Sir William died at Hendon House in 1703, and he was succeeded in the ownership by the Cornwall family; a John Cornwall was there in 1795.

In 1811 it had been purchased by a Mrs. Price, and a Mr. Stafford Price was about that time in possession of the property. In 1890 it was in the occupation of Major Ardwick Burgess, who resided there until his death in 1908.

The present house, though no donbt it has been much altered from what it was in the seventeenth century, still retains many very interesting evidences of its past history. In two of the windows of the dining-room, one facing to the east, and the other to the south, are the arms of the Whichcotes in very fine coloured glass, which, by the care of the late occupiers, have been kept in a very complete state of preservation. The arms are: *Ermine*, Two Boars *gules*, langued and tusked *blue*, with the Badge of Ulster; and impaled with those of the families of Gould and Groves.

89

The old staircase of oak, with small panels and carved balustrades, still remains, probably, much as it was in the time of the Whichcotes, and there is a low pitched entrance hall, the ceiling of which is supported by classical columns. On the roof is the bell which is generally found in houses of that period, with the date 1680 upon it; and in the fruit and vegetable garden is a very fine leaden cistern, ornamented on the sides and dated 1689. This is probably one of the finest pieces of old lead work in that part of the country.

The present mansion, as may be seen from the print of it, has only two stories, but there was at one time a third story with a gabled roof to it. This was removed when Lord Henley occupied the premises, after the purchase of the estate by Mrs. Price, on account, as it is said, of its weight threatening to injure the lower part of the building. There is also a legend to the effect that the third storey was haunted by an apparition in the shape of a lady who carried her head in her hands. However this may have been, the headless creature seems now to have disappeared, and Hendon House has no longer the antiquarian honour of being a haunted house.

It stands in beautifully wooded grounds of about twenty-three acres in extent, situated on the slope of the hill, running down from the village of Hendon nearly to the river Brent. This is now little more than a dirty stream, and the rippling rivulet, rejoicing in the sunshine and the rain, which in the time of Sir William Rawlinson

> Gave shelter to the winged bands
> That haunted then the Brent,

will now before long be reduced to that last sad stage of a stream's degradation, an underground sort of drain. What may be the future of this pleasant little estate with its lordly cedars and its lovely lawns, which was once the residence of a Commissioner of the Great Seal, remains to be seen, but it is not improbable that sooner or later another of those memories of the past, which are with us here to-day, may have disappeared before the dawning of a not very distant to-morrow.

Since the above was written, the anticipations therein fore-shadowed have been realized, and last May the Hendon House estate was sold for building purposes. This will alter the charming and parklike character of that part of Hendon, and

90

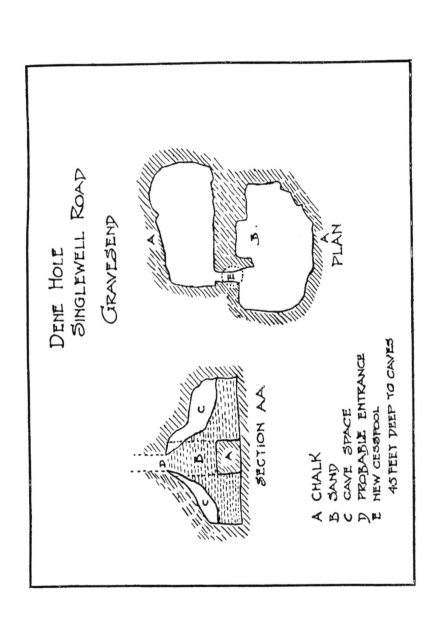

DENE HOLE
SINGLEWELL ROAD
GRAVESEND

A
PLAN

B.

A

SECTION AA

A CHALK
B SAND
C CAVE SPACE
D PROBABLE ENTRANCE
E NEW CESSPOOL
45 FEET DEEP TO CAVES

all that is left to us will be to consider, as the old Romans would say, whether the event

Cretâ an carbone notandum est.

NOTE. The illustration is taken from a scarce print, which has been very kindly lent for the purpose by Mrs. Burgess, the late occupier of Hendon House. This print is undated, but it is probably not later than 1845-1850.

RECENT DENE-HOLE DISCOVERIES.

BY ALEX. J. PHILIP.

THE discoveries of dene-holes during 1907 have been more important than those in any other year since interest was first aroused in these mysterious excavations of the prehistoric period. Unfortunately it has been found impossible to preserve all the specimens discovered. But with two exceptions they have been carefully examined, and it is fitting that the record, together with the evidence obtained from them, should be preserved. For this purpose it is undoubtedly best to deal with them seriatim in the chronological order of their discovery, pointing out new features bearing upon the history and the use of dene-holes, and avoiding as far as possible the controversy, which is still unsettled, as to whether they were granaries, chalk wells, gold mines, or any other of the likely or unlikely purposes which have been suggested from time to time.

The first of these important discoveries of 1907 occurred early in the year at Gravesend. For the purpose of identification I have called this the Gravesend Twin-Chamber Denehole. Its discovery was entirely accidental. The land had been opened up for building and the workmen were engaged in sinking a cesspool. When some fifty feet below the surface, the supposed solid chalk fell away from the feet of the workman, and very much to his surprise he found himself precipitated into this underground cave. Fortunately he was uninjured although considerably startled. There is no known reference in any of the local or county historians to a denehole in this situation. It lies of the south of Windmill Hill, away from the river and completely hidden from it. Probably owing to the slope of the hill the sand and loam had fallen into the cave very evenly and steadily. The original shaft was completely filled and the earth was being forced into the cave at the bottom as from a huge funnel.

An effort was made, largely supported by the then Mayor of the town, J. M. Arnold, Esq., a well-known Kentish antiquary, to raise a sum of money to defray the cost of removing this enormous quantity of sandy loam; unfortunately the project did not receive sufficient support and was abandoned. In the meantime, however, the builder had had a large quantity removed; thus making it possible to take a more detailed survey than would have been the case otherwise. This minute examination showed that in all probability the cave had been sealed up for very many centuries, and there were no signs that it had been put to any use since it was left by its original excavators. In addition it was arranged on a very rare plan. The result was that it has been regarded as one of the most interesting and important specimens known.

The cave was about fifty-five feet below the surface, although at an earlier date the depth was probably greater, as it appears likely that some of the upper soil has found its way into the valley. At the bottom of the loam the shaft is cut through the inevitable three feet of chalk before it widens out into the chamber. It is in the chamber that the great difference between this and the usual Dene-hole was observable. In place of the single chamber or the six chambers arranged like two clover leaves placed base to base, was what is best described as a twin-chamber cave. In the centre and immediately beneath the shaft was a dividing wall of chalk left there in its natural state when the cave was excavated. On the ground level was a communicating gap from one chamber to the other; so that either chamber could be entered from the shaft or goods directed into either chamber, and at the same time it was not necessary to surmount this dividing wall upon every occasion. The chambers were unequal in size. The larger was about thirty feet by twenty-four feet and the smaller twenty-four feet by twenty feet. It was difficult to obtain exact measurements owing to the inequalites of the sand heap, but the figures given are so near that the account of the chambers cannot suffer in any way from the absence of minute measurements. The bones of various animals of the dog tribe were found close to the surface of this huge mound of sand. On excavating this deposit in one portion of the cave it was found to be between nine and ten feet deep, giving a total height in the loftiest part of about eighteen feet. Although the portion cleared was small the various periods could be traced quite easily by the animals' bones and other things found in the sand. Near the floor two or three good flints were found; one of them an excellent specimen of a scraper. On the roof of the smaller chamber, not quite so lofty as the other, was a curious smoothness of the chalk which could have been caused only by the constant rubbing of some fairly hard substance or some other material having the same effect. It was suggested that it had been caused by corn in the ear as it was thrown into the chamber. While its appearance entirely favoured the supposition, it cannot be said with certainty that this is the real explanation. There is no doubt, however, that the most valuable evidence relating to dene-holes is to be found in the marks left by the picks.

Horn, bone, and flint implements were all in use at the same time; that is, the periods overlapped, and different parts of the country had different methods of working. In other words, to render the statement plainer, it may be explained that as soon as the first bronze implement was made all the stone did not immediately suffer destruction, even at the hands of those who appreciated the advantages of bronze. Therefore it is possible that both bone and metal pick impressions might be found on the walls. This is the only explanation available where both types of pick marks are found on the same level of a wall. The Gravesend Twin Chamber Dene-hole showed no sign of these late metal picks. But excellent examples of marks which apparently could have been made only by bone or horn picks were to be seen near the roof. Fortunately I succeeded in obtaining two casts of these in plaster. It was necessary, however, to chop away round the cast before it could be removed, the result was that the impression was immediately destroyed. These pickmarks were only to be seen near the roof; the walls evidently had been smoothed with some flat instruments, probably one of the flint chisel-like implements found near the floor.

The second discovery, due in some measure to accident, cannot be wholly ascribed to chance. In the neighbourhood of the ruins of the once famous Lessness Abbey is a deep well which was believed to be an adapted dene-hole, particularly as another near by had been used for a rubbish-pit and showed no appreciable signs of filling up. On examination it was found that although these wells were probably old they were not dene-holes, nor were they of any very great age, as time goes in estimating the age of dene-holes. In the woods close by a pit about fifteen feet deep bore every evidence of a dene-hole choked with branches of trees and rubbish. A crowbar pushed through revealed the fact that the shaft was continued beneath the obstruction. An endeavour to remove the debris only brought down a still larger quantity from the sides, and a more fitting opportunity was waited for. A number of cup-like depressions close by pointed to the existence of a very large number of specimens. And the iron bar when driven down in the centre of the depression showed that about four feet through the earth was a cavity of some sort. Steady spade work threw open the shafts of two dene-holes, the others being left for a later occasion. The opening of other specimens is to be undertaken; and a sum sufficiently large to pay for the removal and sifting of one or more of the mounds in the caves has been subscribed. The two opened were very similar in appearance and also in their details, so that it will be sufficient to describe one. It may be stated at the same time that they are typical specimens, and have no individual value beyond what may be revealed by the sifting, and the opening of the remaining specimens. The significance of the discovery lies in the number of caves scattered about the immediate neighbourhood, showing unequivocally that, whatever purpose dene-holes were put to, a large settlement of prehistoric people was situated on the spot some three or four thousand years ago.

There could be no doubt whatever that these caves at Abbey Wood had been used for some purpose in comparatively recent times. The chalk had fallen from the roofs and the upper walls in great masses, completely obliterating all signs of tools in the most important parts of the chambers. The pickmarks that were discovered here and there appeared to be those of modern metal tools. It must be admitted, however, that it is extremely difficult if not impossible to identify with certainty the marks of metal tools in chalk of different periods.

The shafts were of the average depth, some sixty feet. The stemple holes, *i.e.*, holes in the side of the shaft for stakes to form a ladder, were extremely good. Three feet of chalk forms the roofs of the caves, which were divided into the six chambers of the double clover leaves. There were no means of gauging the depth of the sand on the floor, but judging from general features the caves were very lofty, so much so that they became awe-inspiring. But this is a very frequent effect of dene-holes, even by those who are not already filled with those romantic theories which have brought so much ridicule upon an interesting and important study. On the top of the mound were articles not much more than a hundred years old. These included some bottles and earthenware of about the very early nineteenth century, a large number of dog, horse, and other animals' bones, together with two somewhat battered examples of the old horn lanterns.

The two specimens which were mentioned as exceptions in the early part of the paper were situated in back gardens at Grays Thurrock. They both caved in suddenly, fortunately without serious result, at different times. While it would have been somewhat dangerous to descend shafts in so precarious a state, an effort would have been made to secure some evidence if the cavities had not been filled in at the earliest moment.

The last of these 1907 discoveries was the shallow dene-hole at Stone, which has been named the Stone Court Dene-hole. By the courtesy of Mr. J. J. Hewitt, every facility has been given for the careful examination of this example. This is fortunate, as it is an important discovery, disproving most decidedly the chalk draw-well theory, which has been for many years the only serious rival to the underground granary theory.

The dene-hole itself was typical and uninteresting in some respects. It was just a six chambered excavation. Near the angle of the roof and the shaft I succeeded in getting a cast of a remarkably good bone pickmark. This spot is the one least likely to be touched by any later workers in the cave, who usually confine their operations to the chambers and their enlargement. And in this case on the end walls of the chambers were marks of picks which could scarcely have been made by bone picks, although they bore little resemblance to the marks made by the modern steel pick.

The great significance of the Stone Court Dene-hole lies in its shallowness. It is barely fifteen feet below the surface, instead of, as is usual, at least fifty. There is no appearance, in fact there appears to be no possibility, of a landslip having taken place. The chief argument of the chalk well theorists, that chalk from a great depth was of more value than that near the surface, is thus rendered nugatory. And, if chalk and chalk only was the object of this laborious excavation, why was the Stone Court Dene-hole sunk at all seeing that only a few yards distant the same bed of chalk outcrops? The question is a significant one.

Many years ago two shallow dene-holes were discovered in the Crayford district; they were eighteen feet from the surface, and the caves were simple single chambers. It is obvious at once that the evidence of the Stone Court Dene-hole is of the utmost importance.

The whole evidence of these discoveries begins to foreshadow the revelation of a picture of a busy, comparatively highly civilized, mercantile race, living in larger or smaller "towns" on the banks of the Thames in North Kent and to a lesser degree in South Essex. It will probably be possible, in the not very distant future, to outline with some certainty and minuteness the life of the prehistoric inhabitants of these parts of our country.

NOTES ON THE HERTFORDSHIRE COUNTY RECORDS.

By Cornelius Nicholls.

AN interesting and historically instructive compilation bearing upon certain phases of social conditions in the Hertfordshire of bygone days, is that of the *Hertfordshire County Records*. For these volumes we are, in the first place, indebted to the Hertfordshire County Council who commissioned the calendaring of the Records in their custody. This work, ably carried out by Mr. W. J. Hardy, F.S.A., deals with the Council's Records from 1620 to 1850, to which are added, by the courtesy of the late Marquis of Salisbury, others of a more ancient date from the muniment room of Hatfield House, going back to the year 1581. Thus, with the exception of matters relating to the separate Liberty of St. Albans, there is a fairly continuous series for nearly two hundred and seventy years. Unfortunately for the completeness of the picture of county life and manners, which would otherwise have been shown, there is generally speaking no information as to the result of the many presentments and indictments forming the bulk of these records.

The following selections may perhaps help to show how great have been the changes in the social life of this country during the period here treated of—changes in manners and customs, laws, commerce, and especially the practice of religion. With regard to the punishment of offenders against the laws, there are here many cases showing with what severity comparatively trifling offences were treated. Religious toleration was non-existent, and would, moreover, have been generally regarded as criminal. In later days we find instances where, if in some cases we are inclined to pity " ejected ministers," we are also reminded how many of these had been previously injected, or " intruded," to the ruin of those they supplanted. As to the housing of the people, it is rather startling to find, in these days of overcrowding, how many " presentments " are made for building cottages " whereunto they have not laid four acres of freehold land according to the statute." There are also many cases of unlawfully exercising certain callings, now free to all, and of others, the very names of which are obsolete and only to be met with, by way of allusion, in the works of old writers. As to these, and to various other matters occurring in the course of the extracts, we have ventured to offer a few sidelights.

Dealing first with entries relating to the reign of Queen Elizabeth, and observing the variations of law and social conditions shown in subsequent reigns, we begin with the year 1589.

1589-90. Gaol Delivery, St. Albans. James Buckston, sentenced to be drawn to the gallows and hanged for clipping money; William Longe, to be hanged for burglary; Richard Bacchus, to be hanged as a cutpurse; Thomas Pasgrave, John Mychell, and Thomas Wheelers, confess themselves guilty of stealing cattle, they claim benefit of clergy and are released. John Gibsons, and John Brokeson, for stealing bread, to be whipped; William Gray and Abery Gray his wife, and Thomas Gill and Alice Gill his wife, indicted as rogues *et executi*.

Presentment: " Mary Pennyfather, of Hipolletts, hath a woman child of the age of fower yeares which could neither goe nor speke, whom she caryed to Thomas Harden, because it is noysed in the country that he is a wyse man and can skyll of many thinges, who told her that her childe was a changelinge, but would in tyme helpe her. The next tyme that she came unto him he bad her to take a nutt and to pick out the curnell and fyll yt with quicksilver, and to stoppe the hole with waxe and to bynd a thred a crosse over the nutte and to lay yt under a pyllow wher the chylde shoulde lye, and that shoulde helpe yt. Her chylde having thereby noe helpe, she repared to him againe, and then he bad her to sett the chylde in a chare uppon her dungell by the space of an houre uppon a sonny day, which she did, and the chylde had noe helpe." The woman gave him sixpence for his reward and promised him more. Others who "repared" to this man were John Bigge of Hipolletts, sick of a fever; Robert Dickinson of "Duddicote [query Codicote], who had a waist-coat purloined; Goodwyfe Strat, of King's Walden, from whom a parcel of new cloth had been stolen; William Kynge of Gamlingay, who had lost two horses; and Mr. Olyver, who was desirous to know who had fired his mother's house at Weston.

1590-91. Indictment of Joan White, wife of Thomas White of Bushey, labourer, as a common witch and enchantress, for devilishly bewitching Marion Man, daughter of William Man, of Bushey, tailor, through which she languished exceedingly from December 20 until June 27 next following, when she died. The jurors say that the said Joan feloniously killed her.

Another case of this kind about the same date, though from another source, gives a curious instance of the old custom of tracking criminals by bloodhounds, a practice still occasionally resorted to in this country.

1590: Information touching certain men taken up in the parish of Edmonton for practising the art of witchcraft and conjuring, "mystic articles were found in their possession, with powders and rats-bane, which the parties that fled strewed in the way, disappointing the bloodhounds thereby."

It is difficult to account satisfactorily for the widespread and deep-rooted belief in this possession of supernatural powers by "wyse" men and women, who, in claiming this power, generally for the gain of very small profit, ran the risk of most cruel punishment. In spite of this, there is no doubt that witchcraft, as an indictable offence, did formerly prevail to an alarming extent. In this country severe laws against it.

were passed in the reigns of Henry VIII, Elizabeth, and James I. Three popes, Alexander VI, 1494; Julius II, 1521; and Julius III in 1522, issued Bulls in its condemnation; but, notwithstanding, it is estimated that in England alone and during the time of the Long Parliament, 3,000 victims were executed for this crime. In the course of two centuries, throughout Germany the appalling number of 100,000 burnings has been recorded, and in France, chiefly about the year 1520, so many that the historian, not trusting himself to figures, sums it all up as "an incredible number."[1] Doubtless many of these suffered by false accusations and by reason of public or private vengeance; some for no more cause than what would now be esteemed mere unpopularity, but in most cases on account of religious fanaticism.

1590-91. Information that Tymothye Phillippis had been examined, concerning the stealing of Northe's sheep, by the constable and others above a dozen times before he was examined by Mr. Spencer, and said, although he be bound to give evidence, he would not appear because the constable and others "make so much a dooe thereabout."

1591. Presentment of Robert Bound of Buntingford West-myll, for absenting himself from the parish church for three months.

Presentment of Thomas ———, yeoman, of the parish of Aston, for striking one Thomas Battes of Aston, "with a staff maliciously, in the chancel of Hitchin Church, drawing blood."

We do not find what was the result of this presentment, but the law enacted that if any person in a church or church-yard should smite or lay violent hands upon another, "he shall be excommunicated *ipso facto*; or if he should strike him with a weapon, he shall, besides being excommunicated, have one of his ears cut off, or in default of losing his ears be branded with the letter F in his cheek."

Presentment of Thomas Smyth of Cottered, labourer, and John Barfoot of the same, bachelor, for buying and engrossing a parcel of grain called a " pese-ryke."

Engrossing, forestalling, and regrating constantly form occasions for presentments in these records. All these practices had the effect of raising the price of goods, to the detriment of the purchaser in the market, by making what is now called

[1] Timperley's Ency., p. 233.

"a corner" in wheat or some other commodity. Under the form of regrating, this offence must have been very prevalent about this time, for Latimer, in a sermon preached before Edward VI, takes occasion to denounce the same which he thus defines: "some farmers will regrate and buy up all the corne that cometh to the market, and lay it up in store, and sell it again at an higher price when they see their time." The "pese-ryke," alluded to above, is a little difficult to define accurately, but it would seem to denote some raised or heaped-up measure of grain. Somewhat in this sense the word Ryke occurs in Burns' *Jolly Beggars*:

> Let me ryke up to dight that tear
> An' go wi' me an' be my dear,
> An' then your every care an' fear
> May whistle owre the lave o't.

Presentment of the Jury. "We present that Richard Emes with one Thomas Davies, the 20th October last past, demanding relief of one Robert Sibthorpe, who, speaking of their disorderly walking, Davies said that the said Sibthorpe and such as he wolde deal with them as the Earl of Leicester wolde have done. Beinge demanded how the Earle wolde have delt with them, he answered, he wolde have hanged three hundred of us in one morninge for demanding of our pay, Sibthorpe said he had some other cause so to doe. Then Davies answered that it was well known what he was, and that he was a traitor. Sibthorpe warned him to take heede what he saide. Then Richard Emes said it was well known both to the Queene and her Councell, for I cuminge over with the Earle of Darbie, when he came out of Flanders, he brought over a scroule in writinge of his treason to this lengthe makinge a marke on his staffe to the length of half a yarde."

This seems an echo of one of the many attempts to destroy the reputation and also the life of Elizabeth's favourite minister, prompted generally by party jealousy and religious animosity; instances of which are chronicled in the State Papers of this reign. To give an example, we find that in 1586, one Lieven Archevier, described as "born at Ghent," gives information touching the design of certain Jesuits to kill the Earl of Leicester, either by poison or other violent means; and about the same time, John Clarke, a prisoner, details "the seditions and vile speeches of one Fishwick, and his plots to burn the Earl's house at Wanstead and to raise a Catholic rebellion; his knowledge of inflammable oils for burning houses; and of the making of mortal poisons and perfumes." These conspiracies and libels aroused the anger of the Queen, who caused a letter to be sent to the Lord Mayor, expressing her indignation at the infamous libels spread against the Earl of Leicester " of which most malicious and wicked imputations, Her Majesty, in her own clear knowledge, doth declare and testify his innocence to all the world. Her Majesty believes in her conscience that none but the Devil himself could believe them to be true." The above is endorsed by Lord Burghley: " A copy of a l're wrytten by Hir Maⁱˢ cõma'dment to ye Mayre of London in defence of ye Er. of Leicestʳ."

Sessions, 1593. Breaking out of Gaol. Verdict: " Wee fynd that there is fower doores belonging to the Gayle goyinge into the gayle as thorowe an entrye, whereof the first doore nexte unto the mayne gayle was cleane broken down, and the second doore beyinge distant from the inner doore aboute two foote and a halfe, beyinge chayned to the inner doore, was broken and the chayne also as they mighte have gonn owte, but they went not beyond the said second doore of the other doores, the inner was shutt still and the forth doore standeth all wayes open in the day time; which brekynge of doores was by Hamond Bateman, Willyam Temple, John Martyne, and John Clarke, with an intent to escape, but whether the breakynge of the said gayle doores as aforesaid be fellonye or no, we refer ourselves to the opinion of the Corte, and if it be fellonye we fynd them all gyltie, and that they had neither goods, chattells, lands, or tenentes at they tyme of the said fellonye or since to our knowledge; and yf it be no fellonye then we fynde ' not gyltie,' and that they broke the first doore and cam into the second doore and brake that to, so whether it be fellonye or not we leave to your worships judgement." The parties are respited. At the Gaol Delivery, Epiphany Sessions, these men were indicted for prison breaking. Those pleading not guilty were remanded. Two of them confessed themselves guilty, claimed benefit of clergy and were discharged:

In the verdict of this rather muddled jury, the only thing which comes out clearly is the claim to Benefit of Clergy, denoting that these two men possessed the then rare accomplishment of being able to read, thereby coming under the denomination *clerici*. From a very early period the Clergy together with their consecrated buildings were exempt from civil jurisdiction, reminiscences of which still linger in the name of Broad Sanctuary, in the precincts of Westminster Abbey. The Church had also demanded and received the same immunity for Laymen of sufficient education; reading (then a rare accomplishment) being considered a sufficient test. This privilege, however, was restricted to first offences, in token of which, the culprit before being handed over to the ecclesiastical authorities, was branded by the gaoler with a hot iron in the "brawn of the left thumb." The meaning of this is very clearly shown by a passage occurring in a description of one of Queen Elizabeth's progresses: "March 18th 1559, Eleven persons, malefactors, rode to hanging; seven men and four women; one of these men was a priest, his crime was for cutting a purse wherein were three shillings; but he was burnt in the hand, or else the book would have saved him."[1]

1592-3. Presentment of John Locke of Barkway, and Francis Umwell of the same, baker, for breaking the assize of bread there—to wit, John Locke made his "twoe pennye lofes" sixteen ounces under weight, and Francis Umwell made his two penny loaves twenty-seven ounces under weight, and his penny loaves six ounces under weight, to the great loss of the public.

The above throws some light on the purchasing power of money at this period, and one can well imagine the size of the penny and two penny loaves, to have borne such a diminution of weight without disappearing altogether. Much evidence as to the cost of provisions is furnished by the articles of agreement made about this time between the Privy Council and the county authorities for the delivery of provisions to the Royal Household. This agreement, subject to a " composition " which no doubt somewhat reduced the market price, states:

"First. That 50 fatt veales of the age of six weeks and upwards shall be delivered the 1st of June at each, iiij*s*. iiij*d*."

" Item. That cxx fat lambes and meet for Her Majesty's service shall be delivered the 20th November at xij*d*."

" Item. That 30 fatt and great porkes and sufficient for Her Majesty's service shall be delivered 20th November at each, iiij*s*."

[1] Nichols, *Progresses of Queen Elizabeth.*

" Item. That 400 quarters of wheate at vjs. viij*d*. the quarter [query bushel] shall be continued according to the old and ancyent composition, and that it shall be lawful for Her Majesty's purveyors for the monthe, to take yearlie within the said sheare by vertue of commission 70 quarters of the best wheate, payinge reddy money for the same, after the rate that of the second price that wheate shall be sold for that sum in the market, or to abate iiijd. for a bushell of the best price of the said market."

A great number of presentments are made with regard to the practice of stopping up rights of way through field-paths, etc., and the unlawful enclosing of common lands. They occur at all periods covered by these records, and are perhaps more numerous than any other kind of offence here chronicled. No wonder that the comparative immunity enjoyed by such offenders should have been at all times the cause of much seething discontent among the people, especially when contrasting this leniency to the wealthy intruders with the frequent hangings of their own class for petty thefts. An early and quaint illustration of how these encroachments would occasionally provoke a serious revolt is given in Grafton's *Chronicle*, where he records that about the fifth year of Henry VIII "The townes men about London, as Islington, Hogsdon, Hackney, Shordiche, and such other, had so enclosed the common fields wyth hedges and dyches, that neyther the young men of the Citie myght shoote nor the auncient persons walke for their pleasure, except eyther their Bowes and Arrowes were broken or taken away, or the substanciall arrested and endyted, saiying that no Londoner shoulde go out of the Citie but in ye high wayes. This saing so grieved the Londoners, that sodeinly in a morning a Turner in a foole's coate came criying thorough the Citie, 'Shovels and Spades'; so many people followed that it was wonder. And within a short space all the hedges about the townes were cast downe and the dyches filled, and every thing made playne. The Kynge's Counsayle, hearyng of this assemblye, came to the Gray-Fryers, nowe called Christe's Hospitall, and sent for the Maior and Counsell of ye Citie to knowe the cause, whyche declared unto them the noysaunce done to the Citizens and their commodities and liberties taken from them, which though they being rulers woulde not, yet the commonaltie which were anoyed, woulde plucke up and remedy. When the Kynge's Counsayle had heard the answer, they dissembled the matter, and commaunded the Maior to see that no other thyng were attempted and to call home the Citizens: who, when they had done their enterprize, came home without any more harme doyng. And so after, the fieldes were never hedged." At a subsequent and milder period of history the enclosure grievance found its expression in the oft quoted lines:

> Why prosecute the vulgar felon
> Who steals the goose from off the common,
> But leave the greater villain loose
> Who steals the common from the goose!

The next presentments show the usual method of procedure in such cases.

1593-94. Presentment: That from time immemorial there has been a common way called a "common fylde gappe" in a field within the parish of Weston, called Hill Syde, through which "common gappe" the inhabitants of Weston were accustomed for all time to pass with their carriages and droves; nevertheless Thomas Harmer, the younger, by force and arms, knowingly and designedly stopped up and barred "le comen gappe" with a great and very deep ditch, and with a quickset hedge.

Presentment: That whereas the inhabitants of Braughinge had long used a certain way and common passage at Brawhinge through a field called Stonye Crofte, when the said field was not lying sown, John Gayler, yeoman, had of late enclosed about six acres with ditches and hedges, being parcel of the said field, and so stopped up the said way.

1593-94. Indictment of John Clarke of Waltham Crosse, smith, for that on October 19th, 1593, at night, viz., between the hours of seven and eight after midday, he burglariously entered the mansion house of Symon Crowche, at Waltham Crosse, and took two cloaks value 20s., one capon, value 6d., and one sack, value 12d., the goods of the said Crowche. Sentenced to be hanged.

Presentment: That the highway between Stapleforde Bridge and *Doggesheade in the Pott* in the parish of Anstye, is decayed.

1594-95. Agreement of the Justices that every High Sheriff of the County at the time of the Assize shall make provision and keep a table for the Justices who shall appear at the same Assizes. Each Justice to pay and contribute for his dinner two shillings and sixpence in money, and for the dinner of his servant eightpence.

1595-96. Order of the Privy Council for the restraint of killing and eating of flesh this next Lent.

Presentment: That John Shotbolte of Yardley, gent., had lately enclosed with a hedge and ditch a part of the common way there, lying in the fields of Yardley.

1596-97. Presentment: That William Kynge of Brawghinge, labourer, on the above date, took "a young mastie bytch" belonging to George Hamond and did flea her, being a live, and so the dog had come to the house of the said George Hamond, without its skin.

Edward Bull affirmed that it was spoken in his hearing upon Cottered Greene, that the Lord Admiral of England had put sand into barrels instead of "powlder" within the ships that the Earl of Essex should go forth withal, and that the Lord Admiral for that was committed to the Tower, but by whom those words were spoken he well remembreth not; and that Thomas Antwissel "should" bring this news from the Court, having been lately there, but who affirmed that he likewise remembreth not. Edward Whytenberry of Cottered, tailor, deposed to similar effect. Thomas Antwissel "confessed (being examined) that he told Whytenberry that (as he knew) there was sand or grease where powder should be, but he thought it was not by the Lord Admiral's means."

1598-1599. Presentment: That Robert Renoldes of Hertford, not having the fear of God before his eyes, entered the yard of Robert Dawson of Hertford, "coryer," and carried away five hides worth 20s.

1599-1600. Presentment of John Pearson and sixteen others (some of them being also unlicensed) for selling beer at the rate of three halfpence per quart.

Petition of the inhabitants of Cheshunt to Sir Henry Coke, Knight, Lord of the manor of Cheshunt, in reference to a recent order for the relief of the poor. As touching the provision of corn, they complain that John Shellye and Thomas Harrys of Cheshunt, "loders," not only buy corn in one market and sell it in another market, unground, but also go from barn to barn, and buy up the corn at the barn doors, so that the petitioners can not buy it for their ready money. They formerly had their corn from Mr. Dakers, the parson, as they needed it, for money, but now, on account of the said forestalling, he carries it not to market.

1600-1601. Presentment: That the pound and the stocks of Weston are not sufficient and ought to be " done " by the Lady Pickerringe, Lady of the same manor.

1601-1602. Presentment: That William Day of Braughing, yeoman, has stopped up an ancient way of passage through his ground to Cockyn Lane, in the said parish, and has cut up the stiles and has " taken away the easementes, with hedging upp and dyching out the Queen's leige people."

As before stated, there are many such like presentments, both with regard to rights of way and the enclosures of common land, greatly to the loss of the poorer classes, too often sufferers in this way from the " oppressor's wrong, the proud man's contumely " ; but no doubt there were also honourable exceptions, of which the following letter, printed in the State Papers of this reign may be cited as a striking example:

1600. Secretary Cecil to William Cock of Hertfordshire: " I had no intention to annoy my neighbours by the enclosure of lands, for which I paid dearly to enlarge my park, and finding they are dissatisfied, I repent what is done. I was assured by those who sounded the dispositions of those interested, that it had the good will of the country, or I would not have attempted it had the land been given me. I offer now how far soever the enclosure has proceeded, to lay it open again, if the parties of whom the land was bought, will return the money, and to secure full compensation to those that had right of common. I request you if there be any peevish person who tries to divert his neighbours' good affection, to assure them that though my place about the Queen prevents my enjoying their acquaintance, I bear them a neighbourly mind. I wish you to over-rule my men, if they injure others to the value of a farthing."

The above quotations bring us to the end of the reign of Queen Elizabeth, and here it may be useful to give, on the

106a

Vange Church.

Pitsea Church.
Photographs by C. W. Forbes.

authority of Hansard's *Parliamentary History*, a list of the prices of provisions prevailing during this time. 1559: Wheat, 8*s.*; rye, 8*s.* 1560: Wheat, 8*s.*; rye, 8*s.*; barley, 5*s.* 2*d.*; oats, 5*s.*; old hay, 12*s.* 6*d.* per load; new hay, 6*s.* 8*d.* 1561: Wheat, 8*s.*; rye, 8*s.*; malt, 5*s.*; oats, 5*s.* 1562: Wheat, 8*s.*; barley, 5*s.*; hay, 13*s.* 4*d.* per load; straw, 6*s.*; claret, £2 10*s.* per hogshead. 1563: Rye, 13*s.* 4*d.*; oats, 5*s.* 1574, a dearth, and wheat was £2 16*s.* per quarter; beef, 1*s.* 10*d.* per stone; and herrings only five for 2*d.*; bay salt (never so dear), 6*s.* the bushel. After harvest wheat was £1 4*s.* and continued so about a year. In 1587 wheat was £3 4*s.* per quarter at London; and, in other places, at 10*s.*, 12*s.* and 13*s.* per bushel occasioned by excessive transportation. In 1594, wheat, £2 16*s*; rye, £2. In 1595 wheat, by great transportation, £2 13*s.* 4*d.*; a hen's egg 1*d.*, or at best, three for 2*d.*; a pound of sweet butter, 7*d.* In 1596 wheat, by reason of great rains, at £4 per quarter; rye, £2 8*s.*; oatmeal, 3*s.* the bushel. In 1597 wheat was £5 4*s.* and fell to £4 per quarter; rye from 9*s.* to 6*s.* per bushel, and then to 3*s.* 2*d.*, and afterwards rose again to the greatest price. Bishop Goodwin says, wheat was once this year at 13*s.* 4*d.* per bushel. In 1598 pepper, 8*s.* per pound; raisins, 6*d.*; Gascoygne wine, 2*s.* 8*d.* per gallon; sweet wine, 4*s.* In 1603 the price of ale and strong beer was settled by Act of Parliament at 1*d.* the quart, and small beer at two quarts for a penny in ale houses.

NOTES ON THE EARLY CHURCHES OF SOUTH ESSEX.

By C. W. FORBES, Member of the Essex Archaeological Society.

[Continued from p. 43.]

ON the south side of the main road between Stanford-le-Hope and Hadleigh, a distance of about ten miles, are four other parishes, besides those of Corringham and Fobbing (which have already been described), viz.: Vange, Pitsea, Bowers Gifford, and South Benfleet.

In this number I propose to take these four parishes, in the above order.

THE EARLY CHURCHES OF SOUTH ESSEX.

VANGE.

Vange is situated partly on a creek of the Thames and partly on the main road that runs between Stanford and Hadleigh. Following this road from Stanford for three miles we arrive at the village. The church, about one hundred yards to the south, is hardly visible in the summer, owing to the trees surrounding the churchyard. It is a very small structure, built of stone and rubble, consisting of a nave and chancel only, with a low wooden bell turret at the west end, containing one bell.

Entrance to the church is by the south door, which has a plain brick porch; the north door has, as is so often the case, been bricked up.

The foundation is ancient, but the present structure dates from the thirteenth century; the windows and bell turret are attributed to the fifteenth century; the plain west window is doubtless a later addition to give light to the small western gallery.

The font is square with arrow marks on the side facing east, and rests on a circular centre pillar with a smaller one at each angle; it is probably very early Norman.

In the east window are some fragments of ancient glass.

Between the chancel and nave is a stone screen running from wall to wall, having a rude arched opening about five feet wide with semicircular head; the whole of this wall at the present time is blank, but doubtless in pre-reformation times it was covered with frescoes, to form a background for the rood.

In the south wall are the remains of the rood stairs and opening for beam.

The chancel screen is about four feet thick, but appears to be hollow.

The registers date from 1558 and are in good condition.

PITSEA.

Continuing on the main road for another mile and a half we reach Pitsea, formerly called Picescia. The parish is situated on a peninsular formed by creeks running into the river; the church, which is quite close to the railway station, is in a very prominent position on the top of a small hill.

According to Domesday Book, at the time of the Conqueror the manor was in the possession of one Ulueva wife of Phin.

Bowers Gifford Church.

South Benfleet Church.
Photographs by C. W. Forbes.

THE EARLY CHURCHES OF SOUTH ESSEX.

The present church of stone and rubble consists of chancel, nave, south porch, and embattled western tower. With the exception of the tower (containing five bells), which is attributed to the thirteenth century, the building is a modern structure, dating from the year 1871.

Inside the altar rails and underneath the south chancel window, almost on a level with the floor, is an interesting brass dated 1588. It is unfortunately much defaced and cracked across the middle; it is believed to have been originally on the chancel floor, but was placed in its present position at the restoration or rebuilding.

The Latin inscription on it reads:

JACIT HIC CONDITA ATQ3 IN HAC TVMBA
SEPVLTA ELIZABETHA VXOR JOH'IS PVRLEVANT,
QVÆ NVPER FVIT ELÍZABETH RAYE.
CHARISSIMA SVO MARITO COMITANS PERAMANS
SEMPER ATQ3 FIDELIS
AMICIS PROPRIIS AMANTISSIMA ET OMNIBVS
ALIIS QVAM BENEVOLENS
SVMMÆ CLEMENTIÆ FLOS,
PIETATISQ3 PATRONA.
MORIENS MVNDO, VIVIT DEO.
CORPORE IN TERRA JACENTE,
SPIRITU IN CÆLO SEDENTE,
OBIIT MORTEM VICESIMO SEXTO
DIE SEPTEMBRIS ANNO DNI 1588
ANNO REGNI ELIZABETHÆ
REGINÆ TRICESIMO.

Translation.

Here lies hidden and buried in this tomb Elizabeth, wife of John Purlevant, whose maiden name was Elizabeth Raye. To her husband she was a very dear wife, attached always, loving and faithful; To her personal friends she was most affectionate and to all others how kind! The flower of all mercy and the patroness of goodness; Dying to the world she lives in God. Her body lies in the earth, her soul rests in Heaven. She passed away on the 26th day of September in the year of our Lord 1588. In the 30th year of the reign of Queen Elizabeth.

The communion plate is interesting; the chalice is of the year 1597, and the paten, which is of the type usually known as a " credence paten," has the hall-mark of 1692.

On the paten are the arms of Sir Samuel Moyer, Knight
(created 1701), of Pitsea Hall, Sheriff of Essex in 1698, who
died in the year 1716. His arms were: silver and two
chevrons gules. He married Rebecca, sister of Alderman
Sir William Jolliffe, whose arms were: silver, a pile azure,
and three right hands on the pile. Both of these arms appear
on the paten, which doubtless formed part of their gift to the
church.

BOWERS GIFFORD.

Leaving Pitsea, which contains little else to interest the
visitor, we proceed on our way to Bowers Gifford. The
parish of Bowers or Burrs is bounded on the south by the
creek which separates Canvey Island from the mainland, and
gives communication to the Thames. The village is under
two miles from Pitsea railway station and principally on the
main road. To reach the church we have to take a narrow
lane to the south for about half a mile until we nearly reach
the railway line between Pitsea and South Benfleet; the
church is on the north side.

The foundation is believed to be very ancient, although no
evidence of an earlier building, so far as is known, exists; it
is stated that prior to the Norman invasion the manor was
held by the Abbey of Westminster.

The present structure is a small stone building dating from
the fourteenth century, consisting of a chancel and nave only,
and at the western end a low tower with a wooden spire containing two bells; on the south-west angle of the tower is a buttress
placed there as a support on account of the sloping nature of
the ground towards the river.

Originally there were three doorways; the west side of
the tower shows traces of one filled in with stone work;
the south door, which has a plain modern wooden porch, is
the only one used, the one on the north side having been
closed up as usual.

On each side of the nave are double and triple light
windows, probably late fourteenth or early fifteenth century.

The east window is filled with modern stained glass; the
chancel has also a double light window of the same period as
those in the nave.

In the chancel is a trefoil head piscina. There is no arch
or screen between chancel and nave. The font is fourteenth

South Benfleet Church.

The Font, Vange.

Photographs by C. W. Forbes.

century, octagonal on an octagonal pillar with very little in the way of ornament.

The most interesting feature in this little church is a mutilated brass to Sir John Gifford, Bart. A modern brass plate states that Sir John Gifford was the son of Sir Robert Gifford, and grandson of William Gifford, at one time Lord of the Manor and patron of the living, who fought at Crécy, and died about the time of the fall of Crécy, *circa* 1347-48. The brass was lost for many years; it was found and restored to the church in 1870, and was repaired and fixed to the north wall of the chancel in 1897. The head of the effigy and the inscription are lost.

There are also five modern brasses to ancestors of Sir Duncan Campbell, dated 1902.

This church, although a small one, is well worth a visit.

SOUTH BENFLEET.

The village of South Benfleet is easily accessible, there being a station here on the railway line running between Fenchurch Street and Southend. If, however, we wish to continue our journey by road, we must return to the highway; a signpost some two miles further points the way to South Benfleet and Canvey Island; turning down here and keeping to the left for, say, another two miles, we come to the church on our right, in the centre of the village.

The parish is situated on the north and east of Hadleigh Bay, the river flowing between it and Canvey Island.

The original Norman church is believed to have been similar to Hadleigh, a description of which will appear in the next number.

The present structure is chiefly fifteenth-century work; it is built of stone and rubble, and consists of a chancel, nave of three bays, with clerestory, north and south aisles, and a low massive tower with a short stunted spire.

The doorway at the west end of the nave, leading into the tower, is Norman, *circa* 1100, the ornamental side facing the interior of the tower; this doorway was the western entrance of the first Norman church.[1]

[1] The description suggests the possibility that we have here the remains of a small Saxon or early Norman church with a central tower. On this supposition, the doorway referred to would have been the chancel arch, not the west door. The chancel arches in these early churches were generally

THE EARLY CHURCHES OF SOUTH ESSEX.

The tower which we now see was erected *circa* 1250. On examination of the exterior we notice a number of Roman tiles worked in with the rubble; the face of each of the buttresses is ornamented with crosses worked in flints and stone, those on the west being red, and on the north and south white. The wooden spire was erected about 150 years back. The tower contains five bells; the tenor weighs nearly 20 cwt., and was cast in 1636; the treble is dated 1664. The door in the north aisle is bricked up. The fifteenth-century porch on the south side is considered to be the finest timbered porch in the county.

The font, which is a modern square one on four pillars, is at the west end of the south aisle; the old font was taken away at the last restoration.

The arcades separating the aisles from the nave are supported on the north side by clustered shafts with moulded caps and bases, those on the south side are octangular.

The present roof is a wooden hammer-beamed flat one of the fifteenth century, the original one was acutely pointed.

In the clerestory are eight corbels which formerly carried the earlier roof; four are sculptured with grotesque figures and four with heads of evangelists.

The nave opens into the chancel with a fine and spacious arch of two reveals, with hollow chamfered edges springing from clustered shafts; the chancel arch and nave pillars on the north side date from *circa* 1240, the pillars on the south side are *circa* 1320.

On the south side of the altar is a piscina with a shelf, within a niche.

The windows on the north side are Perpendicular, and are attributed to the fifteenth century; on the south side they are mostly pointed decorated work of the fourteenth century.

The east end of the south aisle was formerly a chapel, and retains a piscina with large bracket for credence or image.

There are also indications of an altar at east end of north aisle, with a square credence in the wall.

Remains of the rood stairs are to be seen in the wall of the north aisle.

The walls of the aisles were formerly embattled; portions of the battlements still remain on the south side. Portions of the foundations of an early church were found some time ago

very small. St. Peter's, Barton-on-Humber, may be cited as an example. —Editor.

112ª

Boar Place.

From a water-colour drawing.

on the south-east side of the priest's door, now closed. An ancient sepulchral slab, with a raised cross and a French inscription of thirteenth-century date, was also discovered during restoration. Many early memorials are to be found in the church.

The communion cup, with a cover, is dated 1576.

The church belonged from the time of the Conquest to the Abbey of Westminster; the living is now in the hands of the Dean and Chapter.

The list of Vicars dates from 1309.

CANVEY ISLAND

A marshy island defended by high banks erected in 1623, it is joined to South Benfleet at low water by a causeway across Hadleigh Bay. It originally formed part of nine separate parishes in the adjacent country; in 1881 it was formed into a separate ecclesiastical parish.

The present wooden church was erected in 1875 in place of an earlier structure built in 1712; it consists of a chancel, nave, transepts, and small central belfry, with one bell. Of the earlier building some windows and the porch remain.

The registers date from 1819; before that date entries were made at South Benfleet.

[To be continued.]

THE HYDES OF KENT.

By FRED ARMITAGE, Author of *A Short Masonic History*.

WE have no records of stirring strife and battle to tell in these pages, but the history of a nation is not now told in the deeds of the battlefield alone, for commerce and industry have their own story to tell and form no less a part of the nation's life than the epic of the soldier. The history of the ancient Kentish family of Hyde is one which must stir our interest, particularly as the records of much of its history and family doings are clear cut and can be quite easily proved, and we can see the characters living and breathing, loving and dying, under our own eyes.

There are many families of the name of Hyde scattered

throughout England, and naturally enough, for it comes from the Anglo-Saxon word "Hyd," the designation of a piece of land which could be tilled with one plough, and would support one family.

One branch of the Hydes, those of Berkshire, profess to trace their descent direct from King Canute to Sir George Hyde, K.B., of Denchworth near Wantage, Berks, who died 1535, but these sixteenth-century pedigrees are not to be trusted. We have, however, to deal with the Hydes of Kent, concerning whom we have gleaned some little information.

The story starts during the reign of Henry VIII, in the village of Thurgarton, in Nottinghamshire, which is now the site of the palace of the Bishop of Southwell, and is itself the next station to Southwell, on that short line which runs from Newark to Nottingham. At Thurgarton resided Hugh Hyde, who was born about 1529. He was a landed proprietor, and possessed estates in the villages of Langtoft and Baston, which are in the south of the County of Lincoln, not many miles away from Thurgarton; this land descended from father to son in the family for several generations. Hugh is placed at the head of the pedigree of the family of the Hydes of Langtoft in the volume of Lincolnshire Pedigrees issued by the Harleian Society. His arms are given by the Heralds as: gules, a saltire argent between four plates, a chief ermine. His pedigree is also traced in the Heralds' Visitation of London in 1633, the difference between the Lincolnshire and London records being that two different branches of his descendants are followed up.

Hugh Hyde died about 1590, leaving his son John Hyde of Thurgarton surviving him. The son was born in 1551, and was the first of the family to come to the southern counties to live; for we find that he married a lady who lived at Addington in Surrey, in the person of one Mary Leigh, the daughter of John Leigh.

In 1575 was born to them a son, Bernard, who first established himself in London as a Salt Merchant, and lived in Mincing Lane in the Tower Street Ward. It was, of course, quite the usual thing at that time for merchants to live in the city, and there is an interesting note in Strype's edition of Stow's *Survey of London*, which shows us the character of Mincing Lane in days gone by. "Mincing Lane," he says, "antiently called Mincheon, is garnished with very good houses, which for the generality are taken up by Merchants and persons of repute, and the Street is broad and straight coming out of Tower Street, and coming up into Fenchurch Street."

Salt was an article the price of which had risen in 1627 from £2 10s. to £12 "per weight," and as to which there were then considerable profits by reason of the monopoly granted by James I to manufacturers of salt in Shields. Salt was also imported from Spain, and to carry on this branch of trade Bernard had a Wharf or "Key," as he spells it, on the River Thames near Mincing Lane. The Salters' Company had been founded in the year 1558 to guard the interests of the trade, and Bernard Hyde became a member of the Livery, and in 1611 occupied the Chair of Master of the Company. This chair is still in the Company's Hall in St. Swithin's Lane, having been saved from the Great Fire of 1666. On the wall of the Court Room is a full-length oil painting of Bernard Hyde, who appears as a tall imposing man of about sixty, wearing a beard, attired in hose and doublet, with a ruff round his neck, and holding an embroidered gauntlet in his left hand. Immediately beside this picture hangs a contemporary portrait of Charles I, who appointed him to office.

In 1607 Bernard Hyde married Anne Walcot, the daughter of Humphrey Walcot of Walcot, Shropshire. The Walcots were a family with old traditions, for in the Visitation of Shropshire in 1623, no less than ten generations of the Walcots are chronicled, beginning with Sir John Walcot, Knight, who died in the year 1406, in the reign of Henry IV. Their arms in the reign of Henry V were: argent, a chevron between 3 chess rooks, ermines. At last they moved to London, where Humphrey Walcot married Alice, the daughter of Richard Halsey, also of London. Accordingly Humphrey Walcot quartered with his arms those of his wife's family, which were: ermine, on a chief or, a demi-lion issuant, vert. When Bernard Hyde married Anne Walcot he added his wife's arms to his own, which then took the form of the Hyde arms on the dexter side of the shield, and on the sinister side were the quartered arms of Walcot and Halsey. We observe in the *Journal of the Kent Archaeological Society* for 1860 a print of these arms which are described as "the Arms of Hyde impaling Walcot and Helgise quarterly," the word Helgise being an obvious mistake for Halsey. The couple resided over the business premises in Mincing Lane, though their country seat was at Little Ilford, Essex; and they had a family of five children, Bernard born in 1608, Humphrey, John, William, and Anne.

About 1610 Bernard Hyde bought Boar Place, Kent, and the Millbrook Estate adjoining. Boar Place is actually in the Parish of Chiddingstone, next to Sundridge, and at the present time nothing is left of it but one wall in ruins. In the garden, however, stands a lime tree, which has still upon its trunk a shield bearing the Hyde arms.

The history of Boar Place can be traced back through many years to the reign of Henry III, when a family of the name of Boar or Bore lived there. About the year 1421 John Bore conveyed the mansion, which had then become somewhat ruinous, to John Alphew, who rebuilt it, and died possessed of it in 1489. On his death it passed to his daughter Margaret, who married Sir Robert Read, a barrister, who was made a Judge of the Court of King's Bench by Henry VII in 1495, and eleven years later was raised to be Lord Chief Justice of the Court of Common Pleas. Sir Robert lived at Boar Place, which he enlarged. When he died, in January, 1519, he left only female issue, and again the estate passed to a daughter, who is described in one authority as Bridget, in another as Catherine Read. She, like her mother, married a Judge, in the person of Sir Thomas Willoughby, who was appointed a Judge of the Court of Common Pleas, and likewise resided at Boar Place. He died on 29th September, 1545, and is buried in Chiddingstone Church. From him the estate descended to his son, Robert Willoughby, and thereafter to his grandson, Sir Percival Willoughby, who, as we have seen, sold it in 1610 to Commissioner Hyde.

Boar Place was a typical Tudor mansion, forming three sides of a square with a courtyard, in front of which was a moat dividing it from the highway.

Fortunately there are three good views of it in existence. One is contained in that fine old quarto volume Dr. Harris's *History of Kent*, published in 1719, which possesses many double-page wood blocks of country residences. A larger view is preserved in the writer's family, a water-colour drawing, which differs somewhat in detail from the view on the map, due no doubt to alterations made from time to time. An oil painting on panel is also in the possession of Colonel Streatfeild of Chiddingstone.

The fact that Bernard's name is not included in the Heralds' first Visitation of Kent in the year 1619 seems proof positive that he did not occupy his country seat at Boar Place at that period. He habitually lived in town, and attended the Church of St. Dunstan in the East, where he desired to be buried. He was naturally a man with pride of ancestry, and accordingly he went to the College of Arms, where he exhibited the family arms borne by his grandfather, Hugh Hyde; and on 16th September, 1609, he obtained from the Garter King at Arms, Sir William Segar, an examplification or certificate of their authenticity.

In 1609 the large undertaking for supplying London with water brought by a new river from Chadwell and Amwell, Berkshire, was conceived by the leading engineer of the day, Hugh Middleton. He took up a difficult enterprise at his own expense and risk; the work was commenced in 1609 and completed at the end of 1613. When half through his enterprise his means came to an end, and on 2nd May, 1612, he made a bargain with James I for the latter to pay half the cost of the work present and future upon condition of receiving half the profits. Middleton and the King both saw they must take in partners to whom they could sell parts of their ventures, and accordingly the King's moiety and the Adventurers' moiety were each cut up into thirty-six parts, and from time to time Middleton sold these shares to his friends, till out of his thirty-six shares only thirteen remained to him at his death. One share Middleton sold to Bernard Hyde and another to Sir Nicholas Hyde, Lord Chief Justice of the King's Bench. The shares were freehold property, and although cut up into fractions to divide amongst the family on the deaths of their successive owners, part of Commissioner Hyde's share remained in the family for nearly 300 years, till the New River Company was dissolved, and taken over by the Metropolitan Water Board in 1905.

Bernard Hyde now came into touch with a remarkable man, whose name figures largely in the history of those times, Sir John Wolstenholme. He was a great favourite at Court and a prominent City merchant. James I had appointed him a Commissioner of Customs, and in 1619 granted to him and others a lease for eight years of the duties on wines. The lease expired in 1627, and then Sir John got together a little syndicate, of whom Bernard Hyde was one, to act with him as Commissioners of the Customs. The State Papers of the times contain a record of the transaction, and we read that on 3rd September, 1627, the King confirmed the offer of a lease to be granted to Sir John Wolstenholme, Sir Maurice Abbott, Henry Garway, Abraham Jacob, Bernard Hyde, William Garway, Richard Crosham, John Williams, and John Millward, of the customs on wines and corinths, or currants, for three and a half years, with a release for the time past, in consideration of a fine of £12,000 and a loan to the King of £20,000. The King changed his mind before the actual lease was drawn up, and obtained better terms and a heavier rent: for on the 21st November, 1627, the document was sealed, and is stated to be a "Lease of the Customs of wines and currants for 3½ years at the rent of £44,005, and upon the terms contained in the Confirmation before calendared." Sir John Wolstenholme was a close personal friend of Commissioner Hyde, and is mentioned in the latter's will. Commissioner Hyde was obviously constantly at the Custom House, for in his will he refers to a friend of his in the "Wyne office at the Custom House." In 1627 his own Company of the Salters requested him to get from the Custom House some money which was due to them in connection with the salt trade.

Commissioner Bernard's love for landed property did not end with the purchase of Boar Place, for we find that he also purchased in the year .1630 the Manor of Stroud near Rochester. This Manor was granted by the Crown to Sir Robert Cecil, Earl of Salisbury, who died in 1612, leaving it to his son and heir, William, Earl of Salisbury, who sold it to Bernard Hyde, and thence it passed to Bernard's third son, John Hyde.

On 12th December, 1630, Commissioner Hyde executed a Deed of Gift to the Master and Wardens of the Salters' Company, whereby he settled £1,500, represented in after years by £1,900 three per cent. Consols, producing £57 10s. per annum. The income was to be applied as follows:

To a lecturer for a weekly sermon in St. Dunstan's in the East or at St. Mary at Hill, £30; to the poor of the parish where the lecture was said, £5; to ten poor brethren of the company at Christmas, £5; to the poor of the parish of Little Ilford, £1; to fifty-four poor widows or maids out of thirty City parishes, 5s. each, amounting to £13 10s.; to the Master, Wardens, and officers of the Salters' Company, £3. This lecture, thus provided for, was for many years delivered at St. Mary's church, but has now fallen into disuse, and the money is applied to other purposes by the Charity Commissioners.

By his will Bernard Hyde also left £3 to be divided amongst

THE HYDES OF KENT.

the brethren of the Salters' Almshouses in Bread Street, Cheapside, on the day of his funeral. He died on 20th July, 1631 (though the date on his tablet is given as 1630), and was buried in the church of St. Dunstan in the East, one report stating that he was buried "under ye altar." His estate is estimated to have been worth £20,000, equivalent to £100,000 at the present value of money. He, like all the Hydes, left many legacies to charities, and provided for the poor of many city parishes, including St. Botolph, Bishopsgate, St. Botolph, Aldgate, St. Olave, Hart Street, St. Dunstan in the East, St. Sepulchre, and others. He bequeathed mourning to several friends, and in particular he left a legacy to his friend, Sir John Wolstenholme, to pay for a "mourning Cloake for himself and his man," while a lady friend was provided with a mourning gown. The eldest son, Bernard the younger, was at the time of his father's death engaged to be married to a young lady, Hester, the daughter of John Trott of St. Augustin's Fryers (or Austin Friars) in the city of London. Her mother was Catherine Hills, the daughter of Daniell Hills, a merchant of London, who was entitled to a coat of arms, and whose pedigree was set out by the Heralds at their Visitation of London. An agreement for a settlement on the marriage of Bernard and Hester was made by the father of the bridegroom, whereby he arranged to settle £3,000 on his son, but Bernard the father died before the wedding could take place.

To his other sons Commissioner Hyde left £3,000 apiece; Bernard in addition got Boar Place, and the land at Little Ilford, while Humphrey received the Lincolnshire property that had belonged to his great-grandfather Hugh Hyde. Mrs. Anne Hyde survived her husband ten years, dying in 1641, and was likewise buried in St. Dunstan's in the East. Her will is dated 13th January, 1637-8, and was proved on 20th May, 1641; by it she left £3 per annum to be divided amongst six poor widows of St. Dunstan's, besides legacies to the poor of Langtoft, Little Ilford, Chesham, and Chiddingston. She was the eldest of a long family, for one of her brothers was born after her marriage, and her husband stood godfather to the baby who was named after him. Indeed the Commissioner playfully alludes to his namesake as "my brother-in-law and godsonne, Bernard Walcot." Her eldest brother, Humphrey Walcot, was a man of standing, and was appointed High Sheriff of Shropshire in 1631.

[To be continued.]

119

NOTES FROM THE VESTRY MINUTE BOOK OF ST. BENNET, PAUL'S WHARF.

BY HENRY R. PLOMER.

A MONGST the London churches destroyed in the fire of 1666, one of the most interesting, from its associations with the College of Arms, was the church of St. Bennet, Paul's Wharf, in Thames Street. Its early records probably perished with it, the earliest of those now deposited at the Guildhall consisting of the Churchwardens' Accounts from 1565 to 1648, and the Vestry Minute Book beginning in 1572. Of these the more interesting is the Vestry Minute Book, in which the business transacted at the meetings of that body were supposed to be entered. I say "supposed," because up to a certain point the minutes were very badly entered, and only a small part of the work of the Vestry is recorded. Nevertheless the Vestry Book of St. Bennet, Paul's Wharf, has its own distinctive character, and though somewhat late in date, contains much that is interesting to the student of bygone civic life.

The book is a small folio of some five hundred pages, and has been written up from both ends, but is only paged from one, which may be taken as the legitimate commencement of the volume.

The entries begin with a list of the sums collected for the poor from the year 1572 to the year 1596, and the nature of these entries may be gathered from the earliest one, which will also serve as an example of Elizabethan spelling:

> 1572. M^d Resevyd of Ihon Macham and Hare [Harry] Ro ben son, in mone that they dyd gather to the yowes of the powres cheste. xxxjs. iiiid.

The sum annually received varied from £5 7s. 8d. to 2s. 8d., and amongst those who collected the largest amount during their year of office was one Henry Bynneman. This was the printer of that name who had lately come into the parish, and was carrying on business in Thames Street, near Baynard's Castle, having removed from the sign of the Mermaid in Knightrider Street about 1578. Bynneman was noted for the excellence of his work and was largely employed by the booksellers and publishers of those days. His death took place early in 1584.

Nor was Bynneman the only London printer whose name occurs in the records of St. Bennet, Paul's Wharf, there being several other large printing offices in the parish, in Thames Street, Doctors' Commons, and Addling or Addle Hill, whose proprietors at one time and another during the sixteenth and seventeenth centuries, served as officers of the Vestry. It was as one of the "constables" of the parish, that Henry Bynneman had made his collection for the poor box in 1580. In 1586 and 1587 we meet with the name of Thomas East, famous as a printer of music. In the imprint to an undated edition of Sir Thomas Malory's, *La Mort D'Arthur*, he describes the position of his printing office as "betweene Paules wharfe and Baynardes Castle," and it is just possible that it was the same house in which Bynneman had lived. East also rented from the churchwardens of St. Bennet a shed adjoining the church, for which he paid ten shillings a year, but his residence in the parish was short, and he subsequently moved to the sign of the Black Horse in Aldersgate Street. Between 1592 and 1603 John Windet's name occurs in these records either as "constable," or as serving on the wardmote inquest. This printer lived first at the sign of the White Bear in Addling Street, "nigh Baynards Castle," where he was in partnership with John Judson, and later at the Cross Keys on Paul's Wharf. John Windet succeeded John Wolf as official printer to the City of London in 1603. Other printers of note whose names are met with during the seventeenth century are John Raworth, Thomas Newcombe who married John Raworth's widow and succeeded to the business, Thomas Mottershead of Doctors' Commons, and Thomas Ratcliffe his partner.

It would appear that the duties connected with the various offices of constable, scavenger, and the like, were of an arduous nature, for the minutes down to the year 1650 consist of little else than petitions from one and another of those elected, to be excused from serving, on the ground of age or pressure of business. On one occasion two of the Proctors of the Prerogative Court were allowed to compound, for the sum of six pounds apiece, the Vestry considering that if they should be taken from their business "it might prove very prejudicial to the people of this commonwealth."

On another occasion a Mr. George Fielding refused to serve

the office of scavenger or to pay the usual fine for not serving, and the Vestry were compelled to take proceedings against him in the Lord Mayor's Court, with the result that he had to pay a good deal more in the end than he would have done in the first place.

At one period the number of those appealing for exemption increased so much that the Vestry were compelled to make an order increasing the fine for non service, in the case of constables to a minimum of four pounds, and in the case of scavengers to a minimum of six pounds. This order was signed by twenty-three of the parishioners, and it is interesting to note that of this number there were only three who were unable to write.

Being a waterside neighbourhood, there was much poverty in the parish, and the Vestry Book may well be termed the short and simple annals of the poor. Here for example is a note of the proceedings on the 16th June, 1657:

> Imprimis, that goodie Nickolls have hir 18^d made 2s. a weeke.
>
> 2^{ndly} That the overseers tacke care of the widow Dandie and that she have 5s. for the present.
>
> 3^{rdly} That John Thelwall have 20s. for his former servis in warding and attendance on the parrish, as a full discharge.
>
> 4th That goodie Gilberd have 5s. lent her for a stocke.
>
> 5th That goodie Milner have 3s. for keeping of goodie Gilberd for a weeke paid to hir.
>
> 6th That goodie Commins have 3s. grattuitie paid hir.

Another reference to the widow Dandie occurs on the 14th December, 1658, when a payment was made to her in regard that "hir boate and skulls are out of repair, and she expects them to be brought home every hour from mending."

John Bennett was a foundling left in Frying-Pan-Alley on the 1st December, 1652, and he was handed over to George Berd whom the Vestry allowed eighteen pence weekly for his keep. The following year George Berd was allowed ten shillings for the maintenance of the child's clothing, and a quarterly payment of five shillings. Probably the child John Bennett died, for in 1656 George Berd was admitted to the almshouses on Paul's Wharf.

The calls upon the Vestry were many and various, as may be gathered from a few entries culled at random from the book:

It is agreed . . . that Goodwife Pedglar being lately deceased, and her husband not having wherewithall to bury her, the Vestry have thought good to allow him five shillings towards his charges in bying her a shroud, and towards the burying of her.

Ordered . . . that Simon Marbury shall have one flock bed and Bolster with a paire of sheetes and two sheftes.

Ordered that the churchwardens doe forthwith pay unto old Widow Lambert five shillings towards the making upp of some cloathes for her little grand child William Smith, and noe more without further order of this vestry.

Ordered that the two penny loaves given formerlye on the Sabbath daies to Mistress Alsopp, a poore woman of this parish, (bee taken off) and given, and continued to be given, every Sabbath day to the children of one William Fowler, liveinge on St. Bennitts Hill, and at present in a very poore condition till further order of this vestry.

A note of humour is imparted to these otherwise pitiful narratives by the following story of old Mistress Lambert, as set down in the minutes of December, 1659.

Old M^ris Lambert, one of the Almeswomen in the almes houses on St. Petters-hill, appeared at the vestrye, and craved some helpe of maynetenance towardes the keepeinge of a little boy, late of one Smith a tayler, who married one of the daughters of olde M^ris Lambert (to which M^ris Lambert is grandmother) which Smith and his wife are deceased about a yeare and a halfe or two yeares: To whiche the Vestry replyed that they were certified, that the parents of the child did leave behind them, the sume of tenn poundes in ready money, besides twoe ringes and alsoe household stuffe, and asked her where the money was, and the rings and goods, to which shee answered that for the goods there was not much left, but in theire sicknesse, it was sould and pawned . . . and for the rings they were disposed off to buy necessaries for the child . . . but as for the tenn poundes, that was safe, shee knew where it was, but it should remaine where it was, and that it was safe enough, and nobody should have it, for shee had put it upp soe that it lies and is safe and shall bee kept for the good of the child, and to that effect. . . .

In vain the members of the Vestry pointed out to the old dame that the money might be stolen, that it would be much safer in the churchwardens' hands, and that if put out to interest it would be of more use to the child, besides reimbursing the vestry for any present outlay. But, says the churchwarden, "all the perswations of the vestrye to her could not prevaile," so the matter was adjourned to the next vestry meeting, several persons promising to have another interview with the old lady, to try to induce her to give up the money. They might as well have tried to move the church. She refused to give it up or to say where it was hidden.

> Soe that this vestry seeing her stubbornesse herein is resolved, and doth agree and consent, that verye suddenlye shee bee carried(?) inn by the churchwardens and overseers . . . before the Lord Mayor . . . or some other Justices of the Peace within the cittye of London . . . whereby shee may bee perswaded or indeed forced to declare where the said tenn poundes . . . are . . . unlesse within a few daies . . . she doe appeare and declare herself where the money is.

We are left to imagine the pains and penalties that "olde M^{ris} Lambert" brought upon herself, but we doubt whether the vestry ever found that ten pounds.

In 1659 one of the churchwardens was a certain Joseph Gillman, who took a much wider view of his duties than any of his predecessors. During his period of office the minutes were entered more fully than had ever been the case previously, and it is due to his energy that the proceedings respecting Mr. George Fielding and the case of old Mrs. Lambert, are preserved to us. Nor is this all, Joseph Gillman was a bit of an antiquary in his way. He was always complaining that orders made by the vestry in times past had never been entered in the minute book, but that the minutes had been kept privately by the churchwardens. He accordingly sought out any such unrecorded minutes and entered them; with the result that he made a discovery of some importance which he records thus:

> This is to be taken notice of &c. August, 1659. That I Joseph Gillman Churchwarden of St. Bennetts Paul's Wharf London lookinge into the parish booke, I there found sett downe in the time of Mr. Henry Bodeman churchwarden in the yeare . . . 1642. That amongest other things receaved for the use of the poore, that these wordes followeinge were sett downe in writeinge, viz.:
>> Receaved for the guift of Alderman Lambert and Alderman Stiles, fortye shillinges, beinge the dividend part of Eight Pounds, given by them to the ward, which comes soe to bee paid to this Ward of Castle Baynard, once in sixteene yeares. I say receaved £02 00s. 00d.

> Which findeinge soe sett downe (seemed att presentt to bee some thinge a darke business) and I made Inquiry of several housekeepers in the parish and at present could not bee fullye satisfied in the thinge, but makeinge a strict search into it (I found) it is to be paid by the Company of Grocers. . . . And have gained from Mr. Francis Harris, one of the clerkes, belonginge to Grocers-hall, a breviatt at length of the guift, together with the doner's names, and how and when to be distributed, which coppye of it, I thought good to sett downe in this booke belongeinge to the parish, and is written to a word accordinglye, this 25th day of Januarye, 1659.

He then proceeds to set down a minute dated 22nd January, 1590, made by the Alderman, Wardens, and Assistants of the Company of Grocers, to the effect that Richard Lambert, late Alderman, had left a sum of one hundred pounds for the relief and benefit of the poor in all the wards of London, and in accordance with the terms of the bequest they agreed that for the next two years, it should be divided between two young freemen of the Grocer's Company, and so on every two years the recipients being drawn from a different ward each time. A similar sum was also left by Alderman Stile with the same object.

The worthy churchwarden, having finished his copy, adds:

> This is a true Coppye to a word, which I thought good to insert, for a memorandum for the future, and the rather, because that I find heretofore vestry orders have bene kept privatelye in person's handes, and not sett downe in the vestry-booke, to the dishoner of a parishe: Mr. Petter Tomlinson, a former churchwarden hath done it and I leave it to better judgementts whether it ought to bee soe or noe.

Had it not been for the foresight of Joseph Gillman it seems probable that all record of this bequest, at least as regards the Ward of Baynard Castle, would have been lost.

The parish of St. Bennet possessed almshouses in St. Peter's Hill, in Addling Hill, and on Paul's Wharf. There does not appear to be any record as to how they became possessed of those in Addling Hill and Paul's Wharf, but the houses on St. Peter's Hill were the bequest of David Smith, embroiderer, who died in the year 1587, and left by will six newly built houses, to be inhabited by six poor widows of the parish of St. Bennet, Paul's Wharf, which were to be called the poor widows Alley or poore widows Inn. The will is entered at length in the book of bequests (Guildhall MS. 387), and as regards the original the following order was made on the 9th January, 1663-4:

> That there bee a more especiall care taken of the will of Mr. David Smith, Imbroyderer, deceased, then hath beene had, and that it bee distinctly read over in the saide Vestry twice in every yeare, viz. at the choyse of officers for parish affaires, beinge about Easter, and at theire choyse of officers for Ward occasions about Christmas; and that as he was the sole doner of those sixe new built Tenements one St. Peter's Hill in this parish called by him the poore widdows Inn; soe there bee diligent care taken by the churchwardens for the time beinge, that the orders therein bee observed and kept, and securitye bee taken of everye person cominge in, to inhabite in any of the saide sixe houses, according to the intent of the doner, and his meaninge in the saide will, and to prevent further charge or trouble through neglect, as for a precedent Elizabeth Graves widdow, hath done, and that it bee duelye observed for the future vnto which were subscribed our hands.

Needless to say this entry is in the handwriting of Joseph Gillman.

Of the religious troubles of the Commonwealth period, there is only a faint echo in this book. In 1653 a Mr. Allen Geare was appointed minister of the church, but in May of the following year he had evidently ceased to officiate and there is an entry under his hand, resigning his right to the Rectory and an order of the Vestry that an allowance should be made to him for certain things he left behind. He was succeeded by the Rev. John Jackson with whom there appears to have been some trouble at the Restoration, which is recorded in a note by Stephen Trigg, one of the churchwardens.

From this it appears that in the year 1662 Mr. Jackson was suspended by the Chancellor for refusing to read the Common Prayer, and a previous churchwarden had locked the minister out of the church and set two men, one of whom was the porter at the Heralds' College, to keep him out of his desk. Stephen Trigg refused to follow "that envious pattarne" and complains that for that reason he was sorely persecuted and kept out of his moneys nearly half a year. But these and all similar troubles found a common grave in the ashes of the church in that fateful September, 1666.

SOME EAST KENT PARISH HISTORY.

By Peter de Sandwich.

[Continued from p. 45.]

CAPEL LE FERNE.

1569. (Abp. Parker's Visitation.)

CAPLEFERNE is a chapel to Alkham.
Curate:—Dom. John Cadman, Vicar of Alkham.
Householders, 18
Communicants, 61.—(Fol. 55.)

That our Vicar is Vicar at Alkham and Capleferne, and Curate of Folkestone.—(Vol. 1569.)

1570. That our parish being a Chapel annexed to Alkham, ought to be served after this manner: that is to say, the Vicar of Alkham is bounden to do ministrations at all times, and for that he hath all the small tithes of our parish, and for the duly saying of divine service my Lord, his Grace, hath always allowed us and yet doth, a pension of £4, whereof always our Vicar had a marc (13s. 4d.) for receiving of the same, and our clerk the rest for saying our daily Divine Service, until now of late that Mr. Cadman being our Vicar, doth withhold most part of the same from our clerk, whereby we are like to want our divine service, and also the poor man our clerk, driven to live upon the alms of the parish.—(Vol. ii, 1570-71.)[1]

1578. That the church windows be unglazed in divers places and the church porch untiled.

2. They have no poor-man's box, neither was there at any time any collections made and distributed to the poor of the parish.

3. Also they have no chest with locks for keeping of their Register Book; they have no Paraphrases.

4. Our churchyard is un-hedged.

5. They have sold certain stones, both cross-stones and tome [tomb] stones, and kept the money to their own use.

6. That they have taken down a spire steeple of forty or

[1] This volume is in the Probate Office at Canterbury.

fifty feet height which was covered with lead, and sold away certain of the lead, more than ten pounds worth, and five score of it they have in their custody, and some of it now the Churchwardens saith was stolen away, and that they have repaired the church with the money thereof.

7. They have cut down certain trees, sixteen or twenty, whereof some they take for timber, some they burned, and some they sold away.

8. They sold away the timber of the steeple.—(Fol. 9.)

Our Minister doth not instruct the youth in the Catechism; also our Vicar doth not wear a surplice.—(Fol. 11.)

1579. That Ingerham Joll keepeth one mansion-house with a hundred acres of land, which he now doth occupy as a barn, from which the clerk was wont to have sixteenpence every year, and now hath had no wages for the space of six years last past at Michaelmas.—(Vol. 1577-83, fol. 33.)

1580. [See under Badlesmere, vol. vii, p. 212.]

1587. The seats in our church be a little broken and decayed. We have not had our quarter sermons.—(Fol. 42.)

1591. We present our Vicar for not schooling and teaching our children and servants the Catechism and other things, but he promiseth amendment.—(Fol. 129.)

There is no sufficient Book of Common Prayer within the parish, and there is lacking the second Book of Homilies, and no presentment by the churchwardens and sidesmen before this time made there.—(Fol. 130.)

1592. These are to signify to Your Worship that we have, and have had, remaining in our parish of Alkham, at the now dwelling-house of Robert Woollett, two gentlewomen, that is to say, Mr. Daniel Woolett his wife, and one Mistress Norden, sister to Woollett, who have been there in the parish these six weeks, refusing to come to the church, although there was on Palm Sunday warning given to come to a sermon, which Mr. Hull preached the same day, neither did they either come to the church on Easter Day neither did they receive the Holy Communion.—(Fol. 141.)

We present and answer that sometimes we have not Divine Service upon Sundays and Holydays in such order as we should, for our Minister dwelleth not in our parish, by reason whereof he, either being letted by the weather or other business we know not of, cometh not to our church to read and say service accordingly.

2. Our Minister is not resident at this time, neither hath been heretofore.

3. Our Minister doth not catechise so oft as is required of.—(Fol. 141.)

1593. We present we have had no sermons this last year, but our Vicar hath promised we shall have two sermons this next year; but if your Worship will allow us no more, we must be contented.

As touching the catechising of the children of our parish, our Minister doth it, but we have found some fault with him for it, but he hath promised it shall be amended.—(Vol. 1585-92, fol. 175.)

1594. We have all things well, saving Divine Service; we have been very ill served from Christmas last hitherward, for some time we have service, for some time none, and these three last Sundays we have had none at all.

On 25th November it was stated in Court that Mr. Hemming,[1] the Vicar, was not provided at that time of a curate, but since he came he hath served the cure there accordingly, saving when he was necessarily from his benefice. —(Vol. 1585-92, part ii, fol. 37.)

1602. We have nothing to present, saving our chancel of our church, which Mr. Hamon hath promised to repair shortly.—(Fol. 20.)

1609. Our Minister neither readeth service on Wednesdays and Fridays, not being holy days.

Our parishioners have not received so often as is required, but I present Mr. Francis Rogers,[2] our Minister, through

[1] Robert Hemming, B.D., Vicar of Brabourne 1593, but resigned the same year: Alkham, 1594-6; Chislet, 1594-1601; Harbledown, 1597-1601.
[2] He was second son of Richard Rogers, Bishop of Dover (1568-97), and Dean of Canterbury (1584-97). Francis Rogers was Rector of Holy Trinity (Minories), London, 1606-7; Vicar of Alkham with Capel le Ferne, 1607-27; Rector of Denton, 1608-38; St. Margaret's, Canterbury, 1629-38, where he was buried. He married (1) Afra, the daughter of Vincent Boys of Bekesbourne, by whom two daughters; (2) Thomasine Fogge, the

whose neglect (in not appointing the times of receiving so often as that the parishioners might according receive as is required), this hath been.

Our Minister doth not wear the surplice and hood at such times in our parish. On the 15th July he appeared in Court and stated: That if there hath been any neglect of service on Wednesdays and Fridays, the fault was in his curate, who is lately gone from him. He hath had Communions three times a year in the Chapel at Capel-le-ferne, and the fourth time they were to come to the Communion at Alkham, being the mother church, which they neglected to do. He doth not wear his hood when he cometh to Capel-le-Ferne for that it is so far from Alkham, yet he doth wear his surplice and tippett when he preacheth, or administering the Sacrament.—(Vol. 1602-9, fol. 172.)

1610. We have not Divine Service upon Wednesdays and Fridays, and our curate is not licensed by the Bishop.—(Fol. 21.)

1611. That we have not Divine Service upon Holydays and Fridays, according to the form prescribed in the Book of Common Prayer.—(Vol. 1609-18, fol. 36.)

1721. I, Ingram Spearpoint, sole churchwarden of the parish, present William Nethersole the elder and William Nethersole the younger, both of Alkham, farmers of the parsonage of our parish of Capel, for that our chancel is very badly paved, and the walls thereof want white limeing.—(Fol. 47.)

1626. That in our parish he [the curate, Mr. Harbert] hath not so read the Litany, but in Alkham he hath and doth.

2. That our Minister doth only preach once every Sunday, but very shortly he meaneth to catechise the youth.

3. Our Minister would willingly wear such a gown if he were able to buy one, and when he is, he will.—(Vol. 1621-32, fol. 106.)

1635. David Marsh of Capel for his cess for the church, which is 1s. 10d.

widow of George Fogge of Chilham. Thomasine was a daughter of Matthew Gibbon (ob. 1628) of Westcliff, and married (1) . . . Colley; (2) in 1606, George Fogge; and (3) in 1618, this Francis Rogers.—(Hasted, *Hist. of Kent*; *Acta Curia of Archdeacon of Canterbury*, MS. vols.)

We, the Minister, church-wardens and sidesmen of the parish of Capel or Capel le Ferne, do present David Marsh of the same parish, for speaking scandalous speeches of our church or chapel, namely, that John Lushington should have it for a barn, or else it should be an ale-house, and Mr. Pownall's wife should keep the ale-house, and we will come all thither. This is a common reputed fame in our parish and in many men's mouths as spoken by Marsh to many.

Ingram Hogben for not paying of his cess being 4s.— (Fol. 39.)

John Andrews for 8s. 10d., which he refuseth to pay, for that the church cannot be re-paved for want of money.

William Mockett for 2s. 6d.—(Fol. 40.)

1636. We present David Marsh, who raileth at his Minister, church-wardens, and neighbours, for making of a cess for the church, saying, as the fame and common report goeth—" a company of rogues have set their hands to a cess, and trouble honest men to ride about it."

The church wanteth some paveing and the church-yard some railing, which could not be done by reason there hath been controversy about the cess.—(Vol. 1583-1636, fol. 53.)

CHARLTON.

1563. It is presented that they have neither parson, vicar nor curate, whereby they are altogether unserved. Henry Leonard of Dover, farmer.

That Mr. Alexander Mynge of Dover doth keep the church-yard from the church, and thereon doth make pasture.

They have no Register Book and none to keep it.

That Sir John Burvell, Vicar of Alkham, had away the chalice and book and other ornaments belonging to the church, which said Sir John Burvell was the last Minister there.

They have no manner of books, and none doth mind to provide [them].—(Vol. 1562-3.)

1569. (Abp. Parker's Visitation.)
Est ecclesia desolata.
Householders, 6
Communicants, 14.—(Vol. 1574-76, fol. 55.)

SOME EAST KENT PARISH HISTORY.

1574. That the church is ruinously fallen into decay, neither font in reparation, nor books serviceable, nor bell to give the people warning, nor seats to sit in. (Vol. 1574-6, fol. 70.)

1579. Our church is decayed, by reason whereof we have no service there said, nor Sacraments ministered, whereby we are constrained to repair unto St. James' in Dover, unto Mr. Watts, Minister, and there the Sacraments are ministered unto us, and we there have the service of God.—(Vol. 1577-83, fol. 31.)

1580. (See under Badlesmere, vol. vii, p. 212.)

1585. We lack a Bible of the largest volume.—(Fol. 6.)

1588. We present Mr. Watts, Minister of the parish of Charlton, for lacking of Divine Service certain days.

William Mackner, victualler of the parish, for keeping of men in Evening Prayer [time] in his house.

We present William Mackner for speaking against the church, he said it was better to hurl the money down the stream [1] than to be bestowed upon the seats as it was; that it makes them which we have cessed be unwilling to pay, for they say there be some in our parish that said the money that had been given aforetime it were better it had been hurled down the stream; and there be some that have heard William Mackner speak them words and nobody but him, and therefore we cannot judge nobody but him.—(Fol. 50.)

1590. Henry Newman, for shaking abroad four powtes [2] of hay upon the Sabbath-day; but he being at service in the forenoon and afternoon.

Also for the like, Nicholas Boykett and goodwife Milton.

James Kingscote, for mowing on the Sabbath-day stubble for his own use.

Goodman Milton's servant, his name is Harry, for playing at cards in the parish in the service time.—(Fol. 104.)

---

[1] The old church stood close to the east bank of the Dour. See *Some More Memories of Old Dover*, by Miss M. Horsley, for a description of this stream.

[2] A pout is a small round stack of hay or straw; the small heaps are called cocks and the larger ones pouts.—*Dict. Kent Dialect.*

1591. We present Henry Milton, miller, for grinding on the Sabbath-day, being the nineteenth day of September.—(Fol. 134.)

1593. We present our Minister, Mr. Watts, for that upon Whitsunday last we had no Evening Prayer, nor upon the morrow following, and upon divers Sundays and Holydays we have but service once a day, and sometimes none at all.

We have no covering for our Communion Table, nor any cup, nor cushion for our pulpit, nor any box for the poor.—(Vol. 1585-92, fol. 171.)

1594. There is no Communion cup, for the which I do crave some reasonable time to provide the same.—(Fol. 33.)

1601. We do present Henry Milton, who lately was church-warden and clerk of the parish, having in his keeping the Communion Cup, and the cloth for the Communion Table, and now doth withhold them from the church.—(Vol. 1593-1602, part ii, fol. 161.)

1602. On the twenty-sixth day of June, William Watts, the Rector of the parish, appeared in Court and said:—That he is not resident at Charlton according to law; that indeed he dwelleth not upon his parsonage, but is continually abiding every day teaching school in the parish church there.

He was ordered by the Court:—That he do not let to farm his tithes of the parsonage unto Mr. Thomas Monings, his former farmer; and that he be resident upon his parsonage of Charlton according to law.—(Vol. 1600-1602, fol. 206.)

1606. This we do present with the rest:—first, Stephen Constable of the parish of Buckland, with the rest of his company; William Burvill of the same parish; William Blurstone of the parish of Charlton; Thomas Judge of the same, for reaping of pease upon the Sabbath day.—(Fol. 88.)

Abraham Goden, for breaking of the floor of the church, and not making it again.   •

On 3rd November he appeared in Court, and confessed:—That he buried his wife in the parish church of Charlton, where was no pavement but only a floor, and purposeth to lay a stone over her grave, and saith that the floor of or over the same grave was and is made again as before the same burial it was, and saith that he intendeth to pave the same grave or lay a decent stone upon the same.—(Fol. 89.)

We also present Thomas Bing, for working on the Sabbath day.—(Vol. 1602-9, fol. 89.)

1607. We present Abraham Godwine [*sic*], for that he doth not cover his wife's grave in the church.—(Fol. 105.)

Thomas Alison, for not coming orderly to Divine Service in our parish.—(Fol. 106.)

Thomas Webb, miller, doth use to load and grind corn upon holy-days.

On 1st June, when Webb appeared in the Court and confessed:—That he hath sometimes, when there hath been a holyday fallen upon a Saturday, being the common market-day at Dover, ground corn in his mill situate in the parish of Charlton near Dover, but hath not ground any corn in the time of Divine Service upon any holy-day, as he believeth.—(Fol. 108.)

Abraham Godden and his wife of our parish, for that they do not diligently resort to our church to hear Divine Service.—(Fol. 109.)

Mr. Watts, parson there, for that he suffereth the chancel of our church to go to decay, in not repairing of it where and when it needeth, so as it raineth in upon the Communion Table.

Likewise for that he doth but very seldom read service publicly in our church, either upon Sundays or Holydays, but divers times will forsake us and goes elsewhere, and there says service on such days.

1608. That the wife of Thomas Pepper hath been delivered of a child some two months past, and doth refuse to go to the church to give God thanks for her safe delivery in childbirth, according to laws in that behalf provided.—(Vol. 1602-9, fol. 143.)

To be continued.]

The Site of the King's Old Barge-House.
From Agas's map, *temp.* Elizabeth.

THE KING'S OLD BARGEHOUSE.

By Ethel Lega-Weekes.

[Continued from p. 51.]

THE earliest map or plan known to me that shows any houses immediately to westward of the great ditch, is the one that for convenience I refer to as Bray's,[1] it having been in his possession.

Here, in the large corner plot north of the Narrow Wall (the holding, I take it, of "Mr Kent") are three double-gabled houses, and a little tower with a round top which Bray describes as "a cupola," and from which, he says, "a staff with a flag at the end is extended towards the river"; though to my thinking it rather suggests a crane, a common feature of these riverside premises.

Adjoining this plot is "the Prince's Land on the west," the bare state of which might lead us to infer that this plan was drawn before the houses specified in 1649 were erected, but that experience of early maps shows their negative evidence to be of little or no value, whole rows or clusters of houses appearing and disappearing repeatedly, in a series of maps professing to have been drawn within a few years of each other.

The land south of the way is marked "A parte of the Prince's Meadow," and has a cottage in its north-eastern corner, doubtless the one to be referred to below, as "occupied by washerwomen."

To revert to the Survey of October, 1649, the description of "the Prince's Meadow" is followed by:

> WHITE'S WOODYARD: Mr White under-tenant. All that tenement, etc., lying in a place called *the Bargehouses* on the bankside of the river of Thames, in the parish of Lambeth, within the said manor of Kennington; consisting of one messuage, containing foure rooms below stayrs and foure rooms aboove stayrs, one wash-house cont. one room below and one above, one little tenement, cont. two rooms below and one above, and one other little tenement cont. three rooms below and three above, one yard, cont. 1½ acres land, and one great crane; which premises are bounded by one great woodyard now in possession of Mr Kent on the E., the Prince's Mead on the S., one great woodyard in possession of Mr Smith, on the W., and the river Thames on the N.—Worth per an: £28.

[1] See ante, vol. x, p. 164.

135

SMITH'S WOODYARD:—Mr Smith under-tenant. All that tenement, . . . etc., lying in the said place called *the Bargehouses* . . . consisting of one messuage, cont. four rooms below stayres and foure above, one garret, one great yard cont. 1 acre of land, one countinghouse, cont. two rooms, one large crane, and six large sheades, and one pond for water; which premises are bounded with White's Woodyard on the E., the sd. Prince's Meadow on the S., one yard in possession of Mr James Sherley, on the W., and the Thames on the N.— Worth £30.

SHIRLIE'S WOODYARD:—Mr Jas. Shirley[1] under-tenant. All that tenement . . . lying in the said place called *the Bargehouses* . . . consisting of one messuage; a new-built house of deal boards, not fully finished, cont. two rooms below stayrs and three rooms above, one great yard, cont. 3 roods, . . . etc. of land, one parcell of waste ground, and one parcell of waste land lying between the sd. yard and the sluce, cont. 1 acre of ground; bounded with the sd. Smith's Woodyard on the E., the sd. Prince's Meadow on the S., the sd. Sluce upon the W., and the Thames on the N.—Worth £8.

JUDAH WALKER, Undertenant. One little tenement standing in the N.E. corner of the sd. close or parcell of meadowe called the Prince's Meadoues, consisting of three little rooms wherein washerwomen live.—Worth per an., £1 10s.

The last-named must, I think, be identical with the premises referred to in the following extract from Norden's Survey, 1615 (No. 147).

[Official Translation]. Randolph Hanmer, Gent., among other things hath purchased a certain piece of ground, formerly Cockerham's containing by estimation 1½ acres, lying near the river Thames, called the Corner Meadow, lying in the marsh there called Prince's Marsh, in Lambeth and Lambeth Marsh, within the Manor of Kennington, and lying in the north corner of the said Prince's Meadow, next to the garden called Paries Garden, adjoining to the house upon the bank there, and containing from thence in breadth, at the north corner [*i.e.*, from the N.E. corner] towards the west, by a trench there leading to the river Thames, 11 rods; but in

---

[1] In a Surrey Fine of Michaelmas term, 1657, Thomas Sherley, gent., appears as one of several querents to whom James Sherley, Clerk in Holy Orders, and Mary his wife, quit-claimed for £200, three messuages, 2 cottages, 4 gardens, one acre of land, and three wharves with the appurtenances, in Lambeth. In 1662 Stan(wer?)dine Sherley paid tax on nine hearths in Foxhall Liberty, South Lambeth.

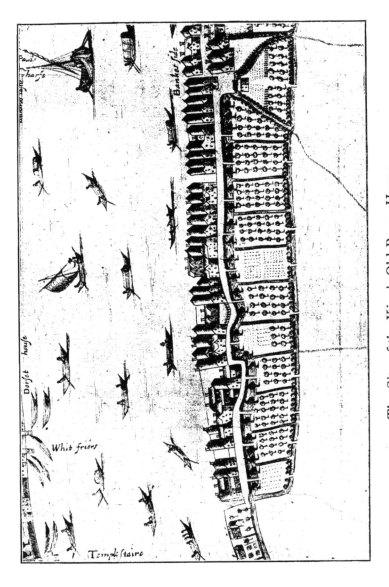

The Site of the King's Old Barge-House.
From Faithorne's map, 1658.

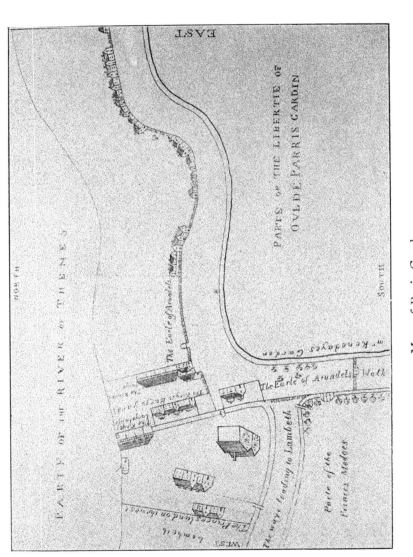

Map of Paris Garden.

From Allen's *History of Lambeth.*

length, by the ditch and Bank of Paryes Garden towards the south, 22 rods; as by four separate posts and boundaries called stakes, fixed in the acre-and-a-half of meadow ground, according to the custom of the said manor, for the separating and better distinguishing of the same, more plainly appears; at the yearly rent of 21*d*.

It will be noticed that although Mr. Kent's woodyard is mentioned as the eastern boundary of the first of the premises lying in "the Bargehouses" described in the Survey of the Manor of Kennington, it is not itself included in that survey; neither is it claimed as a Crown possession by Cromwell's surveyors, who declare the King's Bargehouse to be adjoined on the west by "a timber yard now in the possession of Griffiths Kent."

This I cannot explain; but its situation indisputably identifies Kent's yard with a part—if not the whole—of the enclosure just across the ditch from the King's Barge Yard, as pourtrayed on Bray's plan.

Its holder (who, it will be remembered, eventually purchased the old Bargehouse) was perhaps the son of (if not identical with) one " Griffith Kent,[1] Citizen & Sadler of London," who was a party to an indenture dated December, 1655 (Close Roll, 3865, No. 21), whereby Richard Mountney of London, Merchant, conveyed to Kent certain lands in Bermondsey (described in detail), near St. Saviour's Mill Pond and "the Divell's Neckinger." The indenture mentions, further, one Peter Theobald, as late husband of Mary, the then wife of the said Griffith Kent.

In 1658 Griffith Kent was one of the Auditors of the Accounts of the Overseers of the Poor of Paris Garden (Add. MS. 34110).

The Court Book of the Manor[2] contains the Counterpart (Sched. vi, No. 10) of a Lease dated 1663, from William Angell to Griffith Kent of "a parcell of land, or wharf, lying by the Thames-side in Paris Garden," from Lady-day then last past, for the term of thirty-one years; at the yearly rent of 30*s*.

---

[1] Ducarel states that in 1636 Thomas Kent, Gent., held the Manor House of Kennington. In 1662 Thomas Kent paid tax on 10 hearths in the Prince's Liberty in the parish of Lambeth (Lay Subsidies, Bundle 187, No. 479).
In Lambeth Parish Registers are the entries :
    1629, Oct. 31.—Bur: a dau. of Thomas Kent's, Still-born.
    1674, March 31.—Bur: Lane the son of Mathew Kent.
[2] At Messrs. Lethbridge, Money, and Prior's.

In 1676 the same premises (evidently) were demised, by Angell and others, to Joseph Holden and William Wilkinson, under the description of "a little wharfe by the Thames side, over against the Temple, in lease to Griffiths Kent at 30s. a year."

This item is immediately followed by "A messuage near the Barge House in the occupation of [*blank*] Quinborough, at £4"; and "A piece of ground adjoining, in lease to George Biggs, whereon were three houses built by Biggs."

We may get a fair idea of the general aspect of the tenements collectively known as the Bargehouses, though we cannot identify house by house, from Faithorne's map, which is said to have been surveyed between 1643 and 1647, but to have had features introduced up to the date of its engraving in 1658. This shows several buildings scattered along a strip of land confined between the Thames and the long ditch bordering Narrow Wall, and divided by lesser ditches into three parcels. In the westernmost of these, close to the embouchure of the Cupar's Garden Sluice, stands a long-armed windmill, the wood-saw-mill, said to have been erected during Cromwell's Protectorate,[1] and to have been frequently visited by him as a curious object, the first of its kind in England, though common enough in Holland. The ground in this and the second division is strewn with little rectangles which may be meant for planks, symbolizing timber yards; but in the third there are small squares that may perhaps represent tanks for the whetsters, tenters,[2] or other local trades.

In the map in Strype's *Stow*, 1720, the same strip is cut up into seven holdings, bearing the names respectively (proceeding from Old Barge Stairs) of Squire Shorter,[3] Mr Tibals

---

[1] Manning and Bray, iii, 467.

[2] Bleachers and dyers.

[3] The above-named "Squire" was possibly son of Sir John Shorter, who, as we learn from Robert Woodger Bower's *Sketches of Southwark Old and New*, was Lord Mayor in 1688, and, dying the same year, devised by his will to the poor of the parish of Southwark, the rents of a freehold house and land formerly on the east side of Boddy's Bridge. Sir John was a dissenter, an Anabaptist, and John Bunyan was his Chaplain. The wife of Sir Robert Walpole was his granddaughter. In 1658 John Shorter was one of the auditors of the Paris Garden Overseers' accounts [Add. MS. 34100]. The same year William Angell leased to John Shorter "4 *Putt Galleries* or Shedds, built over the mill-stream upon the wharfe thereof, in Paris Garden, for 99 years, at the yearly rent of 1d." [Old Court Book at Messrs. Lethbridge and Prior's, p. 40.] In 1661, 24th April, William Angell conveyed to John Shorter "a wharfe . . . adjoining to the east

Bruce Castle, Tottenham, 1686.
From an old print.

BRUCE CASTLE, TOTTENHAM.

[*i.e.*, Theobalds] Mr Batcher[1] [*i.e.*, Bachelor; here is a dry dock] Mr Phillips, Mr Baker, Mr Hering, and Sir Peter Rich.

In Roque's map, 1746, a Glass house yard seems to cover the site of Shorter's or perhaps the next tenement. In Summersell's map, 1768, the first division is Capt. Shorter's, the next Mr. James's, and the next to that Mr. Theobald's—a very large timber yard, including a dock, and reaching to " Morris' Causeway " and the " Lord Mayor's Bargehouse."

In Middleton's Survey, 1784, " Shorter's " is, apparently, represented by " No. 11 " (George Russell's wood shed and wharf), while a bare plot, 22 ft. 9 in. wide, intervenes between it and Bargehouse Alley. In Summersell's Survey a division corresponding to this bare plot is demarked from Shorter's by the dotted parochial boundary line, so that it evidently belonged to the old liberty of Paris Garden; whereas the division corresponding to Shorter's, and marked in the latest ordnance map as " Site of the King's Old Bargehouse," belongs to the Duchy.

From comparison of these maps with the Ogilby-Morgan, where the westernmost of the buildings marked " Old Bargehouses " is contiguous to the Alley, and from other evidence considered in this paper, I would submit that the bare plot, and *not* " No. 11 " was the actual site of the " King's Old Bargehouse," as described in the Survey of 1652 (see *ante*, vol. x, p. 173).

BRUCE CASTLE, TOTTENHAM.

By C. Edgar Thomas.

[Continued from p. 60.]

JAMES TOWNSEND added a new east wing to the mansion. He figured very prominently in political circles in his day, and in 1769 was elected an Alderman of the Ward of Bishopsgate, while in 1772-3 he became Lord Mayor

side of Old Paris Garden Stairs, together with the sd. Common Staires or landing-place." [*Ibid.*, Schedule i, No. 35.] For discussion of the term "*Pott Gallery*" see *Notes and Queries*, May (*et seq.*), 1907.

[1] The Lambeth Burial Registers:
1656, April 14.—Joseph the son of Thomas Baccheler, a stranger.
1665, Jan. 3.—Samuel son of John Batcheller.
1667, . . . Katherin the wife of John Batcheller.

of London. In Parliament he represented Calne in Wiltshire, the representation extending to the time of his death. He was acquainted with Lord Shelburne, who, while on a visit to Bruce Castle in 1771, wrote to Lord Chatham. Chatham in his reply spoke of "our worthy warm friend your landlord." His wife died in 1785, and he followed her to the grave four years later, leaving one daughter and one son, James or Henry Hare Townsend, who then came into the estate. As we find in the case of some other old houses, there was an ancient custom connected with Bruce Castle. When a member of the family died the corpse was not carried to its last resting place through the gate, but an opening was made for it to pass through in the outer wall nearest to the church. The church was All Hallows, Tottenham, which is situated opposite the side entrance to the premises. The last time this curious old custom was enacted happened in 1789, when a breach was made in the wall for the body of Alderman Townsend to pass through.

In Dyson's *Tottenham*, 1792, is found the following description of Bruce Castle: "the attic story consists of a large nursery, and 9 good bedchambers, with 2 large closets. The middle story contains a library, 35 ft. by 18 ft.; a billiard room, 31 by 22; 7 neat bedrooms, with 4 dressing rooms; and a store room. The ground floor consists of a commodious hall, 33 by 22; a saloon, 35 by 18; and a handsome staircase; a drawing room, 26 by 19; an eating-room, 30 by 24; a breakfast parlour, 18 by 22; and a dressing-room adjoining; besides apartments for steward, housekeeper, and butler, servants' hall, spacious kitchen, and back stairs, and roomy dry cellaring. Among the detached offices are stables for 12 horses, a treble coach-house with loft, and the whole is supplied with water from a deep well over which is erected a brick tower on the S.W. of the house, the upper part of which is used as a dairy." It will thus be readily seen that the house was of no mean order, but, on the contrary, a fine specimen of what once constituted a nobleman's residence. There used to be a painting of the house before its alteration by the Coleraine family, and this was placed over the mantelpiece in one of the parlours. Curiously enough, this picture shows two more towers like the one mentioned in the preceding description of the mansion, but all of them have now been razed to the ground.

Some time after—during the latter part of the eighteenth century—the whole of the estate was purchased by a Mr. Smith,

Bruce Castle, Tottenham, 1840.

From an old print.

who, however, did not retain it long, but disposed of it to Mr. Ayton Lee. He, in turn, sold it shortly afterwards to his cousin, Richard Lee. Thus within the space of a very few years, the Castle found three purchasers, but fate seems to have ordained that it should not remain long in the possession of any one of them.

Richard Lee resided at Bruce Castle for a short time, and it then became the property of John Eardley Wilmot, one of the Masters in Chancery. This was about 1804. He contrived to extend the property by procuring adjacent land, in all about twenty-five acres. Mr. Wilmot owned the estate until 1813, when it was by his order put up for sale by Messrs. Hoggart and Phillips, then of the Auction Mart. The estate then consisted of, roughly, forty-seven acres, comprising the house, pleasure garden, and paddock, about twenty acres, orchard, farm-yard, and farm-house, about twelve acres; the remaining ground was situated immediately opposite the mansion-house, on the south side of Lordship Lane, extending in a considerable line from east to west. About this time the Land Tax on the property was redeemed; the valuable timber, the worth of which was estimated at £1,100, was also included in the sale. Bruce Castle was not sold by auction, but was bought in at £12,900. It was, however, disposed of by private contract, to Mr. John Ede, a very prosperous city merchant, as is amply proved by the fact that he paid Mr. Wilmot no less than £11,500 for it. This included the fixtures in the house, the park and grounds behind the mansion, and also the valuable timber.

Mr. Ede, on taking possession, entirely demolished the west wing of the house, including the stables and coach-house, and under his direction the remainder of the structure underwent a good and complete repair. There used to be an avenue of fine old elms which ran from the high road to the mansion, and *Bruce Grove* now marks this site. The estate was owned by Mr. Ede until 1827, when he parted with the mansion and fifteen acres of pleasure ground, gardens, etc., to the celebrated Hill family. He also sold part of the land directly in the front of the house, containing about eighteen acres to a Mr. Joseph Fletcher, reserving to himself the hoppet on the west side of the Lane, leading from Lordship Lane to All Hallows Church, and a field opposite on which he built some houses.

The three brothers Hill, Edwin, Frederick, and Rowland, afterwards Sir Rowland Hill, converted the premises into a school, as a branch establishment of "Hazelwood School," Birmingham, which was then conducted by their father, Thomas Wright Hill, and which enjoyed a great reputation as a respectable middle-class boarding school. It can be safely asserted that "Bruce Castle School" soon acquired equal celebrity. It was about this time that the entrance to the house was altered; a new one being made round the side of the premises, the drive being shaped accordingly, whilst the old front door immediately under the ancient clock tower, was bricked up and made to form a retiring or ante-room, jutting off the dining-hall. From the window of this small room one can now enjoy an uninterrupted view of the lawn. The room in which Sir Rowland is said to have thought out his idea of the penny postage, is happily still intact, and possesses a considerable amount of interest.

In 1833 Rowland Hill came to the conclusion that on account of failing health, he must abandon the profession of a schoolmaster; he accordingly withdrew from the school and devoted himself to public life. His brothers Edwin and Frederick did likewise some time after, both of them eventually gaining high positions in the public service. On their retirement the school was successfully conducted by Mr. Arthur Hill, and subsequently by Sir Rowland's nephew, Birkbeck Hill.

Having been in the possession of the Hills for about fifty years, Bruce Castle again changed hand in 1877, the new owner being the Rev. W. Almack, M.A. Sir Rowland Hill in an account of the years he spent at Bruce Castle, written in 1869, says: "Although, however, I separated myself from duties in which I had been engaged for three and twenty years, I have never lost interest in the school, nor ever failed to render it such assistance as lay in my power. I gladly hailed the early return of its prosperity; and at the end of thirty-six years from my withdrawal, I rejoice to see it still flourishing."

As has been before stated, eight years later, and fifty from its opening as a school, Bruce Castle had passed from the possession of the Hill family. In 1892, the Tottenham Urban District Council purchased it from Joshua Pedley, Esq., of White Hart Lane, the amount paid for it being £25,000. The object of the purchase was to secure the historic old place for the public, and so preserve it. The grounds have been made into a public park, and the house has been entirely renovated.

BRUCE CASTLE, TOTTENHAM.

It now contains a valuable and well-arranged museum, and also a reading-room and branch library in connection with the Tottenham Public Libraries. For these purposes two long rooms have been thrown into one, but beyond this, and some redecoration and repairs, it can happily be stated that very little has been done towards reconstruction or so-called restoration. The old fireplaces are still preserved, one of them having the china painting down the sides still intact, while another of later date is closed up. There are two handsome oak staircases, the larger one leading from the hall to the apartments above, being a splendid example of the old wide staircase of long ago ; the other one, situated at the back of the premises, is probably the older of the two. It is not so massive as the front stair, but what it lacks in this respect it makes up for in other features, being beautifully rounded and bearing much handsome carving, some of which has been unfortunately detached. The ancient row of bells still hang in the old place high up at the far end of the hall. Among the apartments upstairs is a gymnasium, besides a few cells in excellent preservation. On the wall over the balcony hangs an oil painting of Bruce Castle as it was in the seventeenth century. The house is still adorned with the clinging ivy and creeper, the growth of centuries, while above all, as firm as ever, stands the old clock tower, with its pretty little balustrade. The ancient mansion is well worth a visit.

HOUGHTON CONQUEST.

By CONSTANCE ISHERWOOD.

[Continued from p. 64.]

ON the north side of the chancel is a large altar tomb of Purbeck stone, inlaid with the brasses of Richard and Isabella Conquest, with their nine sons and five daughters, and of John Conquest, the father of Richard. The two male effigies are represented in early Tudor armour, in simple cuirasses, small placcates, condières, and mail skirts below skirts of taces with tuilles; and the lady is represented in a close-fitting bodice and sleeves, a flowing skirt, and a pedimental head-dress. Each of these three effigies measures twenty-eight inches. Above the knight is a shield, on the sinister side, with the arms of Conquest: Quarterly, *argent* and *sable*, a label of three points, *gules*; impaling: quarterly, I and IV, *checky*, a fess, *ermine*; II and III, a bend, *lozengy*. Below the effigies, in miniature, of the nine sons, is the symbol of St. Luke, a winged ox; and, at the sinister corner, is the symbol of St. Matthew, the angel bearing the Bible. The inscription is as follows:

> Hic jacet Joħes Conquest, armiger, nup dñus de Houghton, et Riĉus Conquest, filius et heres ejusdē Joħis ac Isabella uxor eius qui quidē Riĉus obiit die   Aº dñi Mcccc & ꝑdĉa Isabella obiit 18 Augusti Aº dñi 1493, qu'ꝫ aiãbuz ꝓpicieł dē am̃.

The other brasses represent the effigies of Richard and Elizabeth Conquest, with their six sons and two daughters. The male is represented in Tudor armour, and his lady in a flowing skirt, close-fitting bodice and sleeves, and pedimental head-dress. The inscription is as follows:

> Orate ß mortuis quia moriemur. Hic jacet Riĉus Conquest Armiger, et Elizabeth, uxor eius, qui quidem Riĉus obiit xxviij die mens̃ Julii Anno dñi Milliºcccc, et dict' Elizabeth obiit die   Aº dñi Mºvc: quorũ aiãbuz ꝓpicietur Deus, Amen.

Arms: Per cross, a file of five points, Conquest (over the lady); two swords in saltire, points in chief.

The male line of the Conquest family became extinct on the death of Benedict Conquest, the father of Lady Arundel, and the estate was purchased of them by the father of the Earl of Upper Ossory, of Ampthill Park, in 1741.

The mural monument in memory of the celebrated Dr. Thomas Archer, of Jacobean fame, is characteristic; it represents the bust of the worthy priest, attired in a preacher's gown, with a ruff and a black skull cap. The effigy, which is painted in *proper* colours, is represented as leaning on a pulpit cushion, and as holding the Bible in his left hand. The inscription, in Latin, is as quaint as the monument, and commences by adjuring the reader that, " If things are well within, do not trouble," and goes on to say that, " I have instructed many, while living, now I instruct few. What one day constructs, one day pulls down. So the wonderful fabric of the beautiful world falls down. So man rises, dies, a defenceless worm. O, happy one that I am, who, after being relieved of the burden of the flesh, I have changed uncertainties for realities, and vanities for blessings. Thomas Archer, Chaplain to King James, Rector of this Church for 41 years, placed this in his lifetime, in the year of our Lord, 1620, in the year of his age 76."

The mural tablet in memory of Dr. Zachary Grey, of gray and white marble, is simple and undecorative; it bears this inscription: " Sacred to the Memory of Zachary Grey, L.L.D., late Rector of this Parish, who, with zeal undissembled, served his God, with love and affection endeared himself to his Family, with Sincerity unaffected promoted the Interest of his Friends, and with real Charity and extensive Humanity behaved towards all mankind. He died Nov. 25, 1766. Aged 78." Beside this tablet is that of his wife, bearing this inscription: " Near this Place is interred Susanna Grey, relict of the late Revd Zachary Grey. She died Feb. 3rd, 1771. Aged 82, whose social virtues rendered her dear to all."

The east window is Perpendicular, of five lights; the glass, representing the Crucifixion and the Ascension, was placed " In loving Memory of three Benefactors, Eliza Hargreave, and Mary and Sarah Windle, A.D. 1880."

On either side of the altar are niches of the Decorated period, ornamented with quaint leafy crockets and rose-tipped cusps, and slender shafts in the jambs, with circular capitals. The double piscina is Perpendicular, having a cinquefoil head, supported by slender octagonal shafts in the jambs. Some of the ancient carved oak has been preserved in the choir stalls. In the vestry is a chest or " safe," made of wood, with strong iron bands, and bearing the date 1691. The fine old hammer-beam roof has fortunately been preserved. The windows of the chancel are all Perpendicular, and contain some ancient glass. The rood screen belongs to the same period, and is of oak, carved in a graceful design, after the " window" pattern and painted red, with ornamentations in the form of white and gold flowers. The nave is separated from the aisles by clustered columns, of the Decorated period. The arch mouldings terminate in beautiful corbels, representing the heads of a king and a queen, a bishop, nuns and monks, our Lord, St. John, the beloved disciple, and the Blessed Virgin Mary. The beautiful windows of the north and south aisles belong both to the Decorated and the Early Perpendicular periods. In the upper lights are preserved some valuable bits of ancient stained glass, depicting shields charged with coats of arms.

Over the north door is a fine fresco, " more than life size—colossal," representing St. Christopher bearing his divine burden. The figure is of immense proportions, and eminently striking to the eye; it would be wonderfully interesting to know whose was the hand that limned it, hundreds of years ago. Remains of other frescoes remind us of what the interior of this noble church must have been like in all its former beauty. Over the chancel arch is a representation of the glorified Christ, with an angel on either side, and shields of arms; while on the upper part of the eastern wall of the south aisle the double triangles, or "six-pointed stars," known as Solomon's Seal or David's Shield, are discernible; on the north wall, in a line with the effigy of St. Christopher, is part of an inscription which, however, is not legible.

The font, which is septagonal, is Decorated, the panels of the basin being richly ornamented with "crockets" and "tabernacle work." The seventh panel is rough and un-decorated.

The spacious pre-Reformation pews have fortunately sur-vived past "restorations,"[1] and their decorative standards, carved with cusps and flanked by quaint "buttresses," remain untouched. Recessed in the wall in the south aisle is a Decorated piscina, surmounted by an ogee arch, and in close proximity is a small square niche, which probably served as an aumbry. Square leafy bosses ornament the juncture of the ribs of the ancient oak roof of the nave and the aisles, and traces of colouring are still visible in the aisles.

The tower is separated from the nave by a pointed arch springing from octagonal capitals. Above, high up, projecting from the wall, is a tiny ringer's gallery, with massive oak rails, a rare feature of the interior of Bedfordshire churches. A ring of six bells hangs in the belfry.

Taking leave of the beautiful and venerable church of All Saints, with its cluster of old-world memories, we return to matters mundane, and consider the other features of anti-quarian interest in the parish that have not yet been described.

The Almshouse was erected and endowed in 1632 by Sir Francis Clarke, Kt., the benefactor of Sidney Sussex College, Cambridge, for six poor widows, " out of his desire to con-tribute a perpetual benefit to the inhabitants of Houghton

---

[1] The last being in 1845.

Conquest." Attached to the almshouse is a free school, with a residence for the master.

Bedfordshire pillow lace—which, so tradition tells us, was introduced into the county by Queen Katherine of Arragon, during her residence at Ampthill Castle from 1510 to 1533— is made in the village, and, until quite recently, the lace-makers used to celebrate St. Katherine's Day, 25th November, as the holiday of their craft, "in memory of good Queen Katherine, who, when the trade was dull, burnt all her lace and ordered new to be made."

About two miles from the village of Houghton Conquest, picturesquely situated in a noble park, with fine avenues of oak and chestnut trees and commanding a magnificent view of the Vale of Bedford, stand the ruins of Houghton House, once the palatial residence of Mary Herbert, Countess of Pembroke—"Sidney's sister and Pembroke's mother" (who built it in 1615)—now but the veriest shell of its former greatness, ivy mantled and desolate. By good fortune pictures remain to show us what Houghton House was like in its pristine splendour, when it rose "like an exhalation from the earth" under the direction of Inigo Jones, who reproduced in the *north* front the style of Palladio, which is supposed to be a replica of the Convent della Carita, Venice. The south and west fronts were richly ornamented with colonnades of Doric and Ionic columns, with the pediments and the friezes finely sculptured with the porcupine, the bear and ragged staff, and the lion rampant, the crests of the Sidney, Dudley, and Pembroke families. Square towers, with incurved roofs, stood at the corners of the mansion, and added considerably to its beauty and dignity. The numerous windows, of which nothing remains but the stone framework and the massive mullions, were of the Elizabethan and Jacobean periods. The terraces and the pleasaunces, that formed the fair setting to this mansion, have long since disappeared and no traces remain, except a few holly and yew trees that have survived the general devastation.

Houghton House was purchased by John, Duke of Bedford, in 1738, and was restored and fitted up for his son, the Marquis of Tavistock. He was killed in 1767, by a fall from his horse, and after this sad event no member of the Bedford family cared to reside here. The last occupant was the Earl of Upper Ossory. In 1794 the mansion was dismantled, and part of the materials were used in the building of the Swan Hotel, on the embankment, Bedford.

HOUGHTON CONQUEST.

Mary, Countess of Pembroke, who was a very gifted woman, of high intellectual abilities combined with great personal beauty and exquisite charm of manner, and a brilliant ornament of the Court of Queen Elizabeth, retired to Houghton House, which she erected in her widowhood, and there is an idea that this house was built after some plan or description set forth in the " Arcadia," a tribute of affection to the memory of her brave and noble brother, Sir Philip Sidney. This celebrated lady, according to Coxeter, translated the whole of the Psalms into English metre, being assisted in this work by Dr. Gervase Babington, her lord's chaplain, afterwards Bishop of Exeter, and wrote the " Tragedie of Antonie," " done from the French," bearing the name and date " Ramsbury, Nov. 26, 1590." After the defeat of the Royalist army at Worcester in 1651, the celebrated Christiana, Countess of Devonshire, took up her residence at Houghton House (at this time the seat of her brother, Thomas, Earl of Elgin), and here she lived for three years in comparative seclusion, "lightening her griefs and her expenses," and also taking an active part in planning the restoration of King Charles II. This noble lady, who was the daughter of Edward, Lord Bruce of Kinloss, and wife of William, Earl. of Devonshire, was in constant correspondence with General Monk, who was instrumental in bringing about the restoration of the King, and she also befriended Dr. George Lawson, a staunch Royalist, who was wrongfully ejected from his benefice in Northamptonshire during the Commonwealth. Lady Devonshire lived to see the dream of her life fulfilled, and a great wrong righted; she passed peacefully away at Derby in 1674, truly a " victor after hard won fight." A story is told of how " once even a troop of soldiers were sent to Houghton House to take her prisoner, and convey her to the Tower of London," but, fortunately, she avoided their malevolent designs, and worked on harder than ever at the cause she had so much at heart.

Many are the historic memories that cluster around this stately ruin, majestic even in its decay; and by a writer whose romances of bygone Bedfordshire have delighted many hearts, Houghton House has been immortalized by being identified as the original of the " House Beautiful," seen with the golden vision of the " Immortal Dreamer."

AN EALING TRAGEDY, 1747.

BY J. METHAM WARRENER.

THE district of Castle Bar Hill is now the most fashionable part of Ealing, and its staid and well-to-do inhabitants would doubtless be greatly shocked if any deed of violence were committed in so respectable a quarter.

A century and a half ago it was a lonely and desolate spot. As late as 1825, Cary's Map shows not a single house on the north side of the "Oxford, Cheltenham, Glocester and Milford Road," now the Uxbridge Road, between Acton and Ealing Dean; while at "Castle Bear Hill" there were apparently only two houses, close to the end of Pitshanger Lane. Between this lane and Perivale a large piece of land is marked as "Castle Bear Common."

It was probably on this common that my ancestor, Samuel Verry, was shot by highwaymen in 1747. A Broadside giving an account of the murder was issued in a few days, a copy of which has been handed down in the family and is now in my possession. It runs as follows:

JAN. 24th   A Full and Particular   1747.
ACCOUNT
OF THE
Apprending and Taking
OF
William Groves, and *Noah Groves*.

For the barbarous Murder of Mr. Samuel Verry, a fubftantial Farmer of Oxendon-hill in the Parifh of Perrivale, Middlefex; who going home laft Saturday Night about Seven o'Clock, was attacked clofe by the empty Houfe by Caftle Bar, late in the Poffeffion of Dr. Hollings, near the Uxbridge Road. With the Whole Examination, before the Right Hon the Worfhipful Juftice Clithero, and their Commitment laft Night the one to Newgate, and the other to New-Prison.

The Farmer fhot was Mr. Samuel Verry, an honeft fubftantial Farmer of Oxendon-hill, in the Parifh of Perrivale,

Middlefex; who going home laft Saturday Night about Seven
o'Clock, with his Son, a Youth about Seventeen Years of Age,
was attacked clofe by the empty House by Caftle-bar, late in
the Poffeffion Dr. Hollings, near the Uxbridge-road. Mr.
Verry rode by the Fellows on which they endeavoured to
ftop his Son, but failed, the Boy riding back towards the Sign
of the Feathers, crying *Murder!* Mr. Verry turning back to
look for his Son, was ftopp'd; and one of the Fellows being
about to rob him, Mr. Verry who was fomewhat in Liquor
and a stout Man, ftruck him a violent blow, on which the
other Villain fhot Mr. Verry in the breaft; and robb'd him of
fome part of his Money. Mr. Verry riding back towards the
Feathers, met his Son, who had got affiftance, and told them
that he had been robb'd and fhot, but that he thought himfelf
not much hurt.—And he feem'd very hearty when he had dif-
mounted at the Feathers. But his Friends obferving after
fome time, a great Quantity of Blood in the Chair on which
he fat, he was ftripp'd and a Surgeon fent for, who found he
was fhot in the Left Breaft with a Ball and a Slug. The Ball
went through his Body and was found in his Clothes; the Slug
having been ftopp'd by one of the breaft bones, was taken out.
Mr. Verry continued in his Senfes till he dy'd, which was on
Monday Morning, about Two o'Clock: And in the mean
Time, fettled his Affairs, and earneftly defired all People to
be cautious of travelling late, or making Refiftance if attacked
by fuch Villains.

Wednefday two Fellows were taken up and examined by
James Clithero, Efq; one of his Majefty's Juftices of the Peace
for the County of Middlefex, they having been feen to load
Piftols the fame Evening the Fact was done. And Yefterday
they were re-examined by the faid Gentleman, when he committed one of them, Noah Groves, to New-Prifon, and the
other, William Groves, to Newgate, being charged on a violent
Sufpicion of fhooting the faid Samuel Verry on the King's
Highway.

The above William Groves was formerly an Evidence
againft three Men for fmuggling, who were found guilty, fin'd
and imprifon'd, and all died in Newgate.

THE CHRONICLE OF PAUL'S CROSS.

BY W. PALEY BAILDON, F.S.A.

[Continued from p. 73.]

1541, November 13. "Alexander Seton, a Scotish, and a worther Preacher. . . . This Seton was Chaplain to the Duke of Suffolk, and by him was made free Denison. In his sermon preached at Saint Antholine's, his adversaries picked against him matter containing fifteen objections, or rather cavillations. . . . Touching reconciliation spoken of by Doctor Smith, preaching in the forenoon at *Paul's Cross*, Alexander Seton, preaching at afternoon at Saint Anthonie's [*sic*], and reciting his sayings and Scriptures, reproved him for alledging this saying, *Reconciliamini Deo*, and Englishing the same thus, 'Reconcile your selves to God'; because it is there spoken passively, and not actively, so that there should be nothing in man pertaining to reconciliation, but all in God. Also reproving the said Doctor Smith, for that the said D. said that man by his good works might merit. Which saying of Doctor Smith the said Alexander Seton reproved in the Pulpit at S. Anthonie's [*sic*] the 13 day of November, the year of our Lord 1541, as naughtily spoken. . . . So that in the end, he, with Tolwine aforesaid, was caused to recant at *Paul's Cross*, 1541." (Fox, *Martyrs*, vol. ii, pp. 451, 452.)

1543, July 8. "Allso, the 8 of Julye, beinge Reliques Sonday, three persons recanted at *Paules Crosse*, one called Thomas Beacon alias Theodore Basill,—Wysedome, Curate of Aldermary under Doctor Cromer [Edward Crome], and one Shingleton, all three preistes; and the said Thomas Beacon cutt in peeces, at his sayd recantinge, 11 bookes which he had made and caused to be printed, wherein was certeine heresyes."—(Wriothesley's *Chronicle*, Camden Soc., N. S., vol. ii, p. 142.)

1544, July 6. "This same year also followed the Recantation of John Haywood; who, although he was tached for Treason for denying the King's Supremacy, yet using the

151

clemency of the King, upon his better reformation and amendment, made an open and Solemn Recantation in the face of
all the people, abandoning and renouncing the Pope's usurped
supremacy, and confessing of the King to be chief supream
Head and Governour of this Church of England, all forein
Authority and Jurisdiction being excluded. The tenour and
effect of whose Recantation here followeth." . . . Memorandum that the above recantation was made and publicly
pronounced by the s^d John Haywood, on Sunday, July 6th,
1544, at *Paul's Cross*, at the time of the Sermon.—(Fox,
Martyrs, vol. ii, p. 479.)

1544, July 6. " The 6 day of July,—Hayward recanted his
treason at *Pawles Crosse*, which had bene afore condempned
to death, and brought to be layd on the hardell [hurdle], for
denyinge the Supremacye of the Kinges Majestie against the
Bishop of Rome."—(Wriothesley's *Chronicle*, Camden Soc.,
N. S., vol. ii, p. 148.)

1545, February 8. "This 8th day allso, stoode at *Pawles
Crosse* a preist, with a broad stole of linen cloath, couloured
with drops like bloud, about his necke; which was given him
in pennance by my Lord Chauncellour [Wriothesley], in the
Starre Chamber, for fayninge and counterfeyting a miracle
that he woulde had [been] done whilest he was at Masse, and
pricked his finger [so] that the bloud dropped on the corporasse
and aulter, so that he woulde have made men beleue that the
Hoste of the Body of Christ, by him consecrated, had bledde,
and allso he quaveringe and shakinge at the tyme of consecration; all which he openly declared at *Pawles Crosse*."—
(Wriothesley's *Chronicle*, Camden Soc., N. S., vol. ii, p. 152.)

1545. "This yere, the xxvii daie of June, doctor Crome
preached at *Poules Crosse*, and there openly confessed that he
had been seduced with naughtie bookes, contrary to the true
doctrine of Christe, and in this dooyng he saied he was not
compelled so to saie; neither for feare nor by any other
meanes, but onely of his free and voluntary will."—(Fabyan.)

1545. "And thys yere stode a prest of Kente at *Polles
Crose* for cuttynge of hys fynger and made it to blede on the
hoste at his Masse for a fallse sacrafyce; and also another
prest this yere was sett on the pyllere in Chepe, for makynge

of false letters in the weste contre unto a blynde woman."—
(*Chronicle of the Grey Friars*, p. 48.)

1546, April 11. "Item the xj day of Aprille before was
Passion Sonday, and then preched Doctor Crome in hys
pariche church [St. Mary Aldermary], at the wyche sermond
he preched agayne [against] the Sacrament of the Auter; and
that same tyme he was send for unto the Corte, and there was
exammynd; and the V sarmondes at Ester spake alle agayne
[against] the sayd oppynyons, but namyd not hym. And the
Sonday after the Low Sonday, the wyche was the ix day of
May after, he preched at *Powlles Crosse*, and there sayd he
came not thether to recante nor to denye hys worddes, nor
wolde not. And then he was send for that same day agayne,
and was examynd agayne; and the xxvij day of June after,
wyche was the Sonday after Corpus Christi day, he was com-
andyd to preche at *Powlles Crosse* agayne, and there recantyd
and denyyd hys worddes."—(*Chronicle of the Grey Friars*,
p. 50.)

1546, May 8. "Doctour Crome beeng called and examyned
before the Counsail, present the Bishops of London and
Worcester and such of the Kinges Chaplaynes as the daye
before were appointed to be at his sermon at *Poles Crosse*,
was examyned uppon his rashenes and indirect procedinges,
and therupon committed to a chambre to answere to certeyne
interrogatoryes."—(*Acts of the Privy Council*.)

1546, May 9. Dr. Edward Crome preached. *See* June 27th
post.

1546, May 11. THE COUNCIL TO SIR WILLIAM PETRE.
"Mr. Secretary, after our harty commendacions, yesterday,
in the morning, we had Mr. Crome before us, unto whom,
according to the Kinges Majestes commandent, we objectid
his misbehavour at *Paules Crosse*, contrary to the Kinges
Hieghnes expectacion and his owne promes. Which matter
we engrevid as the qualite thereof wourthily required. . . .
Whereunto when he had aunswered with grete asseverations,
and with a mervaillous constante behavour, that he had so
doon and fulfilled his promes at *Paules Crosse*, as no man
ought to fynde faulte with his doinges, and layenge his hand
on his brest, saide he knew himself better then any other man

153

did, and he thought he had doon so well, as he shuld never have been charged or blamed, but rather comendid therefore. . . ."—(*State Papers*, Henry VIII, vol. i, p. 842.)

1546, May 13. THE COUNCIL TO SIR WILLIAM PETRE.

" Mr. Secretarye, after our right harty commendations. Where thies herers, my Lord of Worcestre [Nicholas Heath], and others the Kinges Majesties Chaplayns, doe repayre at this tyme to his Majestie, to declare unto him the procedinges with Crome sithens [since] our last advertisement, whereunto they shall make you pryvey, we shall require you to helpe them to his Majesties presence, and to know whether his Hieghnes woll heruppon commaunde us any further, touching this matier, then is alredy signefyed unto us. This day we looke for Latymer, the Vicar of St. Brides, and summe others of those that have specially comforted Crome in his folye. Crome, sithens the last depositions sent to his Majestie, hath confessed that Huick, uppon sight of th' articles which he shuld have sett furth at *Pole Crosse*, shewed himself to mislyke the same, and thought they could not be mayntened with good conscyence, and that he doubted not, therfore, but the said Crome could declare them honestly; by the which, and such other thinges as Crome hath confessed, it appereth that he, and summe of those folkes that he named in his depositions, be as much to be blamed, or more, then himself."—(*State Papers*, Henry VIII, vol. i, p. 845.'

[To be continued.]

NOTES AND QUERIES.

RE
tions,
eath]
're at
:inges
eunto
helpe
:r his
ching
.y we
:thers
folye.
hath
:h he
slyke
good
said
such
:t he,
:ions,
State

U NPUBLISHED MSS. RELATING TO THE HOME COUNTIES
IN THE COLLECTION OF P. C. RUSHEN.

[Continued from p. 74.]

1573, Sept. 27. Lease by John Nuttynge of Hendon, yeoman, to Thomas Wood of Great Marlow, Bucks, Glover, of the lessor's small tenement with an orchard, in Great Marlow, then in the lessee's occupation, for 21 years, at 20s. per annum. Covenants by the lessee, for full repairs, not to sub-lease or assign to any but his kindred without license of the lessor, and to plant at least 12 fruit trees in the orchard in the first 3 years.

1598, Aug. 27. Lease by Richard Brenchley to Francis Pope, both of Bobbing, co. Kent, yeomen, of 10 acres of land there, for 3 years at a peppercorn rent. *Counterpart signed by Pope.*

1619, May 20. Lease by John Barker of London, Merchant, to John Greene of Lincoln's Inn, Esq., for 21 years at £10 per annum, of a garden and garden-house occupied by the lessor in the parish of St. Leonard, Shoreditch, adjoining on the east to a garden occupied by Robert Parkhurst, and severed with a new brick wall on the west from a garden occupied by John Turkell, and with another new brick wall on the north from a garden occupied by Thomas Stone, and on the south with a high " tymber pale cantrailed next the alley " leading to the demised premises and to other gardens. *Counterpart with Schedule of fixtures and fittings.*

Memorandum endorsed, that on 22 Jan., 1623, Henry Blount of London, Girdler, assignee of the lessor, in consideration of £17. 10. 0 paid to him, accepted a surrender of the lease and all the estate the exors. of Dame Mary Weld had in the demised premises.

1620, Jan. 1. Lease by Henry Mann alias Towsey, of Quainton, Bucks, yeoman, & Isabel his wife, to Thomas Brice, son of the said Isabel, in consideration of £60, of a tenement occupied by Annis Clarke, widow, and 2 parts of a yardland divided into 3 parts, & common of pasture for 4 horses, 4 kine, & 27 sheep, & 3 acres 1 rood of meadow in the common meadow, occupied by the said Mann, all in Quainton : to hold for 40 years, if either of lessors should live so long. The Lessors are to save the lessee from a lease of the premises made by Isabel, while a widow, to the said Henry, for 40 years, which lease was supposed to be lost.

1683, Oct. 1. Lease by Ann Whittle, widow, of Eastmalling, Kent, as guardian to her five sons, Thurston, William, Robert, Thomas, & George, to Francis Tomlin of Eastmalling, yeoman, for 11 years, at £14 per annum, of 3 pieces of land called Lunsford's Broomes, containing 26 acres, in the lessee's occupation, near Larkefield Heath, in the parish of Eastmalling, & 4 pieces of land containing 7 acres, adjoining Larkefield Heath, in the lessee's occupation, then late of James Dowell.

1689, April 2. Lease by William Warne, scrivener, and John Teale, pewterer, to Nicholas Blackman, blacksmith, for 2 years, at £32 per annum, of a messuage on the east side of Castle Street in the parish of St. Martin's in the Fields, then lately new built, & in the occupation of . . . Hattanvil, tallow chandler, and then occupied by the lessee, with the building behind, and used as a workshop, next to an alley there serving for a passage to other adjacent houses of the lessors. Paper-counterpart, signed by Blackman. Witnesses, Tho. Gilbert, a scrivr in St. Martin's, & Ralph Mayor, a coachmaker there.

1692, Nov. 10. Lease and counterpart lease by Thomas Scott of Shoreditch, Middlesex, brickmaker, to Jonathan Parsons of Stepney, carpenter, for 60 years, at £2 per annum, of a piece of ground 30 feet by 47 feet, on the east side of Denmark St., Stepney, abutting on a house belonging to Isaac & Abraham Hickman on the south, on gardens on the east, on Betts St. on the west, & on another piece of ground belonging to the lessor on the north. Lessee covenants to erect 2 houses on the land.

1692, Nov. 30. Lease by the same lessor to Jeremiah Slow of Stepney, husbandman, for 60 years, at £1. 10 0 per annum, of a piece of ground similarly situated as in the last, & 30 feet by 49 feet, abutting on a tenement belonging to John Oxden on the south, & on a tenement belonging to Richard Sankey on the north. Lessee covenants as in the last lease. *Counterpart.*

1692, Dec. 14. Lease by Isaac Hickman, citizen & leatherseller of London, to James Browne of Stepney, Carpenter, for 60 years, at £4. 10 0 per annum, of a piece of ground similarly situated as in the last, & 41½ feet by 47½ feet, abutting on land of John Edmondson, Saylemaker, on the west, on land of Thomas Scott leased to Parsons on the north, & on land of Isaac Hickman let to Browne on the south. Lessee covenants to erect 3 houses on the land. *Counterpart.*

1720, March 20. Unexecuted lease by Robert Gosling of London, Bookseller, executor of Christian Griffin, widow, late of the same, deceased, & on behalf of Joseph Griffin of Kingsale, Ireland, Gent., to John Ditcher of London, Gent., for 11 years at £30 per annum, of a shop & messuage belonging to the said Joseph in the Old Bayly, London, in the parish of St. Martin, Ludgate, late occupied by . . . Tysoe, Painter, abutting on the north on another messuage of the said Griffin, occupied by John Decker, Glazier. *With Schedule of fixtures.*

1789, April 1. Lease by Richard Barrett of the hamlet of Ratcliff in the parish of Stepney, Middlesex, Boat Builder, to Charles Wainwright of the parish of St. George, Middlesex, Baker, for 30 years at £20 per annum, of two messuages in St. George's, being the north west corner of Cannon St. & the messuage adjoining thereto, occupied by . . . Mushroy & . . . Hadshead.

1804, Feb. 29. Assignment of the unexpired term in the above premises, endorsed on the lease, in consideration of £286, Charles Wainwright to Richard Hester of Windsor, Baker.

1790, Nov. 15. Lease by Thomas Andrewes of East Malling, Kent, Gent., to Sarah Parker of Marden, Kent, widow, for 21 years at £30 per annum, of a messuage with a barn, stable, millhouse, &c., & 5 acres of land in Marden, formerly occupied by Michael Stone, then late by William Parker, & then by the said Sarah. *Counterpart.*

1806, June 2. Lease by Thomas Andrewes of East Malling, Kent, Gent., to Elizabeth Eagles, of Yalding, Kent, widow, for 21 years at £63. 16. 0 per annum, of a messuage, &c., & 63 acres in Yalding, occupied by the lessee.

[To be continued.]

COOK'S COURT.—In *Bleak House* Charles Dickens describes Cook's Court as being situated in Cursitor Street, on the eastern side of Chancery Lane. Obviously he meant Tooks Court, a thoroughfare formerly much patronized by law stationers of the Snagsby type. Why did Dickens mis-name this court? It may not be generally known that a Cook's Court did really exist on the western side of Chancery Lane and adjacent to Lincoln's Inn. This court was demolished some twenty-eight years ago, and was to some extent, like Tooks Court, given over to the law stationery business. The proper Cook's Court was a passage between Searle Street and that part of Carey Street facing the eastern wing of King's College Hospital, now about to be removed to Denmark Hill. This passage was entered from both ends under an archway, and at one period a beadle was stationed there to ensure quietness and to warn off beggars and other undesirables. The site, now bounded by Carey Street on two sides, Portugal Street and Searle Street, is now covered by the block of red brick buildings mostly let out as chambers.

The real Tooks Court is fast disappearing, for H.M. Patent Office has acquired, and is still acquiring, much of the property there to meet its growing demands for more space. A few of the old houses yet remain. The Chiswick Press has been located here since 1827, and, as some evidence of the date of some of the houses, it may be mentioned that No. 14, a lock-up warehouse in the possession of the Chiswick Press, has in the basement a leaden cistern bearing the date 1746, cast in the middle of a geometrical design on the front. Prior to 1827, when Charles Whittingham took a lease of No. 21, that building was occupied by another well-known printer, Richard Valpy, who issued the famous one hundred volumes of classics.—C. T. J.

ROLLS' YARD was, I believe, situated in Chancery Lane, somewhere near or on the spot of the Record Office. Was there not a chapel there, and if so when was it demolished? Has any reference been made in former numbers of this Magazine to this place and chapel? Was there any connection between this and St. Thomas' Liberty of the Rolls, a church formerly standing in Breams Buildings?—J.

REVIEWS.

HISTORY OF THE BOROUGH OF LEWISHAM, with an Itinerary; by Leland L. Duncan, M.V.O., F.S.A. With chapters on the Geology of the District by W. H. Griffin, and on the Local Authorities by A. W. Hiscox, sometime Mayor of the Borough. Charles North, pp. 173.

A valuable contribution to local topography. Founded necessarily on Hasted, it is expanded and enlarged, added to here, corrected there, until Hasted himself would hardly recognize it. The history of Lewisham is longer than most boroughs can boast; from 862 (the first dated document cited is of that year) to the present day, nearly ten centuries and a half, is indeed a record for what was, nearly down to our own time, a small and insignificant village. But unimportant as Lewisham was in the past, its history has considerable interest. Given to the great Abbey of Ghent by Elfrida, daughter of King Alfred, in 918; seized from time to time by various kings, as the property of an alien priory; finally confiscated, for the same reason, in 1414, by Henry V, and given to the Carthusian Priory at Shene; given to Henry VIII in 1531 in exchange for other lands; given subsequently to John Dudley, Earl of Warwick, to Thomas, Lord Seymour of Sudeley, to Cardinal Pole; and by James I to one of his hungry Scotchmen; sold to Reynold Graham in 1640, who bequeathed it to his nephew, George Legge, the ancestor of the Earl of

REVIEWS.

Dartmouth, the present lord of the manor—here is a history, indeed! But Mr. Duncan's book does not stop here. He has unearthed some Court Rolls in the Record Office, and from these he gives us copious extracts, showing the little everyday incidents of life in the fourteenth and fifteenth centuries. We get the little human touches that appeal to us more than alien priories and Scotch earls: how Alice Pod sold bread short in weight, how John Scot drew blood from William Palfreyman, how Robert Lord was fined 3*d.* for digging turves on the common *de la Blakeheth*, and so forth and so on. When we get to the story of Abraham Colfe, the sturdy and enlightened vicar for forty-seven years, 1610 to 1657, we have Mr. Duncan at his best. He handles that worthy man, like Isaac Walton and the frog, as though he loved him, as, indeed, the founder and builder of the Grammar School ought to be revered by Lewisham folk. An exhaustive itinerary follows, which includes a graphic account of the many stirring incidents associated with Blackheath. The book is well illustrated from old prints, maps, and photographs. The Index is not as good as it ought to be.

A LIFE OF JOHN COLET, D.D., Dean of St. Paul's and Founder of St. Paul's School, with an Appendix of some of his English writings; by the late J. H. Lupton, D.D., formerly Surmaster of St. Paul's School and Fellow of St. John's College, Cambridge. New edition. George Bell and Sons; pp. xiv, 323; 8*s.* 6*d.* net.

Twenty-two years have elapsed since Dr. Lupton published his well-known *Life of Colet*; no more fitting celebration of the four hundredth anniversary of the foundation of the great school could have been found than a new edition of the Life of the Founder. Until the first publication of Dr. Lupton's work the worthy Dean had almost been overshadowed by his own school; the pious founder was remembered, the scholar was wellnigh forgotten. This important fact is admirably brought out. Colet was the intimate friend of Erasmus, Sir Thomas More, and most of the enlightened and scholarly men of his day. Indeed, so advanced was he in some of his views, that on one occasion he was accused of heresy by his bishop, on the ground that he had taught that images ought not to be worshipped. Yet More declared "that none more learned or more holy had lived among them for many ages past"; and the pious Carthusian monks of Shene had no objection to receive him among them for his last days. His works are now little read, but were highly valued in his own day. The Statutes and some other papers relating to St. Paul's School are printed in an Appendix. These are well worth reading, both from their quaintness of diction and their extraordinary minuteness of detail. Nothing was too trivial for him; every possible contingency, both for the masters and the scholars, seems to have been anticipated. The story of his severity, not to say brutality, to the children, is absolutely discredited. That he loved children is clear from the "lytell proheme" to his *Accidence*: "Wherfore I praye you, al lytel babys, al lytel chyldren, lerne gladly this lytel treatyse, and commende it dylygently to your memoryes. . . . And lyfte up your lytel whyte bandes for me, which prayeth for you to God." These are not the words of one who ordered the flogging of a child of ten, and stood callously looking on till the boy swooned. No wonder Dr. Lupton is "simply amazed at the credulity" of those who ever believed the story. There is a good Index.

THE ANGLO-SAXON CHRONICLE, newly translated by G. E. C. Gomme, B.A. George Bell and Sons; pp. xvi, 315. 6*s.* net.

All students of our early history should be grateful for this scholarly translation. Mr. Gomme's work is done on sound and common-sense lines. To begin with, we

REVIEWS.

find him throwing over-board a large amount of the pedantic spelling of names, beloved of certain historians. It is a positive relief to read of "Edward" and "Alfred" once more. Place-names are treated in similar fashion; where the identification is certain the modern spelling is used; in other cases, the spelling of the original. The translation is " word for word in the most literal and exact way." Mr. Gomme's collation of the various MSS. is careful and minute, and his twenty pages of notes add very greatly to the value of the book; we gather from them that he has no particular axe to grind, which is as it should be. There is an exhaustive Index.

THE TRAMPING METHODIST, by Sheila Kaye-Smith. George Bell and Sons; pp. 316; 6s.

A story of considerable power and much originality. The scene is mostly in Sussex, the period the eighteenth century, and the subject the early days of Methodism. It is difficult to realize nowadays the scorn and persecution that had to be faced by the early followers of Wesley. It is equally hard to picture the callousness, indifference and downright brutality of many of the clergy of the Church of England; and yet, in spite of this, we cannot help hoping that Miss Kaye-Smith's incidents are not founded on fact. Her style is crisp and lucid, and the descriptions of atmosphere and scenery delicate and poetical. The story itself, though a little melodramatic, is well conceived and will be read with great interest.

THE HISTORY OF WENDOVER in the County of Buckingham; by Leonard H. West, LL.D., Representative of Wendover on the Bucks County Council and Member of the County Education Committee, Aylesbury: "Bucks Advertiser" Office; pp. 89.

An interesting little book. Wendover has almost more than its fair share of celebrities, and for so small a place the list is a remarkable one. Beginning with Roger of Wendover, the historian, we find two other eminent literary men connected with the Borough, Richard Steele and Edmund Burke. John Hampden, of Ship-Money fame, and several others of his family were members of Parliament for Wendover, as also were George Grenville, the instigator of the American Stamp Acts which resulted in the War of Independence, and George Canning. Wendover was the scene of a good many stirring incidents during the Civil War, which are well told. The story of the Vicar's wife in 1643, who made apple pies for the Royalist troops and had perforce to see them consumed by the Roundheads, has a touch of grim humour about it. The work was originally written, we are told, as a lecture, and reprinted in book form; it will be worth while, in a subsequent edition, which is sure to be called for, to get rid of the lecture element altogether. Lectures rarely print well, and some of the defects of arrangement are doubtless due to this cause. Dr. West should also reconsider the statement (p. 62) that Hugh Seymour Conway was a *descendant* of Jane Seymour.

A CRITICAL STUDY OF THE FORM OF LETTERS PATENT FOR INVENTIONS; by Percy C. Rushen, Chartered Patent Agent. Stevens and Sons; pp. 124.

The title sufficiently indicates the nature and scope of this work; the criticism is at once legal, antiquarian, and etymological. Many of Mr. Rushen's suggested improvements are admirable. A learned work, and by no means dry reading.

159

REVIEWS.

THE PRIORY CHURCH OF ST. BARTHOLOMEW-THE-GREAT, SMITH-
FIELD. A Short History of the Foundation, and a Description
of the Fabric, and also of the Church of St. Bartholomew-the-
Less; by George Worley; 42 illustrations. George Bell and
Sons; pp. viii, 82; 1s. 6d. net.

For clearness and conciseness, those two prime factors in a guide book, Mr.
Worley's account of St. Bartholomew's will compare favourably with any of its
predecessors in the well-known "Cathedral Series." The history of the Priory,
from its foundation by Rahere in 1123 down to the present time, the extraordinary
vicissitudes of the Priory Church, and the noble efforts that have preserved what
we see to-day, are well and sympathetically told. The Hospital, with its curious
church of St. Bartholomew-the-Less, has a chapter to itself, and all the facts and
details required by the visitor are carefully recorded. The illustrations are well
chosen, and include reproductions of a number of old prints showing the church at
various dates, the principal monuments, and casts of all the known seals of the
Priory. Some corrections are required in the transcript of the inscription on
page 67, but this minor detail seems all that there is for the most captious critic to
cavil at.

"A MANNOR AND COURT BARON" (Harleian MS. 6714); edited by
Nathaniel J. Hone, with a preface by J. Samuel Green, M.A.,
B.C.L., LL.D., Barrister-at-Law. The Manorial Society; pp. 59.

It is a capital idea to start printing some of the numerous MSS. relating to
manors and copyholds, and we trust that this is but the first of a long series, to
include also the reprinting of some of the scarcer pamphlets on the subject. The
MS. here printed is apparently anonymous. Mr. Green dates it as late sixteenth
or early seventeenth century; it was, therefore, written at a time when the manorial
system had suffered very little change from its first institution in England. The
author, as it seems to us, was clearly a lawyer and well versed in manorial law;
some of the theories he puts forward are not now accepted, but on the whole he is
singularly free from the fantastic notions found in many writers of the period. We
know that barristers of good practice, and even serjeants, were not above acting as
stewards of manors, and we should judge that the author was probably such an
one. The treatise is not always easy reading, and the scarcity of stops does not
tend to make it easier. It is too highly technical to be used as an elementary text-
book, but the advanced student will read it with advantage.

LONDON'S LURE; an Anthology in Prose and Verse. By Helen and
Lewis Melville. George Bell and Sons; pp. 328; 3s. 6d. net.

An interesting collection of prose and poetry, garnered from a wide range of
authors, and grouped under various headings. The items are well selected and
arranged. The title-page and end-papers in pen and ink are very pretty; we would
gladly mention the artist's name—if we could read it!

iii

CONTENTS.

NOTICES.

It is particularly requested that all communications for the Editor be addressed to him *by name* at 5, Stone Buildings, Lincoln's Inn, W.C. All communications for the Publishers should be sent direct to them.

The annual subscription to the Magazine is 6s. 6d. post free. Quarterly Parts, 1s. 6d. net each, by post, 1s. 8d. Cases for binding, 1s. 6d. each, can be obtained from the Publishers.

Copies of some of the Plates which have appeared in the Magazine are for sale, and certain Blocks can also be purchased at moderate prices.

GEORGE BELL & SONS, YORK HOUSE, PORTUGAL ST. W.C.

The **Princess Pocahontas.**
From an old print.

THE PRINCESS POCAHONTAS.

By Alex. J. Philip.

THE discovery of human remains, pronounced by an expert to be those of an Indian female of high degree, near the site of the old chapel of St. Mary, at Gravesend, has done nothing to settle the old dispute as to the burial of Pocahontas, but it has drawn attention to the intensely interesting story of the Indian Princess who came to so untimely an end at Gravesend. It has been a matter of great uncertainty where she was buried, but the question will be dealt with later on in the present article.

Pocahontas, the daughter of the chief, Powhatan, was born at the end of the sixteenth century, most probably in 1595. Her real name was "Matoaka," but, following the practice of her people, who lived in superstitious fear of spirits, this was hidden from the colonists of Virginia, and the better-known name of Pocahontas bestowed upon her. A great deal of misconception regarding the condition and standing of her father has always existed, chiefly owing to the fatuity of King James I. Powhatan was acknowledged as the most powerful of the chiefs living in the vicinity of James River. This fact was communicated to the King, who was unable to appreciate the circumstances of savage life. Powhatan was obviously an emperor; and, to establish the fact, King James sent over a copper-gilt crown and some almost worthless presents. The chief fact thus impressed upon the mind of the savage chief was his own importance. This naturally led to arrogance, a great increase in the magnitude of his unfulfilled promises, and a notable increase in his demands, which were in reality thefts, from the struggling colonists.

Powhatan's story has very little in common with that of Pocahontas, but so much it was necessary to state to make clear the more interesting account of Matoaka.

The other strand of the story was woven in London, by the foundation of the London Virginia Company in 1606.

· John Smith was born in 1580 at Willoughby, in Lincolnshire. He attended school at Alford, but later on was sent to the Grammar School at Louth. On the death of his father, followed soon after by that of his mother, Smith was sent by his guardian, George Mettham, to the office of a shipper named Sendall, at King's Lynn. He soon tired of office work, however, and at fifteen or sixteen years of age, he started out on the high road to fortune. He passed through numerous adventures in various parts of the Continent, then in a very unsettled state. Some of these have been subjected to severe criticism, and their authenticity disputed by some of Smith's commentators. He returned to England in 1604. About this time he was attacked with the "colony" fever. He spent some time in obtaining all the information he could that related to the "New Lands," and in 1606 the London Virginia Company was formed with a royal charter. This was largely due to the exertions of Smith and those whom he had interested in his schemes. On December 19, 1606, three ships were sent out, the "Susan Constant," the admiral's ship, the "Godspeed," and the "Discovery." The voyage was not a happy one. Smith was put in irons, and threatened with hanging.

This fleet, of two ships and a pinnace, for the "Discovery" was only of twenty tons burden, cast anchor in Chesapeake Bay on the 25th of April, 1607. The crews forced a landing in the face of the opposition of the Indians, and opened the sealed orders under which the colonists had sailed. It was then found that Smith had been appointed to a seat on the Council acting in Virginia. In this way the colonists settled in Virginia and founded Jamestown.

While their stores remained the colonists lived on them, eating even their seeds. When these were done, they bewailed their lot and took very few measures to supply their wants. Smith was perhaps the only settler who realized their needs, but even he was unable to do anything to make the colonists thrifty and industrious. For some years this was the history of the men sent out by the London Virginia Company; men, for the most part, failures at home, ignorant of farming and unused to work. They lived on the fat of the stores when a ship reached them, and on the charity of the Indians when they were without food. Their sufferings excited the pity of Pocahontas, and, accompanied by "braves," she brought them corn and other food-stuffs.

These kindnesses were only possible following on the better relations Smith had established with their savage neighbours, when his influence increased. Smith was captured by one of the tribes, when on an exploring expedition. After the "medicine men" failed to arrive at a decision, he was brought before Powhatan, the over-chief, at Wesowocomoco, an Indian village not far from Jamestown.

Powhatan had no serious doubts about the matter, and ordered Smith's execution. Pocahontas pleaded, but in vain, for his release. The primitive method of executing a captive was to lay his head on one stone and beat out his brains with another. Pocahontas at once threw herself on Smith and covered him, and, so the story goes, Powhatan pardoned the captive on condition that two of the culverins should be given to the "braves" who would accompany him to Jamestown. Knowing that they would be unable to carry them away, Smith readily promised this.

The colony had met with so many misfortunes during Smith's captivity, that the settlers were on the point of putting to sea in the pinnace. Smith prevented this, however, and Pocahontas's gifts enabled them to tide over the period intervening before the arrival of the "Phœnix" from England. The London Council sent out gold miners and glass-blowers, but still the colony did not prosper.

Powhatan fixed upon swords and muskets as the only legal tender for the purchase of corn. Of course this was a prohibitive price, and Smith set out on a trading expedition up the river Pannukey. This met with no success, although it was known that the Indians had abundance of corn. So far had the relations between the colonists and the Indians suffered, by the deceit of the latter on the one hand, and the vacillation of the former on the other, that a night attack was planned to exterminate Smith and his comrades just before they returned from this fruitless expedition. Pocahontas learned the secret, and warned Smith of the impending danger. As a result of this, Smith let the enemy know that he had discovered the plan, and so prevented its being put into operation. Already the Indians had begun to view Smith as something more than man, and a surprise seemed the only means of effecting his death. Another attempt was made, with a large number of braves, to secure him, but this also failed.

Soon after, however, Smith was accidentally or intentionally blown up by the explosion of a bag of gunpowder. It was feared that his injuries would prove fatal, but he recovered sufficiently to return to England where he was completely cured. Pocahontas missed her friend, and inquired for him at Jamestown. She was told that Smith was dead, and a newly made grave was pointed out to her as that of the intrepid captain.

The presents of corn ceased from that time, and the interest of the colony so far as Pocahontas is concerned, ceased with this, until 1612.

From this period the story has a greater interest, as Pocahontas is the chief figure in it. The Governors of the Colony had relinquished Smith's vigorous policy, and, in consequence suffered considerably from the arrogance of the chief Powhatan, when Captain Argall, who had entered the river with a store-ship, succeeded in capturing Pocahontas, now about seventeen years old, by a subterfuge, not to call his method by a worse name. For one reason or another, possibly because he knew no harm would come to her, Powhatan refused to redeem his daughter with fresh promises. The princess quickly settled down to the life and ways of the English, with whom indeed she had always shown herself in sympathy. She adopted the dress of the few Englishwomen in the colony, learned the language, and endeavoured to adapt herself to the ways of her captors.

This went on for two years, until the time when she was married to John Rolfe, a prominent colonist. The idea appears to have been that the union would create and cement a friendship between the two peoples. The project appears to have met with some success, as there is no doubt that both before and after her marriage Pocahontas did more than any other to establish amicable relations between her own people and the whites. Rolfe came of an old Norfolk family. He and his first wife had met with bad weather and heavy misfortunes on their voyage to Virginia, with the result that she had succumbed in 1610.

Matoaka, who had been dubbed Pocahontas, was now, in 1614, baptised into the Christian faith in the name of Rebecca, and was then generally known as the Lady Rebecca. This period of her life is commemorated in the mural decorations on the Capitol Buildings at Washington.

A son was born to them, and in 1616 the little family of three undertook the voyage to England, in company with Sir Thomas Dale and a few of Powhatan's "braves," one of whom was instructed by his chief to "count the number of the English." As the daughter of "Emperor" Powhatan, as well as on account of the benefits she had secured for the

THE PRINCESS POCAHONTAS.

Virginian settlers, Pocahontas was well received. Smith had written a pamphlet about her as soon as he had learned of the visit, and this had been sent broadcast about the country. Lady Rebecca was entertained by the Bishop of London, then Dr. King, and presented at the Court of the King, James I.

It was not, however, all plain sailing. James, knowing he had conferred the title of "Emperor" on the old chief, together with a cruse of oil for his anointing, and a copper-gilt crown, was not quite sure that Rolfe had not committed treason by marrying the daughter of a foreign potentate; and so Rolfe came as little as possible before the King's notice. The health of the Princess suffered considerably at this time, and she left London for Brentford, then a place of some renown and beauty, and noted for its healthiness.

Captain Smith, who still enjoyed a sufficiently good income in spite of the misfortunes that had dogged his steps since he left Virginia, had taken up his residence at Brentford, and as a pleasant surprise for the Princess a meeting was arranged between them. Pocahontas was still in ignorance that her friend was still alive, and when she again saw the man whom for so many years she had thought dead, she suffered a severe revulsion of feeling. As the story goes she is supposed to have ejaculated the one word, "Father." The shock of this meeting is said to have broken her heart; but, doubtless, the change from the free air of the Virginian forests to the London of the early seventeenth century had already undermined her health. At all events she did not see Virginia again, and her little son, Thomas, was left behind and brought up by his uncle, Henry Rolfe, until, when he was twenty-five years of age, he too went out to Virginia.

The rest of the pathetic story has a large amount of uncertainty in it. By one account she is said to have left London by the King's ship "George," and to have died before the vessel reached the open sea, being brought ashore at Gravesend. Another version states that she followed the usual practice of passengers of distinction, and travelled from London by coach to pick up the "George" at Gravesend, the last land in England; but was taken suddenly ill at an inn, situated at a corner of what is now Stone Street. It is not known with certainty what malady she died of, but it is very generally believed to have been smallpox. Which version is correct is not a matter of great importance. There is no doubt that she was buried in the river-side town. The following entry in the parish register:—" 1616. March 2j, [old style] Rebecca Wrolfe, wyffe of Thomas Wrolfe, gent., a Virginian lady borne, here was buried in ye Chauncell," would appear not only to settle the fact that she was buried in Gravesend, but to indicate clearly where the body was buried. Unfortunately this is not so. The then Parish Church of St. George's was situated where the present church now stands, and if it could be shown that the "Chauncell" of the register was the same as that in the church, there would be no difficulty in fixing upon the position of the grave, in spite of the fact that the church was destroyed by fire in 1727. The church of St. Mary was then standing where the White Post Inn is now situated, and a comparatively large burial ground surrounded it. At that time the minister of St. George's was the Rev. Nicholas Trankwell, who no doubt performed the Service. St. George's had been made the parish church as early as 1544, by a grant of Henry VIII, but St. Mary's Church still stood.

If the Princess died of the dread disease which was so much feared in England at that time, there is some ground for those who contend that instead of being buried in a vault in the chancel of St. George's, her remains were interred in the farthest point of the burial ground of St. Mary's Church— then nearly a mile from the town and almost isolated. The discovery of the bones already referred to has given great support to this theory; but it can scarcely be described as conclusive. At the same time it must be admitted that very little is known regarding this early church on the outskirts of the town.

The present parish church contains a memorial tablet to the unfortunate Princess, and the Virginians are exceedingly anxious to erect a more enduring and substantial monument to one whom they regard as amongst their greatest women. The project has been broached several times, but up to the present nothing has been done, chiefly on account of the uncertainty surrounding the place of her burial.

SOME ACCOUNT OF SOUTHGATE.

By C. Edgar Thomas.

OF all those districts lining the northern heights of London which have, during the last decade or so, become annexed to the great capital of the world, none, perhaps, has withstood the march of so-called progress so effectively or has been longer in a state of transition, than the pretty little village of Southgate. Neighbouring and out-lying districts, thanks to the speculative builder and other unsentimental wreckers, have been completely robbed of their rurality; in other words swallowed up whole, and thus qualified to become portions of the mighty everspreading metropolis; but Southgate has, for a long time, made a brave fight against such unwarrantable desecration. Even now, surrounded as it is on all sides by sunny suburbia and other outward indications of increasing and excessive modernity, Southgate is still successful in retaining a little of that individuality which characterized it of yore, and we may rejoice that it yet has spots which have altered but little during the last half century.

Standing on a sunny morning by the village green and the quaint old Cherry Tree Inn—with the tall massive trees and surrounding greenery rustling in the gentle breeze, the picturesque old cottages and shops that line the High Street, the spire of the handsome parish church towering far above the highest trees—one might well believe himself anywhere but near modernity as he enjoys its restful calm and quietude. Yet only a few yards down the road there stretches a fashion-able parade of new shops and the ever-present electric tram!

The beauty of this ancient spot has ofttimes been recorded, notably by H. Crabb Robinson, who laudably sang its praises, and Sir Augustus Hare, who devotes a whole chapter to Southgate in his *Story of my Life*, of whom more anon. There is one account, however, that is in no wise omitted in every publication descriptive of the district; to write an article on Southgate without its inclusion, would be only to prove that article hopelessly incomplete. Indeed, so often has it been employed, that it has become almost hackneyed—if such words can be hackneyed! It may not, however, be altogether out of place in this unpretentious survey. I refer to the words of the litterateur and poet, Leigh Hunt, who was born at Southgate. He says : "It is a pleasure to me to know that I was ever born in so sweet a village as Southgate. I first saw light there on the 19th October, 1784. It found me cradled not only in the lap of nature which I love, but in the midst of all the truly English scenery which I love beyond all other. Middlesex in general . . . is a scene of trees and meadows of greenery and nestling cottages, and Southgate is a prime specimen of Middlesex. It is a place lying out of the way of innovation, therefore it has the pure sweet air of antiquity about it."

It must be admitted that these words are sweet, and the name of their distinguished author certainly enhances their value.

Southgate derives its name from its situation at the southern extremity of the once royal Chase of Enfield. In many old books it is referred to as "South Street," but with the lapse of time it received its present appellation. The district was for a long time nothing more than waste and forest land, whilst the perpetuation of such names as "Chase Side," "Chase Road," and "Chase Riding," still serve to connect the neighbourhood with the famous old-time sport indulged in by our ancestors in the great Forest of Middlesex.

Southgate is now a populous district of some 28,000 souls; it is bounded on the north by Enfield and Winchmore Hill, on the south by Wood Green, on the east by Barnet, and on the west by Edmonton.

New Southgate is a district of recent growth lying to the south of the old village, which was formerly designated Colney Hatch. The exact meaning of this term is rather doubtful, but it may be found mentioned in a Court Roll of the time of Henry VII. In all probability it had reference to a gateway or other entrance to the Enfield Chase. Instances of the word "Hatch" may be found elsewhere, notably the "Pilgrims' Hatch," near Brentwood, which is a standing landmark to the great Forest of Waltham.

The Lunatic Asylum of the County of London, which was erected at Colney Hatch in 1841, in conjunction with the advent of the Great Northern Railway, thirty years later, has perhaps done more than anything else to turn the neighbourhood from the pleasing hamlet that it once was, into the modern residential district that it is to-day.

The Asylum, which occupies a site to the west of the railway station, is a plain structure, in the Italian style, devoid of all ornamentation, erected from the designs of

SOME ACCOUNT OF SOUTHGATE.

Mr. S. W. Bankes. It originally occupied something like four acres of ground, but it has since been considerably enlarged. The chapel, a large oblong room, is situated in the centre of the north front of the building. The late Prince Consort laid the foundation stone in 1841, and the institution was opened for the receipt of patients two years later. It will be readily seen that the staff necessary for a large asylum created a great influx to the population of Southgate.

The earliest and most important place of worship in Southgate was the Weld Chapel. Previous to the seventeenth century the inhabitants of the village had journeyed across to Edmonton to perform their devotions ; but in 1615 Sir John Weld, a descendant of the distinguished Weld family of Lulworth Castle, and one of the most important residents of Southgate at that time, erected a chapel to serve the needs of his household and the populace of Southgate, in the grounds of his estate, then called Arnolds. It is recorded that the length of this edifice was 42 feet, while in breadth it measured 20 feet. It was formally consecrated on 24th May, 1615, by Dr. John King, the then Bishop of London. It was established : ". ,. Saving always the right and interest of the mother Church, in the parish whereof the said chapel or oratory aforesaid is placed and situated, in all and singular tithes, oblations, wages, profits, privileges, rights and emoluments whatsoever, ordinary and extraordinary, to the said mother church of right or custom in any wise due or accustomed or belonging or appertaining, and there being reserved to the said John Weld, Esq., his heirs and assigns, free and full power a fit priest from time to time to nominate and appoint to the said chapel, for the performing and celebrating the divine offices aforesaid in the same chapel, by our episcopal authority and of our successors from time to time to be appointed and limited, the assent and consent of the Vicar of the said mother church for the time being, and his successors, first being requested and the oath of the said priest testified, all and which singular things we so reserve by these presents. The inhabitants to receive the sacrament on Easter day at the mother church, and not in the chapel without license, and no baptism or marriage shall be solemnised without the assent and consent of the Vicar of the mother church and the possessor of Arnolds."

It will thus be seen that the patronage of the chapel was given into the hands of its founder and his descendants,

who, in conjunction with the Vicar of the mother church at
Edmonton, were to appoint a curate to its charge, and his
stipend was stipulated as being not less than £13 6s. 8d.
Sir John Weld died eight years later, and by his will directed
that his body was to be buried " in my late erected chapel,
near unto my mansion house, called Arnolds." He also
bequeathed a sum of something like £550 in favour of the
chapel, which was to be invested, and the produce disposed
of in the following manner: "twenty marks to the curate;
twenty marks to poor kindred; twelve pence weekly in bread;
ten shillings to the clerk; the remainder to be employed in
repairing the chapel or increasing the salary of the curate."
If there were no applications to the curate for poor relief, the
twenty marks set apart for that purpose were to go to him.
Sir John also provided for the erection of a domicile in the
neighbourhood for the curate. In 1625 his widow, Dame
Frances Weld, contributed a sum of £20 towards the better
maintenance of the clergyman, and in December of that year
she procured of one Henry Rastell some property in Essex
called Ossett, by means of which the chapel was subsequently
endowed. Some years later a silver cup was presented to the
chapel by Dame Frances,.on the foot of which was engraved,
" The guift of the Lady Frances Weld, anno 1639." In May,
1645, the Weld Chapel came into the possession of Sir William
Acton, Bart., to whom Dame Frances sold it with other property, and the estate of Arnolds. The words of the deed of
conveyance were:

> We give and grant for us and our heirs, unto Sir William
> Acton, Bart., and his heirs and assigns for ever, all our and
> every of our estate, right, tithe, interest, claim and demand
> of in, all to all, that chapel, chancel, seats and burying
> place in the new erected chapel of Edmonton, near to the
> capital messuage called Arnolds, which we have sold to the
> said Sir William Acton, his heirs, and assigns for ever.

It is generally supposed that the price paid by Sir William
Acton for the property was £3,600. It is interesting to note
that in this conveyance no mention is made of the power to
nominate a minister to the chapel, this being eventually the
cause of a dispute. Perhaps Dame Frances Weld reserved
this right, but whether she did or no, it remains a fact that the
family never availed themselves of the privilege. In 1722 the
Rev. William Washbourn, Vicar of Edmonton, made application to Margaret Weld to nominate a minister to the custody

of the chapel, and, on her refusing, he himself appointed the Rev. James Kilner. The chapel was enlarged by the addition of a north aisle in 1715, and for the carrying out of this £311 was raised by public subscription. On the application of the inhabitants of Southgate and the Rev. —— Harrison, the then chaplain, in 1732, the Bishop of London granted a faculty to demolish the minister's house for the purpose of further extending the chapel. Eventually Weld Chapel descended into the hands of Sir George Colebrooke. It would appear that his trustees disposed of it in 1774 to the Rev. Henry Shepherd for £525. This gentleman held it until 1784, when he sold it to the Rev. William Barclay for £1,000; thus making a clear profit of £475. Two years later Mr. Barclay accepted £1,175 for it, from Robert Winbolt, a lawyer, of Enfield. He presented the living to his son, the Rev. Thomas Winbolt, and although he referred to the matter in his will, bequeathing the chapel to his wife, Elizabeth, it seems that he did not draw up a separate nomination in writing. The Rev. T. Winbolt officiated as Incumbent of Weld Chapel until his death in 1813, when his mother, claiming the right of presentation, nominated the Rev. S. W. Curtis, nephew of Sir William Curtis, of Cullands Grove. The Vicar of Edmonton, the Rev. Dawson Warren, on hearing of the appointment, objected. He took possession of the chapel, and gave out that he should keep charge of it until a new incumbent had been legally appointed. An action was begun by Mrs. Winbolt, in the Court of King's Bench, to compel the Vicar to give up the chapel, and it was arranged on the 7th July, 1841, that the suit should be tried; but before the trial, Mrs. Winbolt ceded all right to the chapel to the Vicar of Edmonton, as appears by the following letter:

No. 4, Copthall Buildings.
March 1, 1815.

Sir,

In compliance of the advice of my solicitor, Mr. Wadeson, I hereby acquaint you that I have abandoned this suit, and give up all my pretensions to the right of nominating a clergyman to officiate in the Southgate Chapel.

I am, Sir,
Your obedient Servant,
E. WINBOLT.

To the Rev. Mr. Warren,
Edmonton.

SOME ACCOUNT OF SOUTHGATE.

The Rev. Dawson Warren was thus left in entire possession of the Weld Chapel, and he and his assistant curates continued to officiate until 1829, when the Rev. Thomas Sale was appointed to the charge. He resigned after eight years' service, and was succeeded by the Rev. Vincent Stanton, who made further alterations in the structure in 1830, consisting of a new roof, chancel, and pews, the total cost of which amounted to £1,868 10s. 11d.

Owing to the growth of Southgate, it was found about 1860 that Weld Chapel was quite inadequate to cope with the increasing congregation; so the Rev. James Baird, the then Incumbent, erected a handsome stone edifice in the Early English style, from the designs of Sir Gilbert Scott, R.A. The building is lofty, with north and south aisles and chancel. There are two stained glass windows at the east end of the north aisle, by Burne-Jones, and another at the west end of the south aisle by Rossetti. There are in the church, among others, the following memorial windows:

To the glory of God and in affect. memory of Sarah Maria Walker, a dearly beloved aunt, this window is dedicated by her nephews and niece, Thomas Walker Sale, John Edward Sale, and Mary Lydia Moorhouse, 19 August, 1883.

To the glory of God and in loving memory of Susannah Anne Turner, who, having lived in this parish for 70 years, entered into rest 22 April, 1903. This window is placed by Ada and Arthur Rowland Barker.

Conjugis in memoriam A. M. Bradley, Sep. 1866. Also in loving memory of Revd. Charles Bradley, M.A., who lived for 26 years in this parish and died in London, March 29, 1883, aged 68. "Them also which sleep in Jesus will God bring with him."

There is also a memorial tablet to the Rev. James Baird, the first Vicar of the Church, and a window to his successor, the Rev. C. F. Wilson:

To the glory of God and in loving memory of James Baird, M.A., Vicar of this parish. Died October 1st, 1893, aged 82. This tablet is placed to record his earnest labours for 35 years. Faithful as a preacher, diligent as a pastor, His ready help and care for the sick and aged, with his friendly words, brought

SOME ACCOUNT OF SOUTHGATE.

PEACE AND COMFORT TO MANY A SHADOWED HOME. TO HIS
UNTIRING MEMORY THE RIGHTEOUS SHALL BE IN EVER-
LASTING REMEMBRANCE.

TO THE GLORY OF GOD AND IN AFFECTIONATE MEMORY
OF CYRIL FITZROY WILSON, VICAR OF THIS PARISH 1893-
1898. ENTERED INTO REST 10 FEB. 1898. ERECTED BY THE
PARISHIONERS.

In 1906 Vyell E. Walker, of Arnos Grove, at his own expense, converted the north transept into a Lady Chapel, in
memory of his parents; he died before its completion, and the
following tablet was set up to his memory:

TO THE GLORY OF GOD AND IN LOVING MEMORY OF
VYELL EDWARD WALKER OF ARNOS GROVE THIS CHANCEL
WAS DECORATED AND THE SEDILIA ERECTED BY HIS FRIENDS
AND RELATIONS. A.D. 1907.

The tower contains a peal of fine toned bells, and also a set
of Cambridge chimes, which were installed as a souvenir of
the late Queen Victoria's Jubilee in 1887. Christ Church,
Southgate, is indeed one of the most handsome parish churches
to be seen, standing as it does amidst pleasant surroundings,
with its massive spire towering far above the tallest greenery.
Nothing remains to mark the site of the old Weld Chapel,
except a space in the churchyard devoid of graves.

One of the chief places of interest in Southgate at the present
time is Broomfield Park. The historic old mansion Broomfield,
or Bromfield, House, together with the fine grounds, comprising
about fifty odd acres, was purchased by the Southgate Urban
District Council, in 1903, for the sum of £25,000, and turned
into a public park. The Middlesex County Council contributed
£6,250 towards the purchase. The early history of the site is
shrouded in mystery, but it is generally supposed to have been
a monastery adjacent to the great Forest of Middlesex. The
front of the house looks out on to three large lakes, and there
is no doubt that in the "good old times" the monks could have
been seen fishing here on a Thursday.

It is probable that when Bluff King Hal dealt hardly with
the conventual establishments of the country he granted
Broomfield House to one of his courtiers, a supposition which
is borne out by the fact of the present structure being of Tudor
design. It is said that King James I was in the habit of using
the place as a hunting box whilst following his favourite sport.

SOME ACCOUNT OF SOUTHGATE.

The mansion was for some time the home of the Skeffingtons, and later the Jacksons owned it for three centuries; a descendant of the latter family marrying William Tash, it eventually came into his hands. In later years it was the residence of Sir Ralph Littler, K.C.

The interior of the edifice is very fine, nearly all the walls being panelled with oak, and there is a handsome old oak staircase bearing some exquisite carving. The staircase walls and ceiling are adorned with valuable frescoes, representing the four seasons. These were executed by Sir James Thornhill, who is chiefly remembered for his decorations at St. Paul's, Greenwich Palace, Hampton Court, etc.

The ground floor consists of seven large rooms, a curious little ante-room resembling a secret chamber, and the usual household offices. Here are the drawing-room, dining-room, and a billiard room, the doors of which are of solid oak and of an unusual thickness; at least two of the apartments contain very good oak mantlepieces, ornamented with handsome carving. The floor above contains fifteen smaller rooms.

The spacious grounds contain some very fine trees, notably a long avenue of ancient elms, which is supposed to have formerly been the western approach to the Royal Chase of Enfield. There are also two yew trees considerably over 800 years old, while better examples of Scotch fir and green oak would be difficult to find. As has been previously stated, Broomfield House was purchased from Mr. Powys Sybbe, converted into a public recreation ground, and formally dedicated to "the public as an open space for ever" on 23rd April, 1903. The house is now used as a Secondary School.

Adjoining Broomfield Park are the house and grounds of Arnos Grove, at one time called Arnolds. In 1610 the estate was possessed by Sir John Weld, who has been spoken of previously in connection with the Weld Chapel. The property came by purchase into the hands of Sir William Acton in 1620, and from that time until a century later little is known of its history. At his death Arnos Grove was inherited by his only daughter, who married Sir William Whitmore. Their only son, William, who subsequently became possessed of it, died without issue and bequeathed the estate to a relative, Thomas Whitmore.

In 1720 Mr. James Colebrooke purchased Arnos Grove, his son, Sir George Colebrooke, eventually inheriting it. It would appear that previous to his purchase James Colebrooke took

SOME ACCOUNT OF SOUTHGATE.

a lease of Arnos Grove and other lands in Southgate for a period of three years from Oliver Horseman of Hatton Garden, M.D., executor of Sir Samuel Blewitt of Edmonton, knt., and guardian of his infant son and heir, John Blewitt. The property is described as " All that capitall messuage or mansion house, with the outhouses, orchards, gardens and curtilages thereunto belonging, with the appurtenances, in South Street alias Southgate, late in the possession or occupation of the said Sir Samuell Blewitt," etc. Among the fixtures were " a sideboard with an iron foot," " a hatchment and a picture of the Sargeants yeoman," " twelve pictures of the Apostles and two Escutcheons," " a sideboard with an iron legg," a " Chimney sett with Dutch Tyles," " a Draught of the house in a picture," and " twelve leather bucketts hanging on peggs."

Mr. James Colebrooke is generally supposed to have destroyed the old structure and commenced the erection of a new one, but dying while the work was in progress, his son Sir George completed it. He afterwards sold the mansion and grounds to Abraham Hume, for £10,302 5s.

The next owner was Sir William Mayne, Bart., afterwards created Lord Newhaven, who greatly improved the premises and added a new wing; this being about the year 1776. John Brown, Esq., was the next owner of Arnos Grove, but it was soon purchased from him by Mr. Isaac Walker, and it has remained in the possession of the Walker family to the present time.

The Walkers were great lovers of our national game of cricket, and Tom Walker, a member of the old Hambledon Club is credited with the invention in 1785 of the round or straight arm bowling in distinction to the old underhand method. The discovery was, however, suppressed at the time owing to jealousy and professional prejudice, but it was revived in 1805.

The mansion contains some exceptionally fine apartments, and in the dining and drawing rooms there are two valuable Sicilian jasper mantlepieces, made in Italy, one of them consisting of a magnificent statuary mask of Apollo.

Arnos Grove also boasts a picturesque old staircase decorated by Lanscroon with the triumphal entry of Julius Caesar into Rome; it was also noted for a large and valuable collection of paintings, Etruscan vases, and relics from Herculaneum and Pompeii.

The grounds a century or so ago comprised 100 acres,

covered with beautiful timber, including some cedars of Lebanon, and tall Weymouth pines; the whole being beautifully watered by the New River.

Beaver Hall was another handsome seat of Southgate, occupying a site close to Arnos Grove. It came by purchase into the hands of Mr. John Walker in 1870, and he pulled down the house and included the land in his estate. Formerly the residence of the Schneider family, Beaver Hall was finally possessed by a wealthy railway contractor named Joseph Thornton.

The mansion and park of Cannons or Cullands Grove was situated close to Alderman's Hill, which derived its name from Sir William Curtis, an Alderman of the City of London, and Lord Mayor in 1795. He resided here for many years, and, on being created a Baronet in 1802, was described as "of Cullands Grove, Southgate." Sir William Curtis was born in 1752, and had the distinction of being elected Alderman for Tower Ward when only thirty-three years of age. In 1790 he was elected M.P. for the City, a position which he filled without interruption for twenty-eight years. He was a man of great political importance and influence, and when the Tories became unpopular in 1818, he, as the head of that party, suffered also by losing his seat. To alleviate his disappointment he was offered a peerage as Lord Tenterden, which he promptly refused. Compensation for his defeat, however, was tendered to him at a special meeting of the Drapers' Company—of which he was a Liveryman—at Drapers' Hall, where he was presented with an illuminated address, a gold snuff-box, and a purse containing two hundred guineas. Two years later he received the honour of re-election to Parliament as Member for the City. Sir William was very popular among royalty, and whilst accompanying George IV to Scotland in 1822, the King, as a mark of appreciation, presented him with his portrait, inscribed: "G. R. to his faithful and loyal subject, Sir William Curtis."

He is considered to have been the most caricatured personage of his time, and although a great public man and a mover in the *élite* of Society, it would appear that he was exceedingly ignorant. The following anecdote, which is quoted on the authority of a contemporary historian of the neighbourhood, goes to prove this: " . . . when his royal patron was dining at Cullands Grove, a Mr. Cox being of the party, Sir

Cullands Grove, Southgate, 1801.
From an old print.

ribed as
rtis was
d Alder-
of age,
which he
le was a
hen the
of that
s disap-
n, which
owever,
Drapers'
rs' Hall,
s, a gold
as. Two
rliament
r among
otland in
iim with
subject,

red per-
n and a
he was
s quoted
ighbour-
ron was
arty, Sir

SOME ACCOUNT OF SOUTHGATE.

William proceeded to toast His Majesty and the commoner in one health and in these words 'Here's to the three C's—King, Cox and Curtis.'"

Bowes Park, that latest exponent of all that is up-to-date in modern suburbia, now marks the site of Bowes Manor, at one time the residence of Thomas Wilde, who was Lord Chancellor in 1850, and in that year created Baron Truro of Bowes Manor, Middlesex. The first mention of the property occurs in a deed dated 1397, in which a citizen of London, by name John Northampton, "grants the manors of Bowes and Darnford with Pole House and Fordes" to one William Horsecroft. The manor of Bowes was owned in the reign of Henry IV by Sir John Danbriggecomb, who granted it to Thomas Langley, Bishop of Durham, and Ralph Nevile, Earl of Westmorland. In 1413 Bowes and other manors were conceded to the Crown, and it appears that they were afterwards made over to St. Paul's Cathedral, for in 1428 the Dean and Chapter granted them on lease to one William Bothe. Sir Edward Barkham owned Bowes Manor for some time, and in 1694 Robert Frampton was lessee. Other tenants were John Dashwood King and Sir James Pennyman about 1750, Mr. Hare in 1777, Mr. Berdmore in 1780, and eventually Mr. Julius Hutchinson, from whom it was purchased about 1819 by William Tash, sometime owner of Broomfield House. Afterwards Bowes Manor came into the possession of Lord Truro. He is worthy of notice for the exceptional rapidity with which he rose in the public service. Entering parliament in 1831 as Member for Newmarket, he attained the position of Solicitor-General in 1840; Attorney-General in the following year, and finally Lord Chief Justice of the Common Pleas in 1846. It must be admitted that this was a feat of which any man might be proud. He lost his parliamentary seat, however, in the general election of 1832, but regained it in 1835, and held it until 1841. He was one of the earliest supporters of Sir Rowland Hill's postal reform scheme, which he himself introduced into the House of Commons in 1843; he also supported a measure in the following year for the total suppression of the slave trade. Lord Truro died in 1855, and was buried at St. Lawrence, near Ramsgate. His valuable law library was presented by his widow to the House of Lords. During the time of Lord Truro's possession of Bowes Manor the grounds comprised seventy acres, and to the south of the mansion there was a beautiful grove walk, lined by an avenue of tall and majestic trees. The house, some time before its demolition, was the residence of Alderman Sidney, who served the office of Lord Mayor in 1853-4.

Southgate Grove—or, as it is now designated, Grovelands —was erected at the beginning of the last century by Walker Gray, Esq., who employed as architect Thomas Nash. The building is mainly Ionic in its design, and is encompassed by undulating pleasure grounds, which are very pleasing in their effect as they gradually fall to a piece of water. The mansion can claim the distinction of possessing three names within half a century. Originally called Southgate Grove, the name was changed by J. Donnithorne Taylor—grandfather of the present owner—to Woodlands, and again in 1850 it was re-christened Grovelands. The original gates of the mansion now form the entrance to Broomfield Park, and are inscribed the " village gates."

Southgate House happily still exists, but, beyond its size and beautiful estate, there is little of historic interest attaching to it. One of the Walker family lived and died here in 1853.

It is with regret that one recollects Minchenden House, because it was one of the finest seats that Southgate possessed. The mansion was intimately associated with the Duke of Chandos, who, after the demolition of his other residence, Canons, at Edgware, came to reside at Southgate. It was erected about 1747—a large brick building shut out from the high road by a large wall or fence—by one John Nicholl, who, however, only lived to complete it. His daughter, who inherited the property, married in 1753 James, third Duke of Chandos, who had been appointed Ranger of Enfield Chase. She died in 1768. After her death Minchenden House became the occasional residence of the Dowager Duchess of Chandos until her decease in 1813. The house then came into the possession of the Marquis of Buckingham, through his wife, who was the heiress of the last Duke of Chandos. In 1853 Mr. Isaac Walker became possessed of the property, and in that year he destroyed the house and added the grounds to his estate of Arnos Grove. To reach the entrance of this fine old mansion, one had to traverse a broad gravel path, running by the side of the New River, and then through a shrubbery

Minchenden House, Southgate.
From an old lithograph.

that led on to the lawn. A massive old pollard oak known as the Chandos oak is still in existence, and is said to cover more ground than any other tree in England, its spread measuring no less than 136 feet; it is still increasing.

Although Minchenden House is now no more, there still exists a smaller structure called Minchenden Lodge, originally a small cottage, a little to the north of the site; this was enlarged some time after the demolition of the old mansion, some of its materials being utilized for this purpose. It was here that the late Queen and Prince Consort stayed for refreshment when they laid the foundation stone of Colney Hatch Lunatic Asylum.

Queen Elizabeth's Lodge was for a period of half a century or so inhabited by the Rev. Charles Bradley, the elder brother of the late Dean of Westminster, who conducted a school there. There is a tradition that "Good Queen Bess" was accustomed to watch the hunting from the garden of the Lodge, hence its name. Sir Augustus Hare speaks of it in his *Story of my Life*. He says: "His [Mr. Bradley's] house was an ugly brick villa, standing a little way back from the road, in the pretty village of Southgate, about ten miles from London. . . . The life at Southgate for the next two years was certainly the reverse of luxurious, and I did not get on well with my tutor, owing to his extraordinary peculiarities, and probably to my own faults also; but I feel that mentally I owe everything to Mr. Bradley."

The New River flows through Southgate. With the growth of London at the beginning of the seventeenth century, the means for the supply of pure water had become totally inadequate. Complaints had been raised from time to time, and even Acts of Parliament passed in 1605 and 1606, authorizing the making of a stream from the springs of Anwell and Chadwell in Hertfordshire, to remedy the defect. Nothing seems to have been done, however, until Mr. Hugh Myddleton, who as a member of the Parliamentary Committees appointed to inquire into the matter had given the subject careful study, agreed to undertake the project. He set to work diligently and promised to complete the channel in four years from 1609. At first great opposition was encountered from the several landowners through whose property the stream was to flow. In the following year his adversaries sent a deputation to the House of Commons, and succeeded in getting a Special Committee appointed to inquire into their grievances, but before a report could be made, parliament had dissolved. The opposition of the landed gentry, however, had so severely harassed Myddleton in his task, that in 1611 he was obliged to petition for an extension of time, which was granted him. When the stream was brought to Enfield, just half way to London, he was faced by another and more serious difficulty, namely, lack of funds, and on soliciting parliament and the rich city merchants for assistance he was met by a distinct refusal. Finally, in desperation, he requested James I to furnish him with capital, and the canny Scot, who ever had an eye to business, having become interested in the undertaking by watching the progress of the work from his palace of Theobalds, readily acceded to his request, by agreeing to pay half the cost on condition of receiving half the profit. To these rather harsh terms Myddleton perforce consented, and thus provided with fresh funds he commenced again with renewed vigour, and completed his work in 1613.

On Michaelmas day in that year, the Lord Mayor, Sir Thomas Myddleton—his elder brother—presided over the ceremony at Clerkenwell to celebrate the entrance of the New River into London.* In the following year Myddleton, who had expended the best part of his savings upon the costly undertaking, was obliged to ask the corporation of the City for a loan of £3,000, which was at once granted to him "in consideration of the benefit likely to accrue to the city from his New River." As a reward for the success of his enterprise James I made him a Baronet in 1622.

Sir Hugh Myddleton died in 1631, aged seventy-one years, and was buried in the Church of St. Matthew, Friday Street.

His wife died at Bush Hill some twelve years later, and was interred in the chancel of Edmonton Church.

In its earliest form the New River was a canal about ten feet wide, and four in depth, but it has since been widened and generally improved in the matter of reservoirs, etc.

Charles Lamb, commenting on a friend of his—George Dyer, sometime Editor of the Cambridge edition of the Classics—who had the misfortune to fall into the New River, thus immortalizes the stream in his *Amicus Redivivus*:

> Waters of Sir Hugh Myddleton—what a spark you were like to have extinguished for ever! Your salubrious streams to this city for now near two centuries, would hardly have atoned for what you were in a moment washing away. Mockery of a

river, liquid artifice, wretched conduit! henceforth rank with
canels and sluggish aqueducts. Was it for this, that smit in
boyhood with the explorations of that Abyssinian traveller, I
paced the vales of Anwell to explore your tributary springs,
to trace your salutary waters sparkling through green Hertfordshire and cultured Enfield Parks? (ye have no swans, no
Naiad, no river God) or did the benevolent hoary aspect of
my friend tempt ye to suck him in that ye also might have the
tutelary genius of your waters.

It has been previously stated that Leigh Hunt was born at
Southgate; Eagle Hall, his birthplace, although altered somewhat, is still existing, hidden from view by a line of modern
buildings. Isaac Hunt, the father of the litterateur, was for
some time pastor of a chapel at Lisson Grove, W., and also
an occasional preacher at Southgate, and it is surmised that
in this capacity he attracted the attention of the Duke of
Chandos of Minchenden House. His helpful sermons and
charming personality made a favourable impression on the
Duke, so much, indeed, that he invited him to become tutor
to his nephew, Mr. James Henry Leigh. On the birth of
Mr. Hunt's youngest son in 1784, he was christened, by the
express wish of the Duke, in the names of his father's pupil,
who stood godfather to him, so that his full name became
James Henry Leigh Hunt.

Isaac Hunt founded a school at his residence, Eagle Hall,
and received as pupils sons of the local aristocracy. At his
decease the institution was conducted by Mr. Fleuret, and
eventually by Mr. James Rumsey, who made extensive alterations in enlarging the place. On his retirement about 1856,
his son, Henry Rumsey was appointed to the charge, retiring
himself after some ten years' work. There were two more
masters of the school, and then it ceased to exist.

Southgate school was situated at the northern extremity of
the town; a plain, brick, thatched building supported by the
munificence of Mr. John Walker. It originally consisted of
about 140 pupils, and was open to children irrespective of sect.

One can only conclude with the fervent hope that Southgate
may long remain a place "lying out of the way of innovation,"
as Leigh Hunt so ably put it; at the present day the district
may be described as one of the healthiest, most picturesque,
and most charming suburbs on the beautiful "northern heights."

NOTES ON THE EARLY CHURCHES OF SOUTH ESSEX.

By C. W. FORBES, Member of the Essex Archaeological Society.

[Continued from p. 113.]

HADLEIGH,

OUR next visit is to Hadleigh, anciently called Hadleigh ad Castrum, a village which gives its name to the bay or strait that separates Canvey Island from the mainland; the village is situated about two and a half miles north-east from South Benfleet station, and two miles from Leigh.

The church is a Norman structure, dating from the reign of King Stephen, *circa* 1140, nearly a century before mention is first made of the district as Hadleigh ad Castrum; it therefore claims greater antiquity than the castle erected near here by Hubert de Burgh, Earl of Kent, *temp*. Henry III. It is one of a few churches left in the county with round apsidal endings to the chancel, similar to East Ham.[1] There are, I believe, eight others still in existence, viz.: Great and Little Maplestead, Haversfield, Colchester Castle Chapel, Bamborough Chapel, Little Braxted, Langford, and Copford.

The building consists of a chancel, nave, western wooden spire, and south porch; the walls are very thick, as is usual with Norman structures, measuring about three feet two inches across.

The spire, added in the fifteenth century, was originally shingled, and contained down to the time of Edward VI four bells; there is now only one, which was recast in 1636, which date is on it.

In the chancel are four small Norman windows, and six in the nave, as follows: one in west wall, two in north wall, and three in the south wall. On the north side, near the chancel, is a small Early English lancet window, and opposite, in south wall, one of the Decorated period; besides these we notice two fairly large two-light Perpendicular windows, one on each side.

[1] A description of the church at East Ham was given in the first of this series of articles. See vol. ix, p. 209.

Hadleigh Church.
Photographs by C. W. Forbes.

THE EARLY CHURCHES OF SOUTH ESSEX.

Originally the church had three entrances, north, south, and west; the one on the north, twelfth century, has been blocked up; the south door is of the same date, but has fourteenth-century moulding and a trefoil holy-water stoup added on the exterior; the porch is also attributed to the same period. The small doorway on the west is a plain Norman one. There is also a priest's door on the north side, now blocked up, attributed to the fourteenth century. Dividing the nave from the chancel is a stone wall about three feet thick; it forms part of the original Norman building, and furnishes a good example of a mediaeval stone screen.[1] It was originally pierced with three semicircular arches; the small side openings were, however, filled in with masonry in the early part of the fifteenth century. This masonry was pierced, probably later in the same century, with two very fine cinquefoil openings or hagioscopes,[2] one on each side of the nave; between these openings and the centre arch, in a narrow space of about eleven inches, were minute niches with cusped ogee arches and delicate tracery of the same date; one niche only without tracery now remains on the north side.

The chancel arch presents a fine and striking appearance from its lofty proportions as one looks eastward from the western end of the nave.

In the chancel are two aumbries, and on the north side a lofty Perpendicular niche or credence, with cusped tracery.

The rood screen stood in front of the arch, and the staircase leading to the loft still remains on the north side; it was blocked up and the old door taken away at the restoration in 1855.

The walls of the nave were originally covered with large paintings or frescoes; in the eighteenth century these were covered with whitewash, and on the removal of this whitewash in 1855 portions of the frescoes were discovered. The subjects were St. George and the Dragon, the Virgin and Child, and St. Thomas of Canterbury in full pontificals. They are attributed to the latter end of the twelfth century. Portions of two frescoes that have been preserved are, The Angel and Child, to be seen on the arch of a Norman window on the north side of the nave, and St. Thomas à Becket, fragments of which are to be found on the splay of the lancet window on the same side.

[1] There is a good example of an early stone screen at Vange Church. See *ante*, p. 108.
[2] Many authorities consider that these small openings in screens were for confessionals.—Editor.

The font at the west end, three feet two inches high, has an octagonal bowl, two feet four inches in diameter; the under part is circular, and has a bold torus moulding with trefoil leaves; it stands on three modern ornamental round pillars; the bowl is probably of the same age as the church, twelfth century. Among the church plate is a communion cup (now disused) with a paten cover of the time of Edward VI. It is engraved " Hadle of Essex bi the Castil." An extensive restoration was undertaken in 1855, under the direction of the late Sir G. E. Street, when the roofs of both nave and chancel were renewed; they may probably be facsimiles of the earlier ones, the style being an old one; the walls also were replastered inside.

The altar table, pulpit, prayer desk, and lectern of oak date from 1855, and were all designed by the architect.

The stained glass is modern, and inserted during the latter part of the nineteenth century; that in the Perpendicular window on the south side of the nave is in memory of the wife of Mr. King, who was a noted Essex antiquary. Both this window and a smaller one on the same side in the chancel are worthy of note from their fine colouring; they are the work of Messrs. Cox and Sons of London.

Some little distance to the south of the church are the remains of Hadleigh Castle, built by Hubert de Burgh, Earl of Kent, about 1228. It appears later to have been confiscated by the Crown, and extensive alterations and repairs were made by order of Edward III. The castle was granted from time to time to a royal favourite. Henry VIII made a grant of the castle and lands to Anne of Cleves. In 1551 it was given by Edward VI to Richard, first Baron Rich of Leeze, who for some reason reduced the castle to a ruin; these ruins now consist of two round towers, which are falling to pieces, and portions of the gateway tower and the walls enclosing the courtyard, and still exhibit traces of their former grandeur; they are overrun with shrubs and brushwood, and look very picturesque. The ruins are now the property of the Salvation Army.

EASTWOOD.

Eastwood is a place known to have been in existence as early as the time of Edward the Confessor; it is situated about two miles north-east of Hadleigh.

The ancient church is an interesting old structure, built of

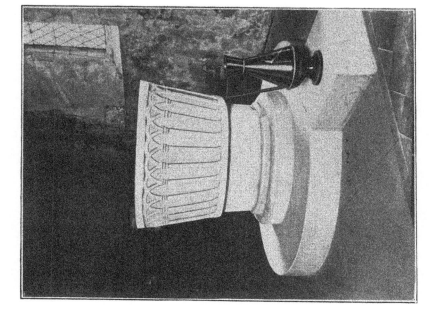

The Font, Eastwood.

The Font, Hadleigh.

Photographs by C. W. Forbes.

part

latter
icular
e wife
h this
el are
ork of

he re-
arl of
ed by
made
ime to
of the
en by
ho for
w con-
d por-
court-
; they
very
lvation

nce as
ituated

uilt of

brick and stone; it is very picturesque in appearance, and the venerable elms in the churchyard add much to the beauty and pleasing seclusion of the site. It consists of a nave, with north and south aisles, a large and lofty chancel, and a tower with a long slender spire at the south-west corner of the edifice, which is rather a rare example in this county.

The spire was originally shingled; now, however, we find it boarded in a very modern style of carpentry. Formerly there were four bells, but only three now exist; two of them are ancient, and have Latin inscriptions. The first reads: "Sancte Gregore, ora pro nobis"; the second, "Sancta Katerina, ora pro nobis"; the third bears the date 1693. The present building dates from the middle of the twelfth century; extensive alterations appear to have been made in the thirteenth and fourteenth centuries. The nave is the oldest part of the church; the original Norman building doubtless consisted of a nave and chancel only. About the end of the thirteenth century the north and south aisles and tower were added; the chancel also appears to have been enlarged about that period, and the low Norman arch supplanted by the lofty Early English one we now see; traces of an early arch are visible at the sides.

The tower was heightened slightly, and the spire added, in the fourteenth century.

The porch of the south door, which is the only entrance into the church, is a red brick Tudor one of the sixteenth century. Over the front at the top is a niche for an image; on the east side of the doorway can be seen the remains of a trefoil holy-water stoup.

The square-headed oaken door at the entrance is very fine and much admired; it is covered with decorative iron work. On one of the iron bands across it, although much worn, one can still read the following inscription in Latin: "Pax regat intrantes, eadem regat egredientes," a literal translation of which is: "May peace direct those who enter, also those who leave."

The north doorway is blocked up; but a similar ancient door (without, however, any inscription), which formerly hung here, now stands in the vestry. The priests' doorway, on the south side of chancel, is also filled in. On entering, the first object of interest one notices is the magnificent old circular font of the Norman period; the exterior round the basin is beautifully carved with interlaced ornamental arcading;

the basin is about four feet in diameter ; the lead lining is said to be as old as the font itself.

The aisles are separated from the nave by two octagonal pillars and three pointed arches on each side. Over those on the north side are the filled-in remains of three small Norman clerestory windows, showing that the dividing wall over the arches is a portion of the original north wall of the church, cut through to form the aisle.

The western end of the north aisle was enclosed by wood-work in the early part of the fifteenth century, a floor being inserted in the enclosure, thus dividing it into two stories or apartments. The lower one was used as a sacristy and the upper chamber as a muniment room; it is quite possible, however, that it was originally built as a priests' house; the floor of the upper part is framed with a well hole as the only means of access ; the wooden trap-door is furnished with a lock of huge proportions; it is lit by two small lancet windows.

The south aisle was at one time used as a chapel ; it may have been a chantry. The remains of a small piscina can be seen in the south wall, and an aumbry in the east wall.

A peculiar feature of this church is the cutting of the two pillars on the south side of the nave, about four ft. from the floor. The first pillar from the chancel has a small portion cut out on the north side, and the second column a similar piece off the south side ; the sacristan was thus enabled, by looking between these two columns, and the hagioscope cut in the stone chancel wall, to ring the Sanctus bell at the Elevation of the Host.

On the south side of the chancel are plain sedilia and the remains of a piscina. There is also near this a low side window ; over this window is an arched recess, probably the remains of a founder's tomb.

A small Jacobean altar table, now disused, is also to be seen in the chancel. Within the altar rails is a brass to Thomas Burrow, who died in 1600.

The benefice of Eastwood belonged at an early period to the Priory of Prittlewell. It is supposed that it was given by the founder, Robert son of Suene; at any rate, the Priory was in possession in the reign of Henry II, during the Arch-bishopric of Thomas à Becket. The church was then a chapel to Prittlewell ; afterwards it became a rectory to which the Prior presented. About 1390 the sanction of the Pope was

1869

Eastwood Church.

Photograph by C. W. Forbes.

procured for its appropriation to the Priory; as, however, this was done without the consent of the King or the bishop of the diocese, they were obliged to obtain a licence from King Richard II, in 1394, to appropriate the churches of Eastwood and North Shoebury to their own use; and, by way of compensation to the Bishop of London, to agree to pay him and his successors 6s. 8d. yearly. This agreement was made in 1398.

The Priory retained possession of the advowson of Eastwood until the suppression of the monasteries, when it came into the possession of the Crown, which has held it unto the present day.

A note with reference to this church is to be found in Archdeacon Hale's *Precedents in causes of office against churchwardens and others*, published in 1841, being "Extracts from the Act Books of the Consistory Court of London." It is stated that in 1612 the church was in a dilapidated condition as regards the roof; and that the "seates were neither fflored, nor well benched"; there was neither "pott or pewter, nor any other mettall to put wine in, for the communion table," etc. Want of money being pleaded as an excuse for not doing the repairs, a commission was granted, to survey "ye decayes," and the making of a rate, to the churchwardens, and to Mr. Vassall, Richard Thorneton, Francis Gates, John Hawkin, Richard Ellis, and other parishioners; they had orders to transmit their proceedings and rate, together with the commission, into the court.

The "pott" above mentioned was a vessel used to contain the wine before consecration.

LEIGH.

Leigh, an ancient place which up to a few years ago was a small fishing village, is situated some three miles to the west of Southend; the church is to be found about half a mile to the south of the main London Road, between Hadleigh and Southend.

Probably a church existed here from an early period, but the present edifice was erected in the latter half of the fifteenth century, in the late Perpendicular style, of Kentish ragstone. It consists of a nave, chancel, north and south aisles, north chapel, and a fine embattled stone tower, eighty feet high at the west end, containing a clock and six bells.

The north door is bricked up; the south door has a porch of red brick, with a sundial dated 1729.

On the south side of the chancel is a priests' doorway.

On the north side the aisle and chapel are of corresponding length, divided from the nave and chancel by six octagonal columns, four in the nave and two in the chancel.

The font is a modern one, apparently a copy of that at Prittlewell.

The church in the past has undergone considerable restoration and reconstruction; first, in the early part of the eighteenth century, when the present porch was added and material alterations made in the chancel, the south window being blocked up; again in 1837; and, lastly, in 1871, when the chancel was lengthened and practically rebuilt, in the Decorated style. The last column dividing the chancel from the north chapel was probably inserted at this time; it is smaller and lower, the arch being more acute.

The windows also are nearly all modern. Between the chancel and the nave is a recess, now filled up, which may have contained the rood stairs, or possibly an aumbry.

There are several brasses with effigies, the earliest being one to Richard Haddok, who died in 1453, and his wife, with seven sons and three daughters. There are also a number of monuments in the church.

[To be continued.]

NOTES FROM ST. BARTHOLOMEW THE LESS.

By A. J. JEWARS.

WITHIN the boundaries of the great Hospital of St. Bartholomew, and directly appertaining to it, is the little church of St. Bartholomew the Less, which has been quite eclipsed by the interest of St. Bartholomew the Great. The structure has been rebuilt in comparatively recent times, and its many modern tablets cause it to appear at first sight to contain nothing worthy of notice. Yet such is not the case; and although we know, from incidental mention of them, that many monuments have disappeared, it is the purpose of

Brass of William Markeby and his wife
(St. Bartholomew the Less, Smithfield).

a porch

onding
tagonal

that at

restora-
hteenth
naterial
being
hen the
in the
chancel
s time;

en the
ch may

t being
fe, with
nber of

THE

l of St
t, is the
ich has
ew the
y recent
at first
not the
f them,
rpose of

Arms granted to Robert Balthorpe.

Arms of Robert Balthorpe
(from his Monument, St. Bartholomew the Less, Smithfield).
Drawn by A. J. Jewars.

NOTES FROM ST. BARTHOLOMEW THE LESS.

this article to show there is still much of interest to the antiquary and collector.

The oldest memorial now to be found is a brass of the fifteenth century, with figures of a gentleman and his wife in the usual dress of the period. The inscription is simple, and remarkable only for the insertion of an English word in a Latin inscription, instead of its usual Latin equivalent. The wording runs: "Hic Jacent Willm̄ Markeby de Londoniis Gentilmā qui obiit 11 die July A. dñi M° cccc xxx ix, et Alicia uxor ei9." Here it will be seen that the inscription has been cut away to destroy the pious request for prayers for the deceased. The man's head has been broken off and not very skilfully rejoined, giving the lower part of the face a curious twisted appearance.

Next to call for attention, in the recess on the south side of the chancel, partly hidden by the organ, is a monument, consisting of a panel with an inscription, above which is the effigy of a gentleman kneeling within an arched canopy, supported by two pillars, while surmounting all is a shield of arms with helmet, crest, and mantling. This commemorates Robert Balthorpe, Sergeant-Surgeon to Queen Elizabeth. The inscription is so delightfully quaint we may surely risk giving it in full:

Here Robert Balthorpe lyes Intomb'd to Elizabeth our Queen,
Who sergeant of the Surgeons sworn near thirty years hath been.
He dyed at Sixty nine of yeares December ninth the Day;
The yeare of Grace eight hundred twice, deducting nine away.
  Let here his rotten bones repose
  Till angell Trumpet sound
  To warn the World of present change
  And raise the dead from ground.
  Vivat post funera virtus.

The ingenuity of getting in all the facts to rhyme is charming. The doctor's will is still more attractive, but it is altogether too long even to give a fair abstract of it. Naturally he mentions some of his assistants and surgical instruments, as, "my lancett that is sett in golde and enamyled"; "my syringe of silver gilted and three pipes of silver and gilted belonging to the same"; "my servaunts that nowe are with me, and have bene my servaunts in time past which do practize and exercise the art of chirurgery." Then there is a box mentioned as having the lock, hinges, and bars over it of "copper gilted." Does any collector possess this? or either the "greate Ringe of golde with my seale of Armes" and "my lesser Ringe of golde with my seale of Armes"? Where are these things?

There is an allusion to his being in the royal service in the paragraph, "my English bible which is at the Courte," also "my bagge with the case and all the instruments and other things that are therein which lyeth for my daily use in my chest wherein I put my linnen at the Courte." Again, the description of sundry articles of dress shows how much richer and more picturesque was the dress of his day than is that of our own. We might quote particulars of his bequest of a silver gilt "bell bowle" to the Company of Barbers and Surgeons, and of money for them to make "a dynner" in their Hall after the funeral, then a general practice; but we must stay our pen.

Strange to say, the arms on this monument, though much discoloured, appear to differ from those granted to Dr. Balthorpe by William Harvey, Clarenceux King of Arms, which are here given.

We have lingered so long with Dr. Balthorpe we must dismiss our next illustration, the rubbing from a brass, the oldest memorial remaining in the church, leaving it to speak for itself.

Under the window at the west end of the church are the remains of a fine altar tomb of late fifteenth-century work; it has been somewhat defaced, and no traces of the brasses are to be found, while the whole tomb was misappropriated by an eighteenth-century surgeon, John Freke, as a memorial of himself and his wife, who was Elizabeth, daughter of Richard Blundell of London. For this purpose a brief Latin inscription has been cut at the back, and a block of stone carved with the arms here depicted let in at the top. The lady died in 1741, and John Freke himself in 1756, intestate; administration to his effects being granted to his only child, Susanna, wife of William Williams.

The accompanying shield of arms is on a floor slab, the helmet and crest are hidden by a fixed safe—the usual disregard of monuments and other objects of interest, when any alterations or restorations in churches are made, is responsible. The inscription records that Thomas Sprigg, citizen and cooper, who died in 1735-6, lies there; as also his relict, Mrs. Sarah Sprigg, who died in 1751-2. The will of Thomas Sprigg con-

Arms on the Freke Monument
(St. Bartholomew the Less).
Drawn by A. J. Jewars.

tains nothing of general interest; he appears to have left no children, as his brothers came in for most of what he had to leave, part of which was in the fatal South Sea Annuities.

To the north of the chancel is a memorial of the wife of Sir Thomas Bodley, the founder of the Bodleian Library at Oxford, but it calls for no special mention.

MAUNDY CELEBRATIONS: ANCIENT AND MODERN.

By CORNELIUS NICHOLLS.

THE following is an attempt to bring together various records relating to the observance of Maundy Thursday and its attendant ceremonials, from the earliest periods to the present time, more especially with regard to our own country. It will be seen how, from its simple inauguration by the founder of Christianity, the Maundy grew into a ceremonious and royal function, practised also by great nobles and princes of the Church, and rising apparently to its fullest development as a State ceremony under the Tudor Queens, Mary and Elizabeth. Shortly after these reigns there was a curtailment of the ceremony, and from the time of James II, that part relating to the washing of the feet of the poor was no longer performed by the monarch in person.

It may be that the detailed quotations here given from old writers—*ipsissima verba*—appear somewhat prolix, yet it is hoped that the quaintness of the original, occasionally preserving by its ancient orthography information beyond that of the immediate narrative, may not be found uninteresting. As observed by Cowper, in one of his letters, " the same idea, which clothed in colloquial language seems childish and even foolish, assumes quite a different air in Latin," so, perhaps, in some such way these descriptions of old customs, given in the actual diction of the times portrayed, may lend to the scene an atmosphere of antiquity and some sense of perspective to the imagination.

Authorities differ as to the derivation of the word "Maundy," some holding that it comes from *maund*, the old name for a basket in which gifts were carried and subsequently distri-

buted. In this sense the word is used· by Shakespeare in
A Lover's Complaint:

> A thousand favours from a maund she drew
> Of amber, crystal, and of beaded jet.

Spelman and others derive the word from this source, thus
seeming to confine the term to that part of the ceremony
which consisted of the giving of alms. But by most writers
it is thought to have been derived from the Latin *mandatum*,
with reference to Our Lord's precept in St. John's Gospel,
"If I then, your Lord and Master, have washed your feet, ye
also ought to wash one another's feet." Thus Bishop Sparrow,
on this subject, writes: "This day Christ washed His disciples'
feet and gave them a commandment to do likewise. Hence
it is called *dies mandati*, mandate or Maundy Thursday";
and it is now generally accepted that from a vernacular
corruption of this Latin form we get our English word
Maundy. It is also to be remembered that in primitive
times obedience to Christ's precept was the chief if not the
only object; the distribution of gifts to the poor being a later
addition.

Other names formerly used for this occasion were "Dies
Coenae Domini," referring to the inauguration of the Lord's
Supper; "Holy Thursday"; "White Thursday"—the Lenten
vestments and hangings of some churches being then changed
from violet to white, in memory of the institution of the
Blessed Sacrament—and "Shere Thursday." This last is so
called from the custom practised by the monks and others of
being then shaven and shorn in preparation for the coming
Easter. As an old writer has it: "For in old Faders' daies
the people wolde that daye shere their hedes and clyppe their
berdes and poll their hedes, and so make theym honest ayenst
Esterday."[1] In addition to this, and giving the practice a
wider significance, was the fact that on this day those people
who had been put out of the Church and subjected to penance
were, if repentant, again reconciled after an ordeal that might
well have given occasion to this rendering of the name. On
the first day of Lent these offenders had been required to
present themselves before the bishop clothed in sackcloth,
with naked feet, and with every accompaniment of abject
humility. Upon entering the church, the penitential Psalms
having been recited, the priests threw ashes upon the

[1] *Liber Festivalis* (1500), cited by Wheatley.

1929

Arms on Tombstone of Thomas Sprigg
(St. Bartholomew the Less, Smithfield).

"penitents," and covered their heads with sackcloth. After this they were driven out of the church, followed by the clergy repeating the curse pronounced against Adam when expelled from Paradise. But with the arrival of Maundy Thursday, all the doors of the church were thrown open, and the penitents, lying outside prostrate on the earth, were welcomed in by the bishop. They then trimmed their heads and beards, took off their penitential weeds, and reclothed themselves in decent apparel in token of their reconciliation.[1]

The extreme severity of many penances that were formerly inflicted, by causing them to be frequently evaded, gave rise to a relaxation of discipline in the form of a commutation of sentences. "A new system of canonical arithmetic was established; and the fast of a day was taxed at the rate of a silver penny for the rich, or 50 paternosters for the illiterate and 50 psalms for the learned."[2] In the eighth century penance might be commuted for alms and prayers; in the tenth, pilgrimages were enjoined, in which a man might never pass two nights in one place, might not eat meat, nor clip his hair or nails. If rich he founded a church, built a bridge, or made roads, or emancipated serfs. In the twelfth century it consisted generally of pilgrimages. In 1389 men in shirts and breeches, women in shifts, holding sacred images, stood during Mass bareheaded and barefooted, and finally made an offering to the priest. In 1554 penitents stood wrapped in a white sheet, with a taper in one hand and a rod in the other, during a sermon, after which they were struck on the head, at Paul's Cross, and so reconciled.[3] This particular penance was inflicted by the Church long after the above date, and was particularly insisted upon throughout the land. In the printed articles, dated 1625, ordered " to be enquired of by the Churchwardens and sworne-men in every parish within the Commissariship of Essex and Hertford ; and presentment thereof to be made to the Commissary, with peculiar answer to every article," the following is the 45th and concluding article: "Lastly, you, the Churchwardens, are at the charge of your parish to provide a convenient large Sheete and a White Wand to be had and kept within your Church or Vestrie, to be used at such times as offenders are censured for their grievous and notorious crimes." Our Commination Service,

---

[1] Bp. Sparrow's *Rationale on Book of Common Prayer*, pp. 117, 126.
[2] Lingard, *Anglo-Saxon Church*, p. 336.
[3] Feasey, *Ancient English Holy-Week Ceremonials*, p. 100.

appointed to be used on the first day of Lent, "and at other times as the Ordinary shall appoint," is all that now remains to remind us of that "Godly Discipline" of primitive times, of which our Prayer Book, in archaic language, still deplores the loss.

In addition to those people who were reconciled after penance, it was customary with many who had kept Lent, to bathe and wash their bodies on Maundy Thursday, in order to appear decently pure and clean "from the filth which their bodies might have contracted from the austerities of Lent."[1]

To what extremes these "austerities" were sometimes carried may be seen from a passage in Bede's *Life of St. Cuthbert*. Describing this Saint's withdrawal from all earthly matters, he says:

> So entirely had he put off all care as to the body, and so had given himself up to the care of the soul alone, that when once he had put on his long hose, which were made of hide, he used to wear them for several months together. Yea, with the exception of once at Easter, it may be said that he never took them off again for a year, until the return of the Pasch, when he was unshod for the ceremony of washing the feet, which is wont to take place on Maundy Thursday. Hence on account of his frequent prayers and genuflections which he performed when thus hosed, it was discovered that he had an oblong and extensive callosity at the juncture of the feet and legs.

The Church's obedience to the *mandatum* has been traced as far back as the fourth century. In the Early English Text Society's transcription of the *South England Legendary* may be found a direct reference to the keeping of Maundy Thursday, in the sixth century, by St. Brendan and his monks. St. Brendan, who died at the age of ninety-four, in the year 578, is there described as a great traveller, and the chief actor in many marvellous adventures. It was on the occasion of his voyage to the "Isle of Sheep," where he arrived with his monks on Maundy Thursday, that the event took place which is here given in a literal translation from the old rhymed version:

So that their ship at the last to that isle drew
On Shire Thursday   .   .   .   .   .
The Procurator came to meet them and welcomed them anon,

---

[1] Bingham, *Antiquities of the Christian Church*, p. 353.

And kissed St. Brendan's feet, and the monks, each one;
                       [the time of day required it]
And set them [sith] to supper, for the day it would so.
And then he washed their feet all, the Maundy for to do.
                       [did stay]
They held there their Maundy, and there they gan stay
On Good Friday all the long day, until Easter Eve.

Other early references to this day are made by Alcuin in the eighth century, who gives the form for its celebration in his Book of Offices; also in an ancient MS. pontifical of the English Church of the tenth century, now preserved in the British Museum.

In addition to the primitive practice of washing one another's feet, it became customary to provide for the poor gifts of clothes, food, and money, together with a substantial meal at the time of their distribution; this last being a recognition by the Church of the previous fasting undergone by the recipients.[1] It would seem, too, that this breaking of the Lenten fast was a concession enjoyed not only by poor Maundy folk. The following verses sarcastically portray a monastic celebration, and are translated from some old and apparently contemporaneous writer—possibly one of those members of the secular clergy who regarded the monks with such well-known jealousy, a jealousy and animosity apparent not only in their writings but also in those monkish caricatures on bosses and corbels still to be seen in various churches throughout the land:

And here the monks their maundies make with sundry solemn rites,
And signs of great humility and wondrous pleasant sights,
Each one the other's feet doth wash and wipe them clean and dry,
With helpful mind and secret fraud, that in their hearts doth lie;
As if that Christ with his examples did these things require,
And not to help our brethren here with zeal and free desire;
Each one supplying other's want, in all things that they may,
As he himself a servant made, to serve us every way.
Then straight the loaves do walk, and pots in every place they skink,[2]
Wherewith the holy fathers oft to pleasant damsels drink.

In the ancient Offices of the Church of England, among the various observances connected with the ceremony, was the passing round of the "loving cup" (called in the Rubric *caritatis potum*) after the washing of feet and the sermon which followed.[3] This *poculum caritatis*, or loving cup, was a survival of the wassail-bowl of Saxon times, which, instead of

---

[1] Stephen, *Common Prayer*, pp. 889-90.
[2] Skink, A.S. *Scenc*, to draw liquor.
[3] Blunt, *Ann. Common Prayer*.

195

being abolished on the introduction of Christianity, was adopted under the above name for use in religious ceremonies.

It is interesting to note that there are in some of our cathedral churches indications still remaining of the places where the ceremony of the washing of feet was performed.

> At York Minster, the Maundy seats are probably those in the north quire aisle; at Worcester in the east alley of the cloisters is a bench table anciently used at the Maundy. On a stone bench in the east cloister at Westminster sat the twelve beggars whose feet the Abbot washed, and under the nosing of the bench, still remain the copper eyes from which hung the carpet on which he knelt during the performance of the ceremony. At Lichfield and probably other cathedrals destitute of cloisters, the maundy ceremony took place in quires; the stalls and aumbries on the north side of the quire at York having probably some connection with the ceremonial.[1]

. In the Middle Ages kings, princes, and nobles kept their Maundy with much ceremony, records of which have been preserved in the accounts of the privy purse expenses of monarchs, the receipts and payments of great houses, and in the ancient chronicles of early historians. The first mention of the monarch's name in this connection appears to be that of Edward II, who, in the nineteenth year of his reign, washed the feet of fifty poor men.[2] In the following reign, Edward III, an order was given, 20th March, 1361, to John de Newbury, to buy and deliver to Thomas de Keynes, the King's Almoner, " 200 ells of cloth of Candlewykstrete, 50 pairs of slippers, 2 short towels of Paris [cloth], and 4 ells of linen of Flanders, for next *Cena Domini*."[3] In the next century, under the head of the privy expenses of Henry VII, there is an entry of six pounds and four pence to thirty-eight poor men, in alms, and one shilling and eight pence for thirty-eight small purses; this number corresponding with the King's age in that year. Who inaugurated the custom of making his benefactions correspond with the number of his own years of age does not clearly appear; but, as we have seen from the foregoing, the practice would seem to date at least as far back as the reign of Edward III in 1361, part of whose gifts consisted of fifty pairs of slippers, he being fifty years old at that time.

[1] Feasey, *Ancient Holy Week Ceremonials*, pp. 107, 109.
[2] Wardrobe Roll, 19 Ed. II, cited by Feasey, p. 110.
[3] Close Roll, 34 Ed. III.

MAUNDY CELEBRATIONS.

In 1502 the privy purse expenses of Elizabeth of York show a disbursement by her of three shillings and a penny for each of thirty-seven poor women upon "Shere Thursday." Also about this time the ceremony was carried out at the Church of St. Mary, Huntingdon, and at Barking Abbey, and doubtless by many others, records of which have perished.

Greatest of the nobles who held yearly celebrations of the Maundy was the fifth Earl of Northumberland (1477-1527). Of this we have a full account by the antiquary Grose, taken from the Northumberland Household Book, edited in 1770 by Bishop Percy. Here is shown minutely the Earl's method of distributing his gifts on that day, not only in his own person, but also for his wife and children. The household, we are told, was established upon the same plan, and with a splendour scarcely inferior to that of the Royal Court; and it is interesting to notice his custom with regard to the royal practice of apportioning the Maundy gifts according to the age of the giver. Here, too, we have a practical illustration of the old motto, " Noblesse oblige," in the constantly recurring formula, " To gyf to as manny as his Lordshipe is yeares of age *and one for the yeare of my Lordis aige to come.*"

Extracted from the voluminous accounts of the expenditure of this house, the following are the items relating exclusively to the Maundy. It will be noticed how curiously they are set out, according to the custom at that time, with an entire absence of punctuation, though with an attempt to supply its place by means of capital letters, and in a form entailing, to a non-legal mind, a vast amount of vain repetition:

> Al Manner of Things Yerly Geven by my Lorde for his Maundy ande my Laidis and his Lordshippis Children As the Consideracion Why more playnly hereafter folowyth.

> Furst My Lorde useth and accustomyth yerely uppon Maundy Thursday when his Lordship is at home to gyf yerly as menny Gownes to as manny Poor Men as my Lorde is Yeres of Aige with Hoodes to them and one for the Yere of my Lordes Aige to Come Of Russet cloth after iij yerddes of Brode Cloth in every Gowne and Hoode Ande after xijd the brode Yerde of Clothe
> Item My Lorde useth ande accustomyth yerly uppon Maundy Thursday when his Lordship is at Home to gyf yerly as manny Sherts of Lynnon Cloth to as manny Poure Men as his Lordshipe is Yers of Aige ande one for the Yere of my Lords Aige

to come After ij yerdes dim. [*dimidius* = half] in every shert and after . . . the yerde

Item My Lorde useth and accustomyth yerly uppon the said Maundy Thursday when his Lordshipe is at Home to gyf yerly as manny Iren Platers [wooden trenchers] after ob. [*obolus*, a halfpenny] the pece with a Cast of Brede and a Certen Meat in it to as manny Poure Men as his Lordship is Yeres of Aige and one for the Yere of my Lordis Aige to come

Item My Lorde useth and accustomyth yerly upon the said Maundy Thursday when his Lordship is at home to gyf yerely as many Eshen [ashen] Cuppis after ob. the pece with Wyne in them to as many Poure Men as his Lordship is Yeres of Aige and one for the Yere of my Lordis Aige to come

Item. My Lorde useth and accustomyth yerly uppon the said Maundy Thursday when his Lordshipe is at home to gyf yerly as manny Pursses of Lether after ob. the pece with as manny Penys in every purse to as many poore men as his Lordshipe is Yeres of Aige and one for the Yere of my Lords Aige to come

Item. My Lorde useth and accustomyth yerely uppon Maundy Thursday to cause to be bought iij Yerdis and iij Quarters of Brode Violett Cloth for a Gowne for his Lordshipe to doo service in Or for them that schall doo service in his Lordshypes Absence After iiij*s* viij*d* the Yerde And to be furrede with Blake Lamb Contenynge ij Keippe and a half after xxx skynnes in a kepe and vj*s* iij*d* the kepe and after ij ob. the skynne and after Lxxv skynns for Furringe of the said Gowne Which Gowne my Lorde werith all the tyme his Lordship doith service And after his Lordship hath don his service at his said Maundy doith gyf to the pourest man that he fyndeth as he thynkyth emongs them all the said Gowne

Item. My Lorde useth and accustomyth yerly upon the said Maundy Thursday to caus to be delyvered to one of my Lordis Chaplayns[1] for my Lady If she be at my Lordis fyndynge and not at her owen To comaunde hym to gyf for her as manny Groits to as manny Poure Men as her Ladyshipe is Yeres of Aige and one for the Yere of hir Aige to come Owte of my Lordis Coffueres if sche be not at hir owen fyndynge

Item. My Lorde useth and accustomyth yerly uppon the said Maundy Thursday to caus to be delyvered to one of my Lordis Chaplayns for my Lordis Eldest Sone the Lord Percy For hym to comaunde to gyf for hym as manny Pens of ij Pens to as manny Poure Men as his Lordshipe is Yeres of Aige and one for the Yere of his Lordshipes aige to come

---

[1] There were eleven priests in the Earl's household.

Item My Lorde useth and accustomyth yerly uppon Maundy Thursday to cause to be delyverit to one of my Lordis Chaplayns for every of my Yonge Maisters My Lordis Yonger Sones To gyf for every of them as manny Pens to as manny Poore Men as every of my said Maisters is yeeres of Aige and for the Yere to come.

As an instance of the way in which the ceremony was observed by a prince of the Church, we find that about the same time as the foregoing illustration, Cardinal Wolsey, in the hey-day of his prosperity, made a grand progress with a body of 160 followers from Richmond to Peterborough, and there kept Maundy Thursday and the Easter celebrations. The event is thus quaintly chronicled by Holinshed:

Then prepared the Cardinal for his journey into the North, and sent to London for liverie clothes for his servants, and so rode from Richmond to Hendon, from thence to a place called the Rie; the next day to Raistone [Royston] where he lodged in the Priorie; the next daie to Huntingdon and there lodged in the Abbeie; the next day to Peterborow and there lodged in the Abbeie, where he abode all the next weeke and there he kept his Easter, his train was in number an hundred and three score persons. Upon Maundie thursdaie he made his maundie, there having nine and fiftie poore men, whose feet he washed, and gave everie one twelve pence in monie, three els of good canvas, a paire of shoes, a cast of red herrings, and three white herrings, and one of them had two shillings.[1]

In this reign also Catherine of Arragon, while Queen, had been accustomed to celebrate the day; but after her divorce she was forbidden by the King to do so (1533), except under the title of Princess Dowager.

In the two next reigns, Mary and Elizabeth, we reach what we have called the highest development of the Maundy as a religious and royal ceremonial, and in reading the account of Queen Mary's observance of the day it is apparent to all, as it was to the narrator, how great was the fervour of her devotion, not only to the form but also to the spirit of the *mandatum*. The account is contained in a letter written by Marco Antonio Faitta, secretary to Cardinal Pole, the Pope's Legate in this country, to his correspondent, a Doctor of Divinity in Venice, and is dated 3rd April, 1556. After writing on other matters, he proceeds:

[1] Holinshed, vol. iii, p. 914.

199

and on Holy Thursday, at 3 o'clock in the afternoon, the most Serene Queen accompanied by the right reverend Legate and by the Council, entered a large hall,[1] at the head of which was my Lord Bishop of Ely, as Dean of the Queen's Chaplains, with the Choristers of her Majesty's chapel. Around the hall on either side there were seated on certain benches, with their feet on stools, many poor women to the number of forty and one, such being the number of the years of the most Serene Queen. Then one of the menials of the Court, having washed the right foot of each of these poor persons, and this function being also next performed by the Under-Almoner, and also by the Grand Almoner, who is the Bishop of Chichester, her Majesty next commenced the ceremony in the following manner:

At the entrance of the Hall, there was a great number of the chief dames and noble ladies of the Court, and they prepared themselves by putting on a long linen apron which reached the ground, and round their necks they placed a towel, the two ends of which remained pendant at full length on either side, each of them carrying a silver ewer, and they had flowers in their hands, the Queen also being arrayed in like manner. Her Majesty knelt down on both her knees before the first of the poor women and taking in her left hand the woman's right foot, she washed it with her own right hand, drying it very thoroughly with the towel which hung at her neck, and having signed it with the cross, she kissed the foot so fervently that it seemed as if she were embracing something very precious. She did the like by all and each of the other poor women, one by one, each of the ladies, her attendants, giving her in turn their basin and ewer and towel; and I vow to you that in all her movements and gestures, and by her manner she seemed to act thus not merely out of ceremony, but from great feeling and devotion. Amongst these demonstrations there was this one remarkable, that in washing the feet, she went the whole length of that long hall from one end to the other, ever on her knees. Having finished and risen on her feet, she went back to the head of the hall and commenced giving in turn to each of the poor women a large wooden platter with enough food for four persons, filled with great pieces of salted fish, and two large loaves, and thus she went a second time distributing these alms. She next returned a third time, to begin again, giving to each of the women a wooden bowl filled with wine, or rather, I think, hippocras; after which for the fourth time she returned and gave to

---

[1] Query, Somerset-House.

each of those poor people a piece of cloth of royal mixture for clothing. Then returning for the fifth time she gave to each a pair of shoes and stockings ; for the sixth time she gave to each a leathern purse, containing fortyone pennies, according to the number of her own years, and which in value may amount to rather more than half an Italian golden crown;[1] finally, going back for the seventh time, she distributed all the aprons and towels which had been carried by those dames and noble ladies, in number forty-one, giving each with her own hand.

Her Majesty then quitted the hall to take off the gown she had worn, and half an hour afterwards she returned, being preceded by an attendant carrying the said gown, and thus she went twice round the hall, examining very closely all the poor women one by one, and then returning for the third time, she gave the said gown to the one who was in fact the poorest and most aged of them all ; and this gown was of the finest purple cloth lined with Marten's fur, and with sleeves so long and wide that they reached the ground. During the ceremony the choristers chaunted the *miserere*, with certain other psalms, reciting at each verse the words: *In diebus illis mulier quæ erat in civitate peccatrix.* I will not omit telling you that on Holy Thursday alms were distributed here in the Court to a great amount to upwards of 3000 persons.[2]

An incidental testimony to the importance known to be attached by the Queen to this Lenten observance occurs in a list of the presents received by her on New Year's Day. These were given, for the most part, by high dignitaries of Church and State, nobles, and titled ladies, and were both numerous and costly; but among gifts, presumably from the more humble members of the Court, such as flowers, fruit, sweetmeats, trinkets, and needlework, it is especially interesting to notice, "a table painted with the Maundy"; and again, "a table of needleworke of the Maundy."[3]

Queen Elizabeth appears to have closely followed the example set by her sister in most particulars, save perhaps as

[1] The golden crown and the Venetian sequin were of equal value, so it is thus seen that in the course of two centuries and a half the standard of the English silver coinage had been so debased that the sequin, which in 1410 could be purchased in London for $30\frac{1}{2}d$. was worth 82 pence in the year 1556. The value of the sequin in English money in 1410 is ascertained by a document registered in the Venetian Calendar, vol. iv, p. 451.

[2] *Calendar of State Papers* (Venetian), vol. vi, p. 428.

[3] J. Nichols, *Illus. Manners and Expences of Ancient Times.*

to the extent of her personal humiliation, and to have made elaborate preparation for her Maundy by Royal Warrant. That for the year 1578 is addressed to the Keeper of the Great Wardrobe in the following terms:

> Wee will and commaund you that immediatelye upon the sight hereof ye do liver or cause to be delyvered to our well beloved servante, Raufe Hope, Yeoman of our Wardrobe of robes, for th'use of our Mawndye, and our sayd Wardrobe theyse parcelles of stuffe followinge, that is to say, first, one hundred thirtye and fyve yerdes of russet cloth, to make fourety and three gownes [*sic*] for fouretye and fyve poore women; and fouretye and fyve peire of single soled showes for them. Item, two hundrethe fyvetye and eight elles of lynen cloth, as well to make smockes for the said poore women, as also to be employed in the service of our said Mawndye. Item, twentie and sixe peire of bearinge and trussinge sheetes of two bredthes and a half of Hollande cloth, and two elles thre quarters longe the pere. Item, thirtye elles of diaper of elle quarter brode; and eighteene napkyns cont' one elle long the pere, for thuse of our said wardrobe. Item, one peire of presse sheetes, of fower bredthes of Holland cloth, and nyne elles long the pere. Item, one curten for a presse, of lynen cloth, cont' seven bredthes and two elles longe. Item, thirtye elles of canvas, and the boultes of stronge rope to trusse the said stuff in, and that ye content and paye for making of the premisses; and also for carriadge of the same from our greate Wardrobe to the place wheare, God willing, we shall make our said Maundye. And theyse our ìres signed with our owne hande, shal be your sufficient warrante and dischardge in this behalf annempst us, our heires and successors.
>
> Geoven under out Signett at our Pallaise at Westm' the 12th day of Marche, the 21st Yeare of our reigne
>
> Jo. Saru.
>
> To our trustie and well beloved servannte, John Forteskewe, esquire, Maister of our Greate Wardrobe
>
> Ex' p̃ N. Pigeon.[1]

For a detailed illustration of Queen Elizabeth's celebration of Maundy Thursday we must go back from the date of this warrant to the year 1572. The Court was at this time held at Greenwich, and the account proceeds:

> First the hall was prepared with a long table on each side, and forms set by them; on the edges of which tables, and

---

[1] J. Nichols, *Illus. Manners, etc., in Ancient Times.*

under these forms were laid carpets and cushions for her Majesty to kneel when she should wash them. There was also another table set across the upper end of the hall, somewhat above the foot pace, for the Chaplain to stand at. A little beneath the midst whereof, and beneath the said foot pace, a stool and cushion of estate was pitched for her Majesty to kneel at during the service time. This done, the holy water, basins, alms, and other things being brought into the hall, and the Chaplain and poor folks having taken the said places, the laundress, armed with a fair towel, and taking a silver basin filled with warm water and sweet flowers, washed their feet all after one another, and wiped the same with his towel, and so making a cross a little above the toes, kissed them. After him within a little while followed the sub-almoner doing likewise, and after him the almoner himself also. Then lastly, her Majesty came into the hall and after some singing and prayers made, and the Gospel of Christs' washing of his disciples' feet read, thirty nine ladies and gentlewomen (for so many were the poor folks, according to the number of yeares complete of her Majesty's age) addressed themselves with aprons and towels to wait upon her Majesty; and she kneeling down upon the cushions and carpets under the feet of the poor women, first washed one foot of every one of them in so many several basins of warm water and sweet flowers, brought to her severally by the said ladies and gentlewomen, then wiped, crossed, and kissed them as the almoner and others had done before. When her Majesty had thus gone through the whole number of thirty-nine (of which twenty sat on the one side of the hall and nineteen on the other) she resorted to the first again, and gave to each one certain yards of broadcloth to make a gown, so passing to them all. Thirdly, she began at the first, and gave to each of them a pair of shoes. Fourthly, to each of them a wooden platter whereon was half a side of salmon, as much ling, six red herrings and cheat [manchet] loaves of bread. Fifthly, she began with the first and gave to each of them a white wooden dish with claret wine. Sixthly, she received of each waiting lady and gentlewoman their towel and apron, and gave to each poor woman one of the same; and after this the ladies and gentlewomen waited no longer, nor served as they had done throughout the courses before. But the treasurer of the Chamber, Mr Heneage, came to her Majesty with thirty nine small white purses wherein were also thirty nine pence (as they say) after the number of years to her Majesty's said age, and of him she received and distributed them severally. Which done she received of him so many leather purses also, each containing twenty shillings for the redemption of her

Majesty's gown which (so men say) by ancient order she ought to give some of them at her pleasure: but she, to avoid the trouble of suit, which accustomably was made for that preferment, had changed that reward into money, to be equally divided among them all, namely, twenty shillings apiece, and she also delivered particularly to the whole company. And so taking her ease upon the cushion of estate, and hearing the choir a little while, her Majesty withdrew herself and the company departed: for it was by that time the sun was setting.[1]

One deviation from long established usage may here be noticed in the procedure of the Queen, who no longer gives away the royal robe. The cause for this would seem to have been some little difficulty as to its bestowal, here delicately alluded to as "the trouble of suit which accustomably was made for that preferment." In one of her earlier celebrations (1559-60) it is recorded that Elizabeth "gave to twenty poor women so many gowns, and one of them had her best gown," a circumstance which fixes this reign as the period when the old custom was abandoned in favour of a money payment "for the redemption of the gown."

Not every year, however, could Elizabeth carry out this elaborate ritual. In 1564 a proclamation was issued remitting the distribution of the Maundy by the Queen in person, though alms were ordered to be given to the poor of Windsor and Eton. The reason assigned was because of the " present time of contagious sickness."[2] There was at this time a terrible visitation of the plague, which appears to have been very fatal in its results, and is thus commented upon by Grafton in his *Chronicle*:

> The infection mervelously encreased in sundry places, but most chiefly in the citie of London, so that there dyed in the sayd citie and suburbs of the same, conteyning 108 parishes, from the sixt day of April unto the last day of November next following, 23660 persons. And at the first entraunce of thys plague into the Cytie, the Maior and his brethren tooke order that at such houses as were infected therewyth, should have a headlesse Crosse, coloure blewe, wyth thys wrytyng under the foote of the same, *Per signum Tau*, set over the streete doore, but these crosses encreased so sore and the citizens were crossed away so fast, that at lengthe they were faine to leave their crosses and to referre ye matter to God's good mercifull hand.

---

[1] J. Nichols, *Royal Progresses*, p. 37.
[2] *Misc. State Papers*, 1561, p. 26.

The accounts of the prayers and ceremonies used by the House of Stuart for Maundy Thursday are preserved in the Royal Cheque Book, from which it appears that the washing of feet was performed by a more expeditious method than that formerly in use. This consisted in sprinkling the feet of the poor with a sprig of hyssop dipped in water, and afterwards wiping and kissing them; the distribution of gifts and the prayers interspersed with anthems being continued as before. The service concluded by the almoner calling for wine to drink the King's health, and bidding the poor to be thankful to God and pray for the King.[1] The last English monarch who thus observed the ancient ceremony of washing the feet of the poor was James II, a brief record of which, to the following effect, is contained in an old book still preserved at Somerset House: "On Maundy Thursday, April 16th, Our Gracious King James ye 2nd, washed, wiped, and kissed the feet of 52 poor men, with wonderful humility."

Under the Hanoverian sovereigns, this part of the ceremony was deputed to the Lord Almoner. The account of the proceedings in the year 1731 is given in the pages of the *Gentleman's Magazine*—this year, by the way, being the first appearance of that valuable (styled by Cowper "immortal") repository of contemporary and other information:

Thursday, April 15th, 1731, being Maundy Thursday, there was distributed at the Banquetting House, Whitehall, to 48 poor men and 48 poor women (the King's age being 48) boiled Beef, shoulders of Mutton, and small bowls of Ale, which is called dinner; after that large wooden platters of Fish and Loaves, viz. undressed, 1 large old Ling,[2] and one large dried Cod; 12 red Herrings, and 4 half quarter Loaves; each person had one platter of this Provision. After which was distributed to them, Shoes, Stockings, Linen and Woollen Cloth and leathern bags with one penny, two penny, three penny and four penny pieces of silver, to each about £4 in value. His Grace the Lord Archbishop of York, Lord High Almoner, performed the ceremony of washing the feet of a certain number of poor people in the Chapel Royal, Whitehall, formerly done by the Kings themselves. •

---

[1] Feasey, p. iii.

[2] *Ling*, now seldom heard of, was formerly much esteemed. Fuller in his *Worthies*, treating of the extent of our fisheries before the Civil Wars, speaks of upwards of 200 ships being engaged, "Chiefly for the taking of Ling, that noble Fish, co-rival in his joule with the surloin of Beef at the tables of Gentlemen."

MAUNDY CELEBRATIONS.

The washing of the feet as a Maundy observance seems to have entirely disappeared since 1736. In that year the Archbishop of York distributed at Whitehall to fifty-three poor persons alms consisting of food, clothing, twenty shillings in lieu of the King's robe, and fifty-three pence for the maundy coin. In the following year, alms, with fifty-four pence were given, the washing being omitted, and since that time it has formed no part of the ceremony. The Yeomen of the Guard, who still attend, were until the last twenty-five years always covered during the service.[1]

To check the bartering which frequently took place with the gifts in kind, they have gradually been replaced by money payments, and now the maundy alms are composed entirely of money, apportioned in the following manner: (1) The gift of pence at the rate of one penny for each year of the sovereign's age, given in a white leather purse; (2) sums of £1 10s. in lieu of provisions, and £1 inclosed in a red leather purse in lieu of the gown formerly given from the royal wardrobe; (3) a further gift of 35s. to the women and 45s. to the men in lieu of clothing, this last gift being inclosed in a paper packet. The ceremony of the distribution of the maundy alms was, with some exceptions during alterations in the building, performed in the Chapel Royal, Whitehall, from 1714 to 1890, and (the chapel having been closed) since that time in Westminster Abbey.[2] The order of service for the Maundy is mainly that used for Matins, interspersed with special anthems having reference to the ceremony.[3]

With regard to the denominations of the silver pieces known as Maundy money, the penny is by far the most ancient and dates back to the time of the Mercian King, Offa (757-796).

Down to and for some time after the reign of King John the penny was the chief coin in general circulation, and, according to the following statement in Harrison's dissertation, prefixed to Holinshed's *Chronicle*, not before the time of Edward I did it take a circular form. Having prefaced his remarks by the naïve confession, "The Saxon Coine before the Conquest is in maner utterlie unknown to me" he proceeds:

[1] Feasey's *Ancient Holy Week Ceremonial.*
[2] Information derived from the Mint.
[3] The service is fully set forth in Stephen's *Book of Common Prayer* under Thursday in Holy Week.

MAUNDY CELEBRATIONS.

> I read that King Edward in the eight year of his reign, did first coin the penie and smallest pieces of silver roundwise which before were square, and wont to beare a double crosse, with a crest, in such sort that the penie might easilie be broken either into halfes or quarters; by which shift onlie the people came by small monies, as half pence and fardings, that otherwise were not stamped nor coined of set purpose.

Round halfpennies, however, were coined during the reigns of Ælfred, Ædweard, and Ædred. They were also issued by John. Silver groats, which had appeared, probably as pattern coins, under Edward I, came into general use during the reign of Edward III, together with the half groat, while the threepenny piece was first issued by Edward VI.

Previous to the time of the Restoration, the Maundy money had always been furnished from the current coin, but under Charles II a new and special issue of small silver pieces was struck (1661) for the express purpose of the Maundy distribution. These coins, of which there were various issues, consisted in the first instance of hammered money, made by hand in the customary manner by striking the die with a hammer or mallet. Afterwards, in 1668, the Maundy money was produced by a new method termed "milling," and took on a new form, in which the various denominations were indicated by an ingenious device of interlinked Cs, the groat having, on the reverse, four Cs surmounted by the crown, and in the spandrels representations of the rose, thistle, fleur-de-lis, and harp; the threepenny piece bore three Cs; the twopenny, two; and the penny, one; these being without the national emblems.[1] Although a process of coining by the machinery of the "mill and screw" had previously been introduced here in 1561, it met with scant encouragement by the Mint authorities, nor did it entirely succeed in displacing the old system, but on its re-introduction by Charles II, milling was permanently adopted for all the coinage; pieces below the value of sixpence (viz., the Maundy coins), however, being produced with the smooth edge which has ever since been the practice.[2]

The novelty of the appearance of milled money on both these occasions would naturally have been much commented upon by the people and appears to have suggested the curious anachronism which occurs in a remark of one of Shakespeare's

---

[1] See illustration. [2] Fourpenny pieces had milled edges.—*Editor*.

characters. In the *Merry Wives of Windsor* Falstaff (*temp.* 1378-1459), addressing Pistol, says: "Pistol, did you pick Master Slender's purse?" to whom Slender replies: "Ay, by these gloves did he (or I would I might never come in mine own great chamber else) of seven groats in mill six-pences," etc.

Returning to our main subject, a brief reference to the more recent celebrations of Maundy Thursday will serve to show the precipitate decline in the ceremonial of this day as contrasted with that of former ages. At present even the etymologies of the name disappear, there being now no sign of either "maund" or *mandatum*, unless, indeed, with regard to the latter, we accept the girding on of perfunctory towels by the Almoner and his assistants as a sufficient indication. Nor, considering that this particular ceremony was in use up to the middle of the eighteenth century, do the modern apologists of the Church, on this matter, seem quite convincing in the statement: "The Church of England in later ages, has considered the commandment to follow our Lord's example in that particular [St. John, xiii, 14] as one which is not of a perpetual obligation."[1]

A report on the day following the most recent observance of Maundy Thursday, at Westminster Abbey, alludes to it as "a last remnant of the custom maintained for centuries." A form of prayer, and the money gifts to the poor, still remain, together with what is described as "a charming and splendid spectacle." But there must be many who regret that obedience to a direct precept should, after the practice of so many centuries, have been abandoned by the Anglican branch of the Catholic Church.

Subjoined are representations of the Maundy coins of Charles II, showing the device of interlinked Cs, together with specimens of those struck during the last year of Queen Victoria and the first year of King Edward VII.

[1] Blunt's *Annotated Prayer Book.*

Maundy Money.

SOME EAST KENT PARISH HISTORY.

By Peter de Sandwich.

[Continued from p. 134.]

CHERITON (now in Elham Deanery).

COLDRED.[1]

1557. (Cardinal Pole's Visitation?)

GEORGE BINGHAM for one pention [pension] which accustomably hath yearly been paid to the vicar of Coldred.

Henry Birche that he with holdeth two acres and a half of land from the Vicar of Coldred, which was given to the Vicars of Coldred for the time being by a deade [deed].

The Parson of Waldershare, for with holding a pension of 6s. by the year accustomed yearly to be paid to the Vicars of Coldred for certain lands lying within the bounds of Coldred, and the said Parson hath tithe thereof.

Margaret, dwelling with Mr. Eton, for that Mary Maudelyn's day [22 July] last past she went out of the church, as soon as the sacring bell was rung.

Mr. Geoffrey Eton, for at the sacring time he looketh upon his book and not upon the sacrament, and that he is a very envying [injuring?] to the church.—(Undated Vol., fols. 11, 44.)

Note.—This is an undated Volume of the reign of Queen Mary.

1560. That the Injunctions is [*sic*] not kept.

That there hath been delivered to Mr. Collins[2] to be burnt, the Communion Book, the Book of Omeles [*sic*], and the Sawter Book.—(Vol. 1560-84, fol. 20.)

1562. The parsonage-house is in great decay, and the church is not served with any curate.—(Vol. 1562-3.)

[1] Anciently in Sandwich Deanery.
[2] Robert Collins (or Colens) was Commissary to Abp. Pole, and Official to the Archdeacon, and deprived in 1559. A Canon of Wingham College at the suppression in 1547, when he received a pension.

1565. The chancel is in great decay and ruin, that is to say, in tiling, glazing and paveing.

That the parsonage-house was taken down by Mr. Geoffrey Eates, and he promised to build up the ruin within eight weeks the which he hath not done, but the timber of the said house lieth waste and suffers much harm.

1569. (Abp. Parker's Visitation.)

Rectory; appropriator, the Abp. of Canterbury.

Vicarage, in same patronage.

Vicar:—Dom Robert Bannister, who is married, does not reside there, but serves the cure himself; has also the vicarage of Shepherdswell in the same [Sandwich] Deanery, where he lives; not a preacher nor licensed to preach, and is not a graduate.

Householders, 13.
Communicants, 61.—(Fol. 21.)

That their parsonage-house is fallen down; the chancel in decay for lack of tiling, glazing and paveing.

The Vicar is not resident, and hath two benefices joining together.—(Vol. 1569.)

1586. The church roof is in decay.

1590. Whereas the church was somewhat in ruin and decayed by the weather, we have repaired some of it as soon as may be.

Our vicarage-house is ruinous, and hath been heretofore presented and not yet reformed.

1592. Our church wants reparations, and we desire time for the amendment of the same.

We present our Vicar, for we have not our quarterly sermons according to the Article, and the use in other parishes.— (Fol. 147.)

1594. The register-book is well kept, but their chest wanteth the locks appointed.

Their church wanteth reparation by reason of the last wind, also the chancel.—(Fol. 16.)

1597. Our chancel windows are out of repair which we present, but know not who ought to repair them.—(Fol. 82.)

1598. Thomas Jekyn being cessed for the necessary repairs of our church, at the sum of 2s. 8d., he refuseth to pay the same.—(Fol. 90.)

1600. George Brett refuseth to pay his cess towards the repair of the church.

The chancel is not sufficiently repaired, nor the church.

1601. Stephen Pilcher refuses to pay his part of the cess made for the use of our church, being the sum of 4s. 8d.— (Fol. 134.)

1604. Concerning the bill aforesaid it is answered by the Churchwarden of the parish of Coldred under his hand, that the church is not repaired as it ought to be, by reason the parishioners cannot agree about a rate, so that he the Churchwarden knoweth not how to have that amended which is amiss, not able himself to disburse such sums of money as thereunto are necessarily required, as also he saith there yet wanteth a new service-book for the cause aforesaid.

1605. Our Communion cloth is not decent. We have not the Ten Commandments. There is no chest for alms given to the poor. Our church wants reparations. The churchyard is not fenced with any other fence than a hedge. The Churchwardens have not given any account for the last year. We have no Table of Degrees of marriages forbidden. We have neither comely pulpit-cloth or cushion. The going of the perambulation of our parish hath been neglected for this year last past.—(Fol. 44.)

Our Minister doth not read the Litany nor the Commination against sinners, neither indeed reads any service on these days in our parish-church.

Our Minister doth not wear the surplice at public-prayers, and but seldom at the ministering of the Communion, neither doth he wear any hood.

We have the Canons, but these have not been read as yet publicly in our parish church.—(Fol. 50.)

1606. Whereas it is ordered in the 59 Canon that servants shall obediently hear and be ordered by the Minister during the time of Catechism. So it is, very notable abuse hath been offered in the church to my person (I mean in regard of my place and office) by John Broadbridge, servant to Richard Minbrie of Coldred, and John Ashley, servant to Steven Pilcher of that parish, who have not only been very negligent in coming, but also most unreverent when they are present, froward in their answers, in behaviour very scoffing, distempering the whole company of youth, refusing to be instructed, either departing out of the church afore we have done, drawing others with them into the churchyard, there to glory in their doings, with neglect of Evening Prayer; or else, when they do stay, they use the place as though it were ordered for scurrility. And especially it is reported and much spoken of by persons very credible, who were much grieved thereat, that Ashley, as soon as I began Evening Prayer and so had my back towards him, made the Communion Table his stool, and then made merry at me, to the offence of many.—(Fol. 56.)

We want a lock and key to the coffer in which our book of christenings, marriages and burials remains.

We have not the Ten Commandments set upon the church, neither is the seat where our Minister sitteth convenient, for there wanteth a desk whereon to lay the books.

We want a door to the pulpit, neither have we a chest for to receive that which is given to the poor.

The floor of the church is not paved, nor have we the table of degrees of marriages forbidden, in our parish church.

We want a pulpit cloth and a large and comely surplice.—(Fol. 62.)

1607. Thomas Jenkin refuseth to pay his cess towards the raparation of our church, the sum of 37s. 6d.

1608. Thomas Jenkin refuses to pay his cess made for the reparation of our church, and certain ornaments in the same to be provided, the sum he is cessed at is 37s.

1609. Our church is not well repaired in default of the Churchwardens, and also the churchyard is unfenced.

We have not a sufficient carpet for our Communion Table. We have no pot of pewter to put the wine in for the Communion; nor a box for the money for the poor.—(Vol. 1602-9.)

1618. Joan Rose, wife of Arnold Rose (or Miller) of the parish of Coldred, for railing and scolding at her neighbours, and especially for railing at our Minister, Mr. Mark Grace-borrow, as the fame is in our parish.—(Fol. 196.)

Edward Jenkin, for not paying his cess towards the reparation of our parish church, he being divers times demanded the said cess, namely the sum of 11s.

Edward Jenkin, when Churchwarden, about four years ago, did disburse about the parish business £3 or thereabouts more than he received by his cesses; and that William Ponet and John Coppin, the succeeding Churchwardens there, or one of them, did pay unto Edward Jenkin in part payment of the £3, the sum of 8s. or thereabouts, and in the name of the parishioners of Coldred did promise payment of the residue, out of such cesses as afterwards should be made in the parish towards the parish business, which now they refuse or deny to pay.—(Fol. 197; vol. 1610-37.)

1623. Richard Smyth of our parish, sidesman, for that he did work at the harrow and rowle [roll] on one of the Holy Days happening in Easter week last past, as the common fame is in our parish, of which offence we came to have notice pointed out, since the presentment ordered at Easter last.—(Fol. 95.)

1631. Our vicarage-house is much gone to decay in the timber work and walls thereof, in Mr. Graceborrow our Vicar's default.—(Fol. 163.)

1633. A part of the fence of our churchyard is at reparations and in decay, in the default as I conceive of Thomas Philpot, esquire, farmer of our parsonage; for that the same part hath heretofore usually been repaired, as occasion required, by the farmer of the parsonage for the time being; and another part of the fence about our churchyard is likewise in decay, in the default of John Pile of our parish, who hath promised speedily to repair the same.—(Fol. 190; vol. 1610-37, part ii.)

[To be continued.]

THE FRIENDS' MEETING AT COGGES-HALL.

By A. B. WALLIS CHAPMAN, D.Sc.

ONE of the most interesting features of the pleasant little town of Coggeshall in Essex is the long-established Friends' Meeting. This particular branch of the Society of Friends has had a continuous existence for more than two hundred and thirty years. Its minute books, which are still extant, date from the year 1672.

These books, which, by the kindness of Mr. Doubleday, of Coggeshall, I have been allowed to examine, give a curious picture of the early growth of this little religious community. Already, in 1672, the Friends in Coggeshall must have been an established body, with recent traditions of courage and of suffering. The imprisonment and death of James Parnell in Colchester Gaol must have been fresh in their memories;[1] but during the years succeeding the commencement of these minutes such persecution as the Members of the Society underwent was less violent, and was chiefly caused by their attitude in regard to the payment of tithes and the ceremony of marriage.

About these points their rules were of the strictest. Indeed, their whole discipline was severe; necessarily so, perhaps, in an infant community maintaining itself with difficulty against the outside world. The earliest entry in the minute-book (11th January, 1671-2) is a declaration against those who sometimes frequented the meeting, but had relapsed into worldliness; against those who were profane or drunken, or cozeners of other men's money; and, above all, against those who " have run to the preists for husbands and for wives." About fifteen persons, who had been admonished in vain, were " disassociated."

Complaints of delinquents who " ran to the preists for a marriage," are of frequent occurrence throughout these early minute-books, though it was the only *legal* method then exist-

---

[1] James Parnell, a youth of nineteen, one of the earliest of the Quaker martyrs, was imprisoned in Colchester Gaol, and there died in 1655. It is said that his death was caused by the brutality of his gaolers.

ing for contracting marriages. That numerous "Friends" were, however, strong enough to defy law and convention on this point is shown by the frequent records of weddings. The second entry is of this nature:

> Upon the first day of the third month, Lawrence Candler and Elizabeth Knight, both of Fearinge, did at the monthly men's meeting lay before freinds . . . their intention of taking each other to husband and wife, and freinds then left buissnes to John Raven and James Carberton to enquire wheather they were cleare from any other person each of them, whoe did upon the third of the fourth month certifie freinds that they made enquiry and did finde them cleare.

After this account there is a ten years' gap, but in 1682 the first entries are those of four marriages; in these cases, however, the record seems to be simply one of marriage "with the consent of friends." There is no question of investigation.

It is noteworthy, as showing the degree of education among the "Friends," that in the majority of cases the bride and bridegroom sign their names, instead of making their marks, the bridegroom signing more frequently than the bride.

The brevity of the notes concerning the batch of marriages in 1682 may possibly arise from the fact that the "Meeting" had scarcely yet established itself in a regular groove. There are occasional hints that some "Friends" had not yet quite accommodated themselves to their new habits; such as when, in 1692, the clerk, by a slip of the pen, writes "December" for "twelfth month." The meeting, too, was still in process of development: in 1692 (when, to judge by the change in the handwriting, a new clerk must have been appointed), the meeting becomes the "men's *and women's* meeting," the first occasion in the records on which both sexes are mentioned as co-equal members of the society. It is a natural corollary from this that a few years later two men and two women Friends are set to investigate the "clearness" of a would-be bride and bridegroom.

In 1692 the Meeting adopted a further method of satisfying itself in the case of marriages by receiving certificates. John Bale of Colchester, wishing to marry Elizabeth Evans, brought three certificates to satisfy the Friends, one from his father and mother, one from London, and one from Colchester, which had been his last place of residence; while, some years later (1703), Joseph Sanderson, of Spittlefield, wishing to marry

215

Elizabeth Bell of Kelvedon, produced a certificate from London, signed by twenty-one Friends. As the sect increased in numbers, these certificates probably became more necessary; for on 5th July, 1698, "It is desired that all friends living out of ye Division in which they intend to take a wife that they do at the first monthly meating they appear at, bring a certificate from there owne meeting unto which they do belong to satisfye ye freinds that all things are cleare."

Such a certificate was by no means always easy to obtain, as George Clark of Halsted found when he applied to the meeting for a certificate. He had "gone to the priest" for his former wife, and "had given no satisfaction"; so he was now desired to wait a month.

From regulating marriages to supervising love-affairs was a short step. On "the 6th 2nd mo. 1695," a Friend was "spoken with" (*i.e.* admonished) about a report concerning himself and a certain widow: "Wee found the man in a very tender frame of spirit, and he did acknowledge that he had given sum ocation by carrying of her abroad . . . and he tould us forasmuch as she hath denied me for to have nothing to do with her concerning marridge which was to our satisfaction"!

All Friends did not, however, take rebuke so meekly when it touched a delicate subject. The widow Page, when admonished in a similar affair by two men and two women, "sleyted our advice . . . It was her owne concern and nobodies ellse!"

A broken engagement was a very serious matter; such a case occurred in 1673, when a young couple, who had previously wished to take each other for husband and wife, "desired to flee each other." The Friends examined the business, and found that there was no contract, so they were willing to leave them free. "Yet afterwards the mother of the mayde said that they had parted them that had made a contract with each other." Whereon ensued renewed investigation; and not till the youth and girl had affirmed *several times* before the meeting that there had never been any contract between them, were they looked on as "clear of each other and each of them had their freedom to take any other as by the Lord they shall be directed." On the whole, a breach of promise suit would probably have been less embarrassing; yet the intervention of the meeting seems sometimes to have been welcomed by lovers, as in the case of Mathew Delle and Betsy Charden in 1697, who, when spoken with about the "grate delay in there intended maridge," said it was "becaus of the surconstances of the house"; and they would be glad of Friends' help to put an end to them. "She say she will not marry till it be ended."

Matrimonial difficulties were not the only causes which the Meeting took under its care. In fact, as the Friends declined to resort to worldly tribunals, the Meeting necessarily became a court of justice and appeal, with, however, only one penalty in its power, that of "disassociation." Persons guilty of profanity, drunkenness, debt, and the taking of oaths, were rebuked and advised by individuals appointed for the purpose by the Meeting: women being usually sent to rebuke women, and men, men. Generally the culprit came voluntarily to confession, as in the case of Thomas Perry in 1704-5, who owned that "he has caused truth to be evil spoken of . . . by contracting of debts more than I could answer . . . for which I have felt the just judgement of God upon me. . . . So I hope I shall be more carefull and not doe anything whereby I may bring Dishonour to Truth and Exercise to them that walk therein. . . . So I desire you may pass my offence so that I may be in Unity with you."

Like the greater world without, this little community had to deal with the question of heresy. In 1699 Thomas Turner and Joseph Simpson were in high argument whether or no a certain George Kieth was an orthodox preacher; Turner affirming, Simpson denying that he "spoke against truth"; and a little later Simpson himself advanced the doctrine that "we shall be saved by the light within us, and doe not own what Christ hath done without us." He declined to be argued out of his opinions, and was finally told severely that "The truth would be Cleere and ye people of it will be cleere of him."

In various other ways did this tiny state within a state show a sense of its responsibilities. In 1703 it commenced to keep a register of births and burials. The care of the poor was early an object of attention. In 1698 Giles Sayer of Colchester came to the monthly meeting in Coggeshall, and did "deliver to the men's freinds, £6; and four pound to the women's monthly meeting in Coggeshall . . . being ten pound given poor people calld Quakers in and about Coggeshall by Sarah Mootham deceased." And this was only one of a series of legacies devised for similar purposes. But the Friends by no means relied on legacies. Collections for the poor were made at stated times; and the zeal of the subscribers appears in the following entry, 30th of the ninth month, 1704. "We whose names are subscribed underneath are freely willing to make good our places on ye days yt are for collection for ye Poor if we should be absent on those days that ye collection is called for"; to which declaration seventeen signatures are appended. The sense of responsibility must have been very strong in these men, most of whom appear to have been farmers, artisans, tradesmen and the like.

The money obtained by legacies and collections was frequently distributed in small weekly pensions to poor Friends. A pretty touch in connection with these pensions was the application of an old woman in 1700, "who did speak to Edward Mines of her owne accord that sixpence a week less might serve her occasion, whereas she used to have two shillings and threepence ye week: this I acquainted friends with at our two meetings." Sometimes a lump sum would be disbursed in gifts; William Abrams, for instance, gave 50s. in 1704, which was distributed among five poor Friends in gifts, varying in amount from £1 to 6d. Sometimes, both the money and the goods of a deceased friend were applied to charity. In 1704 Anne Hazlewood died and the Friends seem to have acted as her executors. They expended £1 6s. 6d. in her funeral; 17s. 6d. for the Queen's taxes and the "Coffen"; and applying the rest to common purposes, they laid out, for Samuel Clarke's son, 13s. 9d., paid the half year's rent of Mary Addem, 14s., lent to one Friend to reimburse another, 3s. 9d., and for a new collection book, 3s. The total was £3 18s. 6d., and the Meeting still had sevenpence in hand. In addition to this, however, certain kitchen utensils of Anne Hazlewood's were lent to another Friend; to wit, "A Glass case, A puter dish, 3 earthern dishes, a ketle, a porage pott, a skillet, a frying pann, a stooll and a Tea-mill."

The relief of the poor must have formed the largest part of the financial affairs of the meeting; but the Friends had other and serious calls; such, for instance, as the rent of the meeting-house chamber itself; this rent though not high, ten shillings a year, had in 1704 been in arrears for eight years. Then, too, there were gifts to other Meetings, as when "Coxall subscribed 20s. towards repairing the meeting house at Coulne." There was, of course, the cost of lights for their own meeting, and its furnishing, though this was probably scanty; in 1703 they paid five shillings and sixpence to Edward Mines for "two tables and Tressels and a chair in ye Meeting House." Another piece of furniture was provided in 1706: "It is agreed by this meeting there should be a cubard either at the stand or upon the shelf to lock up our books in as friends do think conveant." These books may have been certain volumes which appear to have been lent out among members of the Society. Among them were George Foxe's *Journal* and *Epistles*, and Thomas Ellwood's *Foundation of Tithes*.

This last work touches a burning question of the day: the greatest difficulty under which the little society laboured was the resistance they felt it necessary to make to the payment of tithes; and the consequent troubles of many individual members are recorded in these books. About 1700 appears, "A Coppey of the suffering of Andrew Hills. Upon the 9th and 22nd day of 6th mo. Andrew Hills of Fearinge had taken from him by John Hamon and Robert Guyon and other seruants to Henry Abbott Junor of Earles Coulne, tieth farmer under John Cotton, Impropreator, out of corn, thirty-four pounds; two loads of barley, a load of peese £6."

The Friends were earnestly encouraged to keep up their resistance. Richard Adely was "exorted" to faithfulness in the matter and to be very careful to "keep his sone clear." If tithes were paid for any person, it was regarded as a reproach against them. In 1701 Thomas Houchen "protested with weeping eyes that he knew nothing of his brother and his sons paying Richard Hane for James Boyes . . . and when he came to Feering and did see his Tumbrell and his mares which were distrained from him for tythes, he was struck at the sight of it and did say he did hoope he should in some time moore get out of that snarld case . . . speaking with weeping eyes."

But despite all difficulties with tithe-collectors outside and recalcitrant members inside, the little community flourished; by 1724 it had fairly settled down into an even course of life, a vigorous body itself, and a centre for numerous lesser meetings in the neighbourhood. It continued to grow throughout the eighteenth century, developing among its members such habits of strict discipline and neighbourly co-operation, such a deep sense of individual and common responsibility, as must have gone far to render them true citizens of the wider national state.

DOWNING STREET AND ITS EARLY HISTORY.

By Percy C. Rushen.

READERS of a certain popular London daily were recently reminded of the obscure origin and topographical history of the world-renowned Downing Street. Bearing in mind that this obscure street is the heart of our Empire, it is astonishing how little throwing a light on its early history is to be found recorded apart from the great official names associated with it. This being the case, the contents of an old deed dealing with the unpretentious property formerly standing against the street and of which a part still remains as the official residence of the Premier, will be of interest and perhaps of value.

The deed is dated 8th June, 1803, and made between James Martin, formerly of Whitehall, late of Downing Street, and then of Great George Street, Westminster, of the one part, and the United Company of Merchants of England trading to the East Indies, of the other part. The recitals are lengthy, and from them a good deal of information may be gathered.

It appears that by Letters Patent, dated 5th February, 1752, King George II leased to Sir Jacob Gerrard Downing, in consideration of a fine of £1,000 and a rent of £9 per annum, for a term which with that then in being would make up fifty years, a piece of ground at the west end of Downing Street, abutting on the east on a house then lately repaired or rebuilt by the Crown for the first Commissioner of the Treasury; on the north on the wall of the garden of the latter; on the west on the wall of St. James's Park; and on the south on the large area at the upper end of the street in part, and on a garden belonging to Mr. Beard for the other part, and of these dimensions, 119 ft. on the west, 128 ft. on the north, 63½ ft. on the east, and on the south 57½ ft. next the said area, and 67 ft. next the garden; together with the four houses standing on the site and the terrace adjoining and enjoyed therewith, the houses being occupied by Sir Watkin Williams Wynn, Baronet, the Duke of Bolton, Mr. Delaval, and the Bishop of St. David's; together with two other pieces of ground with the houses thereon. Sir Jacob Downing died about 1764, leaving his relict,

Dame Margaret, sole executrix of his will, which was proved by her in the Canterbury Court. Dame Margaret afterwards married George Bowyer, Esq., and being entitled to the premises as residuary legatee of her first husband's will, she, by her settlement, dated 10th November, 1768, assigned the same to William Greaves, Beaupre Bell, Thomas Ryder, Henry Mountford, and John Rose, as trustees for her sole use after marriage. By Letters Patent dated 9th May, 1772, King George III, in consideration of £267 paid by the trustees, granted another lease of the premises to them for seventeen years, from 16th February, 1803, at the increased rent of £15 per annum, until 1803 and from that date £75 per annum. By a deed, dated 24th November, 1772, the lease was assigned to William Masered of Hertford Street, St. George's, Hanover Square, for £10,500, of which £2,500 was advanced by the trustees on mortgage of the lease. The house next to the Park by a deed dated 25th May, 1775, was leased by Masered for thirty years to William Hunt of Well Street, St. Marylebone, Builder, at £210 per annum, being then occupied by Major-General Simon Fraser, formerly by Sir John Cust, Baronet, and Dame Elthreda his widow; the adjoining house then being occupied by Sir John Eden, Baronet, formerly by the Earl of Scarborough. In the following month, Hunt assigned his premises to General Fraser for £2,100, of which £1,500 was advanced by Hunt on mortgage of them. By deed, dated 17th May, 1777, Bowyer and Masered conveyed the head lease of General Fraser's house to him in consideration of £2,800 to Masered and £700 to Bowyer in reduction of Masered's mortgage. General Fraser died 8th February, 1782, and his executors, together with the assignee of his mortgagee, conveyed Fraser's house to James Martin, by deed, dated 8th April, 1783, in consideration of £1,492 10s. to the executors and £1,500 to the mortgagee. Then, by the deed of 8th June, 1803, the said Martin conveys to the company the house of which he was thus possessed for £6,650, apparently showing a very handsome profit.

On the deed is indorsed another, dated 2nd April, 1804, by which the East India Company assigned the premises to William Chinnery, Esq., one of the chief clerks in the office of the Lord Commissioners of the Treasury, on behalf of his Majesty, in consideration of £9,433 public money, a transaction showing another handsome profit to the vendor.

No doubt the premises of which the Premier's official residence formed part were built by **Sir Jacob Downing** during the term which seems to have been granted to him prior to **1752,** and in consequence of his being lessee of all or most of the frontage in the street his name has been perpetuated in the name of the thoroughfare.

THE HISTORY AND PEDIGREE OF THE FAMILY OF AUCHER, A.D. 853-1726.

By A. Leland Noel.

THIS was one of the few Saxon families which maintained their position as landed gentry, in spite of the almost universal change in the ownership of land resulting from the Norman Conquest.

First, as regards the spelling of the name, which, running back as the family does to remote Saxon times, has experienced even more than the usual mutations.

It appears in the following variations:

In Latin—Aucherus, Alcherus, Aulcherus.
In Anglo-Saxon—Ealher, Ealcher.
In Norman French—Fitzaucher.
In English—Auger, Aucher.

A.D. 853.—The first representative who appears in history is an Anglo-Saxon Earl, appointed by King Ethelwulf[1] to lead the men of Kent against the Danes.

The Danes having been defeated, in 852, by kings Ethelwulf and Athelstan, renewed the war in 853, by invading the Isle of Thanet. They landed at Sandwich with a considerable force, and, being attacked by *Earl Ealcher* at the head of the Kentish men and Earl Hulda leading the *posse comitatus* of Surrey, an obstinate battle was fought, in which many lives were lost, among the killed being Earl Ealcher himself. This Kentish Earl, as commander of the forces of the county, had what we should call " brevet rank " as duke.

At the time of the Conquest the names of two of the family appear; one as a benefactor of St. Saviour's, Bermondsey, and one as holding the Manor of Bosenham in Sussex, by grant from William I. •

---

[1] The father of Alfred the Great.

TORY.

luring the
r to 1753,
ost of the
ted in the

? THE

ch main-
te of the
nd result-

, running
s experi-

n history
lwulf[1] to

?thelwulf
the Isle
ble force,
: Kentish
f Surrey
vere lost
Kentish
what we

le family
lsey, and
by grant

THE FAMILY OF AUCHER.

What connection they had with the first Earl of Kent it is impossible to say, and the interval between 853 and 1066 being so considerable, the claim of descent, though possibly good and even probably so, cannot be verified.

The next name that appears is that of *William Fitzaucher*, to whom Henry II (1154-1189) gave the fourth part of a knight's fee in Essex, and in the reign of his son, King John (1199-1216), a Fitzaucher appears as the owner of the Manor of Losenham in Kent. Whether he was the same person as William of Essex, or was his son, cannot be shown; but we are told that William's grandson, Richard, was one of the Kentish gentlemen who attended Henry III in the expedition he made into Wales in 1258.

Meantime, in 1241, a *Sir Thomas Fitzaucher* founded the Carmelite Friary of St. Mary's, Losenham, and I think it was he who, as "Thomas filius Alcheri," was named among the holders of fees in Kent in 1254, as holding of the Prior of Leeds (Ledes).

In 1274 Henry son of Richard Fitzaucher did homage to the Abbat of Waltham for Copped Hall, Shingled Hall, Langfare, and other lands in Essex. And about the same time Henry III granted him free warren in all his lands in the counties of Essex, Cambridge, Wilts, and Southampton.[1]

1300. The name of Henry Fitzaucher occurs in the roll of Kentish men who were with Edward I at the siege of Carlaverock in Scotland; he was there made a knight banneret.

In the next reign, that of Edward II, we find an Aucher as hereditary forester of Waltham Forest in Essex, and another as a Baron of the Realm of Thorpe, co. York.

There was also one *Peter Aucher*, called "valet" (equivalent to our modern "gentleman of the bedchamber") to King Edward II. He, fearing lest he might be accounted of the Order of the Templars on account of his long beard, and possibly on account of his friendship with Roger the rector of Godmersham (who in 1294 was thinking of entering the Order) obtained a letter from the King certifying that he was his "valet" and was not, nor ever had been, a member of that Order.[2]

[1] He appears to have had property in several counties, but we are told that his principal seat was Copped Hall. His arms in the Charles Roll of Arms, A.D. 1250-1300, are, ermine, on a chief azure, 3 lions rampant or.

[2] It will be remembered that the Knight Templars were at this time under the shadow of the awful charges made against them. Under pressure from his father-in-law, Philip the Fair, King of France, Edward II in

223

THE FAMILY OF AUCHER.

In the reign of Edward II the owner of the Manor of Losenham was

Nicholas Aucher. He married a daughter of —— Oxenbridge of Breed, Sussex, by whom he had one son and one daughter.

    I. Henry, who succeeded to Losenham.

    (i) Agnes, who appears in Edward III's time as the defendant in a lawsuit brought against her by Isabella, wife of Henry Aucher of Losenham. This, I take it, was Isabel At Towne, who married Agnes' nephew, Henry; see below.

Nicholas was succeeded by his son,

Henry Aucher of Losenham, who married Elizabeth, daughter of John Digge[1] of Barham, and through her he became possessed of the Manor of Digges Court in the parish of Westwell, as well as that of Lowden or Little Maytham.

In 1347 he paid aid for making the Black Prince a knight, for both manors, as well as for land in the Hundred of Rolvenden (Rolvindenne), in company with his father Nicholas, and for land in the Hundred of Tenterden in his own name.

In 1367 he was one of those appointed to inquire into the age of William de Septvans, as a tenant of Edward III; among his coadjutors were Thomas Colepeper and Geffrey Colepeper. He was succeeded by his son (or grandson).

Henry Aucher, of Losenham and Digges Court. He paid aid in 1403 at the marriage of Blanch, the sister of King Henry IV.

He was twice married: 1st, to Isabel At Towne of Throwley; and, 2nd, to Joan, daughter of Thomas St. Leger of Otterden.

By his first wife he had two sons:

    I. Thomas, heir to Losenham.

    II. Robert, heir to Digges Court.

By his second wife he had an only son, Henry, who succeeded to Otterden in right of his mother.

The eldest son of the first marriage was:

Thomas Aucher of Losenham. He married and had a son, who succeeded as

Henry Aucher of Losenham. He (as Henry Auger) is in the list of Kentish gentry in 1492.

December, 1307, imprisoned all the Templars then in England, to await the trial which was afterwards held in Paris in 1309. In view of the inhuman tortures used to extort confessions, we cannot wonder at Peter Aucher's anxiety to dissociate himself with the doomed Order.

[1] This John Digge was probably the son of Adonerus de Digges.

THE FAMILY OF AUCHER.

He married Elizabeth, daughter of Sir John Guldeford, of Halden, by whom he had an only daughter, Anne, who by marriage carried the estate of Losenham and the Manor of Lowden, or Little Maytham, to Walter Colepeper, second son of Sir John Colepeper of Bedgebury.

DIGGES COURT

The second son of Henry Aucher's first marriage inherited the estate of Digges Court in the parish of Westwell, as *Robert Aucher* of Digges Court.

He married Joane ——, by whom he had two sons, i. Henry, ii. James.

His descendants lived at Digges Court until the end of the seventeenth century, when it was sold to one Godden, who in 1700 sold it to William Bokenham of Rochester; his descendant sold it in 1719 to Henry May, Recorder of Chichester, who sold it to Thomas May of Godmersham, who took the name of Knight, and dying in 1781 left it to his son, Thomas Knight of Godmersham.

OTTERDEN

Henry Aucher of Losenham; by right of his wife, Joane St. Leger, became possessed of Otterden. Otterden (in Domesday, Otringedene) was granted by William I to Odo, Bishop of Baieux, his half-brother. It afterwards came into the hands of Lawrence de Ottringden, who died in the reign of Edward II (1307-1327), leaving an only daughter, who married one of the Peyforers, from whom the manor passed to the family of Potyn. Nicholas Potyn left an only daughter, Juliana (*temp.* Richard II), who married Thomas St. Leger, second son of Ralph St. Leger of Ulcomb, M.P. for Kent in 1377. He (Thomas St. Leger) lived at Otterden and died there in 1408. His daughter, Joane, married Henry Aucher, as above, and through her he obtained several other manors.

EASTHALL. This estate was sold by Thomas de la Pine in the reign of Richard II to Thomas St. Leger, and Henry Aucher in 1453 sold it to Humphrey Evans, whose descendant, Alicia Evans, carried it by marriage to Thomas Hales, whose son Christopher Hales sold it in 1522 to Sir Anthony Aucher (see *post*).

NEWHALL, in the parish of Minster. This manor Henry Aucher sold to Sir William Cromer, Lord Mayor of London in 1433.

THE FAMILY OF AUCHER.

EVERSLEY This manor in the reign of Henry III (1216-1272) belonged to Brian de Eversley. Afterwards it belonged to the families of Peyforer and Potyn, and through them it passed to Thomas St. Leger and to the Auchers, who in Elizabeth's reign sold it to the Sondes.

EMLEY. This manor was held by Fulk de Peyforer in 1277, and in the next century his descendant, Juliana, carried it by marriage to Thomas St. Leger. It was sold by Henry Aucher to Sir William Cromer. Henry Aucher was succeeded by his son

Henry Aucher of Otterden Place, who was living there in 1441. He married Alicia Bolyn, and by her had a son.

John Aucher of Otterden Place. He (as John Auger) was one of the trustees under the will of James a Bourne of Dodyngton, made in 1467. And, also as John Auger, he appears in the list of Kentish gentry in 1492. He married Alice Church, by whom he had three sons and two daughters.

    I. James, heir to Otterden.
    II. William, died *s.p.*[1]
    III. Marmaduke, who married a daughter of one Gilbole.
    (1) Elizabeth, who married Thomas Besham of Sissinghurst. .
    (2) Jane, who married Thomas Corbet.

He died 23rd April, 1503, and was buried in Otterden Church, being succeeded by his son

James Aucher of Otterden Place. He married Alice, daughter of Thomas Hills of Eggarton, near Godmersham, by whom he had one son and one daughter.

    I. Anthony, heir to Otterden.
    (1) Susan, who married James Aucher.[2]

---

[1] It seems probable that this was the William Aucher to whom there is a brass in Rainham Church, with the following inscription: "Pray for the souls of Wᵐ Aucher and Elizabeth his wife, which William died 23 December, 1514, on whose soul may God have mercy."

[2] This must be, I think, the James Aucher known as "of Cheriton," who bought the small manor of Sweet Arden, in the parish of Cheriton, of James Man in 1550. Whose son he was I cannot say. Hasted says: "his descendant Anthony Aucher, of Bishopsbourne, in 1691 sold it (the Manor of Sweet Arden") to Richard Topcliff"; but he is, I think, confusing "James of Cheriton" with "James of Otterden." At all events he is wrong in the date 1691, as Godwin Topcliffe of Hythe, the son of the purchaser, resold it in 1619 to Robert Broadnax of Cheriton. This is confirmed by the *Archæologia Cantiana*, where (vol. xvii, p. 365) it is stated that "The Revᵈ Richard Topcliffe, Rector of Cheriton 1584-1602, bought of Anthʸ Aucher cir. 1591 Bank House farm and Sweet Arden

He died January 6, 1508, and was buried at Otterden near his father.[1] He was succeeded by his only son

Sir Anthony Aucher of Otterden Place. He married Affra, daughter of William Cornwallis of Norfolk, by whom he had four sons:

    I. John, heir to Otterden.
    II. Edward, of Bourne Place.
    III. Thomas, died *s.p.*
    IV. William, of Nonington.[2]

Sir Anthony Aucher had almost as many transactions in land as his friend and neighbour, Thomas Colepeper of Bedgebury, and so I have transferred the particulars to an appendix.

In 1540 he was appointed with William Goldwell to enquire into a charge of disloyalty against the Rev. William Marshall, parson of Mersham. In 1542 he was a contributor to the loan to King Henry VIII. He was subsequently appointed Auditor and Supervisor as well as an Assistant of the dissolved Priory of Christ Church, Canterbury. This appointment may or may not have a connection with the contribution to the loan; but he appears to have been of the school of the Vicar of Bray, for we find him in Mary's reign Master of the Jewel House (juelhouse) to receive goods of Colleges and Chantries. He was killed at the siege of Calais in 1557, and was succeeded by his eldest son

John Aucher of Otterden Place. He married a daughter of Sir William Kellaway, by whom he left an only daughter, Anne, who in the reign of Elizabeth married Sir Humphrey Gilbert,[3] and so carried Otterden and sundry other manors

Manor." How the property passed from James of Cheriton in 1550 to Anthony of Bishopsbourne in 1591 is not clear. Possibly it was another Anthony, perhaps a son of James of Cheriton.

[1] There is some confusion in dates here. James Aucher's widow, Alice, is said to have married secondly, James Hardres of Hardres Court, who died in 1490; whereas by the above she did not become a widow until 1508.

[2] This may have been the William Aucber who was patron of the Rectory of Badlesmere, and presented the Rev. Richard Yates to the living, 31st March, 1579. Perhaps he was acting for his niece, Anne, who married Sir Humphrey Gilbert, who sold the Manor of Badlesmere in 1581. There was another William, known as "William Aucher of God-mersham," who, on 6th October, 1590, presented Paul Chapman to the Rectory of Hurst, Romney. Possibly these two Williams are identical, but if so they could not be identical with William of Nonington.

[3] Sir Humphrey Gilbert was half-brother to Sir Walter Raleigh. He was knighted in 1577, and he is most memorable as having made the firs

into his possession. He sold Otterden to William Lewin, LL.D., who lived there, but died in London, 15th April, 1598, and was buried in St. Leonard's, Shoreditch, a monument to him being erected in Otterden Church. His son, Sir Justinian Lewin, lived at Otterden, and died there, 28th June, 1620. Sir Justinian married Elizabeth, daughter of Sir Arthur Capel of Hertford, Bart., and left an only daughter, who by marriage carried the property to Richard Rogers of Brianstone, Somerset, whose daughter, Elizabeth, by marriage carried it first to Charles Cavendish, Lord Mansfield (son of William Cavendish, Duke of Newcastle), and secondly to Charles Stuart, Duke of Richmond and Lenox, who sold it to Sir George Curteis, who lived and died at Otterden, being buried in the church, October, 1702. His granddaughter, Anne Curteis, by marriage carried it to Thomas Wheler, D.D., Prebendary of Durham, and afterwards to Humphrey Walcot, who sold it to Granville Wheler, the younger brother of his wife's first husband. Granville Wheler died at Otterden in May, 1770, and the property passed to his son, Granville Hastings Wheler.

HAUTBOURNE OR BOURNE PLACE
MANOR OF BISHOPSBOURNE

John de Bourne had a charter of Free Warren granted to him by Edward I in 1289. His descendant carried the Manor of Bourne by marriage to the family of Shelving,[1] whence it was commonly called Shelvingsbourne. A daughter of this family carried it by marriage to Edward Haut, when it came to be known as Hautbourne. His daughter, Elizabeth, carried it by marriage to Thomas Colepeper, who in 1544, sold it, together with the Manor of Bishopsbourne which he had obtained by exchange from the Archbishop of Canterbury, to Sir Anthony Aucher, who at his death in 1558 left them to his second son.

Edward Aucher of Bourne Place. He married, Mabel daughter of Sir Thomas Wrothe, by whom he had one son and one daughter.

I. Anthony, heir to Bourne Place.

settlement in Newfoundland: and, in the foundation of England's first colony, given a date for the birth of the British Empire.

[1] Descended from John de Shelving of Woodnesborough, who died in 1412.

(1) Elizabeth, who married Sir William Lovelace of Bethersden.[1]

On Edward Aucher's death he was succeeded by his only son,

Anthony Aucher of Bourne Place, who was High Sheriff of Kent in 1570. He married twice, and by his second wife, Margaret, daughter of Edwin Sandys, Archbishop of York, (who died 1609) he had two sons and two daughters.

    I. Anthony, heir to Bourne Place.

    II. Edwin, of Willesborough.[2]

    (1) Elizabeth, who married first, Sir William Hammond of St. Alban's Court, and second (in 1624), the Very Rev. Walter Balcauqual, Dean of Rochester.

    (2) Margaret, who married Sir Roger James.

He died 13th January, 1609-10, and was succeeded by

Sir Anthony Aucher of Bourne Place. This Anthony in 1604 (*i.e.* during his father's lifetime) is said to have fled to the continent, in company of Sir Thomas Hardres, to avoid his creditors—their lands being compulsorily sold by Act of Parliament. This appears, however, to have been but a temporary difficulty, for in 1620 he was High Sheriff of Kent; and before 1630 he sold to Sir James Hales, the Manor of Staplegate alias Nackington, which he had bought of Walter Waller. He married Hester, daughter of Peter Collet of London. He died in 1637 and was succeeded by his only son

Sir Anthony Aucher of Bourne Place. He married Elizabeth, daughter of Robert Hatton, who died in 1648,[3] and secondly,

[1] The Bethersden Parish books mention William Lovelace as paying in 1558 twenty shillings towards cost of a new great bell for the church. And in 1591, the churchwardens acknowledge the receipt from " Mrs. Lovelace of 5s. that she did give towards mendynge of the ledde of the church." This Elizabeth Lovelace *née* Aucher, was buried in Canterbury Cathedral, 3rd December, 1627. Sir William Lovelace died in 1629, leaving by his wife, Elizabeth Aucher, a son known as Sir William Lovelace of Woolrich, who married Anne, daughter of Sir William Barnes, and by her had a son, Sir Richard Lovelace of Lovelace Place. He died in 1658, leaving an only daughter, Margaret, who married a son of Lord Chief Justice Coke.

[2] He married Mary, daughter of John Gibbon, and their son, the Rev. John Aucher, was Prebendary of Canterbury.

[3] In the year that his first wife died (1648) his name appears in the following list of the leaders of the Royalist rising in Kent:

Sir Gamaliel Dudley, Sir George Lisle, Sir William Compton, Sir Robert Tracey, Col. Leigh, Sir John Many, Sir James Hales, Sir William Many, Sir Richard Hardres, Col. Washington, Col. L'Estrange, Col. Hacker, Sir Anthony Aucher, Sir William Brockman of Beechborough, Sir Thomas Colepeper of St. Stephen's, Darrell of Scotney Castle, Sir

Elizabeth, daughter of Sir Thomas Hewitt, by whom he had four sons and two daughters.

I. Anthony, heir to Bourne Place.

II. Hewitt, heir to his brother.

III. Rev. Robert, of Queen's College, Oxford.

IV. Hatton, Administrator of the goods of his brother Robert.

(1) Elizabeth, who married John Corbett, LL.D.

(2) Hester, who married Ralph Blomer, D.D., Prebendary of Canterbury, by whom she had a daughter, Anne Blomer, who married James Teale, and had a son, Isaac M. Teale, and a daughter, Mary Teale, who married General Sir Charles Shipley and left three daughters: (1) Katherine Jane Shipley, who married Colonel Edward Warner; (2) Augusta Mary Shipley, who married Alexander Manning; (3) Elizabeth Cole Shipley, who married Henry, Earl of Buchan.

He was created a Baronet by Charles II in 1666. In 1673, the Advowson of the Rectory of East Church Minster was granted by Charles II to Sir Henry Palmer of Wingham, Bart., and eleven other gentlemen, of whom Sir Anthony Aucher of Bishopsbourne was one. The trustees presented Sir Anthony's third son, the Rev. Robert Aucher, to the living, and on his death in or about 1682, his younger brother Hatton as his Administrator (with I presume the consent of the twelve trustees) presented Anthony Woolrick to the Vicarage: he appears to have held it only two years, for in 1684 the trustees presented the Rev. James Jeffreys to the living, who, dying in 1689, was succeeded by the Rev. William Mills, who held it for ten years. Sir Anthony died in May, 1692, aged seventy-eight,[1] and was succeeded by his son,

Sir Anthony Aucher, second Baronet. He died a minor in 1694, when the title and estate passed to his next brother,

Sir Hewitt Aucher, third Baronet. The only mention of him I have found is in Dr. John Harris's *History of Kent*, who,

---

Thomas Godfrey of Heppington, Edward Hales of Tunsted, Anthony and Francis Hammond of St. Alban's Court, Francis Lovelace, Sir Henry and Sir Thomas Palmer of Beaksbourne, Sir Thomas Payton of Knowlton, Mr. James Dowell, Mr. George Newman, and Mr. Whelton.

[1] His widow, Elizabeth (*née* Hewitt) in 1707 sold to Sir Henry Furness of Waldershare, Bart., a large tract of woodland, some 1,100 acres, once called North Blean and afterwards Abbats Blean, as belonging to the Abbat and convent of Faversham.

writing in 1719, says "Sir Hewitt Aucher has a very fine new-built brick house in this parish," *i.e.* Bishopsbourne. He died unmarried in 1726, when the title became extinct and the estate passed to his eldest sister.

Elizabeth Corbett, wife of John Corbett, LL.D. At her death[1] she left five daughters as co-heirs.

    (1) Catherine, who married, as his second wife,[2] Stephen Beckingham. He, in 1752, bought up the shares of his four sisters-in-law, and left the whole estate to his son, the Rev. John Charles Beckingham, who at his death left an only daughter Louisa,[3] who, on 6th September, 1802, married Edward Taylor of Bifrons, M.P. for Canterbury, 1807-1814.[4]

    (2) Elizabeth, who married Thomas Dinward.

    (3) Frances, who married Sir William Hardres, Bart.

    (4) Antonina, who married Ignatius Geoghagen.

    (5) Margaret Hannah Roberta, who married William Hougham of Barton Court, by whom she had one son and one daughter.

The son, William Hougham of Barton Court, died in 1828, *s. p.*

The daughter, Catherine Hougham, married the Rev. Richard Sandys, and by him had one son and one daughter.

The son, Richard Edwin Sandys, Lieut. R.N., was killed at Copenhagen in 1801.

The daughter, Catherine, married in 1803 John Chesshyre. Captain R.N., and so carried Barton Court to that family.

APPENDIX. MANORS AND PROPERTY ACQUIRED BY SIR ANTHONY AUCHER, 1540-1557.

The Manor of Liminge was in the hands of the See of Canterbury, and Archbishop Ralph, in 1114, charged it with 1*d.* per day towards supplying the lepers in the Hospital at

---

[1] She died in 1764, aged eighty-two.

[2] His first wife was a Miss Cox by whom he had a son, Stephen Beckingham, who married Mary, daughter of John Sawbridge of Ollanteigh.

[3] Mrs. Taylor of Bifrons, as the eldest co-heir of the last baronet of the Hardres family, has a dagger given by Henry VIII to Sir Thomas Hardres, with whom he was hunting in Hardres Park when Sir Thomas was ranger thereof.

[4] Bifrons was sold to the Marquess Conyngham, and Bourne Place to Matthew Bell.

Harbledown with drink. In 1540 Archbishop Cranmer exchanged it with the King for other property. The King granted the manor, together with the advowsons of Liminge, Stanford, and Paddlesworth, to Sir Anthony Aucher of Otterden, to hold in chief at a rental of £4 7s. 2d. After his death in 1557 it passed to his eldest son, John, and so to his granddaughter. Joane, wife of Sir Humphrey Gilbert. The property consisted of the manor and park of Liminge, and 300 acres in Elham, Postling, Bethersden, Woodchurch, and Orleston, with the advowsons of Liminge, Paulford, and Stamford. It afterwards reverted to the Bishopsbourne branch of the Aucher family, and was sold by Sir Anthony Aucher of Bourne Place, soon after the death of Charles I, to Sir John Roberts of Canterbury, Knt., who died in 1658; it then passed through several hands to the Rev. Ralph Price, who held it in 1790.

Folkestone.—In 1540 Henry VIII devised the vicarage and parish church of Folkestone, "with all its rights profits and emoluments," to Thomas, Lord Cromwell, who assigned his interests to Anthony Aucher. But the fee remaining with the King, they were granted in 1551 by Edward VI to Edward, Lord Clinton, and they afterwards came into the possession of the See of Canterbury.   .

Swingfield.—The land in the parish of Swingfield, which had belonged to the Knights of St. John of Jerusalem, on the dissolution of the Order in 1541, was granted in 1542 by Henry VIII to Sir Anthony Aucher of Otterden, who, in 1552, passed it to Sir Henry Palmer of Wingham.

Bilcherst.—The Manor of Bilcherst in the parish of Hawking was granted in 1542 by Henry VIII to Sir Anthony Aucher, who sold it to Thomas Smersole.

Higham.—The Manor of Higham, in the parish of Patrixbourne, was sold by Thomas Colepeper of Bedgebury in 1543 to Sir Anthony Aucher, whose descendant, Sir Hewitt Aucher, dying in 1726, bequeathed it to his sister Elizabeth, wife of Thomas Corbett, LL.D., whose daughter sold it to James Hallet, who was living there in 1790.

Kingston.—The Manor of Kingston, near Bridge, was granted by Edward IV to Roger, Lord Wentworth, whose descendant Richard, Lord Wentworth, sold it in 1530 to Thomas Cole-

THE FAMILY OF AUCHER.

peper, who, in 1533, sold it to Sir Anthony Aucher; his descendant, Sir Anthony Aucher, Bart., sold it in 1647 to Thomas Gibbon of Westcliffe.

Mottenden.—The Manor of Mottenden (Modinden) in the parish of Headcorn was granted by Henry VIII in 1545 to Sir Anthony Aucher in chief, and was assigned by him in 1553 to Sir Walter Handley, who in the same year passed it to his son-in-law, Thomas Colepeper of Bedgebury.

Wildmarsh.—Wildmarsh (or Wolmarsh) in the parish of Stone, belonging to the Abbey of Faversham, was granted by Henry VIII in 1545 to Sir Anthony Aucher, from whom it passed to his granddaughter, Anne, wife of Sir Humphrey Gilbert.

Postling.—The Manor of Postling was in Domesday part of the possessions of Hugh de Montford. It subsequently passed through the families of De Colembers, De Delves, and Fitz-Alan, till in 1547 it was sold to Sir Anthony Aucher, from whom it passed to Sir Humphrey Gilbert, who in 1579 sold it to Thomas Smith of Westenhanger, ancestor of the Viscounts Strangford, from whom it passed to Thomas Gomeldon of Sellinge, and finally was sold to the trustees of Sir Windham Knatchbull, Bart., who, dying in 1768, left it to his heir, and so to Sir Edward Knatchbull, Bart., of Hatch.

Ashford.—The Manor of Ashford (in Domesday Essetesford), was granted by Edward VI in 1550 to Thomas Colepeper of Bedgebury, and was assigned by him (without license from the King) to Sir Anthony Aucher, who in 1555, mortgaged it with other property to Sir Andrew Judde of London, and not being able to redeem them, they passed into the possession of Sir Andrew. The property was afterwards broken up and passed into several hands.[1]

Plumford.—The estate of Plumford in the parish of Ospringe belonged to St. Stephen's, Westminster, and was granted by

---

[1] It is stated (*Archæologia Cantiana*, vol. xvii, p. 193) that Thomas Smythe of Westenhanger, commonly called Customer Smythe (as being an officer in the Customs), bought the Manor of Ashford of Sir Anthony Aucher. This does not tally with the above, unless the sale was made through Sir Andrew Judde.

Edward VI in 1547 to Sir Anthony Aucher, who sold it to Thomas Colepeper, who sold it to John Greenstreet. This, together with the adjoining estate of Painters, which John Greenstreet had also bought, were sold by a descendant of his to Sir Henry Furness of Waldershare, Bart., whose son, Sir Robert Furness, married Arabella, daughter of the Earl of Rockingham, by whom he had a daughter, Catherine, who became the ultimate heir of these two estates. She married, first, Lewis, Earl of Rockingham, and second (in 1751), Francis, Earl of Guildford. She died in 1766, leaving the property to her second husband, whose heir is the present proprietor.

Cobham.—A messuage and four acres in Cobham were granted by Henry VIII in 1547 to Sir Anthony Aucher, to be held in chief.

Statisfield.—The Manor of Statisfield (in Domesday, Stane-felde) was bought by Sir Anthony Aucher of Sir Anthony St. Leger (*temp.* Edward VI), and his son, Sir Anthony, sold it (*temp.* James I) to one Salter, from whom it passed to Richard Webbe of Elham, and thence through the Head baronets to Dr. John Lynch, who held it in 1790.

Badlesmere.—The Manor of Badlesmere, with 2,000 acres in Badlesmere, Sheldwich, Selling, Chelloch, Throwley, and Leveland, was bought by Sir Anthony Aucher in 1549 of Sir Robert Southwell, Master of the Rolls to Henry VIII. Sir Anthony's granddaughter, Anne, carried it by marriage to Sir Humphrey Gilbert, who sold it in 1581 to Sir Michael Sondes of Throwley, from whom it descended to the present Earl Sondes.

Old Surrenden alias Bethersden.—This Manor belonged to the College of Wye, and at the suppression of the religious houses was granted by Henry VIII to Sir Maurice Dennys, Captain of Calais, who in 1549 sold it to Sir Anthony Aucher, who in 1551 sold it to Philip Chowte,[1] Standard Bearer to Henry VIII at the siege of Boulogne, whose descendant, Sir George Choute, Bart., dying in 1721, left it to Sir Edward Austen of Tenterden, Bart., who sold it to Thomas Best.

[1] Sometimes spelt Choute, and on a monument in Holingbourne Church spelt Chovet.

THE FAMILY OF AUCHER.

East Hall or Easthall.—East Hall in the parish of Murston was in 1552 bought of Christopher Hales by Sir Anthony Aucher, who the next year sold it to Thomas Gardyner, who in 1568 sold it to Thomas Norden, who sold it to William Pordage of Rodmersham, from whose descendant it passed to Richard Hazard.

Rigsell.—Twenty-four acres known as Rigsell in the parish of Statisfield, belonging to the Priory of Leeds, were held by Sir Anthony Aucher in 1558, and by Sir Humphrey Gilbert in 1574.

Rollys.—A part of the Manor of Dyve Court, known as Rollys, was at one time held by Sir Anthony Aucher, and afterwards by Peter Greenstreet.

NOTES AND QUERIES.

DENE-HOLES (vol. xi, p. 91).—I am glad to see that you have taken up this interesting question. Surely, with the evidence that has been accumulated of recent years, it is time that the experts came to some agreement as to their date and object. I should like to ask what is the earliest use of the term Dene Hole, and what is the precise meaning and derivation of *dene*. I have heard them called *Dane* Holes.—J. R., *Gravesend.*

REPLIES.

THE CULPEPERS IN KENT (vol. xi, p. 32).—There is a slight inaccuracy in this interesting article. It is stated on page 35, that Preston Hall, Aylesford, was sold to Mr. E. L. Bates, who sold it to Mr. Henry Brassey, and that the latter pulled down the old Hall. The purchaser was Mr. Edward Ladd Betts, a partner in the great firm of Peto, Betts, and Brassey. It was Mr. Betts who pulled down the old Hall and built the present house. On his death Mr. Henry Brassey purchased the estate, and lived and died there.

HERBERT MONCKTON, *Maidstone.*

DENE-HOLES (vol. xi, p. 91).—A Fellow of the Society of Antiquaries yesterday called my attention to an article on *Dene-Holes* in your last number, where I was surprised to see it stated (p. 93) that the pick marks in the Dene-Hole found by Mr. P. J. Martin on Windmill Hill, Gravesend, were made with deer horn, or, at any rate, were not modern metal pick marks. On referring to my notes of 23rd September, 1907, when Mr. Norman Brooks and I thoroughly explored the old chalk well, I find the following: "Now as to the nature of the walls of these caverns, they were very roughly hewn, as at Bexley and Hangman's Wood, and unusually rich in pick marks. We examined about forty of these, and in places where the chalk was damp, found them very clear, some an inch deep, some two inches deep, or more. Many were quite square, with clear cut sides, gradually tapering to a point. Others were more rounded, but still inclining to the square form, as if the once square implement was much worn. Hence we could form no other conclusion than that the holes or marks were made with a metal pick (*i.e.*, of bronze or iron), not of horn, bone, or flint." This report appeared in a Northfleet paper at the time. It is important that the fact should be known, otherwise a false antiquity would be given to a very commonplace chalk excavation, which excavations are quite common both in Kent and Essex.

J. W. HAYES, *West Thurrock Vicarage, Grays, Essex.*

ROLLS YARD AND CHAPEL (vol. xi, p. 157).—No reference to this place and the Chapel appears to have been made in former numbers of this Magazine, but an interesting article on "The Rolls House and Chapel," by Mr. W. J. Hardy, F.S.A., appeared in vol. ii (pp. 49-68) of the *Middlesex and Hertfordshire Notes and Queries*, which Magazine was the precursor of the *Home Counties Magazine*.

The Record Office Museum now stands on the site of the Rolls Chapel; it contains some of the monuments, notably the beautiful one by Torrigiano to Dr. John Young, who was appointed Master of the Rolls in 1508. The museum is well worth a visit.

There was no connection between the Rolls Chapel and St. Thomas's Church in Bream's Buildings. The District called the Liberty of the Rolls was without a church of its own before St. Thomas's was built in 1842, up to which time the Church of St. Dunstan in the West had been used by the parishioners.

St. Thomas's was a modest looking brick building, having a stone Norman arched doorway in Bream's buildings, and a door at the rear in Church Passage, opening into the vestry. The church was erected partly by subscriptions of the residents and business men in the Liberty, and was consecrated on 13th July, 1842, by the Bishop of London. The interior was striking on account of its fine old oak panelling and pewing, which had formerly been in the Temple Church and was purchased from the Temple together with the carved oak communion table. The latter, I was informed, was carved by Grinling Gibbons, and was presented to the Temple by Sir Christopher Wren. If my

REVIEWS.

information is correct, the table and some of the handsomely carved pew doors have found a resting place in St. Dunstan's Church. Owing to much of the residential part of the Liberty being improved away, the congregation of St. Thomas's dwindled almost to vanishing point, and the church being no longer required was demolished in 1887.

Church Passage, which now appears to be a misnomer, had previous to the erection of the church been known as " White's Alley;" it was many years before the old inhabitants got reconciled to the change, and for a long time they persisted in calling it by its old name.

C. M. PHILLIPS.

REVIEWS.

PEWTER MARKS AND OLD PEWTER WARE, DOM-ESTIC AND ECCLESIASTICAL, with about 100 illustrations, 200 facsimile marks, and 1000 full descriptions of touches from the Touch Plates at Pewterers' Hall, as well as other marks obtained from various sources; list of members of the Pewterers' Company from 1450 to the present time, etc. By Christopher A. Markham, F.S.A. Reeves and Turner; pp. xv, 316; 21s.

A good many books have appeared on Pewter during the last few years, of very varying merit; but many of these can hardly be said to be more than descriptive. They are, for the most part, nicely " got up " and pleasantly written, and have so many hundred pretty pictures. The present work has all these qualities, and a good deal more—it is a practical work by a practical man, and has nothing about it of the "illustrated gift-book " order.

After a sufficient account of the history of the craft, in which some of the early statutes are printed in full, we find an excellent descriptive section on domestic pewter, with many apt quotations from inventories, plays, and other sources; the section on ecclesiastical pewter is equally good. Chapters on the manufacture of pewter, the various alloys used, and some very useful hints on cleaning and repairing, complete this part of the work.

The sections following deal with the maker's marks or "touches" as they were called. The system adopted, the regulations of the company, and the frequent evasions and disputes, are all fully and clearly dealt with. Then we have a most useful list of the Freemen of the Pewterers' Company, from 1450 until almost the present time; this list fills more than thirty-three pages. Finally there is a detailed account of the fine remaining "Touch Plates," with either an illustration or a description of every mark recorded upon them. It is impossible to speak too highly of the value of this work; it does for the amateur of pewter what Chaffers and others have done for the collectors of china and silver. The illustrations of various specimens are well chosen; most are from photographs, but not a few from drawings by the author, who has a very pretty "touch" of his own, both with pen and brush. There is a good index.

237

REVIEWS.

SURREY ARCHAEOLOGICAL COLLECTIONS; vol. 23; pp. xlvi, 228.

The first article in this volume is a very useful catalogue of the armorial ledger grave-stones in St. Saviour's Church, Southwark, by Mr. A. Ridley Bax, F.S.A. A rubbing is given of the arms in each case, and voluminous extracts from wills. Mr. R. A. Roberts continues his copies of the Inventories of Church Goods in the time of Edward VI. The most noteworthy feature in this instalment is the return for the parish of Gatton; it was made by Dame Elizabeth Copley, and she certified that "she has nother church wardens nor syde men within the parishe of Gatton, but only hyr selff and hyr familye of hyr place and hathe byn so longe tyme of memorye." The good lady exhibited an inventory made by Sir Roger Copley, her late husband, which includes "a bell not lowde inowghe to be hard a flight schotte agaynst the wynde." Mr. Malden contributes an interesting and scholarly paper on the operations of the Civil War in Surrey in 1642. Mr. P. Woods' history of the Rectory Manor of Godalming is a valuable addition to Surrey topography. These small ecclesiastical manors within manors were very numerous, but as a rule little is known of their history. Mr. Woods was fortunate enough to find a document, which is not strictly speaking a "custumal" but rather a survey, being a list of tenants with the services due from each one. Such documents are not too common, and should always be printed, though this particular one presents no special features.

Mr. P. M. Johnston, F.S.A., has another of his exhaustive monographs on Surrey churches. West Horsley, the church now treated of, has not the same amount of architectural interest as Stoke D'Abernon, but Mr. Johnston thinks that portions of a pre-Conquest building are still remaining. Papers by Mr. Reginald A. Smith, F.S.A., on Romano-British Remains at Cobham, by Mr. C. H. Jenkinson on Temple Elfold, by Mr. George Clinch, F.G.S., on the Lumley Monuments at Cheam, and by Mr. G. F. Hill on Roman Coins found at Brooklands, complete a first-rate volume.

THE ROMAN MEASURES IN THE DOMESDAY SURVEY OF MIDDLESEX, by Montagu Sharpe. Brentford Printing and Publishing Co.; pp. 26; 2s. 6d. net., post free.

We gladly welcome another of Mr. Sharpe's scholarly contributions on ancient Middlesex. The present essay, which forms Chapter XVI of the author's work, *Some Antiquities of Middlesex*, is an attempt to show the continuity of the Roman measurements down to the time of the great Domeesday Survey, and, as a natural consequence, the existence, in main lines at any rate, of the Roman laying out and planning of roads, fields, and other sub-divisions. The latter question was dealt with to a great extent in Mr. Sharpe's previous chapter, on "the Roman Centuriation of the Middlesex District" (see *Home Counties Magazine*, vol. x, p. 160), and he is here principally concerned with the measures. Starting with the assumption (based on his previous chapter), that the Domesday virgate is the equivalent of the Roman *centuria*, Mr. Sharpe gives us some very remarkable figures. Comparing the Domesday calculation with the modern acreage, he show a difference for the whole county of a little over 271 acres in a total of over 141,876 acres. The nearness of the result shows that Mr. Sharpe's estimate, based on the hide of 125 acres, instead of the more usual 120, cannot be far out, and as the 125 acres equals four *centuriae*, we consider that a strong case is made out, so far as Middlesex is concerned. But, as is well known, the area of the field hide varied in different districts.

With regard to the question of the survival of Roman institutions and customs, as opposed to measurements and physical objects, we must confess that we cannot agree with all Mr. Sharpe's conclusions. For the Saxon settlers to occupy fields and roads without alteration is one thing, for them to accept all the rights claimed

REVIEWS.

by the Romano-British *coloni*, is another. There are no doubt certain similarities between the Roman and the old English systems, but even so it does not necessarily follow that one is derived from the other, and in any case they are, in our opinion, too few to bear the serious weight of argument that is sometimes put upon them.

FARNHAM, ESSEX, PAST AND PRESENT; by J. G. Geare, M.A., Rector of Farnham. George Allen and Sons; pp. 201; 2s. 6d. net.

Farnham and its Rector are alike to be congratulated on this excellent little book, which is one of the best of the smaller parish histories that we have ever seen. The author seems to have exhausted all the printed sources of information, and in addition to have collected a considerable amount of material by original research The result is that we have a fairly consecutive history of the parish and its various manors from the Conquest to the present day. There are gaps in the history, as there are in most cases, but Mr. Geare treats these as a sober historian should; he gives us his suggestion, without any attempt to state as fact more than he can prove from his evidence. Moreover (excellent man!) he gives references to his documents. The descriptive portions are equally good; his chapters on the parish registers, rectors, churchwardens, briefs and charities, recusants, etc., all show careful and accurate study, wide reading, and sound antiquarian knowledge. We do not agree with all the author's suggested derivations of field-names, but that is hardly to be expected, since there is no branch of archaeology in which there is so much room for difference of opinion. The index is poor and unworthy; with this sole exception, we have nothing but praise for the author and his book.

DENEHOLES AND OTHER CHALK EXCAVATIONS, their origin and uses. By the Rev. J. W. Hayes. Reprinted from the *Journal of the Royal Anthropological Institute*, vol. 39. 1s. 6d.

We print in this number a note by Mr. Hayes on the Gravesend Dene-Holes, and a perusal of his paper shows that he has made special and careful study of the question. He gives a mass of evidence to show that Dene-Holes are simply excavations for the purpose of getting chalk, and not a few of his witnesses have actually assisted in the operation. We find his arguments too cogent to be resisted, and we think he might have strengthened his case by laying more stress on the negative side of the evidence. How comes it if these excavations were granaries that no store of corn has been found in any one of them? If they were refuges, how is it that no instance has been found of a group of skeletons huddled up in a corner? If they were made for getting flints, how is it that no store of flints, collected but not removed, has ever been noted? Mr. Hayes has done good service by giving us this lucid summing up.

A HANDLIST TO THE SURNAMES represented by Inscriptions in the Hundred of Edwinstree, co. Herts, recorded in 1907. Compiled by W. B. Gerish; pp. 16; 1s. net.

We have here an index to monumental inscriptions within the eighteen parishes comprising the Hundred of Edwinstree, including churches, churchyards, nonconformist and other burial-grounds. The value of such a list is very great, not only to the genealogist but also to the lawyer, since the result of a lawsuit may frequently depend on the knowledge of a particular gravestone. This list gives surnames and

239

REVIEWS.

parishes only, but Mr. Gerish states that the manuscript lists may be freely consulted at his house at Bishop's Stortford, and that he will answer inquiries if a stamped and addressed envelope be sent to him. We congratulate Mr. Gerish on his enterprise and industry, and trust that he will find many imitators in other counties.

TYBURN GALLOWS, by G. L. Gomme, F.S.A.; pp. 24; 2*d*.

Not the least valuable part of the educational work done by the London County Council is the series of historical booklets of which the present monograph forms one. While making free use of Mr. Mark's work, *Tyburn Tree: its History and Annals* [see *ante*, p. 76], and other authorities, Mr. Gomme has given a number of most valuable extracts from the records of the Dean and Chapter of Westminster. The manor of "le Hyde," now Hyde Park, belonged to the Abbey, and from the old leases and other documents cited, it is conclusively shown that a gallows existed at the spot as far back as 1478, and probably much earlier, and that the name Tyburn was applied to the locality as early as 1440, and probably as early as 1356. Due acknowledgment is made to Mr. Herbert Sieveking, M.R.C.S., who first suggested that the site of the Tyburn Gallows should be suitably indicated.

THE ARCHER GUIDE TO BIRCHINGTON, compiled by Gilbert Miller. Archer Printing Co.; pp. 52; 3*d*.

This is quite a good little guide-book, and contains also brief descriptions of Westgate, Minster, Margate, Broadstairs, and other places in the neighbourhood. It is pleasantly written, and contains just the right amount of historical and antiquarian detail for the seaside visitor. Mr. B. C. Dexter contributes some pretty pen-and-ink sketches, but the half-tone illustrations printed in the text are not a success.

HERTFORDSHIRE COUNTY RECORDS.

The County Council are engaged in calendaring the documents in their custody and have now issued a Calendar, in two Volumes, to the

SESSIONS ROLLS, 1561 to 1850.

Compiled by MESSRS. HARDY & PAGE, and edited by
W. J. HARDY, F.S.A.

Each Volume has a full•Index; the First Volume contains a
Preface.

The documents calendared illustrate the

HISTORY (Social, Political, and Ecclesiastical),
TOPOGRAPHY, and
GENEALOGY

of the County. The volume, strongly bound in green cloth, can be obtained from MESSRS. SIMSON & COMPANY, Limited, Booksellers, Hertford; or from the leading London Booksellers

PRICE OF THE TWO VOLUMES, £1 10s.

London Topographical Society

President: THE RIGHT HON. THE EARL OF ROSEBERY, K.G.

The London Topographical Society was founded for the publication of material illustrating the history and topography of the City and County of London from the earliest times to the present day. This object is affected by:

(*a*) The reproduction of Maps, Views, and Plans of the Capital as a whole and of localities within its area at different periods.

(*b*) The publication of documents and data of every description.

(*c*) A yearly record of demolitions and topographical changes.

The Annual Subscription to the Society is One Guinea. Copies of the works produced by the Society are distributed each year to the Members in return for their subscriptions. Members subscribing for a complete set of the publications are presented with a Portfolio to contain the Views, Maps, and Plans.

LIST OF THE WORKS ISSUED BY THE SOCEITY:

VAN DEN WYNGAERDE'S VIEW OF LONDON, *circa* 1550, measuring 10 feet long by 17 inches. In seven sheets.

HOEFNAGEL'S PLAN OF LONDON, from Braun and Hogenberg's "Civitates Orbis Terrarum," 1572. One sheet.

ILLUSTRATED TOPOGRAPHICAL RECORD. First, Second, and Third Series.

VISSCHER'S VIEW OF LONDON, 1616. In four sheets.

PORTER'S MAP OF LONDON AND WESTMINSTER, *circa* 1660. Two sheets.

NORDEN'S MAPS OF LONDON AND WESTMINSTER, 1593. One sheet.

KENSINGTON TURNPIKE TRUST PLANS. A continuous picture of the Road between Hyde Park Corner and Addison Road in 1811. In thirty sheets.

PLAN OF WHITEHALL, 1682, with modern Ground-plan. One sheet.

ANNUAL RECORD. The official organ of the Society. Vol. I. *Continued for subsequent years as "London Topographical Record."*

LONDON TOPOGRAPICAL RECORD. Vols. II. III. and IV.

WEST-CENTRAL LONDON, *circa* 1645. Hollar's Bird's-eye View of the area now known as the West Central district. One sheet.

KIP'S PROSPECT OF THE CITY OF LONDON, WESTMINSTER, AND ST. JAMES'S PARK, 1710. Twelve Sheets.

MORDEN AND LEA'S MAP OF LONDON, 1682. Twelve Sheets.

AGAS'S MAP OF LONDON, *circa* 1560. Eight Sheets.

FAITHORNE'S MAP OF LONDON, 1658. Eight sheets.

HOLLAR'S VIEW OF LONDON, 1647. Seven sheets.

PUBLICATIONS FOR 1908.

WREN'S DRAWINGS OF OLD ST. PAUL'S.

UNIQUE MAP, ENGRAVED BY HOLLAR, OF LONDON AFTER THE GREAT FIRE, 1667.

LONDON TOPOGRAPHICAL RECORD. Vol. V.

For Prospectus and inquiries address:

BERNARD GOMME, *Secretary,*

32 GEORGE STREET, HANOVER SQUARE, W

CONTENTS.

NOTICES.

It is particularly requested that all communications for the Editor be addressed to him *by name* at 5, Stone Buildings, Lincoln's Inn, W.C. All communications for the Publishers should be sent direct to them.

The annual subscription to the Magazine is 6*s.* 6*d.* post free. Quarterly Parts, 1*s.* 6*d.* net each, by post, 1*s.* 8*d.* Cases for binding, 1*s.* 6*d.* each, can be obtained from the Publishers.

Copies of some of the Plates which have appeared in the Magazine are for sale, and certain Blocks can also be purchased at moderate prices.

GEORGE BELL & SONS, YORK HOUSE, PORTUGAL ST. W.C.

St. Martin's, Ludgate.

From an old print.

THE RECORDS OF SAINT MARTIN'S, LUDGATE.

BY HENRY R. PLOMER.

THE historians of London give but a meagre history of the church of St. Martin's, Ludgate. John Stow, generally the best of authorities, passes it over with singular brevity, and does not appear to have known anything about its first foundation, or early benefactors. He takes us back no further than the year 1418, and his successors have added little or nothing to his record of the church. Yet the present building is the third that has stood on the site, the first of which was built in the twelfth century, and there exists to-day amongst the church records deposited in the Guildhall Library an almost unbroken series of records belonging to St. Martin's Church, from the year 1220 to the present day. The earlier ones are contained in a volume which, by some extraordinary oversight, is lettered "St. Martin's Ludgate, Vestry Book from the year 1568 to 1715." This volume consists of two books bound together, the earlier one being of vellum and containing copies of inventories, indentures, inquisitions, deeds of gift, and other documents, the earliest of which dates back to the year 1220. The handwriting is that of the fifteenth century, and the entries were made without any regard to chronological order, but just as the originals came out of the church chest. The latest of these early documents is dated 1485. I am inclined to think that the copies were begun by Nicholas Frost, who was churchwarden of St. Martin's in the eleventh year of Henry IV (1409-10). There is then a gap in the entries of about ninety years, when the Vestry Minutes begin in 1568, continuing down to 1688. The second portion of the volume is of paper, and contains the continuation of the Vestry Minutes from 17th August, 1688, down to the year 1715.

In this book, then, we have the history of the church, not for only for one hundred and forty-seven years, as the dates on the cover would have us believe, but for very nearly five hundred years! Unfortunately, when the volume was put into its present binding, probably in the eighteenth century, it was badly cropped by the binder.

Of the records contained in the earlier portion of this book one, and only one, has, I believe, ever been printed, and that is the fifteenth-century inventory of church goods, which was edited by the Rev. E. S. Dewick, F.S.A., and published in the *Transactions of the St. Paul's Ecclesiological Society* for 1905 (pp. 117-128). In the following article I propose to lay before the reader some of the more important and interesting of the unpublished documents in this book, and I shall do so as far as possible in their chronological sequence.

The place of honour is claimed by the two following undated deeds of gift:

> Omnibus Christi fidelibus ad quos presens scriptum pervenerit, Osbertus Plumbarius salutem, Novit universitas vestra me divine caritatis intuitu et pro salute anime mee dedisse et per superscripti carta mea confirmasse Deo et ecclesie Sancti Martini de Ludgate decem et octo denarios quieti et annui redditus in puram et perpetuam elemosinam ad inveniendum in dicta ecclesia unum cereum percipiendos annuatim de domo illa in qua mansi, que est de feodo Hospitalis Sancti Bartholomei, ad duos terminos anni, scilicet ad festum Sancti Michaeli nonem denarios et ad Pascham nonem denarios, sine occasione. Et volo quod capellanus et parochia dicte ecclesie beati Martini habeant liberam potestatem intrandi et distringendi dictam domum pro illis decem et octo denariis redditus si opus fuerit. Hos autem decem et octo denarios quieti et annui redditus ego Osbertus predictus et heredes mei prenominate' ecclesie inperpetuum sicut nostram puram et perpetuam elemosinam contra omnes gentes debemus warantizare. Et ut hec mea donacio warantia et presentis carte mee confirmacio perpetue firmitatis robur obtineat presens scriptum sigilli mei testimonio roboravi. Hiis testibus, Aldred' capellano, Penticost' aurifabro, Michaele venditore librorum, Johanne Calicer Rogero diacono, Nicholao Petrario, Johanne de Westm'[?] Ricardo Capellano, Thome Allutario, Rogero clerico, et aliis.
>
> Redditus xviij denariorum per annum de concessione Osberti plumbarii ad inveniendum unum cereum in ecclesia Sancti Martini de Ludgate. [Fol. 17.]

We can fix the date of this gift, with some degree of confidence, as before the year 1223, for amongst the records of St. Paul's Cathedral (calendared by Sir H. Maxwell Lyte and printed as an appendix to the ninth Report of the Historical Manuscripts Commission) is a deed of sale by Jordan son of Edwin, which is witnessed by Alderman Pentecost the goldsmith, Michael *qui vendit libros*, and John *qui ligat libros.* Osbert the plumber is also mentioned in the next document calendared, and to which the above date is assigned.

From the occurrence of many of the same witnesses to the second deed it is clearly of the same date, although there are many other names, not the least interesting being that of " Walter who builds walls ":

> Sciant presentes¹ et futuri quod ego, Wygot monetarius, consensu et assensu Matilde uxoris mee, et pro salute anime mee et antecessorum et successorum meorum, dedi et concessi et hac presenti carta mea confirmavi Deo et ecclesie Beati Martini de Ludgate, in puram et perpetuam elemosinam, sex denarios quieti redditus ad lumen inveniendum in predicta ecclesia, scilicet de terra quam Radulfus de Fonte tenuit de me in eadem parochia, Unde idem Radulfus vel heredes sui vel quicunque predictam terram tenebunt reddent predicte ecclesie annuatim ad festum Sancti Johannis Baptiste tres denarios et ad Nativitatem Domini tres denarios. Hos autem predictos sex denarios quieti redditus ego, dictus Wygot, et heredes mei warantizabimus predicte ecclesie contra omnes homines et feminas imperpetuum. Et quia volo quod hec mea donacio concessio firma et stabilis imperpetuum permaneat presentem paginam sigillo meo roboravi. Hiis testibus, Ada de capello ecclesie Sancti Martini, Herveo Diacono, Galfrido Baron, Willelmo Clerico, Radulfo de Fonte, Willelmo Carpentario, Waltero qui facit muros, Andree Framur', Willelmo Thyers, Pentecost' aurifabro, Willelmo Plumbario, Osberto Plumbario, Galfrido Capellano, Nicholao Petrario, et multis aliis.
>
> Redditus sex denariorum de dono Wygot monetarii ad inveniendum lumen in ecclesia Sancti Martini de Ludgate. [Fol. 17*d*.]

Another early benefactor to the church was " Master Michael of London," who died in the year 1269. In " the 19th year of Edward the son of Henry " (*i.e.*, Edward I, 1291), on the Monday next after the Feast of St. Edward, an extract from his will was sworn to by Richard de Hokele, one of his executors, and Walter de Ege. By this he left a sum of five marks a year for the income of one chaplain, to say the divine offices for his soul and the souls of his parents for ever. This sum was to be taken out of the rents of a certain house and shop left to him by his father, which were situated in the parish of St. Martin's parva, "juxta muros de Ludgate," and "ex altera parte via in eadem parochia," and which were then in the occupation of Richard de Herdfeild and Stephen Capellanus. He appointed three of the best and most faithful men in the parish, namely, Richard de Hokele, William le Waleys, and Osbert *le chalicer*, to see the obit established in the church of St. Martin. Nearly a century later Edward III ordered an inquest to be taken of the property held of the Crown by the said Master Michael of London. This inquiry was taken before John Lovekyn, Mayor of the City of London and the King's Escheator, on October 1, 41 Edward III (1368). The jurors were Robert Tetteworth, Robert Messenden, Thomas atte Crouch, John Dene, Robert Mortimer, Richard Harewe, Nicholas Reding, John Wilby, John Burton, William Botelmaker, Robert Mauncel, and Thomas Davy. They said that Master Michael died in the year 1269, but upon what day they were ignorant, and after referring to his bequest, declared that the house was then (1368) in the occupation of Peter atte Mershe and Geoffry Boneyre, and the shop in that of Robert Spenser, and that the chantry had been duly founded and the said five marks received by the churchwardens of St. Martin's, who at the time the inquiry was taken were John Dene and Robert Spenser, "sporier." (Fol. 9d., 10d.) From Dr. Sharpe's *Calendar of Letter Book G*, (London, 1905), we get a few more glimpses of some of the citizens of London mentioned in this inquisition. Thomas atte Crouche was a "sporier," who, on June 17, 1353, was nominated one of the guardians of a daughter of Thomas le Horner (p. 9). A year or two afterwards he is found acting as collector in the Ward of Farndone, or Farringdon Without, of a benevolence (p. 59). In 1360 he witnesses an indenture (p. 121), and in 1371 a writ was issued to the Mayor and Sheriffs forbidding them to put Thomas atte Crouche upon assizes, juries, etc., should he prove to be over seventy years of age (p. 285).

Geoffry Boneyre or Bonere was a "paternostrer." He was executor to the will of William Bonere, "paternoster," and was summoned to render due accounts concerning the property left by the deceased, some of which was in the parish of St. Martin within Ludgate (p. 114). He died before November, 1368. Robert Spenser figures in 1369 as one of the collectors of a subsidy for the Ward of Farringdon Without.

Extracts from a large number of wills are transcribed in this volume. Most of them were enrolled on the Hastings Rolls and are noted in Dr. Sharpe's *Calendar*; but whereas in the latter the abstracts are very brief, in these extracts we get full particulars of the bequests to the church. For example, the following is the will of Richard le Long, goldsmith of London, made in 1349, and proved on the ix kalends of May in the same year.

In Dei nomine, Amen! Ego, Ricardus le Longe, civis et aurifaber London', sanis mente et bona memoria, die dominica in qua cantatur *quasi modo geniti*,[1] Anno domini millesimo CCC quadragesimo nono, condo testamentum meum in hunc modum. In primis lego animam meam Deo Omnipotenti, Beate Marie, et omnibus sanctis, et corpus meum ad sepeliendum in ecclesiam Sancti Martini juxta Ludgate dicte civitatis. Item, lego summo altari ejusdem ecclesie ij*s*., pro decimis et oblacionibus meis oblitis. Item, lego fabrice dicte ecclesie xij*d*. Item, maiori clerico vj*d*., minori clerico iij*d*. Item, lego Alicie uxori mee residuum omnium bonorum meorum, ut ipsa disponat pro exequiis meis secundum voluntatem suam, prout melius videat Deo placere, et ad salutem anime mee et anime sue proficere. Item, lego dicte Alicie uxori mee duas schopas cum solariis supra edificatis et cum omnibus pertinenciis habendas et tenendas predictas duas schopas cum pertinenciis prefate Alicie ad totam vitam suam; Et post decessum dicte Alicie lego predictas duas schopas cum pertinentiis Roberto de Miscenden et Edithe, uxori sue et filie mee, et heredibus de corpore dicte Edithe legitime exeuntibus. Et si contingat qd dicta Editha sine herede de corpore suo legitimo procreato obierit, ex tunc volo et ordino quod post decessum predictorum Roberti et Edithe predicte due shope cum solariis et suis pertinenciis per Rectorem predicte ecclesie et per tres probos et legales homines ejusdem parochie vel per visum et ordinacionem eorum allocentur, reparentur et sustineantur, meliori modo quo eis viderint perficere, et pecunia inde recepta, excerptis expensis pro reparacione et emendacione earundem schoparum, per eosdem cuidem capellano divina celebranti in eadem ecclesia annuatim, secundum quod attingere poterit errogetur imperpetuum pro animabus Nicholai et Agnetis, patris et matris mee, ac eciam pro anima mea et Alicie uxoris mee, et animabus omni fidelium defunctorum. Hujus autem testamenti mei execucionem faciendam istos constituo executores meos, videlicet, predictas Aliciam uxorem meam et Editham filiam meam. In cujus rei testimonium sigillum presentibus apposui. Dat' et del' London', die et anno supradictis, et anno regni Regis Edwardi tercii post conquestum vicesimo tercio.

Probatus [per juramentum] Hugonis de Lemynton et Galfridi de Wychyngham. [Fol. 16.]

In Letter Book F (p. 6), is a list of names of the citizens of London who lent money for making presents to the King and Queen during the mayoralty of John de Pulteneye, 1336-37,

---

[1] Quasimodo Sunday is Low Sunday, the next after Easter.

in which Richard le Long, there described as a "pessoner,"[1] gave no less a sum than 100s. equivalent to £50 or £60 of our present money. Geoffry de Wychyngham, one of the attesting witnesses to the will, was a notable man. He was sometimes called Geoffry "le Tableter," a mercer by trade, and in 1346 was elected as Member of Parliament for the City of London. He was Mayor of the City in 1345. (Sharpe, *Calendar, Letter Book F*, pp. 119, *et seq.*)

Another fourteenth-century will is that of Robert Howner, Citizen and Brewer, who desired to be buried in the church of St. Martin, and left a sum of two marks annually to the rector and churchwardens, to found a chantry. This sum was to be levied on his brewhouse and other tenements in the parish, which he held of the Prioress of Dartford. The indenture of lease between the Prioress of Dartford and Robert Howner is also entered, dated in July, 1371. The premises were in the parish of St. Martin without Ludgate, and the lease was for sixty years at a rent of sixty-six shillings.

Adam Haket, bowyer, died in 1378; his widow released to Thomas Prenteys and John Haxay, then churchwardens of St. Martin's, a rent of seven shillings a year from a house called "the Walssheman on the hoop," and a further rent of 5s. 6d. from a tenement in the parish, which Robert Bray held of her late husband.

Another house, mentioned in a list of the rentals of the church at this time, was "the Horshed without Ludgate in Fleet Street," then inhabited by John Kyng, barber.

There is another interesting series of documents relating to Roger Payn, "sporier," including his admission to the freedom of the City of London, a grant to him by John de Stratton and Isabel, his wife, of lands in the parish, and his will and codicil proved in the Archdeaconry Court of London on April 7, 1405. With this, and other fifteenth-century documents in this wonderful volume, I hope to deal in another article.

[1] This is probably a different individual. *Pessoner* is a fishmonger, modern French, *poissonnier*.—EDITOR.

Chelmsford in 1762.

"With the Judges' Procession on the day of Entrance,

A CHELMSFORD CIRCLE IN THE SEVEN-TEENTH CENTURY.

By CLOTILDA MARSON.

SOME regret was felt by lovers of the picturesque when Chelmsford was chosen as the See of the new Diocese of Essex. Yet though the place has not many beautiful old buildings, it lies in the midst of a district very rich in memories of the past. In the seventeenth century Essex had almost the highest rateable value among the wealthy eastern counties, and was full of timbered halls and pargetted ceilings. "The Nobility," says Sir John Bramston in his *Autobiography*, "came very often to the Saturday market sermons, as did two Earls of Sussex who lived at Woodham Walter." This passage refers to Maldon, but Chelmsford was near to the Earls of Warwick (and afterwards of Manchester) at Leighs, and to Monck's son, the Duke of Albemarle, at New Hall. Thanks to the old memoirs it is possible to become very intimate with the Chelmsford circle of those long-ago days. Unfortunately, there is nothing to equal the *Verney Memoirs* among the old books, and after we have crossed that living stage it is not easy at first to move among the pale wax-works of other authors. Lady Verney's rare gift of selection has made the Denton and the Verney sisters as real as Mrs. Tulliver and Mrs. Glegg in the *Mill on the Floss*. With Sir Ralph Verney's warm-hearted sister, Cary Gardiner, we can become as intimate as with Pepys himself. There is a great charm in her liberal spelling, as when she unconsciously dubs the baby Old Pretender "the Prince of Wails." Her conscious comments on passing history, as on the Revolution of 1688, are no less valuable. In 1689 she writes: " I confes popery wod A bin much wors, for that wod A destroyed thousands of bodies and souls and estates in a short time; bot I heare there is great discontents now. I have sent you the King's speech which I liked and disliked, hee being subject to sinsures, as well as his meanest subject."

When we have closed with reluctance the last of the four volumes of the *Verney Papers*, there is some consolation in discovering that the Verney family had many roots in other counties, and, among others, in Essex. Cary Gardiner often goes to stay there with her sister Betty, the wife of the Vicar of Great Badow, near Chelmsford. Sir John Bramston's brother, Sir Moundeford Bramston, lived at Bassets, in the next hamlet of Little Badow. The Bramstons and their kin were dotted about all over Essex, and the Verneys and the Stewkeleys were frequent guests in those old wainscotted parlours.

In the Autobiography of Mary Rich, Countess of Warwick, we get a good idea of Puritan thought and feeling in the homes and parsonages round Leighs. But *The Autobiography of Sir John Bramston* has more links with everyday seventeenth-century life; the quiet royalist ladies in it are more like the Verney sisters than puritan Madam Walker in the moated Rectory at Fyfield, near as it was to Sir John Bramston's Essex home of Skreens. Doubtless Abigail Bramston could "draw spirits in an alembic or cold still and make pastry, angelots, and other cream-cheese" as well as Madam Walker, but we fancy that she was less tied by observances, and would foot it with the rest when Mr. Petre sent over his priest from Ingatestone:—"I had heard him play his part in music," says Sir John, "and he had often played to us while we were dancing." Carlyle condemns the *Autobiography* because of its long-winded incoherence, quoting meanwhile a most vivid passage about Cromwell's troopers springing out of the corn on the young Bramstons as they carry their father's message to York in 1642. The book is terribly rambling and involved, yet between its pages there lie pictures of every kind of seventeenth-century life, and a record of pious royalists who were willing to suffer death, hunger, and imprisonment for their beliefs.

The headquarters of the family was the timbered house of Skreens, near Chelmsford, but their kin were dotted over the whole county. Sir John does not write for the printer but rambles on for his own grandchildren; as the memories throng in on his mind, the pages rustle, and we seem to hear the hoofs of the six gray and four black horses, as the two shut "calesses" rattle through Oxford to join the Prince of Orange in November, 1688; and we can see the spar-hawk, with which Sir John loved to go fowling, poised above the fields round Skreens.

The sister of Sir Ralph Verney, who lived near Sir Moundeford Bramston at Little Badow, was that Betty who married late, and who always had such difficulties in finding lodgings where her hair could be satisfactorily dressed. " I am con-

Sir John Bramston, C.J.K.B.

From the painting in the National Portrait Gallery.

fident going to plow would not mack me more sick than the reaching up of my arms does," she says. The Verney family considered she had thrown herself away by marrying Mr. Charles Adams, Rector of Great Badow, and she was herself "willing to Ack knolig upon her knees this great folt of hers." Her sister Cary deplores the "rash ackt," but condones it by remembering that Lady Mary Bertie married Dr. Hewitt, who was "bot a chapling." Betty Adams is the Mrs. Gummidge of the *Verney Papers*; when the grand sisters or aunts die, they leave their silver plate to "the Quollity," but "much lumber" to poor Betty Adams. "I am glad the elections and coronation is over," she writes in 1685, "thay forgot to tolk of aney thing els, but nothing can make me forget my soroes."

Sir John Bramston's father was a judge, who, like Sir Ralph Verney, was not altogether a *persona grata* either to King or Parliament. Carlyle quotes the account of how Charles I sent for him to York in 1642, and the Parliament refused to allow him to go. Consequently, he was supplanted in his office of Chief Justice; and until the ruffling wind of civil war had blown over, he lived quietly at Skreens, where he kept a patriarchal board for fifty of his family and their connections, even to the Lord Brabazon from Ireland. At first they "all had for nothinge," but at length the kind old judge was driven to let the clan contribute toward the table, and the "hey and grass" for the horses.

The autobiographer was the eldest son of the judge, and a distinguished lawyer. He had been friend and chamber-fellow of the great Lord Clarendon, whose portrait is at Skreens, as is also the writ from James, Duke of York, in 1667, bidding Sir John, as Vice-Admiral, hinder the escape of the fallen Earl from any of the ports, creeks, or places within his jurisdiction. "The drums and trumpets blew my gown over my eares," says Sir John, "the Judges making a nose of wax of the law, and wresting it to serve turns." Consequently, he sold his chamber in the Temple and quitted his gown. The beauty of the old memoir lies partly in the real piety displayed by this very uncanting family. Cromwell was not slow to recognize the sterling worth of the old judge; but though he urged him earnestly to resume the office of Chief Justice, the old man could not forget the dead King, and preferred obscurity to place and power.

There are many curious particulars in the book about doctors, illnesses, and medicines. Old Judge Bramston's first wife was Bridget Moundeford, daughter of Dr. Thomas Moundeford, physician to James I. Perhaps this relationship gave Sir John his intense interest in diseases and their remedies, and has given us glimpses of Dr. Turberville, the friend of Pepys, Dr. Scarborow, the friend of Cowley, and Harvey, who recommended fasting against the gout. "Dr. Harvie hath starved himself these twentie years and yet hath the gout," said one Mr. Coppin; to which Sir John Bramston replied: "If to fast and have gout be all one with to eat and have gout, I will doe as I have done"—and he lived to the age of eighty-nine with scarce a twinge of it!

In the *Verney Papers*, Cary Gardiner, a connection by marriage with Sir John Bramston's sister, Lady Dorothy Palmer, takes her daughter Peg to see Dr. Turberville at Crewkerne. Poor Peg's eye "labours with 4 diseases," described in full by Cary's graphic pen. Cary is always sanguine, and she hopes that Dr. Turberville will "butify Peg's left eye." With her usual inconsequence Cary trusts less to Dr. Turberville's skill than to the fact that "his birth is very good, which makes mee believe hee will perform what he has promised." In the end Peg throws over Dr. Turberville for a "mountybank," to whom a good character has been given by Prince Rupert. Towards the end of the *Autobiography* (which fills 400 closely-printed pages) we read how his daughter, Lady Andrew Jenour of Bigods, near Dunmow, in Essex, comes to his Soho house, in Greek Street, to stay with him. She has a terrible fungus on her eye, and has been two years under the care of Dr. Turberville at, Salisbury. An "issue" on the shoulder relieves her for a time, and then the waters of Northhall, a Hertfordshire spring, are tried. Cowley's friend, Sir Charles Scarborow, advises "the hummums," which seems to have been a kind of Turkish bath, but the poor lady proved too weak to bear such a prescription, and soon died. She is one of the band of quiet gentlewomen who fit in so well with the Doll Leeks, and Lady Hobarts and Aunt Ishams of the *Verney Papers*. Another kindly picture is that of Sir John's sister, Lady Katharine Dyke. She was long a widow, and highly honoured by her son, Sir Thomas Dyke, for whose family she made a London home. She died in the eighth year of William and Mary, days when one does not expect minute church observances. Yet "since she came to dwell in town, if she were in health, or not hindered by ill weather she was at Morning or Evening Prayer in the church or tabernacle daily, as well working days as holidays and Sundays."

Sir John's other sister, Lady Dorothy Palmer, reminds us yet more of Aunt Isham in the *Verney Papers*, with her silver pocket nutmeg-grater, or Aunt Pen Osborne, who was so skilled in domestic medicine. Lady Osborne used to mix white hellebore root and grated nutmeg for a cold in the head, "to take as you do snuff, it clears the brain"; another of her recipes for a like complaint was "Conserve of Reddrosis." Lady Dorothy Palmer, once of Hill, was also clever at making home medicines. She lived to be a widow of eighty-one, passing from a daughter's summer home in Bedfordshire to another daughter's winter home in Basingshaw Street. God had blessed her with many cures in Bedfordshire, Sir John says, and wherever she came the poor flocked to her. An ungrateful husband left her ill-dowered, but she was always full of kind works. She would have no physician, but caused what she had to be made at home. On the death of her London son-in-law she was at a loss for a home, but her sister, Lady Dyke, sends to say:—"Bring your bed and come to me, you shall set it up in my dining-room and we will be together."

The ways of the sisters sound old fashioned now, but their piety is as fragrant as the herbs and the red roses they gathered by the old Essex garden-walls. As we read of their useful quiet lives we think of Margaret Blagge in Evelyn's pages, who "trussed up her little fardle like the two daughters whom the angell hastened and conducted," and left the wicked Court of Charles II. Doubtless in the Essex cathedral of the future there will be many living stones joined now to the Church Triumphant, and fit to be had in everlasting remembrance:

> And our chaste lamps we hourly trim,
> Lest the great Bridegroom find them dim.

These words of Andrew Marvell's fit well for Sir John Bramston's sisters and daughters, but there are stirring and lively pages in the biography as well as quiet ones. As the old man sat, pen in hand, in the "Low Parlour" at Skreens, or with the rumble of London coaches in his ear at Greek Street, the "old unhappy far-off things and battles long ago" passed in review. There was the Uncle Stepkin, who had drained Wapping Marshes, and then lost many of the profits of his toil through the "hungerie courtiers" of James I. His son, Peter Stepkin, was at Edge Hill fight, "strooke his colonel, and was sentenced to death, but escaped." Cousin William Bramston left Cambridge and the Temple for armed fields, endured great hardship in the siege of Colchester, and finally died under Sir John Bramston's protection at Skreens. Thomas Palmer, a nephew, takes his doctor's degree at Padua, and settles at Cambridge.

The kinsfolk are not always of unblemished character. Some of them are as shady as Lady Hobart's nephew, Dick Hals, the highwayman, whom she helps to escape, and for whom she borrows a flaxen "wigg" from Sir Ralph Verney. Sir John Bramston visits his shady kinsfolk in the Fleet Prison, as elsewhere, and does his kindly best for them, as he had done for Lady Hobart's highwayman nephew when he was shut up in Chelmsford Gaol. The Essex clergy had persuaded Dick Hals to turn informer, and the poor highwayman writes from Chelmsford Gaol bitterly regretting this cowardice, and longing for "my state of innocency, I meane while I was a pure theife, without blott or blemish." The same kindly charity was shown by Sir John to a cousin, Theodosia Stepkin of Wapping, who had three husbands, one of them an East India merchant who "courted her with jewels and fine things." Her credit was blasted in the end because she forged some deeds.

Sir John's own mother, a "beautiful, comely person," died when he was a delicate lad at a Squeers-like school at Blackmore End in Essex, kept by a preaching Mr. Walmsly, who had pies baked of the pigeons trapped by his boys at Smith's Hall, and beat little Moundeford Bramston with fifty strokes of a heavy elm rod, merely because he (Walmsly) was in a temper with his wife. During the punishment the big brother was away minding the master's cattle and conning his task. From school John Bramston went to Wadham College, a foundation with advantages for Essex boys, since Dorothy Wadham was by birth an Essex Petre of the Ingatestone family. The judge's young family was brought up by a wonderful old Moundeford grandmother, who came to look after them in the large city house in Philip Lane. She lived to be ninety-four, was very straight and upright, grave and comely, but, like so many able women, not tall. She was a skilful needlewoman, and wrought many chairs and cushions for her grandchildren, in spite of which she could read without spectacles, and walk without a staff till her last short sickness. Sir John's retentive memory passed on the tradition of another mother in Israel. Mrs. Moundeford's mother, Elizabeth Hill, *née* Locke, had been the twentieth child of a London citizen, and had suffered perils by land and sea in the Marian persecution. She had fled to Antwerp, taking with her " but one feather-bed," and submitted to Catholic baptism for her children, with the permission of Latimer and Ridley, trying to give the rite a Protestant tincture by " putting sugar instead of salt into the handkercher which was to be delivered to the priest." She had two husbands, one Richard Hill and the second Nicholas Bullingham, Bishop of Worcester.

Sir John recalls a stirring adventure in 1631, when his father bade the lad, then a youth of twenty, accompany him on a journey to Ireland, undertaken with the object of winning as his second wife a lady who had been his first love. Judge Bramston makes Hill, in Bedfordshire, the home of his daughter Lady Palmer, the first stage in his journey. This was the same home as that to which fifteen-year-old Cary Verney rode in her honeymoon days, from the Verney nest at the Peach in Covent Garden, with her husband Captain Thomas Gardiner. One of Captain Gardiner's sisters seems to have been married to a brother or a son of Sir William Palmer, for Cary was much at Hill until her first husband's sad death in a skirmish at Ethrop in 1643.

From Hill Judge Bramston and his son have a most adventurous journey, by Penmaenmawr to Beaumaris and Holyhead. They are nearly overtaken by the tide as they gallop over the sands to Beaumaris Ferry from Chester, where they had left their coach. They were nearly put to a swimming bout on horseback, like that of Mistress Alice Thornton over Swale-water when in flood, but at last the drinking ferrymen appeared, and they were shipped in safety. At Holyhead the Welsh parson had prepared an English sermon for the travellers, but they had to leave it and their dinner in the lurch, and take advantage of an auspicious Sunday wind.

Judge Bramston had known the lady he was wooing in Queen Elizabeth's days, when she stayed as a young girl at Munden Hall, near Chelmsford, with her sister Aylmer, wife of good old Bishop Aylmer's eldest son. In those days Lord Brabazon refused his daughter to plain John Bramston and sent her to Ireland, where she married first a knight and then a bishop. In 1631 she is again a widow, and the travellers ride, with bare-legged running Irish footmen alongside, to pay their court to the Lady Elizabeth Brereton. "When I saw her," Sir John says, "I confess I wondered at my Father's love. She was low, fatt, red-faced: her dress too was a hatt and a ruff which she never changed to her death. But my Father, seeing me change countenance, told me it was not beautie but virtue he courted. I believe she had been hand-some in her youth: she had a delicate fine hand, white and plumpe, and indeed proved a good wife and step-mother too." This indifference to the outer man by the graver sort in the seventeenth century may be paralleled in the case of Sir William Temple and many others.

The journey home, too, was not without adventure. As the cavalcade rode over the sands from Beaumaris to Conway, the stout bride in her ruff was perched on horseback behind her young step-son; unthinkingly she pulled off her glove and with it accidentally let fall her wedding-ring. The im-perious lady at once made her serving-man dismount and fish for the ring in the sand, and when he could not reach it leapt from her horse and refused to move without it. The man was made to strip his arm and fish again, while he and she sank to their knees in the yielding sand. At last patience was rewarded, the ring was found, and the party moved on again, climbing like flies over the side of the beetling rock until they reached Conway. We wish that Sir John gave more particulars of the home life in Philip Lane and Boswell Court, but he only says that his step-mother died in 1647, and lies buried in Roxwell Church.

In Commonwealth days the judge and his son showed kind-ness to Dr. Michelson, Rector of Chelmsford and Moulsham, who was evicted from his living partly by the agency of the Puritan Henry Mildmay, of Graces in Badow. This man was the implacable political enemy of Sir John Bramston. "Dr. Michelson was one day burying a corps," says Sir John, "with the Book of Common Prayer in his hand; the rabble threw him into the grave, and had buried him and the booke doubt-less (for they began to throw earth on him), had not some of the wiser townsmen rescued him." The poor man was se-questered and had to flee to Holland, creeping home at last to live sparely at Writtle, on the charity of the Bramstons and of Dr. Warner, Bishop of Rochester.

In 1654 the old judge died. He had been a little rash "in eating of a goose," in the house of his son Moundeford, at Bassets, in Little Badow. He had then walked from Bassets to Tofts, "and talking with the old Lady Barrington, that impertinent everlasting talker, he whispered me, he felt himself not well." Dr. Leonard and the judge's Kentish daughter, Mary Porter, came to see him, but he was seventy-seven years old, and the illness could not be shaken off. After a few days the end came at Skreens. "And diligently to live after Thy commandments—what a word is that diligently," he said to Dr. Michelson. Soon after he received the Absolution and died. He was buried at Roxwell, near Skreens. Cowley wrote his epitaph:

> Ambitione, ira, donoque potentior omni
> Qui judex aliis lex fuit ipse sibi.

It was lonely for Sir John at Skreens after his father's death, for his own happy married life with Alderman Abdy's daughter Alice had not been a long one, though the poor lady bore him ten children between November, 1635, and her death in February, 1647. Sir John only paints his portraits in pastel: they are not Dutch in their accuracy and detail, like Lady Verney's pictures, nor has he that felicity of phrase which makes every Verney letter so luminous, that we long for the unwritten works of scapegrace Tom Verney more than for fresh volumes from Sir Thomas Browne. Sir John cannot match Cary Gardiner's second husband, John Stewkeley, who describes his growing group of babies at Preshaw by saying: "Here are many white aprons that have long strings." Yet we seem to see gentle Alice Bramston sketched with a few pale touches by the husband writing so many years after she left him. She died in 1647, he in 1700, and he never married again. "She was a most careful indulgent Mother to her children," he says, "and heard them the catechism, Lord's prayer, commandments and creed, constantly every morning, as well as some psalms and chapters. She would daylie dress one or more of the gyrles with her own hands. She was a very observant wife. I scarce ever went a journey but she wept." In the winter of 1647 she came up to her husband's London house in the Charterhouse Yard. When she was shopping at Thorowgood's, the linendraper's, a football came through the window and struck the young wife, who was ailing from some "shogg or jolt or fright coming up from Skreens,—for she was very fearful in a coach." These complications defied the skill of Dr. Prujean and all the physicians, and when her baby was born she died. Sir John took his two motherless girls to Mrs. Salmon's school at Hackney, where they probably learned "Jappaning," and we will hope also "all accomplishments that will render them considerable and lovely in the sight of God and man," as did Molly Verney at Mrs. Priest's school at Chelsea.

Sir John's weaker side was his sternness towards Dissenters, whom he calls "fanaticks." He would scarcely have appreciated Thomas Ellwood of Thame, the young Quaker who stood so many "whirrets" on the ear from his father for keeping his hat on, and felt such pangs in his innocent heart for having gone a back way to avoid affronting the town magnates, and so having "shunned the Cross." Yet Sir John recognizes the generosity of Mr. Ellis Crispe, a "fanatick" who helps him in his great dilemma in 1672, when his enemy, Henry Mildmay, hatches a little Popish plot for Sir John's own special benefit, and suborns a Portuguese false witness, called Macedo, to swear that Sir John is a Papist, and has a permit from the Pope to worship the devil!

Sir John writes comparatively little about the reign of Charles II, though he describes the King's apoplexy, and the application of a fire-pan and burning amber to his head. After Charles II's death, we get many most interesting diary-entries during the stirring times of James II, and the puzzling dilemmas of William and Mary's reign. Sir John pays many heavy fines before he takes the new oaths, but at last he submits, feeling that King James's desertion of the kingdom has abrogated the old oaths. "Marrie, if he doe returne, I think our allegiance will also returne to him," writes the old man in those days of questioning of hearts.

Perhaps the most vivid of the many life-like glimpses of James II's short reign is the story of King James's hunt at New Hall, near Chelmsford. It is May, 1686. His Majesty is about to visit the Duke of Albemarle, the unworthy son of the great General Monck. The King is in fine company: there is young Prince George of Denmark, his daughter Anne's husband, the Earl of Feversham, with Sedgemoor laurels not yet withered, Lord Dartmouth, and others. "The great lords, being on the other side of the wood, heard not the hounds, and so several cast out and never reacht the hounds. But the stagg came out of the wood near by Moulsham Hall, where the King was, ran near to Wanstead, and the King was in at the death. This put him in a good humour, and he would have his fellow-hunters to sup with him at New Hall, with spendthrift Albemarle and his flighty Newcastle duchess." Next spring the Duke made a great hit by recovering the wrecked Spanish galleon and £200,000 of Spanish gold lost sixty years before and encrusted with rust and coral. King James had his share, and was doubtless glad of it.

On the second day of the hunt the stag leaps the pale and runs to the Roothings. His Majesty keeps near the dogs, though the ditches are broad and deep, and the hedges high. He is again much pleased that the lords are cast out, and Lord Dartmouth sends a messenger to Copt Hall, to the Earl of Dorset, to say the King will dine there. It turns out that the Earl is away, and the messenger meets the Countess and her mother, Lady Northampton, going a-visiting in their coach. The Countess is much perturbed, for the cook and butler are gone to the fair at Waltham. She hurries home, however, has locks and doors broken open, and by the time the King has washed, and viewed the house and gardens, a handsome collation is prepared. On the way back to London the King meets the Earl of Dorset, who bemoans his ill-fortune in missing the King:—"Make no excuses, it was exceeding well and very handsome," answers James. In a few months the clouds have drawn across the fresh May sky, and the Countess's uncle, Henry Compton, Bishop of London, is suspended. Three short years more, and Bishop Compton, in place of Sancroft, the nonjuror, is setting the crown on the heads of William and Mary.

One of the kindest of Sir John's neighbours was Lady Jane Abdy, of Albyns, near Navestock. There is an amusing page in the *Verney Papers* when twenty-one-year old Jane Nicholas, the daughter of Dr. Denton's only child Nancy, marries "the old gallant," Sir John Abdy of Albyns. He must, indeed, have been an old man in 1687, as he was a brother of Sir John Bramston's wife Alice. Edmund Verney is much against the match. "Cosen Jinny cannot love an old man," he writes, thinking perhaps of spoiled lives, of his own poor lunatic wife Mary, at the White House, and Mary Eure, whom he had loved so passionately, but might never wed. "Doctor's Nancy" wisely leaves the decision to Jinny, "for 'tis she must live with him." Sir John Bramston tells us that the marriage took place in Henry VII's Chapel on 10th May, 1687, in a high wind—so high indeed that on the 12th the tide was kept back and men walked down the bed of the Thames from Westminster to Whitehall. Lady Verney tells us that Jinny's short four years' marriage was a happy one. When baby Jane is born nothing will please Lady Abdy but that Sir Ralph Verney should be godfather, as he had been to the baby's mother and grandmother.

A CHELMSFORD CIRCLE.

We hear of many happy gatherings at Albyns. Lady Abdy
has the Adams and Stewkeley girls to stay with her, and tries
to make them all enjoy themselves. Delightful Dr. Denton
is much at home there, "lolling on bed or couch," or busy
writing prescriptions for Sir Ralph of "a syrup of Scabious
with whey or gorse, boiled with damask roses." Sir John
Bramston is equally fond of visiting Albyns, and describes a
dangerous coach accident he met with when returning from a
visit to her and her brother, Sir John Nicholas. The seventeenth-century folk were always up and down those country
roads. Lady Warwick reads a good book in her coach coming
up from Leighs. The humbler folk travel by carriers' carts,
which "come and go from Dunmow in Essex on Thursdays
and Fridays, and do lodge at the Saracen's Head in Gracious
Street."

The last convivial meeting we read of is on Sir John's
eighty-eighth birthday, in August, 1699, when he flies from
the dust and dirt, caused by the rebuilding of the "Low Parlour," to Lady Jane Abdy's at Albyns. She takes his visit "ex-
treame kindly," and invites all the Bramston kin in the neighbourhood to a family dinner, among them a Mr. Pennington,
married to an Abdy sister, and possibly a relation of Thomas
Ellwood's Quaker friend, Isaac Pennington. The noble company of Bramstons filled two tables, which Lady Abdy loaded
with good cheer. But in the hot August weather the good old
man exerted himself by too much walking. He thanks some
callers, who have given him a swan and two cygnets, and
then falls into an ague. In spite of Gascon Water, Weald
Powder, and Syrup of Gillyflowers, he never really "has his
health" again. He prays God that he may pass with no dis-
quiet of mind, or torturing pain, and then breaks off to say,
"But why doe I direct my Maker? Take me, oh, God! when
and how Thou pleasest." One more entry ends the diary:
"I have been ill with cold a week, and I was in feare I should
not have been able to goe to church on Christmas Day; but I
thanck God I went, and received the Communion at the rails
(this being the first time the Communion hath been celebrated
since the table was railed in and the pulpit removed), and I
praise God I have been free from the cold ever since."

This is the last record of the kind old lawyer and vice-
admiral. On February 14, 1700, he died, and was buried in the
chancel of Roxwell Church.

The book is not easy to read, because it is so ill-arranged

and so incoherent, yet it is full of good things. When we think of his sketch of his god-son, Richard Wyseman of Torrell's Hall—"the first seen on the wall at Buda, stroke down with a simeter and not seen after"—we know that Sir John Bramston had the heart and the eye which make history live. The book has not those dear stage-properties of the *Verney Papers*—the dogs Gamboy and Fleury—the little lists of " buttoned handkerchers, Tortus-shell agendas, cherry marmalad," and other human things of a vanished past. Yet we have the kindly picture of an old Chelmsford gentleman, who walked about the Essex ways, keenly anxious, if possible, to serve both God and the King.

SOME EAST KENT PARISH HISTORY.

By Peter de Sandwich.

[Continued from p. 213.]

DENTON.[1]

1560.

THEY have no Curate. The Parson is not resident. The chancel is in decay. That their parson hath another benefice called Bredgar.—(Fol. 22; vol. 1560-84.)

1561. That the Catechism is not taught, for be cause [*sic*] the youth come not to the church.

That John Broke, gentleman, hath in his keeping a cow belonging to the church.—(Fol. 86; vol. 1561-2.)

1563. It is presented that they have no chest for rhe poor.

That their Rector is not resident.

They lack the Homily for the gange-days [*i.e.* Rogation].—(Vol. 1562-3.)

1569. (Archbishop Parker's Visitation.)

Rectory; in patronage of Mr. Coole.

Rector:—Dom. John Lytherer; he is married, does not reside there, has more benefices, but not in the Diocese of Canterbury, not a preacher nor licensed to preach, not a graduate.

[1] Formerly in Elham Deanery.

Curate:—Dom John Sempyer, Rector of Wootton.
      Householders, 6.
      Communicants, 25.—(Vol. 1569.)

1580.—*See under* Badlesmere, vol. vii, p. 212.

1586.—We present that the churchyard is unenclosed, and the porch at reparation.—(Fol. 2.)

1590.—Our church is not sufficiently repaired, also the chancel.
  Our Minister, Mr. Twisden, for that he weareth not the surplice according to the law.—(Fol. 51.)

1591.—The churchwardens, for that they have been a long while, and yet are without a surplice for their Minister to wear.—(Fol. 67.)

1592. We say that our Minister doth but seldom say the Litany on Fridays and Holydays.
  2. Our Minister doth not every second Sunday teach the catechism, but doth once a quarter.
  On the 5 June, when the Rector appeared in Court he said:—There are but nine houses which are inhabited within the parish, and that on Holydays he readeth the Litany, and that on Fridays he readeth the Litany when any of the parishioners do come to the church.—(Fol. 79.)

1597. That Mr. James Broker, late of Barham, in his last will gave certain legacies to charitable uses to our parish, which is not discharged, whether the fault be in Mr. Thomas Fineux, his executor, or in his heirs, we refer you to the consideration of the will in record in your Court.[1]

1598. We present Mr. Robert Twisden, our Minister, for that he doth not use the surplice as is required to be done, nor hath he of long time worn the same.
  He hath not used to say any service on the holy-days or festival-days.
  We present our Minister for that he doth not use to read the Articles, as is required to be done.—(Fol. 155.)

[1] For the will of this James Brooker, buried in Denton Church, February 7, 1594; see *Archeologia Cantiana*, vol. vi, 290.

SOME EAST KENT PARISH HISTORY.

William Meere, for that he the principal person, the lord, as he called himself, after a masking manner, with his brother and one Richard, whose name we further know not, apparelled like a fool sundry times, especially one Sunday the last Harvest, did disturb our Minister with their pageant and revelery in the church, to the offence of God and the congregation there.

That the said William Meere there one Sunday in the month of September last, in Evening Prayer time, went out of the church to a dancing, notwithstanding he was diswarned by our Minister.—(Fol. 164.)

1599. William Verrier, the last churchwarden, hath two church kine in his hands, which he hath not delivered nor put the parish in assurance by sureties for them, according to the custom of the parish.—(Fol. 174; vol. 1585-1636.)

1605. We have no service on Wednesdays and Fridays.

We think our Minister doth not cross children in baptism, for he useth not the words and confesseth he hath not hitherto done it.

He doth sometimes wear the surplice and sometimes doth not.

Our chancel wants some reparation of tiling.

On June 28, 1605, when Robert Twisden, the Rector, appeared in Court, he confessed:—That by reason of the smallness of his parish he hath sometimes omitted to read service on Wednesdays and Fridays, and for that many times none of his parish do on these days resort to church; but he saith that hereafter he will more carefully perform this duty in reading service on Wednesdays and Fridays. That heretofore he did not sign the children that were baptised by him with the sign of the cross, but saith that of late he hath conferred with Mr. Archdeacon of Canterbury about the using of the sign of the cross in baptism, and that he is now resolved to use the same, and hereafter will use it. He confessed that he hath sometimes omitted to wear the surplice, but he will hereafter wear the same more orderly. He confessed that the chancel of the church wanteth some reparation of tileing.—(Fol. 56.)

We have no convenient cover-cloth for our Communion Table. Our church wants some reparation of tiling, and we have no cushion cloth to our pulpit.—(Fol. 59.)

261

SOME EAST KENT PARISH HISTORY.

1607. We think our Minister doth not sign children with the sign of the cross in baptism.

2. He doth sometimes wear the surplice and sometimes omitteth it.

3. Our Minister doth sometimes omit some part of Divine Service.

On December 4, 1607, when Robert Twisden appeared, he confessed:—That he doth not sign the children in Baptism with the sign of the cross. So the Judge admonished him— That at the next baptising of any child by him in the said parish he do use and sign the child with the sign of the cross, and also use all other ceremonies and duties set down in the Book of Common Prayer; and that he do wear his surplice according as by law he is bound; and also do read the whole service according to the Book of Common Prayer.—(Fol. 111.)

We have no such clerk as can read, but a poor man, James Browne, that cleaneth the church, ringeth the bells, maketh the graves, and hath the accustomed duties. We do present him.—(Fol. 112.)

1608. We have a Bible, but not of the largest volume. We have a pulpit, but no covering.—(Fol. 135.)

Widow Mershe of the parish of Acrise, for that she refuseth to pay her cess towards the reparation of our steeple, which sum is 13s. 4d., being lawfully demanded by me, Thomas Harnett, churchwarden of the parish of Denton.—(Fol. 145; vol. 1602-9.)

1611. Our chancel and vicarage-house wanteth some reparations, and Mr. Rogers craveth a day for the doing thereof. —(Fol. 36.)

That Mr. John Cassell doth teach Sir Francis Swan his children in his own house, which to do whether he be licensed or not I cannot answer.

Our churchyard wanteth such a fencing as heretofore it hath had, for which I crave a day.—(Fol. 37.)

We have not the Table of Degrees of marriages-forbidden, as by this article is required.

Thomas Giles is a neglecter of Divine Service, an ale-house haunter, a common swearer, and a blasphemer and railer on his neighbours.—(Fol. 38.)

1613. That our parsonage-house, barn and out-houses are

very greatly decayed, in default of Mr. Francis Rogers, our Parson.—(Fol. 71.)

1615. We have no sentences of Scripture on the walls.

We have no Communion cup, for Sir Francis Swan, knight, did keep it for us, and one night that cup with much more plate was stolen by thieves, his house being broken up, and the said Sir Francis doth provide one until we can be fitted better.

We have no procession kept.

We have no prayers on Wednesdays and Fridays, our prayers are two chapters and two psalms, and the surplice is never worn.

We have no signing with the cross in baptism.

We have no catechising.—(Fol. 125; vol. 1609-18.)

1620. On January 8, Robert Preble, churchwarden of Denton, presented one Mr. Bachelor, a supposed minister, for that somewhat before Michaelmas last past he did administer the Holy Communion in our parish church to many of the parishioners then and there assembled, he not wearing the surplice, not yet being a licensed minister, as the fame or report is in our said parish, and where he now resideth I do not know.—(Fol. 33.)

On April 12, it was stated in Court:—That Samuel Bachelor serveth the cure of Denton, and so hath done many months last past, without any lawful authority from the Ordinary, having never subscribed the Articles of Religion according to the Canons and constitution of the Church of England; and yet nevertheless is not contented to be quiet and peaceable in the church, but both by his sermons and practise in administering of the Sacraments violateth the order of the Book of Common Prayer established by the laws of this realm; and namely, in the administration of the Lord's Supper, he administereth to such only as sit, and refuseth to administer to such as kneel; and in his sermons inveigheth against the cross in baptism; and in the solemnization of matrimony he useth not the ring, according to the order prescribed in the Book of Common Prayer.

1621. That Mr. Harbert, our Curate, in the administration of baptism doth sometimes omit to sign the children with the sign of the cross upon their foreheads, and sometimes doth it

263

according to the Book of Common Prayer, viz: Hezekias the son of Thomas Marshall of our parish he did omit to sign with the sign of the cross, as the fame is in our parish. But Silvester the son of Edward Dickson he did sign with the sign of the cross.

2. Sometimes in the administration of the Sacrament our Minister doth wear the surplice, and sometimes doth not wear it, but in reading prayers never that I know of doth wear it.

3. Our Minister doth not, nor hath not instructed and examined the ignorant persons and youth of the parish, in the catechism set forth in the Book of Common Prayer, upon any Sunday and Holy-day as he is required.—(Fol. 37.)

1622. Mr. Harbert, our Curate, for that he hath administered the Holy Communion without wearing of his surplice, being on the 25 November, 1621. Also for not catechising the youth and ignorant of our parish; and that he never in his service reads the ten Commandments, nor most part of the Divine Service, neither hath ever read the Book of Canons since he came to our parish.—(Fol. 53.)

Thomas Cowell and his wife, Richard Richardson and his wife, Richard Rye, and Mr. Harbert's man-servant, whose name I cannot learn, for that when they received the Holy Communion they did not reverently kneel, being on the 25 November, 1621.—(Fol. 54.)

Mr. Abiezar Harbert, our Curate, for christening of Robert Jull's son, and not signing him with the sign of the cross. Also that he hath been our Curate about two years, and during which time he hath never read the Book of Canons in our parish.—(Fol. 66; vol. 1619-22.)

1635. To the 36:—he hath not any of these, nor weareth any of them, but weareth a civil black cloake when he preacheth and prayeth, and no other.—(Fol. 20; vol. 1585-1636, part ii.)

On April 3, 1690. William Cramp applied to the Court and said:—There is still due to him for work and material done and used by him about repairing the bell-loft of Denton aforesaid, and for putting up a new frame for the bells, the sum of £16, wherefore he humbly prayed that Francis Baker and William Godfrey may be ordered to make a cess and reimburse him the said sum, in the presence of the same Baker and Godfrey. They however alleged that there appears but a small quantity of timber to be used about the work, and that the timber and workmanship cannot be near worth that sum, and that if William Cramp will be content to have the same surveyed, he to chuse one or two workmen and they the like, they will pay him what the said workmen shall adjudge the timber and workmanship to be worth. Whereupon the Judge ordered them to consent to such a survey, and monished the parties to have such survey taken betwixt this and the next court day and in case the said Baker and Godfrey did not agree to pay Cramp the money the surveyors should adjudge, that they do bring into this Court the survey, and then appear to see and hear further order therein.

On May 14 both Baker and Godfrey appeared and said that they had been ready to consent to a survey as was ordered, and that Cramp hath not as yet named any person to them to survey on his part, and that they are ready to consent whenever Cramp will name his day and man, upon giving them four days' notice of the day happening.

On October 22 Cramp came into the Court, and alleged that Francis Baker aforementioned, and Captain Whorwood, who was churchwarden when the work aforementioned was done, had agreed that a survey should be taken on a Thursday happening in or about July last, and that the persons whom Captain Whorwood and he (Cramp) nominated did attend, and was ready to consent to such a survey on the said Thursday; and Baker his man appeared not, though the said Baker was sent to and desired to come and be present, but he refused to come, and Cramp offered himself ready to make oath thereof, and prayed allowance of the money due to him, in the presence of William Godfrey; whom the Judge did monish to make a church cess at twelve pence in the pound, which Godfrey said would amount to about £12, and to collect the same and pay to Cramp the one half of the money due to him as aforesaid, and the other half thereof at Lady-day next, and to certify thereof at Easter next.—(Fol. 131; vol. 1670-93.)

[To be continued.]

THE EARLY HISTORY OF LITTLE BERKHAMSTEAD, HERTS.

By C. E. JOHNSTON.

THE village of Little Berkhamstead is on the hill south of the Lea Valley, between Hertford and Hatfield, some 375 feet above the sea level. Its name (in Anglo-Saxon, *Beorhhamstede*, the homestead-on-the-hill) well describes its position. In common with neighbouring parishes, its lands run from the high ground down to the river in the valley below, which forms its northern boundary: on the west it is bounded by Bayford Parish, on the east by Essendon, and on the south by Hatfield. The present area of the parish is 1586½ acres, but there was formerly an outlying portion of about 108 acres at Claypits Farm, on the road to Broxbourne; this is now in the civil parish of Bayford, but still pays tithe to Little Berkhamstead.

Though never of much importance, Little Berkhamstead is a place of great antiquity; it belonged to the alms of King Edward the Confessor, and all the kings his predecessors, and was assessed at five hides, which just before the Norman Conquest were divided amongst three holders: Semar, a priest, held two hides; Leuefa (Leofgifu), a widow, held two; and Wlfric Werden, one; it was then worth 100 shillings yearly.

It is now held[1] that it was here or near by, and not at Great Berkhamstead, that William the Conqueror, after his encircling movement round London subsequent to the Battle of Hastings, met Edgar Atheling and the Saxon leaders from London and received their submission. This incident took place near *Beorcham*, just as London came in sight. It would certainly seem that the invading army passed through Little Berkhamstead, as its yearly value was reduced to 50 shillings, when the Conqueror bestowed it on one of his followers, Harduin d'Eschalers,[2] and this would, no doubt, be due to waste and pillage, as by 1086 the value was once more 100 shillings.

The fief which Harduin received from the Conqueror lay in Cambridgeshire and Hertfordshire, and the *caput* of his barony

[1] *English Historical Review*, January, 1898.
[2] The Latinized form of the name was *de Escalariis*, or *Scalariis*, which historians converted into de Scalers; it was derived, perhaps, from Ecalles in Normandy.

was in Cambridgeshire; in Hertfordshire his lands were assessed at some 40 hides, besides 14 houses in the borough of Hertford; it was a characteristic of his scattered estates that he displaced a great number of small holders. He and his wife, Odel, gave the Manor of Bramfield, Herts, to the Abbey of St. Albans. Harduin died, it is said, in 1086, and he left his fief in equal shares to his two sons, Richard and Hugh; they were each, it appears, responsible for the services of fifteen knights, so that Harduin must have held his fief for thirty knights.

Little Berkhamstead fell to the share of Hugh d'Eschalers, the younger son, and he gave the church of Little Berkhamstead and those of Reed and Wyddial, Herts, and Whaddon, Cambs (all inherited from his father), to the Cluniac Priory of St. Pancras at Lewes, where he eventually became a monk, on which his son, Henry, succeeded to his lands and confirmed the grant to the Priory, adding thereto 10 shillings rent in Whaddon.[1] Henry in his turn was succeeded by his son, Hugh, who also confirmed the grants to the Priory.

Meanwhile the elder branch of the family was represented by William d'Eschalers, son of Stephen and grandson of Richard, and second cousin, therefore, of Hugh; William considered that, as descendant of the elder son, he had a right to all his great grandfather, Harduin's, lands, and a grand Assize[2] was accordingly held between the cousins about the end of the twelfth century concerning 2 carucates of land in Whaddon, 3 in Reed, 3 in Wyddial, and 2 in Berkhamstead, and the services of sundry knights. The jury found that when Henry I died, in 1135, Harduin's sons each held the lands he had left them, and that these lands had since descended from father to son in each case. Hugh, therefore, won the day.

Hugh d'Eschalers appears in the *Testa de Nevill*, under " Serjeanties in the time of Henry III," as holding Berkhamstead for one knight's fee,[3] which pertained to his barony. He had three sons, Henry, Geoffrey, and John. Henry succeeded his father, and went to Palestine, assigning the Manor of Wyddial to his wife Maude, for her maintenance in his absence. In 1220 she complained that she was much vexed in her tenure of the manor by Jews, to whom her husband

---

[1] Cartulary of Lewes in the Cottonian MSS.
[2] *Abbreviatio Placitorum*, 7 Ric. I to 9 John.
[3] Note that the assessment of the manor is no longer 5 hides, but one knight's fee, or 2 carucates.

was in debt (probably for his crusading outfit), and the sheriff was directed to have the vexation stopped.[1]

Henry d'Eschalers died in Palestine, and in 1221 his brother, Geoffrey, did homage and paid £100 relief for his lands. An interesting, but far from estimable, person now comes for a brief space into the history of the manor: in 1223 Geoffrey d'Eschalers (his younger brother, John, consenting) granted[2] to Falkes de Breauté for 10 marks of silver the Manor of Little Berkhamstead in demesnes and rents, in villeinage, homage, and freemen's services, and all other appurtenances, to hold for ever of Geoffrey and his heirs, at a yearly rental of a pair of gilt spurs or sixpence at Easter for all service save foreign service.

Falkes de Breauté was a Norman of low origin, who had secured the favour of King John; he should have been banished on the signing of Magna Carta, but was instead raised to greater power for his services to John against the Barons. He was given to wife Margaret, daughter and heiress of Warine Fitz Gerald and widow of Baldwin de Redvers of Devon, with the custody of his stepson, young Baldwin de Redvers. This marriage and wardship gave him a great position, and he further obtained the custody of several castles and the shrievalty of six counties. He was thus in a position of great power at the beginning of Henry III's reign. He committed so many excesses that it could no longer be tolerated, and Hubert de Burgh, the justiciar, demanded the restoration of the castles, honours, and wardships pertaining to the Crown, which Falkes had in his possession. It was only on a threat of excommunication that he complied. He was then tried, found guilty of more than thirty acts of wrongful disseisin, and sentenced to pay a heavy fine. This so incensed him that he seized one of the justices who had given the sentence, and imprisoned him in Bedford Castle, then held by his brother, William de Breauté. Falkes himself retreated to Wales; he was excommunicated and his lands were seized; this was in June, 1224. Bedford Castle was captured in the following August, after a desperate defence, and William de Breauté was hanged. Soon after Falkes was captured and threw himself on the King's mercy, pleading his services to King John. By a deed dated August 25, 1224, Falkes made complete submission and surrendered all his estates; his wife pleaded that she had been

---

[1] Close Rolls.　　　　[2] *Pedes Finium*, 7 Hen. III, Herts, No. 63.

married to him against her will; she was granted a divorce and her own estates were restored to her. In 1225 Falkes was sentenced to banishment from England for ever, and his excommunication was removed. He set out for Rome to solicit the Pope's intervention, and Honorius III wrote to the King and to the Archbishop of Canterbury on his behalf;[1] but nothing came of it, as in 1226 Falkes died abroad. His fall was the end of the influence in England of the foreigners brought in by King John.[2]

Little Berkhamstead thus came into the hands of the King; Henry III promptly restored to Thomas Saut of Cheverel rents of 2 marks and 2 pence in Berkhamstead, which had been granted him by Henry d'Eschalers, and of which he had been wrongfully disseised by Falkes de Breauté.[3] In April, 1225, orders were sent[4] to the Sheriff of Herts to pull down without delay Falkes' houses at Little Berkhamstead, and to cart them to Hertford Castle, where they were to be re-erected. In the following July the King granted Falkes' land there, during pleasure, to John Marescall for his maintenance in the King's service; and in August, Falkes' houses having been removed to Hertford Castle, the sheriff was directed to leave the ancient hall and ancient chapel, brewery and stable (*veterem Aulam et veterem Capellam, bracinum et marescalciam*) till further orders, and not to allow any waste or destruction of the houses, meadows, or corn belonging there, and to let the King know the expense incurred in tilling and sowing the land.

On July 18, 1226, orders were given that at a convenient season the stable-house (*domum marescalcie*) of Little Berkhamstead should be removed to Hertford and erected in a suitable place within the castle. On July 30 the sheriff was directed (notwithstanding the order to take into the King's hands the land of Little Berkhamstead which John Marescall had of the King's bailiff) to allow the said John to have his own goods and chattels there, and to harvest the corn which he had had sown there, and to have the labour due in that vill for harvesting corn that autumn. The same day orders were sent to the sheriff to give seisin of the said land to Nicholas de Moeles, to whom the King had granted it, during pleasure, for his maintenance in the King's service.

[1] Papal Letters, 1226.
[2] For further details about Falkes, *see* Matthew Paris, *Chronica Majora* and *D. N. B.*
[3] Close Rolls, 1224.   [4] Close Rolls.

Two years later (August 11, 1228) the King granted the manor to Nicholas de Moeles and his heirs entirely; unfortunately the membrane on which the grant is enrolled is defective and the terms of the grant cannot be exactly ascertained. From the old *Calendar of Charter Rolls* (published in 1803) we learn that it was a grant to Nicholas de Moeles of all the land in Little Berkhamstead formerly held by Falkes de Breauté, and Chauncy, in his *Antiquities of Hertfordshire* (1700), states that the manor was granted to Nicholas, "to hold of the King in fee or to whom he should give or assign the same, rendring yearly to the King at Easter a pair of gilt spurs, or sixpence, for all services, and that their tenants of the land shall be quit from all suits at the County and Hundred Court:" this tallies with the parts of the original grant still remaining. The exemption of the tenants from suits at the Hundred and County Courts was a privilege of tenants in royal manors.

It will be seen that Geoffrey d'Eschalers's right to the manor appears to have been forfeited as well as Falkes', and the heirs of Nicholas de Moeles certainly held it of the King in chief; but in the *Testa de Nevill*, amongst knights who were tenants-in-chief in other counties but not in Herts, we find Nicholas de Moeles holding Little Berkhamstead, value £10; and in 1235 Nicholas de Moeles of Berkhamstead paid one mark scutage at Hertford by Walter Marescall, his steward, for one knight's fee *of the fee of Geoffrey d'Eschalers*. It would seem that some question about this may have arisen later, as, in 1252, an inquisition was held to find out whether Falkes' two carucates of land in Little Berkhamstead had been in the King's hands for a year and a day or not, and of whom he held that land; the jury found that it had been in the King's hands for a year and a day, and that the land was held of Geoffrey d'Eschalers.[1] A felon's lands were forfeited to the Crown for a year and a day, on the principle that the overlord had not exercised due care in the choice of a tenant, and afterwards the lands reverted to the overlord, but in this case the d'Eschalers family certainly ceased to have any right to the manor by the time of Nicholas de Moeles' son, and the grant to Nicholas was made direct by the King.

The exact origin of Nicholas de Moeles is uncertain. The lordship of Moeles (now Meulles) in Normandy had belonged

---

[1] Cussans in his *History of Hertfordshire* quotes this as an inquisition *post mortem* on Falkes de Breauté.

to Baldwin FitzGilbert, Sheriff of Devon after the Conquest, who was sometimes styled Baldwin de Moeles: a Roger de Moeles was a tenant of his in Devon in 1086 and a Roger de Moeles appears in the Devonshire Pipe Roll of 1140. Nicholas (or Colin, as he was also called) first appears in 1215 in the King's service; on one occasion he is called "King's clerk," and he was often employed in confidential affairs. In 1225 he was sent with some ecclesiastical dignitaries on a mission to the Duke of Austria, and the following year he was sent to Poitou to Earl Richard, the King's brother, and remained in Gascony till 1227. In 1229 he is called *miles noster familiaris*. The same year the King sent to the custodians of the bishopric of Ely to allow Nicholas de Moeles six beeches and four oaks from Hatfield Park, for timber, perhaps for replacing the buildings at Little Berkhamstead, which had been removed to Hertford Castle.

Nicholas had grants of various manors from the King, amongst others King's Kerswell and Diptford, Devon. Some time before 1231 he married Hawise, daughter of James de Newmarch, who brought to him the manors of Cadbury and Maperton, Somerset. By this marriage he had apparently two sons, Roger and James, and two daughters, Maud, who married Richard del Ortiay, and Agnes, who married William de Braose.

He had been made Sheriff of Hampshire and Warden of Winchester Castle in 1228, but he had to surrender the Shrievalty in 1232 to Peter des Roches, Bishop of Winchester, Henry III's worthless favourite; he regained it, however, on the Bishop's dismissal from power in 1234, and he was also given charge of the Channel Islands.

At the coronation of Eleanor of Provence, Henry's queen, in 1236, Nicholas de Moeles and Richard Siward, *milites strenui*, carried the royal sceptres, "not by right, as there is no right to this service, but by the King's choice." Later, he was further favoured, as his son, James, was allowed to be educated with Prince Edward.

In 1242 he accompanied the King to Poitou, and was sent on an unsuccessful mission to Louis IX, to arrange a truce. From 1243 to 1245 he was Seneschal of Gascony, and waged a successful war against Thibaut, King of Navarre. In 1251, he was sent to Gascony to investigate charges against Simon de Montfort. He was governor of various castles at different times, and in 1258 was Warden of the Cinque Ports. The last mention of him[1] is in 1263, and he must have died before 1268, as in that year his son, Roger de Moeles, had a grant of a weekly market and a fair at King's Kerswell, Devon, which had belonged to Nicholas. We may assume that Little Berkhamstead cannot have seen very much of Nicholas de Moeles, as he was so constantly employed in the King's service: it was, moreover, the only manor which he held in that part of the country.

In 1274 an inquisition taken at Hertford[2] found that Nicholas had made encroachment at Little Berkhamstead by appropriating to himself half an acre of land of the King's demesne (presumably in the adjoining royal manors of Bayford or Essendon), "which his son now holds," and that Roger de Moeles had made encroachment by cutting down ten trees on a boundary (*divisa*) of the King's between Essendon and Berkhamstead. Further, Walter de Essex, while sheriff, had taken two of Roger's horses, worth two marks, and still retained them, contrary to the King's command.

In 1278 complaint was made before the Justices Itinerant that the men of Little Berkhamstead and Hertingfordbury were wont to fish in the water of Little Berkhamstead (*i.e.* the River Lea) with fishing-nets, but that Roger de Moeles now for ten years elapsed has restrained them.[3]

Roger de Moeles fought in the Welsh wars of Edward I. He had free warren in his demesne lands at Little Berkhamstead in 1290; and, by inquisition taken after his death in 1295, it was found that he held the manor in chief of the King, by the service of a pair of gilt spurs, worth sixpence, and that John de Moeles, aged twenty-six, was his son and heir. The latter was summoned to Parliament as a baron by writ: he married a daughter of Lord Grey de Ruthyn (?), named apparently Maude,[4] and had three sons, Nicholas, Roger, and John. On his death in 1310 he was succeeded by Nicholas, who was just of age, and who was also summoned to Parliament by writ. This Nicholas married Margaret Courtenay, sister of the Earl of Devon, and in 1313 settled the manor of Little Berkhamstead on himself and his wife for their lives, with remainder, in default of issue between them,

---

[1] See *D.N.B.* and Matthew Paris, *Chronica Majora*, for further details concerning Nicholas de Moeles. Matthew Paris calls him *miles strenuissimus et circumspectus*.

[2] Hundred Rolls.   [3] Assize Rolls.

[4] Feet of Fines, Somerset, 1303.

to his right heirs,[1] so that, on his death without issue in 1316, his widow succeeded to Little Berkhamstead in addition to manors in Devon and Somerset assigned her by the King as dower.[2] The remainder of his lands went to his brother,[3] Roger, who, however, died without issue in 1325, leaving a widow, Alice (daughter and heiress of William le Prouz), and was succeeded by the third brother, John. There were thus two widows to be provided for out of the estates, and John de Moeles' inheritance was somewhat curtailed on that account: Margaret, widow of Nicholas, at all events survived him, but we need not follow her history, as in 1328 she exchanged the manor of Little Berkhamstead with John de Moeles for some of his lands in Devonshire.[4]

John de Moeles did homage for his brother's lands in September, 1325;[5] he married Joan, daughter of Sir Richard Lovel of Castle Cary, who had had custody of his lands for the short period till he came of age. Sir John de Moeles, who had been made a Knight of the Bath, died in 1337, leaving two daughters to divide his property. The elder daughter, Muriel, aged fifteen, was already married to Thomas de Courtenay, younger son of the Earl of Devon, and her pourparty of inheritance was delivered to her and her husband. Little Berkhamstead fell to the portion of Isabel, the younger daughter, aged thirteen, who, being heiress of a tenant-in-chief, under age and unmarried, became a ward of the King. That same year, however, she married, without the King's leave, William de Botreaux, an elderly man, who was the owner of many manors in the south-west of England, chiefly in Cornwall,[6] Devon, and Somerset; the King, therefore, refused to give up her lands and gave the custody of them to Thomas de Ferrers to hold until she should come of age.[7] It was not, however, till 1347 that seisin of her pourparty was given to her and her husband, including Little Berkhamstead.[8]

William de Botreaux died in 1349, leaving a son William, aged twelve, and the King thus again had the wardship of the heir to Little Berkhamstead, the custody of which he gave to William Volant for 25 marks yearly during William's minority.[9]

---

[1] *Ped. Fin.* Herts, and *Inq. ad quod damnum*, 6 Edw. II.
[2] Close Rolls.
[3] He has been erroneously stated to be *son* of Nicholas.
[4] Patent Rolls. [5] Close Rolls, 1337.
[6] The name of this family survives in Boscastle, originally Botreaux Castle, in Cornwall. [7] Close Rolls, 1337.
[8] Close Rolls, 1347. [9] *Rot. Orig. Abbrev.*

EARLY HISTORY OF LITTLE BERKHAMSTEAD.

William de Botreaux, the younger, made proof of age in 1359, and had livery of his lands: he married Elizabeth, daughter of Sir Ralph D'Aubeny, and had four sons, William, Thomas, Ralph, and John. In 1375 he granted the manor of Little Berkhamstead to Edmund de Hyndon for twelve years, at the annual rent of a rose at Midsummer: and later in the same year an inquisition[1] at Hertford found that Sir William de Botreaux might, without prejudice to the King, grant the manor (valued at 100 shillings yearly) to Edmund de Hyndon for life and for a year after Edmund's death to the executors of his will, to hold of the King by the usual services, the manor to revert afterwards wholly to de Botreaux and his heirs. Hyndon's tenure ceased in or before 1384, as in that year Sir William granted[2] the manor, excepting 100 acres of woodland, to William Framelyngham, Citizen and Skinner of London, for ten years, at an annual rent of a rose at Mid-summer for the first six years, and after that 20 marks yearly; and in 1385 he extended the lease to twenty years in all. It was no doubt more profitable to lease manors than to work them, in view of the labour troubles due to the Black Death and the Peasants' Revolt.

In 1385 Sir William de Botreaux settled Little Berkham-stead on himself and his wife, with remainder to his sons, and, in default of them or their heirs, to his sister Elizabeth, wife of Robert de Palton.[3] At Sir William's death, in 1391, it was found that William Framelyngham held the manor, then worth £10 yearly, the hundred acres of woodland being worth 2s. yearly. The eldest son, Sir William de Botreaux, who was aged twenty-three and more in 1391, had married Elizabeth, daughter and heiress of John de St. Lo; he died in 1394, leaving a son, William, aged five, and with this last William ended the senior male line of the family, as he had only a daughter, Margaret, who married Sir Robert Hungerford, second Baron Hungerford, and carried the Botreaux estates into that family.

Little Berkhamstead, however, passed into other hands, for in 1402 it was found[4] that John Norbury, Esquire, held the manor of the King in socage *sine medio*, and that it was worth £18 a year, and he paid 18s. towards the aid for marrying the

---

[1] *Inq. ad quod damnum*, 49 Ed. III.
[2] *Inq. post mortem*, 15 Ric. II, Sir William de Botreaux.
[3] Feet of Fines (Divers Counties), 1385.
[4] Lay Subsidies, Herts, 120-54.

King's eldest daughter, Blanche. Exactly when or by what means Norbury got possession of the manor is not clear. It was still held by the de Botreaux family in 1399, as is shown by a suit recorded in the last *De Banco* Roll of Richard II's reign, brought by the King, as guardian of William de Botreaux, with reference to the advowson of Little Berkhamstead.

John Norbury[1] was a cadet of a Cheshire family,[2] and was a squire to John of Gaunt. He was one of the three English captains mentioned in Froissart's *Chronicle*, who in 1385 arrived at Lisbon from Bordeaux with "three great ships of men of war and English archers, good men of arms and well used in the feats of war," and rendered valiant aid to King John of Portugal against the King of Castile at the battle of Aljubarrota.

In 1387 Norbury acquired the manor of Bedwell[3] in Essendon, which adjoins Little Berkhamstead: Essendon was a royal manor which had been granted to John of Gaunt by Edward III. In 1390 he accompanied Henry, Earl of Derby, son of John of Gaunt, on the "Crusade" of the Teutonic Knights against Lithuania. The following year he was Knight of the Shire for Hertfordshire, and was then receiving £20 a year as squire to the Earl of Derby. He accompanied Henry on his banishment in 1398, and was in attendance on him in Paris in June, 1399; the following month he landed in Yorkshire with Henry, who ostensibly came to claim his father's estates and soon collected an army. Richard II surrendered to Henry on August 19, and on September 3 Norbury was appointed Treasurer of the Exchequer during pleasure.[4] The King was lodged in the Tower of London, where Norbury was one of the witnesses of his abdication; and on September 30, when Henry was accepted as King by Parliament, Norbury's appointment as treasurer was confirmed. Later he received a grant of £40 yearly, the office of Keeper of the King's Privy Wardrobe within the Tower, the Castle and Lordship of Ledes, Kent, the Captaincy of Guisnes Castle in Normandy, and a manor and castle in Ireland, and Ralph, Earl of Westmorland, granted him £60 yearly.[4]

In February, 1400, Norbury was a commissioner for holding special courts of inquiry into cases of treason in London and the neighbourhood.[4] In May, 1401, he vacated the office of

[1] The name was also spelt Northbury or Northbery.
[2] Ormerod's *History of Cheshire*.   [3] Ancient Deeds, P.R.O.
[4] Patent Rolls.

Treasurer, but he remained high in the King's favour, and in 1404 was one of seven commoners in the Privy Council. In 1405 he was recommended, with others, to the King's favour by the Commons for his " *bon et gréable service* " in joining in Henry's adventure in 1399. In 1406 he was sent on an embassy to France with Henry Beaufort, Bishop of Winchester; in this year he vacated the Captaincy of Guisnes. He had amassed wealth, as he advanced £1,000, a considerable sum then, for the pay of the Guisnes garrison, and he lent the King £3,000 more in 1407 and 1408.

It was doubtless through Henry's favour, as guardian of William de Botreaux, that Norbury had been able to acquire the manor of Little Berkhamstead. In 1406 he had license[1] to inclose 800 acres of land and wood in his manors of Bedwell and Little Berkhamstead with palings, a wall, hedge, or ditch, at his will, and make thereof a park, and stock it with wild and other animals; together with free warren in all his demesne lands in Essendon and Little Berkhamstead, so that no one should hunt there without permission, under penalty of £10 fine to the King.

Norbury's first wife was named Petronilla (or Parnel); by her he had two daughters—Joan, married to Nicholas Usk, Treasurer to John of Gaunt, and the other married to William Parker, a London alderman; for the last Norbury negotiated a second marriage, in 1404, with Sir Richard St. Maur. Some time between 1405 and 1410 Norbury married Elizabeth, elder sister of Sir Ralph Boteler of Sudeley, and widow of Sir William Heron, Lord Say, who usually styled herself Elizabeth, Lady Say; by this marriage he had two sons, Henry, godson of Henry IV, and John.

Norbury was a witness to Henry IV's will, made in 1409. In 1412 he was assessed for a subsidy on £100, yearly value of land in Sawbridgeworth, Essendon, Little Berkhamstead, Hoddesdon, and Cheshunt in Herts.[2] The land in Sawbridgeworth, an ancient possession of the Says, perhaps came to him with his second wife. In this year he was granted the alien priory of Lewisham and Greenwich for life, with remainder to his two sons for their lives, during the war with France, and also the manor and advowson of Cheshunt, Herts, with remainder to his wife and their sons. In 1415 Sir William

---

[1] Charter Rolls, 7 Hen. IV.
[2] Lay Subsidies, Essex and Herts, 240-261, 13 Hen. IV.

Botreaux conveyed the manor of Little Berkhamstead[1] to John Norbury and others, and the heirs of John Norbury, for 300 silver marks; this was presumably simply a confirmation of Norbury's title, Sir William Botreaux having been under age when Norbury first acquired it.

The date of John Norbury's death is uncertain. He was buried beside his first wife in an alabaster tomb in the Greyfriars' Church, London, where he was described as *valens armiger, strenuus et probus vir, quondam magnus thesaurarius Regni Anglie*, and his wife as *devotissima mater ordinis*.[2]

It is not clear who succeeded to the manor of Little Berkhamstead; his son, Sir Henry Norbury, does not appear in connection with it, and there are few records about it at this time. It probably passed to his widow, Elizabeth, Lady Say, for her life; she afterwards married Sir John Montgomery of Faulkbourne, Essex (d. 1449), to whom she bore two sons and a daughter; she was godmother of Edward IV, and, on his accession to the throne, had the manor of Cheshunt confirmed to her for life. She died in 1464, and was buried at Erbury in Warwickshire. In 1465 her grandson, John Norbury, son of Sir Henry, succeeded to the lands which had been his grandfather's.[3]

From this it would appear that Sir Henry Norbury was dead; he had been in the French wars under Somerset, and was taken prisoner at Formigny in 1450, but was exchanged for the surrender of Vire, of which town he was captain; in 1455 he was a commissioner for raising money in Surrey for the defence of Calais. His connection with Surrey was through his marriage to Anne Croyser, heiress of the manor of Stoke d'Abernon. He and his wife were buried in the Norbury tomb in the Greyfriars' Church, as was also his younger brother, John, who seems to have been in Henry VI's household.

In 1466 Sir John Norbury conveyed the manor of Bedwell, together with 620 acres of land, and 40s. rent in Essendon, Hatfield, Bayford, North Mimms, Northaw, and Cheshunt, by recovery,[4] to Sir John Say, Speaker of the House of Commons, who must have bought the manor of Little Berkhamstead from him about the same time, and also acquired from Robert Lowthe the adjacent manors of Hornbeamgate and Blounts,

[1] *Ped. Fin.* (Divers Counties), 3 Hen. V, No. 33.
[2] *Coll. Top. et Gen.*, vol. v, MS. of inscriptions in Greyfriars' Church.
[3] Patent Rolls.
[4] De Banco Roll, No. 818, Hilary, 5 Edw. IV, m. 278d.

and the advowson of the Lowthe's Chantry in Hatfield Church; these last two manors became practically incorporated with Bedwell under the name of Bedwell Lowthes. Sir John Say thus acquired a compact group of manors, of which Bedwell was apparently the head, and provided the lord's residence; there is a fine rental of these manors at the Record Office, taken for Sir John Say in 1468.

John Say began his career in the King's household, where he was King's Serjeant and Yeoman of the Chamber in 1444, when he was appointed Coroner of the Marshalsea with a grant of £10 a year; in 1445 he became Keeper of the Privy Palace of Westminster, with an allowance of 6d. a day. He married Elizabeth, daughter of Lawrence Cheyney, Esq., of Fen Ditton, Cambs, and widow of Sir Frederick Tilney,[1] of Boston, Lincs; it was no doubt through this connection that Say was elected M.P. for Cambridge in 1447 and 1449; in the latter year he was Speaker of the House of Commons.

In 1448 Say acquired, through trustees, a group of manors in Broxbourne, Hoddesdon, Amwell, Wormley, and Cheshunt, Herts, centred round the manor of Baas, which became his principal residence; the site of the old manor house can be seen near Base Hill, just outside Broxbournebury Park.

John Say was one of the unpopular courtiers against whom the insurgents under Cade, in 1450, directed their displeasure, and in the "Dirge of the Commons of Kent" two lines were devoted to him:

> John Say synge *Dominus regit me*
> *Nichyll michi deerit*[2] for owt that I can se.

He was one of those indicted of treason at the Guildhall after Cade's entry into London, but was acquitted; and in 1451, "John Say, late of London, Squier," was amongst those presented to the King by the Commons for misbehaviour, with the request that he would remove them from about his person and forbid them coming within twelve miles of the Court; Henry consented to banish some of them from his presence for a year, but insisted on retaining those accustomed to attend on him personally. Say was Knight of the Shire for Herts in 1453 and 1455, and was a commissioner for raising money in Herts for the defence of Calais in 1455. He trimmed when

---

[1] By her first marriage she was great-grandmother of Anne Boleyn.
[2] *Psalm* xxiii.

Edward IV came to the throne, and was made a Knight of the Bath in 1465, at the coronation of Elizabeth Woodville; he was again Knight of the Shire for Herts and Speaker of the House of Commons in 1463 and 1467.

Sir John Say was certainly related to the Barons Say, whose senior male line died out in 1382, but the exact connection has not been established; the Says had held for many generations the manor of Sawbridgeworth, Herts, which passed to the Herons by marriage; in 1468 John Heron died possessed of that manor, without known heirs, and leaving a widow who had a life interest in it, and the trustees of the manor conveyed the reversion of it to Sir John Say and others. Various conjectures have been made as to Say's parentage; he probably came of a junior branch of the Barons Say, and may have been son of William Say, who was King's Serjeant and Yeoman Usher of the Chamber to Henry VI, 1422-55. He had two brothers, William and Thomas; William, who was described as *de foris Aldgate, London*, was Fellow of New College, Oxford, from 1426 to 1442, Prebendary of St. Paul's, 1447, and Dean of St. Paul's from 1457 till his death in 1468; he was a Privy Councillor in 1464, and was Rector of the Fraternity in the Shrowds or Jesus Chapel at St. Paul's, where he was buried.

Lady Say died in 1473, and was buried in Broxbourne Church in a Purbeck marble tomb, on which are brass figures of her and Sir John Say. The legend describes her as "a woman of noble blode and most noble in gode maners." Sir John Say married secondly, in 1477, the widow of Lord Wenlock, and died on April 12, 1478, survived for a few months by his second wife. He was buried in Broxbourne Church. He died possessed of ten manors and other lands in Herts, seven manors in Essex, three in Norfolk, and one in Rutlandshire; he left three sons and four married daughters, and was succeeded by his eldest son, William, who had been in the household of his uncle, Dean Say, as appears by the latter's will.

William Say was Sheriff of Herts in 1482-3, and was made a Knight of the Bath by Richard III on the Sunday before his coronation. He married Genevieve, daughter and heiress of John Hill, of Spaxton, Somerset, by whom he had two surviving children—Elizabeth, who married William Blount, fourth Lord Mountjoy, the friend and pupil of Erasmus, and Mary, who married Henry Bourchier, second Earl of Essex.

EARLY HISTORY OF LITTLE BERKHAMSTEAD.

In 1506 Sir William Say settled[1] the manors of Bedwell and Little 'Berkhamstead and other property after his death on Lord Mountjoy (whose wife was then dead), with remainder to Lord Mountjoy's daughter Gertrude.

Sir William Say died in 1529, and was buried in a chapel which he had built at Broxbourne Church; he left by will 13s. 4d. to the poor of Little Berkhamstead, and a vestment of the value of 20s. to the Church.

Lord Mountjoy died in 1535, and Bedwell and Little Berkhamstead passed to his daughter Gertrude, wife of Henry Courtenay, Marquis of Exeter, first cousin of Henry VIII. The Marquis was executed for high treason in 1539; his widow was also attainted, and her lands were forfeited; she was pardoned in 1540, died in 1557, and lies buried in Wimborne Minster. Bedwell and Little Berkhamstead were never restored to her, and remained for a time in the possession of the Crown.

NOTES ON THE EARLY CHURCHES OF SOUTH ESSEX.

By C. W. FORBES, Member of the Essex Archaeological Society.

[Continued from p. 188.]

PRITTLEWELL.

ONE of the most ancient villages in Essex is that of Prittlewell, the mother parish of the now populous town of Southend, which up to comparatively recent years was a small fishing village.

The church is one of the largest, and, from an architectural point of view, one of the finest in the county. It is built principally of Kentish ragstone; many Roman tiles, however, can be seen in the north wall, and in the wall surrounding the churchyard.

The church consists of a nave, chancel, south aisle, which has an eastern or Jesus Chapel, south porch, and a splendid embattled western tower. The tower contains a clock and a very fine peal of ten bells, some of which are modern; of these

[1] Close Roll 370, No. 10, 1st July, 21 Hen. VII.

Prittlewell Church

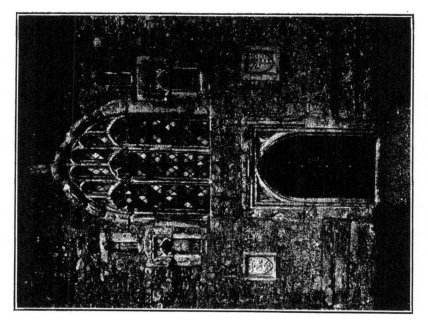

West Door, Little Wakering.

The Font, Prittlewell.

Photographs by C. W. Forbes.

one bears the name of the diocese of St. Albans, and another that of Edward the Seventh, *Fidei defensor.*

The outer walls of the building are surmounted by a rich and singularly perfect embattled parapet of flint and stone chequer-work.

The west door, now closed, is fifteenth century; in the wall at the sides are two niches for images. All the windows in the church are of the same period.

Taken as a whole, the structure may be said to date from the latter part of the fourteenth and the early fifteenth centuries, but remains exist of eleventh and twelfth century work.

The glory of Prittlewell is its tower, four stories high, surmounted by an embattled parapet, each angle being finished with an octangular turret and richly crocketed pinnacles; it is attributed to the beginning of the fifteenth century.

There is every probability that a church existed here from the early Norman period; the north wall of the nave and the chancel is undoubtedly Norman work, being composed of rubble interspersed with Roman bricks or tiles. Portions also of the three westernmost arches, dividing the nave from the aisle, are attributed to the twelfth century; the restorations carried out in 1872, by the late Ewen Christian, disclosed the fact that they cut through a wall of much greater age, containing remains of Norman work. The north wall also shows traces of an arch now bricked up.

With the exception of the above, the entire church appears to have been rebuilt in the Perpendicular Period.

When the aisle was added the westernmost portion of the original south wall was apparently cut through, as the three easternmost arches are higher and the columns more slender than those at the western end, which shows remains of the original wall at the top over the arches. Over the south porch is a priest's chamber, the entrance to this being by means of a small door and stairs in the south wall on the eastern side of the interior of the nave.

The south door is a very fine specimen of oak carving; remains of a holy-water stoup can be seen outside on the east side.

The south aisle of the chancel is known as the Jesus Chapel, it contains a piscina, also a niche by the side of the window.

The font, of the late Perpendicular Period, has an octangular basin, on the sides of which are heraldic shields and the Tudor rose dimidiated with a pomegranate, said to commemorate the marriage either of Prince Arthur and Catherine of Aragon or King Henry the Eighth with the same lady.[1]

Over the pulpit in the north aisle are some remains of the stairs which led to the rood loft.

Some little distance to the north of the church stood the ancient Priory of Cluniac monks, founded, it is stated, in the reign of Henry II by Robert de Essex or Fitz Swain.

The priory was subordinate to the monastery of that order at Lewes in Sussex; at the Dissolution it held seven monks, with a revenue stated to be worth £194 14*s*. 3*d*.

The few remains that are still in existence are in private hands and difficult of access.

SUTTON.

About two miles to the north-east of Prittlewell is the village of Sutton. The church, which stands in a very picturesque position just off the road, is a stone structure of Norman foundation, and consists of a nave, chancel, south porch, and a stunted wooden turret at the west end containing one bell.

The outer walls belong to the early Norman church, also the two small windows in the centre of the walls of the nave on opposite sides.

There are two fairly large Decorated windows in the nave, on opposite sides, and a similar one in the west wall. The windows in the chancel are Early English lancets, there being one on the north, two on the south, and three on the east side.

The south doorway belongs to the thirteenth century; it has been considerably restored. Over it is a plain porch, built of brick, timber, and plaster, dated 1633; the interior of this porch is panelled with wood taken from the old high seventeenth-century pews which were at one time in the nave, one of the panels being dated 1647.

The arch separating the chancel from the nave is a very fine specimen of late Norman work. The remains of a plain Pointed sedilia may be seen in the chancel.

The font is interesting, and consists of a square basin with five Pointed arches on each side; it is supported by a large centre pillar, with a smaller one at each corner, having moulded caps and bases. The basin is of Early English design and is attributed to the thirteenth century, the pillars, however, have

---

[1] The Tudor rose is also to be seen on the font at Orsett.

Sutton Church.

Photograph by C. W. Forbes.

The Font, Shopland.

The Font, Sutton.

Photographs by C. W. Forbes.

all the appearance of being modern work, and probably belong to the restoration which took place in 1869.

SHOPLAND.

After leaving Sutton we follow the road round, keeping to the right, for another two miles, and arrive at the scattered village of Shopland. The church is some distance from the road on the right, and is to be found after traversing a path across some fields, opposite a farmhouse. The churches of Sutton and Shopland are now combined, under the rectory of Sutton, services being held in the churches alternately; this is owing to the population of these two villages being very small and much scattered, that of Shopland being about sixty persons.

The church, built of brick and stone, is of a similar structure to Sutton, consisting of a nave, chancel, south porch, and a low wooden spire with one bell. The bell is inscribed, " Peter Hawkes made me 1608." The north side of the nave and chancel is the oldest part of the building, as on examination one can trace a doorway in the nave and a priest's door in the chancel, now filled in; there is also one Norman niche window left in the nave on this side.

Of the other windows there is a small fourteenth-century one on the south side of the chancel, and two double-light windows on opposite sides of the nave, of the Perpendicular Period.

The east window is a large four-light window, considerably restored and modernized; it is difficult to say what it was originally.

The south door is fourteenth century, and has a fine timber porch, attributed to the same period.

The interior of the nave is interesting, as it is still seated with the old high-backed family pews of the seventeenth century, similar to those which were at one time in the church at Sutton.

The font is of the same shape and size as that at Sutton, the side facing south is decorated with a beautiful interlaced arcading of a similar design to that on the font at Eastwood, the other three sides being quite plain. The basin rests on five circular columns, with moulded caps and bases; as no late restoration has taken place at this church, they are considered to be part of the original work. Those at Sutton being of similar design are probably copies of these; I am, however, unable to get any information as to the age of these supporting pillars. The basin of the font is late Norman.

There is no chancel arch separating the chancel from the nave, both being about the same height. In the chancel is a trefoil-headed piscina, and near it a narrow plain-pointed sedilia.

On the floor of the nave, near the font, can be seen the remains of an ancient brass to Thomas de Stapel, Serjeant at Arms to King Edward the Third; he died in 1371. The inscription in Norman French is now very much obliterated and partly covered in by the pews; a translation of it runs thus: "Thomas de Stapel, some time Serjeant at Arms to our Lord the King, who died on the second day of March, 1371, rests here. God have mercy on his soul, Amen."

This brass, I am informed, was originally on the floor in the chancel near the altar, where he is supposed to have been buried.

Shopland church was at one time attached to the Priory of St. Osyth.

LITTLE WAKERING.

Returning to the main road after leaving Shopland church, and keeping to the left, we shortly notice a signpost directing us to Little Wakering, a parish in which are included Little Potton and New England Islands, and a part of Wallasea Island. The church, as are nearly all in this part of Essex, is of Norman foundation; it is now, however, chiefly a stone structure in the Perpendicular style of the fifteenth century, the only early work which can now be traced are two small Norman niche-windows on the north side, one in the nave, and one in the chancel.

The building consists of a chancel, nave, south porch, and a rather fine western tower, with a shingled spire containing three ancient undated bells. The upper part of the tower has an embattled parapet worked in chequers of stone and flint; under the steps inside the tower is what is supposed to have been a large aumbry, used no doubt for storing the church plate.

There were originally three doorways; the west door is closed and traces of a north door can be seen from the exterior, also a priest's door now closed on the north side of the chancel.

The nave contains three other windows, a large fourteenth-

284

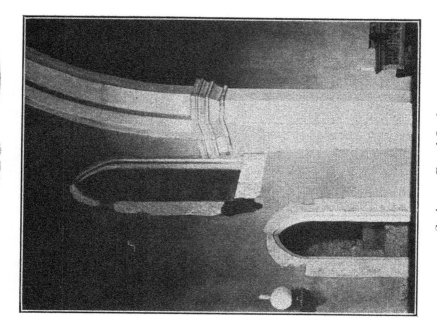

Stairs to Rood Loft.
Little Wakering.

Little Wakering.

Photographs by C. W. Forbes.

century Decorated one on the south side, and two two-light Perpendicular ones, one on each side.

The east window, probably a small fifteenth-century one, was enlarged and rebuilt, and filled with stained glass, as a memorial to Henry Wix of Walthamstow, in 1880.

Over the west Perpendicular door is a fine large window of the same period, and on each side of this are two niches for images, one large and one small. The lower ones still contain the original iron hooks by which these images were fastened at the back. On each side of the doorway are shields with the arms of the patrons. The shield on the north side bears the arms of the Wakering family, the squires of the neighbourhood, the mitre which has been added indicates John Wakering, who was Bishop of Norwich from 1416 to 1425. That on the south side bears the arms of Ann, Countess of Stafford, daughter and heiress of her father, Thomas of Woodstock, Duke of Gloucester, youngest son of Edward the Third. She was first married to the fifth Earl of Stafford, who was killed at the battle of Shrewsbury in 1403; she then married Sir William Bourchier, created in 1419 Earl of Eu in Normandy; she died in 1438.

From these shields it is possible to fix the time of the erection of the tower, which would be *circa* 1416.

On examination therefore we can trace two distinct periods which materially altered the construction of the church, first, in the twelfth century and secondly in the early part of the fifteenth, when the windows which we now see were inserted and the tower erected, doubtless at the combined cost of the Bishop of Norwich and the Countess of Stafford.

Entering the church by the south door, attributed to the fourteenth century, we note in the right-hand corner, just inside the entrance, a large round holy-water stoup.

On the north side of the nave is a recessed arch, which is presumed to have contained the founder's tomb. Near this, between the nave and the chancel, are the rood stairs, with a portion of the beam which at one time went across the chancel to carry the Rood.

In the chancel, on the south side, is a fourteenth-century piscina, with a rose basin, also a plain sedilia.

In 1878 the chancel was restored, and the floor raised and relaid.

The living is in the gift of St. Bartholomew's Hospital.

[To be continued.]

STAR CHAMBER CASES, No. VI.

COBHAM v. JURDAN AND OTHERS.

EASTER TERM, 10 HENRY VII, 1495.

(Star Chamber Proceedings, Henry VII, No. 31.)

TO the most reuerent Fader in God and full gode and gracious lord the Lord Cardynall and Archebisshop of Caunterbury, Chaunceler of Englond:

In the most lamentablest wyse shewith and complayneth unto your most noble grace your humble and dayly Oratrice, Johane late wyf of Reynold Cobham, son and heire of John Cobham, That where as the seid Reynold at the tyme of the Espousels had bitwene him and your seid Oratrice endowyd her in the maner of Gatewyk with th' appurtenances, To have to her for terme of her lyf, The remaynder therof to their Childern, as by the Copye of a dede entayled it appereth: It is so, gracious lord, that diuers persones of the Contrey there, that is to wete, John Jurdan, John Lecheford, Richard Saunder, Thomas White and Thomas Hever of Cukfeld, now by subtill and Crafty meanes have and occupie the seid Maner, londes and tenementes, and therof taken the profites to their uses, ayenst alle right and consciens, notwithstandyng your seid oratrice hath often required theyme of paiement of the issues and profites therof, And thei sumtyme rewarde and refresshe, seiyng unto her that thei geve it to her for almes; but of her duete, according as her seid husbond hath grauntyd her, she canne not be truly contentid, but dayly delayed and mokkyd. And ovir that, thei seyen that thei have bought the seid maner and londes, but what thei have paide for the same no man canne tell. Which Reynold Cobham, husbond to your seid Oratrice, sodenly decessid, And sithen his decesse the seid persones have occupied the seid maner and londes, and therof taken the profites this xxiiij yeres and more, and what he borowyd of theyme your seid Oratrice can not telle. And the same Reynold left your seid Oratrice at the tyme of his decesse V children upon her hondes, having no Frendes to do for theyme, and so she and her childern have lyvyd sithen her husbonde's decesse in gret penuerye and myserye, to her grete

286

inward sorow and hevynesse, and to the uttir disherityng of alle her childern. Please it your noble grace the premisses tenderly to consyder and the grete wrong that the seid persones dayly do unto her and her childern, And also how the seid persones dayly manasse and threte her for askyng of her right, And also how thei will no thing shewe whye and wherby thei shuld so kepe the seid maner and londes, And ovir that manasse and threte the husbond of your seid Oratrice, for askyng of her duete, to murdre and slee, so that he dare not come thider to aske or demaunde his seid wyve's right. And therupon of your most gracious and blessid disposicion to cause the seid persones to appere afore your grace and the noble lordes of the Kynge's Counsell to answere to the premisses, And to bryng inne bifore your grace alle suche wrytynges and evidences wherby thei ought to witholde and kepe from your seid Oratrice her seid dower, and therin to set suche order and direccion for her and her childern that thei may from hensforth peisibly have and enjoye their seid maner and londes, according to their title and right. And this for the love of God and in the wey of Charite. And she shall evir pray to God for your most noble grace.

[Endorsed.]

Termino Pasche, anno x^{mo}, [1495].

Johanna Cobham, vidua, contra Johannem Jourdan, Johannem Lecheford, et alios.

This is the ansuer of Nicholas Jurden[1] to the byll of Complaynt of Johane Cobham, late the wyef of Raynold Cobham.

The said Nicholas sayth that the matter conteyned in the said bill is matter fayned, to the Intent wrongfully to Trobull and vex the said Nicholas Jurden withoutt Colour or cause by hym Committyd, contrary to all Rygth and good consciens. For he saith that he nor no noder persons ever hade poscession or Interest or toke proffettes of the said manor or any parte ther of to his Use, as in the said byll of Complaynt is surmittid; but he of the possession of the said manor and of every parte of the same Manor wtterly disclaymyth. All wiche Matter he is redi to prowe as this Court will awarde, and prayth to be Dismissed owtt of this Cowrte with his resonabull Costes and damages that he hath susteyned by this his Wrongfull wexacion.

[1] Apparently the person called John Jurdan in the Bill.

This is the answer of John Lachefford to the bill of complaynt
of Johane, latte the wieff of Raynolde Cobham.

The said John sayth that the bill of complaynt of the said
Johane is wnttrue and matter Fayned, to the Intent to Trobull
and vex the said John, Contrary untto the lawe, Rigth and
good conciens; and also the matter conteyned in the said
byll apperith matter determinabull att the Comen lawe, wher
wntto he prayth to be directyd. Nevertheles, for declaracion
of the Trowgth and ferther answer wntto the same, the said
John sayth that one Raynold Cobham, latt husbond wntto the
said Jobane, nowe Complaynantt, was seasied of Certen londes
and tenementes Called Massette and Flottgatis londe, somtyme
parcell of the Manor of Gattwyke, in his demen as of Fee;
and so seasied, for a certen som of money bytwexe the said
Raynold and the said John aggreed, bargayned and sold the
said parcele of lond to the said John, to have to hym and to
his hyers for evermor; and the said Raynold, accordyng to
the said bargayn, infeoffed the said John ther of in fee; in to
whos possession the said Jobane Cobham after the deth of the
said Raynold, her said latt husbond, in her Widuhod, for a
Certeyn some of money of the said John rescevyed, by her
dede, redy to be schewed, relessed to the said John all the
rygth and title that sche hadde in the said parcell of lond.
Withowtt that that the said John hath any oder londes than
is afore reherssed parcell of the said manor of Gattwyk;
and withoutt that that the said Raynold att the tyme of the
espowselx indowed the said Johane in the said manor or in
any parte ther of; and withoutt that the said John ever
manassed or thretened the said Johane or els her husbond, in
maner and forme as in the said bill of complaynt is surmitted.
All wiche matter he is redy to prove as this [Court] will
awarde, and prayth to be dismetted owtt of this Courte with
his reasonabull Costes and damages that he hath susteyned for
this his Wrongfull Wexacion.

This is the answer of John Sawnder[1] to the bill of complaynt
of Johane Cobham, late the wyef of Raynold Cobham.

The said John sayth that the matter conteyned in the said
bill is matter fayned, to the Intent Wrongfully to Trobull and
vexe the said John Sawnder, withoutt Colour or Cawse by
hym Committyd, Contrary to all Rygth and good Consciens.

---

[1] Apparently the person called Richard Saunder in the Bill.

For he sayth that he nor no oder persons ever hade possession or interest or toke proffettes of the said manor or any parte ther of to his Use, as in the said bill of Complaynt is surmittyd, but he of the poscession of the said Manor and of every parte of the said Manor utterly dysclaymyth. All wiche Matter he is Redy to prowe as this Courte will award, and prayth to be dismissed owt of this Cowrte with his resonabull Costes and damages that he hath susteyned by this his wrongfull vexacion.

[This document is marked *vacat*.]

This is the answer of Thomas Whitt to the bill of complayntt of Johane Cobham, latte the wyeff of Raynold Cobham.

The said Thomas sayth that the matter conteyned in the said bill of complayntt is wntrue and matter fayned, to Trobule and vex the said Thomas, and also determinabull att the Comen Lawe, wher wntto he prayth to be directed. Neverthele, For declaracion of Trowght [truth] and ferther answer, saothe that the said Raynold was seasied of a parcell lond called the Warelond, somtyme parcell of the manor of Gate-wyke, in his demen as of Fee; and so seased therof, longe tyme affore the espouselx bytwexe the said Raynold and the said Johane hadde, infeoffedd one Thomas Whitt, Fader wntto the said Thomas nowe defendant, to have to him and to his hyers for evermor; by force wherof the said Thomas the Fader was ther of seased in his demen as of Fee, and dyed seased, after whos dethe the said Thomas nowe defendant entrid in to the said parcell of lond as sone and hyer to the said Thomas the fader, and therof was seased in his demen as of fee. And ferthermor the said Thomas saith that the said Raynold was seased of a nother parcell of lond called the Wykelond, somtyme parcell of the said manor of Gattewyk, in his demen as of fee, and so seissed therof infeoffed the said Thomas Whitt the fader, to have to hyme and to his heyrs for evermore, by force wherof the said Thomas the fader was therof seased in his demen as of Fee, and so therof seased died, after whos dethe the said Thomas nowe defendant entred into the said parcell of lond as sone and heir to the said Thomas the fader, and ther of was seased in his demen as of fee; in to whos possession oon John Cursam, nowe husbond wntto the said Johane, by his dede, Redy to bee shewed forth, relessed to the said Thomas nowe defendant all his Rigth and title that he badde in the said parcell of lond called the Wyklond by reson of dowre concernyng the said Johane, his wyeff, of the possession of the said Raynold, her latt husbond. Withoutt that the said Thomas hath any oder londes than is afore rehersed, parcell of the said manor of Gatwyke; and withoutt that the said Thomas ever manassed or thretened the said Johane or her said nowe husbond in maner and fourme as in the said bill of complaynt is surmitted. All wyche matters he is redy to prove as this Courte will awarde, and prayth to be dysmeted owtt of this Courte with his resonabull Costes and damages that he hath susteyned for this his wrongfull vexacion in this behalf.

This is the answer of Thomas Hewer to the bill of complaynte of Johane, latte the wyeff of Raynold Cobham.

The said Thomas sayth that the byll of complaynt of the said Johane is wntrue and matter fayned, to the Intent to trobull and vex the said Thomas, contrary wntto the lawe, Rigth and good Conciens; and also the matter conteyned in the said bill apperyth matter detminabull att the Comen Lawe, wher wntto he prayth to be directyd. Nevertheles, for declaracion of the Trowgth and ferder answer wntto the same, the said Thomas sayth that one Raynold Cobham, latt husbond wntto the said Johane nowe Complaynant, was seasied of certeyn londes and tenementes called Bristoklonde, somtyme parcell of the manor of Gattwyke, in his demen as of Fee, and so seasied, for a certeyn some of money bitwexe the said Raynold and the said Thomas aggred, bargayned and sold the said parcell of lond to the said Thomas, to have to hym and to his hyers for evermor; and the sayd Raynold, accordynge to the said bargayn, inffeoffed the said Thomas there of in fee. Withoutt that the said Thomas hath any oder londes than is affore rehurssed, parcell of the sayd manor of Gatwyk; and withoutt that that the said Raynold att the tyme of the espouselx indoued the said Johane in the said maner or in any parte ther of; and withoutt that the said Thomas ever manassed or thretened the said Johane or els her husbond in maner and forme as in the said bill of complayntt is surmitted. All wyche matter he is redy to prove as this Courte will award, and prayth to be dysmeted owtt of this Cowrte with his resonabull Costes and damages that he hath susteyned by this his Wrongfull wexacion.

DEPOSITIONS.

Ultimo Junii, anno, etc., decimo [1495].

John Lechford, sworn, vpon the bill of Jobane Cobham put agenst him and others, and his ansuer upon the same, deposith that Raynold Cobham, husband whiles he lyved to the complainant, sold to divers persons the manor of Gatwyke, that is to sey;—to this deponent a parte, that is to sey, xv acres, which lye not to gether but in ij parcellis, and they be holden in chef of th' abbot of Chersey, which hath of the same iijs. iiijd. by the yer for quyte rent. This deponente's Fader had first the said xv acres of the said Raynold in morgage, and so had this deponent after his deceas for the terme of v yeres, and lent to the said Raynold upon it vjs. viijd.; and after that he bought of him the hegge rowys of the same ground, which shold have ben fellyd; but sone after that, the same Raynold, befor the lapse of the said v yeres, being in a necessite sold the same xv acres to this deponent for the Sum of xxs., which he paied at the lyverye and season to him made, and so this deponent had bothe the land and the hegge rowys, as to him full bought and sold without payment of any more money, and it hath enjoyed and occupied from v yeres before the deth of the said Raynold, which deceasyd xxiiij^ti yeres past, untill this day and yet occupieth the same. The same John saith that he never herd of any entaile of the said landys untill now of late, how be it he saith that oute of time of mynd it hath ben in the handys of the Cobhams; this deponent knew Raynold in possession of Gatwyke fro the time of his discreion untill he dyed, and he was upo lx^ti yeres old or more when he dyed; and before that, as he herd his fader and other old men say, the fader of the same Rainold and his fader before him. This deponent hath as he saith noon other tytle unto the said land only bi the said bargayn; how be it he hath herd sey that the Fader of Herry Jurden purchasid the maner aforesaid and it hath recoverd in the law bi a recoverye, in which recoverye be comprised the said xv acres or part of thaim, and this deponent knew not of it untill now late he hath a Release of th' oldest sonne of Raynold, and also of the plentif as he saith.

Thomas Hever, sworn, saith that he hath of the Maner of Gatwik as mich land as amownteth to xxs. a yere, and somtime xld. more, above all charges; and he saith that he bought the

same of Raynold Cobham for many yeres goon for the Sum
of xxiiij*li*., which he paid to the same Raynold in fatt Oxyn,
shepe, kene, and Swyne, and some money, homuch he is not
now remembrid; he saith also that he hath a Releas of th' oldest
sonne of Raynold aforsaid of the same land, for which he had
money and an hors, all in valew xl*s*.; and after that the complainant made him a releas of the same, for a Ryall; he saith
also that John Jorden recoveryd, as this deponent herd say of
late, the hole maner of Gatwyk, with all th' appurtenances, this
deponent and other that had bargaigned for parcellis of the
same land with Raynold aforsaid it not knowing. This deponent herd not of any Taile of the land aforsaid but of
Richard Cobham, whom he herd sey so a xvj or xx yeres
goon; treu it is, he saith, that it ben occupied by the Cobhams
for time that noo mynd is.

Thomas White, sworn, saith that he hath [as] mich of the
said land as is worth xx*s*. by yere, and he saith that his Fader
purchasyd it of Raynold Cobham at ij purchaces, the worth of
x*s*. by yere before the same Raynold was weddyd to the complaynant, that other x*s*. worth by yere syth that time; and his
fader enfeoffyd this deponent and other to this deponente's
use in the same land, and so this deponent, as by his fader
will, hath the said land; he saith farther that the fader of this
deponent paid to the complainant xl*d*. by yere for hir dower
of x*s*. worth, and so dyd this deponent du after his decease,
untill she released him for xx*s*., which he paied hir more then
a dosen yeres goon; from which time she askyd this deponent
no moor money; this deponent hath noon other title but as
he hath deposed; whether ther were entaile of the land he
knowith not, but ever the Cobhams had it untill Raynold
alayened it.

NOTE.—The Cardinal Archbishop to whom the Bill is addressed was John
Morton. He was appointed Archbishop of Canterbury in 1486, Lord
Chancellor in 1487, Cardinal in 1493, and died in 1500.

Gatwick is a hamlet in the parish of Charlwood, near Godalming,
well known to many people of recent years from the race-course started
there in 1891. Very little is known of its history. Neither Manning and
Bray nor Brayley and Britton mention the Cobhams in connection with
it; both state that the Jordans had possessed the manor for centuries,
and account for this by suggesting the marriage of a Jordan with an
imaginary heiress of the de Gatwick family.

Nothing appears to be known of this branch of the Cobham family.

BETHNAL GREEN.

By L. M. Biden.

I T is not often that one comes across a two-centuries title to property, and most people would turn from such a document muttering to themselves about it being "dry-as-dust"; yet the following notes from an abstract of title going back to 1680 may be of interest to the general reader and of value to the historian and genealogist.

It relates to nearly twenty-seven acres of land at Bethnal Green, and, to locate the property, I may mention that the Middlesex Chapel in the Hackney Road was built on part of it in 1798.

In 1680 the land consisted of four green fields, called Milk-house Bridge Field, containing 11*ac*. 1*r*. 34*p*. (the general reader may skip details like the acreage, etc., as they are not intended for him but for the historian); Birding Bush Field, containing 7*ac*. 3*r*. 34*p*.; Crab Tree Close, containing 4*ac*. 0*r*. 20*p*.; and Three Acre Close, containing 3*ac*. 1*r*. 0*p*. Birding Bush is to me an uncommon way of spelling the name; here it is never spelt Bird-in-Bush, as in Camberwell and elsewhere, and it may indicate the existence of a bush shelter behind which wild-fowl shooters concealed themselves.

Prior to 1790, when building commenced, no houses are mentioned as being on the land, but there is mention of "Summerhouses." These must have been in connection with tea gardens, for the land is called Garden ground; it was not far from the great city, and the name "Milkhouse" suggests a place where refreshments could be obtained.

Prior to June, 1680, the land had been held by one Humphrey Blake, under a lease for 99 years, and in that month Christopher Todd and Ann, his wife (the daughter of Humphrey Blake the elder), and Robert Blake, her brother, sold the lease for £1,040 to James Smithsby, a "Woolen Draper" of Westminster. Nehemiah and Joseph Blissett con-curred in the sale, apparently as mortgagees. The ground rent is not stated, but would be about £4. Taking money as being worth six per cent. in those days, we find the land had a rental value of about £66 (£62 being six per cent. on £1,040, with £4 ground rent), or say £2 10*s*. per acre, much more than a mere agricultural rent.

In February, 1681, Smithsby acquired the freehold at the

price of £85, and it is this amount that makes me put the ground rent at £4. The vendors were Philadelphia, Lady Wentworth (widow and relict of Thomas, late Lord Wentworth, deceased), and Henrietta Maria, Lady Wentworth, Baroness of Nettlested, sole daughter and heiress of the said Thomas, Lord Wentworth, deceased, and granddaughter and heir of Thomas, late Earl of Cleveland, deceased.

The land was described as parcel of the Manor of Stepney; the alternative name of Stebenheath does not appear till a deed of 1718, when "alias Stebunhills" also is given.

Smithsby, a name taken from the village of that name, died soon after, leaving a widow and two daughters, all three of whom married. The widow became Dame Margaret Hamilton, the daughter Margaret married Sir Francis Head, Baronet; her sister Ann married Hans Hamilton of Hamilton Bawne, Ireland, who afterwards became a Baronet, so that his wife bore the same title as her mother. Dame Ann Hamilton left only one child, a daughter Ann, who married James Campbell, a merchant of London, and they subsequently took the surname of Hamilton. Mrs. Ann Campbell Hamilton died in January, 1771, a widow, and without leaving issue; and thus ended the line of Smithsby's younger daughter and co-heiress.

Turning to her sister, Dâme Margaret Head, I find that her property was settled on her younger children by a deed dated October 13, 1697, made between Sir Francis and Dame Margaret Head of the first part, Sir John Poley, Knight, John Greene, Esquire, John Lynd, Esquire, William Poley, Esquire, and Richard Head, Esquire (the trustees), of the second part, and Frances Poley, widow, of the third part. Sir Francis Head does not seem to have been rich, or perhaps he had been of a free spending nature, for he as executor of the will of his grandfather, Sir Richard Head, converted his grandfather's estate to his own use, and being called to account for the money left to his aunt, Mrs. Frances Poley, and her family, he was unable to pay. So his wife, Dame Margaret, gave security over the property she was entitled to on the death of her mother, Dame Margaret Hamilton, but stipulated that her property should be settled on her younger children, "who had no other provision." The money owing to the Poleys was duly paid, so if Sir Francis had been over-free with money in his youth, at least he pulled up in time, and, aided by his wife, made amends for his extravagance, and justified his grandfather's trust.

BETHNAL GREEN.

Here two chart pedigrees may help to make matters clear.

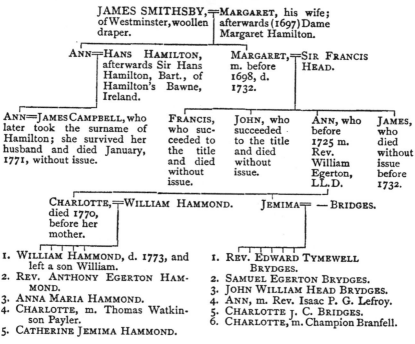

JAMES SMITHSBY,⹏MARGARET, his wife;
of Westminster, woollen | afterwards (1697) Dame
draper. | Margaret Hamilton.

ANN⹏HANS HAMILTON,   MARGARET,⹏SIR FRANCIS
afterwards Sir Hans   m. before   HEAD.
Hamilton, Bart., of   1698, d.
Hamilton's Bawne,   1732.
Ireland.

ANN⹏JAMES CAMPBELL, who | FRANCIS, | JOHN, who | ANN, who | JAMES,
later took the surname of | who suc- | succeeded | before | who
Hamilton; she survived her | ceeded to | to the title | 1725 m. | died
husband and died January, | the title | and died | Rev. | without
1771, without issue. | and died | without | William | issue
| without | issue. | Egerton, | before
| issue. | | LL.D. | 1732.

CHARLOTTE,⹏WILLIAM HAMMOND.   JEMIMA⹏ — BRIDGES.
died 1770,
before her
mother.

1. WILLIAM HAMMOND, d. 1773, and   1. REV. EDWARD TYMEWELL
left a son William.   BRYDGES.
2. REV. ANTHONY EGERTON HAM-   2. SAMUEL EGERTON BRYDGES.
MOND.   3. JOHN WILLIAM HEAD BRYDGES.
3. ANNA MARIA HAMMOND.   4. ANN, m. Rev. Isaac P. G. Lefroy.
4. CHARLOTTE, m. Thomas Watkin-   5. CHARLOTTE J. C. BRIDGES.
son Payler.   6. CHARLOTTE, m. Champion Branfell.
5. CATHERINE JEMIMA HAMMOND.

SIR RICHARD HEAD.

A son, who pre-   FRANCES⹏— POLEY.   A daughter, married
deceased his father.   John Boys.

FRANCIS, who succeeded to   1. RICHARD POLEY.
the title and married Mar-   2. ELIZABETH POLEY.
garet Smithsby; d. 1725.   3. WILLIAM POLEY.
                             4. BRIDGET POLEY.

Sir Francis Head died in 1725, and his son Francis dying, leaving no issue, the next son, John, succeeded to the title. He died in 1769, "late of Canterbury," also without issue. James, the remaining son, predeceased his father. Their sister, Anne, married the Reverend William Egerton, LL.D., by whom she had two daughters—Jemima and Charlotte. The former married Edward Bridges of Wooton, Kent; her son, the Reverend Edward Tymewell Bridges, unsuccessfully claimed a peerage, and perhaps was responsible for altering the family name to Brydges. Anyone desiring earlier information as to the Brydges family may refer to the evidence filed in this peerage case. Samuel Egerton Brydges was not unknown as an author.

Charlotte Egerton married William Hammond, and left two sons and three daughters; in their time the Smithsby property once more became united, for Mrs. Ann Campbell Hamilton left her moiety to Lady Jane Head, the widow of Sir John, for life, then to the Hammond and Brydges families, who, in 1789, concurred in selling the property to John Allport.

I note that in 1789 Mrs. Jemima Bridges, widow, preferred to spell her name in the old way; also the Common Recovery, to which she was a party, included "a moiety of one 36th part of 10 messuages, 160ac. of land covered with water and one cut and stream of water and watercourses, with the appurtenances, situate in the parish of St. Matthew, Bethnal Green, and several other parishes"; in other words, the recovery included half of a New River share, probably Smithsby owned this share.

Prior to the purchase by Allport the property for nearly a century belonged to various people in undivided shares, which were willed away, from time to time, in a somewhat perplexing fashion. I absolve Smithsby from any blame for this, for he made no will; at all events if he made a will it did not include this and other property, as his two daughters are described as his co-heiresses. The historian must pardon my mentioning this for the benefit of the general reader.

Sir John Head, as one of the younger children, and Mrs. Egerton, as another, each became entitled to a quarter-share in the property of Grandfather Smithsby under the said settlement. I like that word "said"; lawyers are accused of tautology because it so often occurs in their deeds, but is it not shorter to say "the said settlement," than "the settlement of Lady Margaret Head's property?" Sir John by his will, proved December 12, 1769, left his real estate (otherwise his freehold property) to his wife Jane for life, and then to his nephews in law, Edward Brydges and William Hammond. The next day, December 13, Sir John's cousin, Mrs. Ann Campbell-Hamilton, made her will, and left her half-share of Grandfather Smithsby's property to Lady Head for life, and then half was to go to Mrs. Hammond and her children, and half to Mrs. Jemima Bridges and her children; Mrs. Hamilton was determined her sex should have her share rather than the husbands.

Sir John's sister, Mrs. Egerton, was dead, or no doubt she would have been mentioned.

In February, 1789, the property was disentailed (by Lease and Release), and a Common Recovery was suffered (1789, Roll 173), Augustine Greenland of Newman Street, St. Mary-le-Bow, gentleman, being plaintiff, and Joseph Ward deforciant, with Jemima Bridges and William Hammond as vouchees. The property is described as one moiety of " 22 messuages, 20 gardens, 20 acres of land, and 20 acres of meadow," also a moiety of a New River share, by the description already given. Two months later six and a half acres of the land were sold to John Allport, the tenant, for £1,400, and conveyed to him by Lease and Release, dated April 21 and 22, 1789; various members of the Bridges (or Brydges) and Hammond families concurred in order to convey their fractional shares; Thomas Lacey was the trustee to bar dower, and a Fine was levied.

During the forty years preceding 1789 I find as tenants successively the names of Christopher Raymond, Thomas Robinson Blissett, Robert Newell, Richard Attkins, William Hopcraft, and then John Allport. Other changes had taken place since Smithsby's time. The Parish of St. Matthew had been formed out of parts of St. Dunstan, Stepney, and St. Leonard, Shoreditch, and the land was stated to adjoin the late turnpike road from London to Hackney, and to be next land of Andrew Pritchard. Why was it called *the late* turnpike road? Had a new one superseded it? In 1797 the Middlesex Chapel was built on part of the land by the Reverend John Jeffries Church, to whom in January, 1798, a building Lease was granted by Allport, who reserved to himself a corner at the north-east of the basement story as a vault or tomb. Allport died in 1807. I cannot say if he was buried in his vault; his son John, who died in 1817, aged forty-two, was buried at the church of St. Leonard, Shoreditch.

In February, 1804, Lacey, the trustee to bar dower, died and was buried in St. Sepulchre's, Cole Abbey, and Allport went to the trouble and expense of a fresh deed to bar the right to dower of Mary his wife, she concurring. Richard Simons, of Wood Street, Cheapside, ribbon manufacturer, was appointed the trustee. I do not know why Allport did this, as by his will made shortly after, he appointed his wife, his son John, his son-in-law Henry Strattin and James Abbiss, of Bishopsgate Street, hardwareman, to be his executors, and he gave her a life interest. Abbiss was buried in April, 1812, at St. Helen's, Bishopsgate, and the widow, Mary Allport, in January, 1826, at Shoreditch.

Now I come to something I cannot understand. In 1822 a bricklayer, named John Poole, took a building agreement of land in Chapel Street, King Street, and Queen Street, at £1 per plot, and for some years was busy building cottages with fifteen-foot frontages, which he sold at rates varying from £33 to £27 each. However he could do it I don't know; £150 nowadays would be nearer the mark. It reminds me of the fable of the rival broom sellers, one of whom wondered that he should be undersold by the other, seeing that he omitted to pay for his materials; but his rival went one better, for he stole his brooms ready made. But at Bethnal Green there was no royal dockyard whence John could obtain his materials free, neither could he have stolen the houses ready made.

ALONG THE KENTISH BORDER.

By Charles V. O'Neil.

TRAVELLERS by the Brighton Railway from London Bridge can hardly have failed to observe the sudden change from London to what has at any rate an appearance of country, immediately upon passing New Cross Station; a transition from the unattractive surroundings of a singularly dreary corner of the metropolis to green banks and glimpses of trees, which at least encourage the feeling that the real country is not far away. If the trees and hedges seem to have struggled against bricks and mortar with a greater measure of success than elsewhere along this line of railway, which runs very near the border line between Kent and Surrey, it is probably because it was laid out at a comparatively remote period, through what was then open country, and has formed a formidable barrier necessitating expensive roads and bridges if the crowded suburbs on either hand were to be linked up. The bridges between New Cross and the outskirts of Croydon are very few in number, and it is to this I think that we mainly owe the pleasant outlook from the carriage windows between New Cross and Norwood.

ALONG THE KENTISH BORDER.

One can, however, hardly expect to find a real country walk within the County of London, and to get well beyond the houses it is necessary to go below Croydon, which for various reasons, notably its ample service of trains, forms an admirable starting-point; and just as the process of "suburbanization" seems to have been exceptionally retarded to the north of that town, so if we turn towards the south east we shall come upon a delightful tract of hill country running down the border line between Surrey and Kent that is absolutely unspoilt, and, in its remoteness from the rush of the present "tube" loving age, seems at least half a century behind the Caterham Valley and the Brighton Road, only a few miles away.

I am confident that a day on the hills between Croydon and the southern face of the North Downs will be a revelation to many, even of those who are fairly well acquainted with Surrey and its scenery.

It will be found most convenient, and save a certain amount of road walking, to leave the train at South Croydon, where some steps in the left-hand corner of the station yard lead down to a road. Passing under the bridge, this road, which a very few years ago was merely a rough chalky track, and is even now not entirely lined with houses, so that there is still a pleasant view across the meadows on the right towards Crohamhurst, must be followed to its termination at Croham Farm, where a somewhat misleading finger-post points to the track on the right as a bridle-way to Selsdon. As a matter of fact this farm track should almost at once be abandoned for a somewhat insignificant path, which rises slightly, and is soon enclosed between a wire fence and a high hedge, with a shallow valley on the left, rising on the other side to the fine woods of Ballards.

At the outset, on looking back, there is a pretty glimpse of Croydon, with the Town Hall tower standing out conspicuously above the houses, but this is quickly left behind and soon there is scarcely a house in sight. When the path becomes a farm road and bears to the right, a track must be followed which runs through a wood in front. This is a delightful enough spot to tempt the most ardent rambler to linger, even though he may have traversed but a couple of miles.

On leaving the wood, turn to the left, along the Selsdon Road, until the chimney of the Croydon Waterworks is seen over the rising ground on the right, in which direction a path is to be followed towards the waterworks. These are placed at the entrance to a long green valley, for some distance almost bare of trees—a striking contrast to the well-wooded country just passed through. The lane through the valley, which is known as Featherbed Lane, must be followed for nearly a mile until a finger-post points the way, on the left, to Lodge Lane. Upon reaching the top of a sharp rise, bear to the right, and then to the left round the farm, Addington Lodge, and pass along a short approach-lane to a road, where are a few old cottages, forming part of the scattered parish of Addington.

In passing along Featherbed Lane, two bridle-ways will have been noticed on the right, leading to Farley, and those who are only out for a short afternoon stroll will find the first of these, a very few yards beyond the waterworks, as wild and unfrequented a track as could be desired. It is necessary literally to force a way through the bushes in places, but it is well worth the trouble. It is doubtful whether there is anywhere round London so primitive a village as Farley, with its population of little more than a hundred, and its few gray cottages clustered round a miniature village green. The manor and advowson have belonged to Merton College, Oxford, since its foundation in the thirteenth century. The church, which lies across the fields almost half-a mile to the east, is very small, and shows traces of Norman and Early English work. From Farley there are various ways of reaching the railway stations in the Caterham Valley. All are attractive, and this part of the country is well furnished with finger-posts, so detailed directions seem unnecessary. The distance from Croydon to Upper Warlingham Station, through Farley, would be about eight miles.

Before resuming the main route at Addington Lodge, I should like to draw attention to a way of reaching that point by a footpath from Elmers End, which is extremely picturesque, and has so far remained unaffected by the rapid growth of Croydon and its suburbs.

The path, described as "To Shirley," starts from the hamlet of Upper Elmers End, about half a mile from the railway station, and leads through pastures and woodland to Shirley. Here turn to the right, then to the left to Shirley Church, and again take the left-hand road to Addington Village.

Addington, which consists of a tiny village set in the midst of a large parish, with a scanty and scattered population, is best known by reason of its purchase for the Archbishops

300

of Canterbury, who have made it their country home for nearly a century. How firmly established this connection has become is evidenced by the fact that the parishes of Croydon and Addington, with West Wickham in Kent, still remain under the direct jurisdiction of the Archbishop, although they are now completely isolated from the rest of the diocese, and he still holds the right of presentation to the two former livings.

Opposite Addington Church, which contains memorials to several of the Archbishops, a lane leads to the Addington Lodge approach-road mentioned above, and another pleasant round may be made by turning down past the farm, across Featherbed Lane, and through the woods to Farley Church and Upper Warlingham, the distance being only a little more than from Croydon, as previously given.

To proceed at last from Addington Lodge, the road at the end of the approach (turning of course to the right) leads past some more old cottages, and in about a mile crosses the border into Kent, the point being marked by several boundary signs of various descriptions.

The country by now has become greener, and we soon reach a pretty open cross-road; here the way is to the right, the lane forming the boundary between Kent and Surrey. It is grass-grown in places, and is evidently but little used, but it is exceedingly pretty, and after some distance descends through a delightful patch of woodland to a spot overlooking a deep green combe. There is a little triangular clearing to the left, which is intensely alluring on a hot afternoon.

The lane here bears abruptly to the right, and in about a mile reaches Chelsham Court, from which place a return route will be found below, but our way is to the left, along a somewhat obscure and evidently little used bridle-way. A very short distance further on, a little swing gate will be seen, low down on the right—it is very easily missed—and from here a path leads down into the combe and up the other side to a farm called Norheads. It is not very easy to find the way when nearing the house, but by bearing to the right, past the back of the buildings, a stile will be seen from which a footpath leads out into a lane. Here bear to the right, and in about a mile another old farm, Bedlestead, said to have formerly been a manor house, is reached.

From this point there are two return routes to Chelsham Court; either to turn to the right along the lane in front of the farm and up Hessier's Hill, turning to the left at the top; or to pass through the farmyard and follow a path at the back, which bears rather to the right down into the valley, and rising on the other side becomes a narrow hedged track, very much overgrown in places. At the top, Chelsham Court is a short distance to the left, and here we may pick up the threads of the three return routes I have indicated.

Just beyond the house a road bears to the right, on the left side of which, under some trees, a footpath will be seen which leads direct to Worms Heath, a wild stretch of common on some of the highest ground in the North Downs.

On the heath, away to the left, the remains of a British Camp may be seen, but the direct route towards the Caterham Valley is straight ahead, the path cannot be mistaken, until the Westerham Road is reached. This road, which is bordered with fine trees, is to be followed as far as the "Hare and Hounds Inn," where a little lane will be found running off the left-hand corner of the green. After a short distance the lane begins to fall slightly, and a gate on the right—usually open—gives access to a hillside path, overlooking a beautiful valley. The path must be followed to a stile close to some cross-roads; the only place where any doubt can exist being just when a farm is seen below on the left; here the path bears a little to the right, and up a bank to a stile in a corner. If preferred, instead of turning in at the open gate mentioned above, the lane may be followed to the cross-roads, bearing to the right at the only doubtful spot. This is an exceptionally beautiful woodland lane, and it is hard to say whether it or the hillside path is the most delightful. At the cross-roads it is straight on under the railway viaduct to the Godstone Road in the Caterham Valley, where there are railway stations to left and right.

Those who, on reaching Bedlested, feel inclined to go yet farther afield—and the best is still to come—can reach Tatsfield by turning to the left along the lane past the farm, until, in about half a mile, they reach a footpath on the left, which leads to Westmore Green, the centre of practically all there is of Tatsfield. This is one of the very few absolutely unspoilt villages round London, and I can imagine no more perfect realization of the idea of "Old England" than to look out over Westmore Green from the windows of the inn early in the morning on a Sunday in summer; no more peaceful spot can be conceived.

ALONG THE KENTISH BORDER.

The church, which is rather more than half a mile away, round to the left by the inn, and then across fields to the right, has recently been described in detail in this magazine (vol. x, p. 15), and the writer has drawn attention to the magnificent view from the churchyard, which is certainly worth a long tramp, although I am of opinion that there are others in the neighbourhood which are even finer.

Westerham may be seen from here, on the lower ground to the left, and may be reached in about three miles by turning to the right outside the church, and taking the second of two roads which branch off to the left, practically at the same spot. This leads direct to Westerham.

The cross-road soon met with is said to be undoubtedly a portion of the " Pilgrims' Way," and a farm hard by is known as Pilgrims' Lodge.

Those who will may, of course, follow the border line of Kent beyond Westerham, over the High Chart and down Crockham Hill to Edenbridge, Hever, or beyond, but this is rather far for a day's ramble, and stations are few and trains infrequent. Without proceeding further afield, however, there is a grand walk from Tatsfield Church along the brow of the Downs to the Godstone Road near Caterham, which will, I feel confident, be considered the finest part of the walk. For this route, turn to the right at the cross roads below Tatsfield Church, and follow the road (Clark's Lane) for about three quarters of a mile, until reaching the second turning on the right. This is the lane which passes Bedlested Farm, and rather over a mile may be saved by omitting a visit to Tatsfield.

Immediately opposite the lane is a field gate, without any indication that there is a right of way through it, but it nevertheless gives access to a public footpath, and to Cold Harbour Beeches, a noble clump of trees a few yards to the left, which stand at an elevation of 881 feet. This is the highest point of the North Downs (of course excluding Leith Hill from that category), and nearly 100 feet higher than Tatsfield Church; the view is magnificent, though there is not the glimpse of Kent which we had at Tatsfield.

From the field gate mentioned above, a path, which is quite invisible for some distance, runs over the hill towards the trees on the right, then, descending abruptly, joins the road to Titsey.

Titsey Church, the spire of which can be seen from the top of the hill, was built nearly fifty years ago, from Mr. Pearson's designs, to replace an insignificant building which had been erected eighty-five years before in lieu of an ancient structure ruthlessly demolished by the then Lord of the Manor because it was too near his house. Titsey is said to be a village, but it is hard to know where to find it. There are only about a dozen cottages, no shops, no post office. There was once an inn, "The Grasshopper," but it has disappeared, and the building is now a school.

There is a "Grasshopper Inn" a mile or more away, between Westerham and Limpsfield, but in Tatsfield Parish; so possibly some bygone landlord may have transferred his business and somewhat unusual sign[1] to what he considered would be a more remunerative location.

Two famous families have in the past been associated with Titsey, the Greshams and the Leveson Gowers. In Titsey Park is the site of a Roman villa, and through it the Pilgrims' Way is said to have passed.

Returning to the gate by Cold Harbour Beeches, and turning to the left, we keep straight on at the woodland cross roads on Botley Hill, or if preferred the road may be followed up Titsey Hill, when it is necessary to turn to the left at the top.

For nearly a mile there is a wood on the left, and the only view is to the north, over an expanse of rolling hills, but when the wood ends a magnificent prospect is opened up. The road follows the very brink of the hills, and all the way to the Godstone Road, four miles away, it is open on the left, except for patches of woodland here and there. Delightful though it may be to sit down at some spot, such as Cold Harbour Beeches, and drink in a far-spreading prospect of smiling country, there comes a moment when one must leave and the view is at once blotted out; but to my mind the delight is doubled, and more than doubled, when it is possible to tramp on for an hour or more, and all the while to enjoy a panorama of some of the fairest scenery in England. It is this that lends such a charm to the old hill track from Dorking to Guildford, and to the Portsmouth Road between, say, Thursley and Liphook.

Precise directions for reaching the Godstone Road are hardly necessary. All that is required is to keep as near to the edge of the hills as possible without descending, unless it

---

[1] The grasshopper was the crest of Sir Thomas Gresham.—EDITOR.

is desired to reach Oxted Station, to which there are several routes—some very muddy—indicated by finger-posts.

About two miles from Botley Hill there is a turning on the right to Woldingham, which has a railway station (about two miles from this point), but very few trains.

This was until a few years ago a very thinly inhabited parish, with the smallest church in the county, situated on one of the highest points therein, but London has now discovered the beauty of the neighbourhood, and many new houses have sprung up, though it must be confessed that in the main they have been designed to harmonize with their surroundings, and there seems to be no immediate fear of the district becoming " suburbanized."

Our hillside track after many windings in its final descent runs into an abandoned portion of the old Godstone Road, only a few hundred yards from the present highway. Turning to the right the latter is soon reached, and Caterham is about a mile further on.

The total distance from Croydon or Elmers End, would, I should say, be sixteen or seventeen miles. I have not walked it with a pedometer, but I do not think this is an underestimate.

If returning from Bedlested to Upper Warlingham Station (which has the best train service in the Caterham Valley) the distance would be approximately twelve to thirteen miles.

It is not possible within the limits of a short article to lay down directions in such detail as the various ramble books provide, but I fancy what I have noted will in the main prove adequate. Those who wish thoroughly to explore this picturesque and unspoilt district will find most of the routes I have suggested—with many others—in the various " Walker Miles " ramble books, though some are given in the reverse direction; and in the immediate neighbourhood of Croydon, Evans and Sharpe's *Field-path Rambles*, with their handy charts for each walk, which were long out of print, but have happily been reissued, will be useful; but what is badly needed for the entire Surrey hill country from the Kentish border to Hindhead is a trustworthy series of field-path maps, on the lines of those issued for the Northern Heights Footpaths Preservation Committee. It has been said for some years that such maps were in preparation, but they have not yet materialized.

The new Ordnance Survey maps, though vastly superior to the old ones, only indicate footpaths in a very partial and perplexing manner. Presumably those are inserted which are considered to be the most important, though this would appear not to be always acted upon, and in the meantime there is every fear that little used but undoubted public paths may become lost.

Fortunately the local councils are mostly on the alert, and this is particularly the case in the wide district managed by the Croydon Rural Council, which is most diligent in the matter of footpaths and finger-posts, and there is little fear that in this area at any rate the rights and interests of the public will be allowed to suffer.

MORGAN JONES; A BERKSHIRE MISER.

BY M. J. PEARMAN.

THE Berkshire miser was of course the notorious Elwes. His great wealth, his position as M.P. for the county, and other circumstances, entitle him to the unenviable distinction. But different as Elwes and Jones in so many respects were, there was one point, besides their miserliness, in which they were alike. The performance of public duties was the best feature in the character of each. Elwes was a good representative, being justly respected for attention to his parliamentary duties. It was matter for regret, on account of the consequent deterioration of his character, as for other reasons, that he was induced to retire from public life; absorbed in his private affairs he developed without check his innate sordidness.

As Curate of Blewbury, on the main road between Reading and Wantage, Jones was esteemed for his public ministrations. He inculcated peace and goodwill, and enforced his teaching by example. Whatever dissensions might arise among his parishioners, he was never mixed up with their quarrels; and it is somewhat remarkable, that during the many years he resided in Blewbury, he was never in a Court of Justice, nor even brought before a Magistrate. His teaching could not, indeed, be called the Gospel in its essential fullness, but it was a clear and definite *something*; and was probably so far superior to the teaching of many of his country contemporaries. In those days, as George Eliot says, the doctrines had not come up. The inculcation, therefore, of peace and good-will had a certain value, even though the motive were obscured. His preaching was plain and practical. His funeral sermons were admired by his congregation, who would have liked to see some of them in print. But it does not seem that they offered to be at the expense of printing; an omission which prevented their wishes from being gratified. Jones was very industrious, having written with his own hand upwards of one thousand sermons.

To speak of a miser's liberality seems paradoxical. But it is a fact that, grudging as he usually was to himself and others, he was a regular subscriber to several religious societies. Besides, he had been known on several occasions to give a pound or two to necessitous persons. His conduct therefore compares very favourably with that of numbers who, free from miserliness, contribute nothing to religious or philanthropic purposes.

Jones lived severely alone, having in his house no servant of any kind, nor even a dog or cat. Whether he had any books, to speak of, is doubtful. But probably he had, as he was credited with a good knowledge of English and Latin authors. He had other necessary occupations, such as the cooking of his dinner, which, however, was a very simple affair. His diet consisted, as he said, of two necessaries, bread and bacon, and one luxury, tea. For some while after taking up his residence at Blewbury he boarded with a family; and during that time he was, as the Psalmist observes, in a different connection, " fat and well-liking." But after he took to housekeeping he fell away frightfully, grudging himself, as he grudged others, food and drink. This tendency to starve oneself, which was not, I think, so marked a trait in the character of Elwes, distinguished Mrs. Meggot, Elwes' mother, in a very marked degree. Though possessed of such great wealth, she died, I believe, simply of inanition. But Jones did not carry his abstinence to such an extreme. He was like Elwes, who had naturally a vast appetite, fond of nice things. This preference or fancy he indulged, whenever he could do so, at other people's expense.

In the matter of dress he was not fastidious. He was Curate of Blewbury for upwards of forty-three years; and it hardly seems credible that for the whole of that period the same hat and coat served him for his everyday dress. The hat by constant use became greatly the worse for wear, but he was enabled by chance to remedy the defect. For, coming one day across the fields from Upton, he found an old hat stuck up for a scare-crow. He carried it home, and with the material furnished by it repaired the one he wore. The transaction strikes us as decidedly dirty, but its repulsiveness hardly seems equal to that of a somewhat similar economy practised by Elwes; *he* picked up in the road an old discarded wig, and *wore it*!

When Jones came from Aston Keys in 1781, his coat was an old surtout. After some time he turned it inside out and had it made up into a *common* one. Whenever a rent appeared in it, he tacked it together with his own hands, for he was considered expert with the needle. Eventually it got reduced to a jacket, covered with patches. In this extraordinary attire he did *not* appear in public, except when he forgot himself. He had a good store of shirts, but would only use one. This was washed every few months at the cost of 4*d.*

He was patient of cold. Except for cooking purposes he seldom indulged in a fire; and that was so small that it might easily have been covered under a half-gallon measure. He carefully gathered all the sticks he could find in the church-yard, and lopped his shrubs and trees, to make this fire. At the approach of night he retired to bed for warmth, but usually went without a candle.

He was not insensible as to the opinions of others respecting him. For many years he partook readily of ale, when he could get it without cost; but on one occasion at a wedding his doing so was noticed by some of those present and commented on. This displeased him, and he made a vow never again to taste alcoholic drink. This resolution he kept strictly and honestly, notwithstanding all solicitations to the contrary.

Though his means were small, Jones must have saved considerable property. The Curacy was worth £50 a year, exclusive of the fees and house. He had also £30 a year from private property. For the last twenty years of his life his expenses were estimated at less than 2*s.* 6*d.* a week. The fees being in excess of that amount, he was enabled to save the remainder of his income. His bankers were Child and Co. of Fleet Street.

His memory, which had been excellent, having failed him, and also his other faculties, he resigned the Curacy in 1824. He was obliged to leave the Vicarage in consequence, and also Blewbury itself because no man would accommodate him gratis. He had shown great affection to a boy in the place, who requited his kindness by robbing him of more than £100. He therefore communicated with his relations in Wales, who took him back to his native place.

THE CHRONICLE OF PAUL'S CROSS.

By W. PALEY BAILDON, F.S.A.

[Continued from p. 154.]

1546, June 25. "William Gray, plommer, who in light sorte without consideracion attempted to conferre with Doctour Crome in the tyme of his examynacion, and before he had executed his promesse to the Kinges Majeste for a playnes [*sic*] at *Pols Crosse*, was for that attemptate committed to custodie, and was this daye uppon repentance of his foly, and with a good lesson, dismissed, being bounde in the somme of Vᶜ markes t'appere at any tyme within xij moneth t'answere to that maye be objected unto him."—(*Privy Council.*)

1546, June 27. "The twentie-seaventh daie of June, Dr. Crome preached at *Paules Crosse*, and their recanted upon certaine articles that he had sett to his hand the 20th of Aprill last past; and [he] should have recanted at a sermon that he made at *Paules Crosse* the nynth daie of Maie, which was the Soundaie next after Lowe Soundaie, and did not; wherupon he was examyned before the Kinges Counsell, and remayned euer synce in warde with one of the Kinges Councell till this daie that he recanted and confessed that he had sett his hand to the said articles. At which sermon was present Lord Wriothesley, Lord Chauncelor of Englande, Duke of Norfolke, Lord Great Master of the Kinges Howseholde, with divers other of the Kinges Councell, with the Major [Mayor] and Aldermen, and a great awdience of people; and after his sermon he was discharged."—(Wriothesley's *Chronicle*, vol. i, p. 166.)

1546, July 12. "The twelfe daie of Julie were arraigned at the Guildhall for heresey, John Hemley, priest, de Essex, John Lasell, gentleman, on of the Sewers of the Kinges Chamber, and Georg Blage, gentleman, a man of faire landes;

which said persons that daie were first endited of heresie against the Sacrament of the Aulter, and ymediatlie arraygned on the same, the priest and Lasceles not denying the same their opinions, but confessing them guiltie; and Mr. Blage abode the triall of twelve men, for he was sent for to my Lord Chauncelor's [Wriothesley's] but the night before, and this daie sent to Newgate not halfe an howre or he was brought to the Hall, nor knew not wherfore he was taken, for he was never examyned before he came to his arraignemente; where was witnes against him Sir Hugh Calveley, knight, and Edward Littleton, gentleman, who accused him for wordes spoken against the Sacrament of the Alter, in Powles Church, the Soundaie next after Lowe Soundaie, which daie Doctor Crome preached at *Poules Crosse*; and so [he] was condempned by twelve men. And all three had judgment to be brent, and after judgment geaven they were commanded to Newgate."— (Wriothesley's *Chronicle*, vol. i, p. 169.) Hemley and Lasceles were burned at Smithfield on 16th July, in company with Anne Askew and another; Blage was pardoned.

1546, July 16. "And the xvj day of July was burnyd in Smythfelde for grett herrysy . . . Hemmysley, a prest, wyche was an Observand Freere of Richemond, Anne Askew, other-wyse callyd Anne Kyme by hare husband, John Lassellys, a gentylman of Furnevalles Inne, and a taylor of Colchester. And Nicolas Schaxton, some tyme Byshopp of Salsbery, was one of the same company, and was in Newgat, and had jugge-ment with them, . . . Blacke, gentylman, and Christopher Whytt of the Inner Tempull; these iij had their pardon. And Schaxtone preched at their burnynge; and there satt on a scaffold, that was made for the nonse, the Lord Chaunsler [Wriothesley], with the Dewke of Norfoke and other of the Cownsell, with the Lorde Mayer, dyvers Aldermen and Shreffes, and the Jugges."

"Item the furst day of August after, preched at *Powlles Cross* the sayd Nicolas Schaxton, and there recantyd, and wepte sore, and made grete lamentacion for hys offens, and pray[ed] the pepulle alle there to forgeve hym hys mysse insample [bad example] that he had gevyn un to the pepulle." —(*Chronicle of the Grey Friars*, p. 51.)

1546, August 1. "The first daie of August, the daie for the election of the Sheriffes, and being Soundaie, Doctor Shaxton preached at *Poules Crosse*, and their declared how he fell into the hereticall opinion of the Sacrament of the Aulter, and of his reconciliation, which he declared with weepinge eies, exhorting the people to beware by him, and to abolish such hereticall bookes of English, which was the occasion of his fall. And because he preached that daie at the *Crosse*, the election of the Sheriffe was putt of till afternoune of the same daie."—(Wriothesley's *Chronicle*, vol. i, p. 170.)

1546, September 26. "Item the xxvj day of September was burnyd at *Pawlles Crosse* a gret multytude of Ynglych bokes, as testamenttes and other bokes, the wych ware forbodyn by Proclamacyon by the Kynges commandment before, thorrow [throughout] alle hys domynyon."—(*Chronicle of the Grey Friars*, p. 52.)

1546, September 26. "The twentie-sixth daie of September were burned openlie at *Poules Crosse* certaine bookes of heresie latelie condemned by Proclamation at the sermon tyme."— (Wriothesley's *Chronicle*, vol. i, p. 175.)

1547, January 30. "The 30th of Januarie the church of the lat Gray Friars in London was opened, and masse song therin; and that daie preached at *Poules Crosse* the Bishopp of Rochester [Henry Holbeach], who declared the Kinges gift geaven to the Cittie of London for the releeving of the poore people, which had geven unto them, by Patent under his Seale, Sainct Bartholomewes Spittell, the church of the Gray Fryars, the church of Sainct Nicholas Flee Shambles, and the church of Sainct Etons [St. Ewin's], to be made one parish church within the Grey Fryars, and withall for the mayntenance of the same and releeving of the poore, fiue hundreth markes by yeare for eaver, and the said church had geven him by name the name of 'Christ Church, founded by King Henrie the Eight.'"—(Wriothesley's *Chronicle*, vol. i, p. 177; Stow, *Annales*, p. 592, where the date is given as January 3.)

1547, April. "Also the same moneth of Aprill, D. Glasier, preaching at *Paul's Crosse*, affirmed there y^t the Lent was not ordained of God to be fasted, neither ye eating of flesh to be forborn, but that the same was a politike ordinance of men, and mought therefore bee broken by men, at their pleasures." —(Stow, *Annales*, p. 594.)

THE CHRONICLE OF PAUL'S CROSS.

1547, May 15. "The fiftenth daie of Maie, 1547, Doctor [Smith] of Wydington College [Whittington's College and Hospital] preached at *Poules Crosse*, and their recanted and burned tow bookes which he had latelie sett fourth, one of traditions and another of unwrytten verities; and there he professed a new sincere doctrine, contrarie to his old papisticall ordre, as his articles in wryting playnelie sheweth."— (Wriothesley, *Chronicle*, vol. i, p. 184; Stow, *Annales*, p. 594.)

1547, November 17. "Item the xvij day of the same monythe, at nyghte, was pullyd downe the Rode in Powlles, with Mary and John, with all the images in the Churche, and too of the men that labord at yt was slayne, and dyvers other sore hurtte. Item also at that same time was pullyd downe throrrow [throughout] alle the Kynges domynyon, in every churche, alle Roddes with alle images, and every precher preched in their sermons agayne alle images. Also the new yeres day after preched Doctor Latemer, that some tyme was Byshop of Wysseter, preched at *Powlles Crosse*, and too sondayes followyn."—(*Chronicle of the Grey Friars*, p. 55.)

1547, November 27. "The xxvijth daie of November, being the first soundaie of Advent, preached at *Poules Crosse* Doctor Barlowe, Bishopp of Sainct Davides, where he shewed a picture of the resurrection of our Lord, made with vices which putt out his legges of sepulchree, and blessed with his hand, and turned his heade; and their stoode afore the pilpitt the imag of our Ladie, which they of Poules had lapped in seerecloth, which was hid in a corner of Poules Church, and found by the Visitors in their Visitation. And in his sermon he declared the great abhomination of idolatrie in images, with other fayned ceremonies, contrarie to Scripture, to the extolling of Godes glorie, and to the great compfort of the awdience. After the sermon, the boyes brooke the idolls in peaces."— (Wriothesley's *Chronicle*, vol. ii, p. 1.)

1547. "Item alle thoys prechers that prechyd at *Powlles Crosse* at that tyme spake moche agayne [against] the Bysshope of Wynchester [Gardiner]; and also Cardmaker [John Cardmaker, Vicar of St. Bride's], that rede in Powlles iij tymes a weke, had more or lesse of hym. . . . Item at this tyme was moche prechyng thorro alle Ynglonde agayne [against] the Sacrament of the Auter, saue only M. Laygton, and he preched, in every place that he prechyd, agayne them alle. And so was moche contraversy and moche besynes in Powlles every Sonday, and syttyng in the Churche, and of none that were honest persons, but boyes and persons of lyttylle reputacion; and wolde haue made moche mor, yf there had not a way bene tane [taken]. And at the last, the xxviij day of December followyng, there was a Proclamacyon that none of bothe partyes shulde preche unto soche tyme as the Counselle had determyned soche thynges as they were in hond with alle; for as that tyme dyuers of the Bysshoppes sat at Cherse Abbe [Chertsey Abbey] for dyuers matters of the Kynge and the Counselle."—(*Chronicle of the Grey Friars*, p. 56.)

1548, January 1, 8. "In the first of Januarie, doct. Latimer preached at *Paule's Crosse*, which was the first sermon by him preached in almost eight yeeres before; for, at the making of the 6 articles, hee being bishop of Worcester would not consent unto them, and therefore was commaunded to silence, and gaue up his bishoppricke: he also preached at *Paul's Crosse* on the 8 of January, wher he affirmed that whatsoever the cleargie commanded ought to be obeyed."—(Stow, *Annales*, p. 595.)

[To be continued.]

NOTES AND QUERIES.

L EYTON.—We are glad to see that the placing of commemorative tablets to distinguished citizens is spreading in the neighbourhood of London. In October last two such tablets were unveiled to two persons, widely differing in position, yet each worthy of remembrance. The first of these, to the memory of Cardinal Wiseman, was placed on Etloe House, Church Road, Leyton, where the Cardinal spent the last fifteen years of his life, was unveiled by Archbishop Bourne. It bears the following inscription: "Cardinal Wiseman, first Roman Catholic Archbishop of Westminster, lived here 1858-1864. Erected by the L. U. D. R. A. 1909." The second tablet, to the memory of Mary Fletcher, the well-known Wesleyan Methodist, has been placed on No. 538, High Road, Leytonstone, built on the spot where the dwelling stood in which she carried on her beneficent work from 1763 to 1768. It was unveiled by the Rev. F. M. Macdonald, Ex-President of the Wesleyan Conference.

NOTES AND QUERIES.

SAFFRON WALDEN.—A series of historical scenes illustrating the history of Saffron Walden is being prepared. A committee under the presidency of the Right Hon. Lord Braybrooke has been working for some time, and a council of guarantors is being formed in order to guard against loss in the undertaking. The parts have been written by Mr. L. Cranmer-Byng, and Mr. Herbert Mahon, Mus. Bac., has been appointed Musical Director. The performance is expected to take place on 31 March and 1 April, 1910. The following is a draft of the "Scenes" intended to be produced: 1. *Romano-British Scene*: Tribesmen making submission to Romans. 2. *Saxon Scene*: Ansgar's Banquet. 3. *Norman Scene*: Funeral of Geoffrey de Mandeville. 4. *Edwardian Scene*: (*a*) Pilgrim bringing Saffron Bulb from the East; (*b*) Saffron Dance. 5. *Elizabethan Scene*: Queen Elizabeth receiving the Walden Council at Audley End. 6. *Cromwellian Scene*: Cromwell and the Generals at the Sun Inn. 7. *Stuart Scene*: Pepys and the Mazer Bowl at the Almshouses. 8. The Flying Serpent of Henham. 9. (*a*) Queen Catherine preparing for Walden Fair; (*b*) Queen Catherine and her Attendants at the Fair. (With Morris Dance, Songs, etc.) Miss L. D. Bell, Dorset House, Saffron Walden, is the Honorary Secretary.—THOMAS W. HUCK.

MAUNDY MONEY.—The editorial note on page 207 to the paper by Mr. Cornelius Nicholls on "Maundy Celebrations," viz., "fourpenny pieces had milled edges," is not as clear as it might have been. As Mr. Nicholls states, the *Maundy* coins, including the groats or fourpenny pieces, were, and are, issued with smooth edges. Groats *for general currency* were issued under William IV and Victoria with the edges milled. The groats issued for currency bore on the reverse a figure of Britannia, seated, instead of the figure 4 crowned.—P. CARLYON-BRITTON.

REPLIES.

DENE-HOLES (vol. xi, pp. 91, 235).—In your November number I notice three items relating to Dene-Holes. One of these is a letter from my very good friend Mr. Hayes. I should like to point out that he did not visit the Gravesend Dene-Hole until some time after it had been opened and the men were working in it. Mr. Hayes and I have had several discussions on the subject of Dene-Holes, without either having succeeded in convincing the other. I have casts of two of the holes which cannot possibly have been made by metal picks. I have numerous casts of pick-marks from other so-called Dene-holes which have no resemblance whatever to those from the Gravesend Dene-Hole. I have also photographs of the walls of the Gravesend Dene-Hole, which, when magnified, show no resemblance to the scored walls of modern chalk pits. In conjunction with Mr. Hayes' letter one must take the review of Mr. Hayes' lecture, reprinted from the "Journal of the Royal Anthropological Institute." I was present at the lecture, and I have the reprint. Mr. Hayes, to my mind, has fallen into an error in logic. Because many chalk pits of recent years have been called, falsely, Dene-Holes, he says, therefore, that all Dene-Holes are modern chalk pits. I have on the stocks a book dealing exhaustively with the subject, in which I think the mass of evidence will be sufficient to refute the " modern chalk pit " theory. This book was announced some time ago in the press. Unfortunately, owing to ill-health, I have been unable to complete it. When finished I hope it will satisfy your other correspondent, " J. R., Gravesend."—ALEX. J. PHILIP.

ROLLS YARD AND CHAPEL (vol. xi, pp. 157, 236).—Referring to Mr. C. M. Phillips' reply to my query, I thank him for the information contained therein, which is very interesting. I used to attend the Church of St. Thomas in the Liberty of the Rolls in the late sixties, but I was not then old enough to appreciate some of the antiquarian points he now mentions. There is, however, one query in my own mind as to whether Church Passage was ever called White's Alley, because I distinctly remember that in the south-east corner of Bream's Buildings, which formed almost a quadrangle when entered from under the archway in Chancery Lane, that there was a labyrinth of courts which one had to go through in order to get into Fetter Lane, and that one of these courts was White's Alley. This remained so up to the time when the neighbourhood was cleared for improvement, some twenty odd years ago, whereas Church Passage was, and still is, on the north side of Bream's Buildings. It may be that prior to 1842 Church Passage was called White's Alley, but it is a coincidence that there was another White's Alley not very far off and yet not in the same building line.—J.

REVIEWS.

OXFORD AND CAMBRIDGE, delineated by Hanslip Fletcher, with Introduction by J. Willis Clark, M.A., Registrary of the University of Cambridge, and Notes by various writers. Sir Isaac Pitman and Sons; pp. xiv, 290; 63 illustrations; 21s. net.

The numerous topographical works written round a set of illustrations are of very varied merit. The bulk of them are of little value either from the literary or artistic point of view, and of none from that of the antiquary and historian. The recipe for these seems to be something of this sort: Take an artist, his skill is not

REVIEWS.

very material; commission him to make a given number of sketches; having got these, hand them over to some one to "write up"; if he can write decent English, so much the better, but it is by no means essential; let him spend a few days at the British Museum, consulting the folio county histories, and making free use of the descriptive portions of Kelly's Directories; if something very superior is desired, have a three-colour frontispiece, with a brilliant scarlet as the predominating tint; serve hot upon highly-glazed "art" paper—and make the best bargain you can for the "remainders." There is, however, as the cookery books have it, another way, where the artist can see and draw, and the writers are not mere scissors-and-paste men; and then we have a book which is a delight, a permanent and valuable addition to any one's library. The present volume takes a high place among the best works of its kind; indeed, we cannot for the moment think of any which we would rank as its superior. Mr. Fletcher is well known as one of the best black-and-white artists of the younger generation, and he has given us in this book some of the best work he has ever done. Most of the drawings are a combination of line and wash, which in Mr. Fletcher's able hands yield most charming results; there is something of the pure etching in these beautiful drawings, and now and then a suggestion of the old-fashioned combination of etching and aquatint. The interior of the Divinity School at Oxford, with its fan-tracery roof, is a masterpiece of careful drawing and skilful light and shade; while of the aquatint-like effects, Neville's Court at Trinity, Cambridge, is extremely clever, in its broad simplicity and wonderful suggestion of bright sunshine. The line drawings (with one exception) are good examples of the artist's vigorous pen-work.

The "contributors of notes," as they are modestly called, are writers intimately connected with the two Universities; for the most part each one deals with a single college. The result is a series of short but singularly interesting histories, clear, authentic, and scholarly, told with absolute independence, emphasizing the salient points in the record of each foundation, and mentioning some of the famous *alumni* who have added lustre to its bede-roll.

Mr. Willis Clark, in addition to his notes on four of the Cambridge Colleges, contributes an introduction to the volume. In the short space of twenty-four pages he contrives to give a most lucid account of what a university is, what a college is, how each arose, when each was founded, and how colleges came by their resemblances and differences, both of structure and constitution. An admirable essay in miniature, it forms a worthy prelude to a notable book.

THE GROWTH OF THE ENGLISH HOUSE, a Short History of its Architectural Development from 1100 to 1800, by J. Alfred Gotch, F.S.A., F.R.I.B.A. Batsford; pp. viii, 336; 7s. 6d. net.

The object of this work is, in the author's own words, "to tell the story of the growth of the English house, from its first appearance in a permanent form, down to the time of our grandfathers, when it lost much of its interest." It is a fascinating story, and though intended, we gather, primarily as a popular handbook, the student of architecture and social development will find it most instructive. We fancy, too, that it would be a welcome gift for the intelligent schoolboy, while the average "grown-up" will find something new in every chapter. Take the subject of stone keeps, for instance. We were all brought up to believe that the keep was primarily a prison and a last refuge for the hard-pressed garrison; its basement was always pictured as full of groaning and half-starved prisoners. We have all thrilled in imagination at the thought, on visiting such a castle. Not a bit of it, says Mr. Gotch; the keep was the ordinary home of the lord and his family, and a comfortless place it must have been, according to our modern notions. Fancy delicate women and children living in these great stone-vaulted chambers, with nothing to keep out the wind but wooden shutters, and with but one fireplace on

REVIEWS.

each floor. Truly, our ancestors were a hardy race. It seems a far cry from a Norman keep to a suburban villa, yet the "hall" of the latter, degenerated to a mere lobby or passage, is the undoubted descendant of that of the former. The fortified manor-house was the next stage of development, and the main difference between it and the castle-keep was that the apartments were placed side by side instead of one a-top of another. But the hall still continued to be the sleeping, eating, and living-room of the household; only the owner had a separate bedroom. The change of the hall grows out of the change of habits. When the whole household, family, guests, retainers, and all, no longer dined together, the great hall was too large for ordinary meals, and a separate dining-room became customary. But, as of old, the main door opened into the hall, so with the later fashion it opened into a large apartment, still called the hall, though no longer used for meals. The rest is clear; any tiny passage or vestibule into which a front-door opens is a "hall," and has an undoubted pedigree from Norman times. We have not space to follow Mr. Gotch further in his most successful work. There are over 200 illustrations and plans, a chronological list of the principal castles and houses, a useful glossary, and a good index. The book is got up with Mr. Batsford's usual skill and taste.

PARISH CHURCHES ON THE SITES OF ROMANO-BRITISH CHAPELS, and the lines of the Roman Survey; with nine Maps; by Montagu Sharpe. Brentford Printing Co.; pp. 12; 2s. net.

Mr. Sharpe's critical investigations into the early history of Middlesex are always worthy of careful attention and study. The present article, the scope of which is sufficiently indicated in the title, is, so far as we are aware, an entirely new suggestion, and at first sight a little startling. We confess that we were somewhat incredulous. Early prejudices die hard, and we half-unconsciously harked back to the history taught in the days of our youth. The Angles and Saxons, as then seen, were ramping and roaring savages, seeking whom and what they might devour and destroy. Where then, we asked, were these supposed Romano-British chapels? Savages they were, doubtless, as opposed to the Britons, at any rate in the neighbourhood of large towns, but they were eminently practical people; they destroyed what they had no use for, but after the period of settlement arrived we may well suppose that a conservative reaction set in, and that destruction for destruction's sake ceased. Be this as it may, we have evidence, preserved by Bede, that temples still existed in Britain a century and a half after the commencement of the Saxon settlement, and that in sufficient numbers to form the subject of a Papal letter. On June 17th, 601, Abbot Mellitus, who was then going to Britain, received a letter from the Pope containing a message to Augustine. The message has all the appearance of being an answer to some letter or inquiry from the great missionary priest. "Tell the most Reverend Bishop Augustine" (it begins) "what I have upon mature deliberation on the affairs of the English determined upon, viz.: that the temples of the idols of that nation ought not to be destroyed, but let the idols that are in them be destroyed." He then goes on to describe how they are to be purified and sanctified: "for if these temples are well built, it is requisite that they be converted from the worship of devils to the service of the true God." Here, then, are our temples, apparently in considerable numbers, and some of them fit for conversion to Christian worship with but little alteration. This is the impression left on our mind by the consideration of the whole tenor of this remarkable document. "Little Arthur" and "Mrs. Markham" are indeed untrustworthy guides. The evidence on which Mr. Sharpe relies to show the identity of site with parish churches is mostly contained in his nine maps, which we strongly advise our readers to study for themselves. They deal with the Isles of Wight, Sheppey, and Thanet, the Hundred of Dengie in Essex, the districts round Silchester, York, Lincoln,

REVIEWS.

and Cirencester, and the south-eastern part of Hertfordshire. The results are of great interest, and if Mr. Sharpe has not hit upon a hitherto unrecognized fact in our history, which we believe he has, then he has been deceived by a most remarkable series of coincidences. One argument, not mentioned by Mr. Sharpe, confirms his views, and that is the frequent finding of Roman coins in churchyards. We have not space to go into this here, but we shall be pleased if our readers will send us notes of any churchyards where this has occurred.

THE GENEALOGISTS' LEGAL DICTIONARY, by Percy C. Rushen. The Genealogists' Pocket Library, vol. vi; pp. 104; 2s. 6d. net.

The genealogist will have to enlarge or multiply his pockets, for here is a sixth volume to join its five predecessors. Most of the terms cropping up in searches among records will be found here, and the explanations are fairly clear and concise. Indeed, some of them are too concise. For instance, under "License to alienate," we read "see Mortmain," and no more. But for genealogical purposes licenses in mortmain are not of great importance. A reference should have been given to the records of the old "Alienation Office," where are recorded the licenses to alienate which all tenants of the Crown had to obtain before transferring their property so held. These contain references to sales, settlements, feoffments to uses, and other matters which often contain useful matter for the family historian. In a second edition both expansions and omissions will be an improvement.

GENERAL INDEX.

Names of contributors are printed in italics.

A

Archery, 74.
Armitage, Fred, 113.
Ashley Family, 28.
Aucher Family, 222.

B

Baildon, W. Paley, F.S.A., 68, 151, 309.
Bargehouse, The King's Old, 46, 135.
Barnard, Sir John, Lord Mayor, 1.
Benfleet, South, Essex, 111.
Berkhamstead, Little, Herts, 266.
Berkshire Miser, 306.
Biden, L. M., 293.
Bolland, W. C., 65.
Bolton, W., 75.
Bowers Gifford, Essex, 110.
Brasses: Harefield, 26, 28, 30, 32.
     ,,   St. Bartholomew the Less, 188.
Bruce Castle, Tottenham, 54, 139.
Buckland, Kent, 44.

C

Capel le Ferne, Kent, 127.
Carlyon-Britton, P. W., F.S.A., 314.
Chapman, A. B. Wallis, D.Sc., 214.
Charlton, Kent, 131.
Chelmsford, 247.
Chesfield, Herts, 19.
Cobham Family, 286.
Coggeshall, Essex, Friends at, 214.
Coldred, Kent, 209.
Culpeper Family, 32, 235.

D

Dene-Holes, 91, 235, 314.
Denton, Kent, 259.

E

Ealing Tragedy, 149.
Eastwood, Essex, 184.
Emslie, J. P., 75.
Essex, South, Early Churches of, 38, 107, 182, 280.

F

Finchley, Font at, 75.
Foord, Alfred Stanley, 7.
Forbes, C. W., 38, 107, 182, 280.

G

Gatwick, Surrey, 286.
Globe Playhouse Memorial, 52.
Gravesend, Kent, 91.

H

Hadleigh, Essex, 182.
Hampstead Assembly Rooms, 7, 74.
     ,,   Wells, 16.
Harefield, Middlesex, 24.
Hayes, J. W., 236.
Heal, A., 75.
Hendon, Middlesex, 81.
Hertfordshire Archers, 74.
     ,,   County Records, 96.
Home Counties, Unpublished MSS., 73, 155.
Houghton Conquest, Beds, 60, 143.
Huck, Thomas W., 314.
Hyde Family, 113.

I

Isherwood, Constance, 60, 143.

J

J., 157, 315.
J., C. T., 157.

INDEX.

CHISWICK PRESS: PRINTED BY C. WHITTINGHAM AND CO., TOOKS COURT, CHANCERY LANE, E.C.

A

LIST OF ILLUSTRATIONS.

Lightning Source UK Ltd.
Milton Keynes UK
UKHW011807190219
337571UK00010B/1573/P